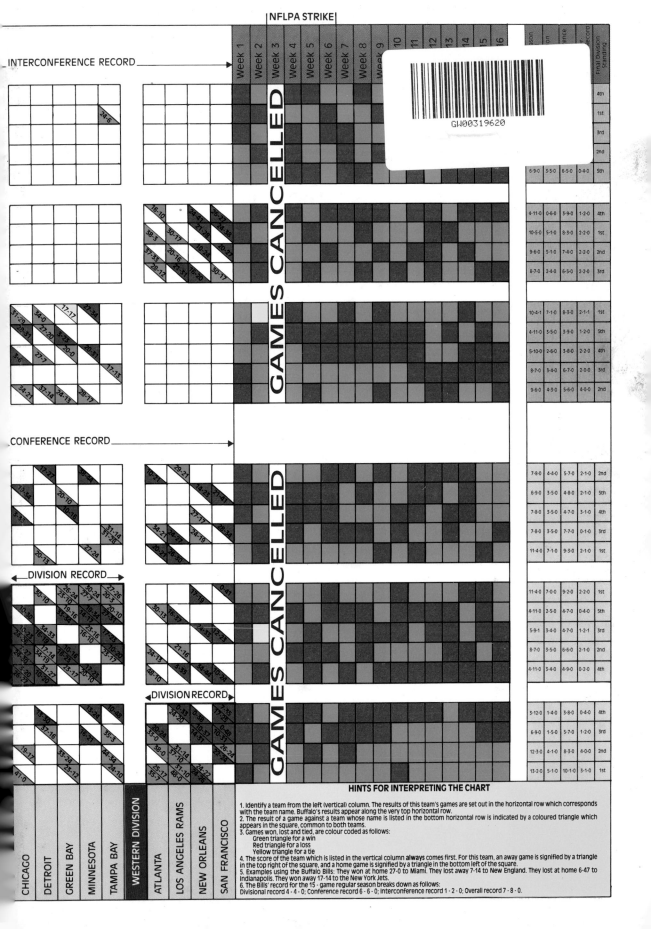

NFLPA STRIKE

INTERCONFERENCE RECORD

CONFERENCE RECORD

DIVISION RECORD

DIVISION RECORD

GAMES CANCELLED

GAMES CANCELLED

GAMES CANCELLED

Week 1 · Week 2 · Week 3 · Week 4 · Week 5 · Week 6 · Week 7 · Week 8 · Week 9 · 10 · 11 · 12 · 13 · 14 · 15 · 16

Final Division Standing

CHICAGO · DETROIT · GREEN BAY · MINNESOTA · TAMPA BAY · WESTERN DIVISION · ATLANTA · LOS ANGELES RAMS · NEW ORLEANS · SAN FRANCISCO

HINTS FOR INTERPRETING THE CHART

1. Identify a team from the left (vertical) column. The results of this team's games are set out in the horizontal row which corresponds with the team name. Buffalo's results appear along the very top horizontal row.
2. The result of a game against a team whose name is listed in the bottom horizontal row is indicated by a coloured triangle which appears in the square, common to both teams.
3. Games won, lost and tied, are colour coded as follows:
   Green triangle for a win
   Red triangle for a loss
   Yellow triangle for a tie
4. The score of the team which is listed in the vertical column **always** comes first. For this team, an away game is signified by a triangle in the top right of the square, and a home game is signified by a triangle in the bottom left of the square.
5. Examples using the Buffalo Bills: They won at home 27-0 to Miami. They lost away 7-14 to New England. They lost at home 6-47 to Indianapolis. They won away 17-14 to the New York Jets.
6. The Bills' record for the 15 - game regular season breaks down as follows:
Divisional record 4 - 4 - 0; Conference record 6 - 6 - 0; Interconference record 1 - 2 - 0; Overall record 7 - 8 - 0.

GW00319620

INTERPRETING THE 1987 RESULTS CHART (See inside front cover)

The chart colour-codes the result of every game in the 1987 regular season. For each club, the results of its games are listed in the horizontal row which corresponds both with its name in the left (vertical) column and the name of its opponent in the bottom (horizontal) row.

The result of every game is indicated by a triangle, coloured green for a win, red for a loss and yellow for a tie. In every square, the position of the triangle indicates either a home or an away game. For a home game, the triangle is at the bottom left of a square, while for an away game it is at the top right.

Looking at the results for the Buffalo Bills, we see that, against teams within their own division, they won one home game and three away games. Against the AFC Central, they lost away to Cleveland and won at home against Houston. In games against AFC West teams, they had a home victory over Denver but lost away to the Raiders. Finally, against NFC East clubs, at home, they beat the Giants but lost to Washington, and they lost away to Philadelphia.

In the 1987 season, there was only one tied game, Denver at Green Bay.

INTERPRETING THE ALL-TIME HEAD-TO-HEAD CHART (See inside back cover)

The numbers in the boxes represent the all-time won-lost-tied record of the team in the left (vertical) column against the team in the top (horizontal) row. Thus, Buffalo has won nine, lost thirty-four and tied one game in the series against Miami. The colour of the box indicates the current status.

A green box indicates that the team is leading in the series.

A red box indicates that the team is behind in the series.

A yellow box indicates that the series is tied.

Thus, Buffalo is tied with Indianapolis, trails Miami and is ahead against Denver.

AMERICAN FOOTBALL
BOOK 6

AMERICAN FOOTBALL
BOOK 6

KEN THOMAS

Macdonald   Queen Anne Press
In association with
Channel Four Television Company Limited

ACKNOWLEDGEMENTS

Reflecting on all the people without whose help I could not hope to write this book, it seems almost an impertinence that my name alone should appear on the front cover. Thankfully, in this section, I am able to express my gratitude.

I begin with the two young men who, for almost ten years, have supported me with increasing commitment and efficiency. By now they will be well known to readers of this book as Roger Smith and Nick Wridgway. Roger, who was the first British fan of the Dallas Cowboys, is quite the best 'reader' of the pro game I have ever met. When Roger says, 'Did you see that move?' he invariably means, 'You'd better re-run that tape because you've missed something important.' In more practical terms, he makes a valuable contribution by supplying me with the all-time statistics, for which I am extremely grateful. Nick, the Assistant Editor of *Touchdown* magazine, has grown to understand me quite well. The time was when, with some trepidation, he would venture to correct my errors of fact. These days, in anticipation, he tips me off before I make them. As always, Nick, you have my gratitude.

Over the years I have come to lean heavily on the knowledge of a growing band of American experts.

The first was Beau Riffenburgh of NFL Properties Inc., with which organisation his status is that of Senior Writer and who wrote the most recent edition of the *Official NFL Encyclopedia*. Larry Eldridge, Jr, a former NFL colleague of Beau, is now the Sports Information Director at the University of Pittsburgh and allows me unlimited access to his treasure chest of quotations. Turning to the NFL in New York City, both Pete Abitante and his close colleague, Rich Mauch, have given generously of their time and patience. Gentlemen, how you manage to tolerate my intrusions I do not know.

As usual, Sharon Kuthe and Kevin Terrell organised the supply of photographic material with outstanding efficiency.

A little closer to home, Celia Kent and Simon Webb, of Queen Anne Press, somehow have managed to survive their annual exposure to my insufferability, for which they have my thanks. That's also true of Mrs Susanna Yager, the Publishing and Merchandising Manager of Channel Four Television, who has a formula for that sort of thing – tolerating me with a degree of kindness that I value greatly.

Finally, there's Janie, my wife, who continues to be a source of inspiration and support. Thanks, love.

K.T. June 1988

A **Queen Anne Press** Book

© Ken Thomas 1988

Fist published in Great Britain in 1988 by
Queen Anne Press, a division of
Macdonald & Co (Publishers) Ltd
3rd Floor
Greater London House
Hampstead Road
London
NW1 7QX

The American Football Book is associated with Channel Four Television's coverage of the sport produced by Cheerleader Productions Limited.

(TM) NFL Properties (UK) Ltd

Cover photographs – Front: Super Bowl XXII *All-Sport*
Back: Super Bowl XXII *All-Sport*

British Library Cataloguing in Publication Data

Thomas, Ken
American football book 6.
1. American football
I. Title
796.332

ISBN 0-356-15876-4

Typeset by SX Composing Ltd

Printed and bound in Great Britain by
Purnell Book Production Ltd
Member of BPCC plc

PHOTOGRAPHS

All photographs have been supplied by courtesy of the NFL. The following photographers took the pictures on the pages indicated: The Allens 149; All-Sport 97; Charles AquaViva 36, 95; John Betancourt 44T, 143; James Biever 34; John Biever 47; Vernon Biever Contents page, 61; David Boss 117; Clifton Boutelle 59; Peter Brouillet 35L, 48, 49B, 93, 111; Rob Brown 63; T. J. Croke 19; Scott Cunningham 22, 62, 147; J. Edler 141; Malcolm Emmons 29L, 40; Nate Fine 58; Richard Gentile 137; George Gojkovich 89, 113; Peter Groh 31, 145; Jon Hayt 121; George Jardine 83; Paul Jasienski 9R, 153; Ali Jorge 131; Al Kooistra 32, 103; Long Photography 51; Amos Love 91; John McDonough Title page, 25, 107, 125; Richard Mackson 6, 45, 86; Ed Mahan 23; Al Messerschmidt 37, 42B, 49T, 109, 123, 139; Bill Mount 13T; PRM 50, 115; George Robarge 21, 99, 119, 127; Bob Rosato 10, 38, 42T, 101; George Rose 1, 30, 155; Ron Ross 129; Manny Rubio 14, 128, 151; John Sandhaus 33; Robert Shaver 11B, 16; Paul Spinelli 1, 17T, 18, 43, 105; Damian Strohmeyer 28, 35R, 39, 88; Alan Schwarz 29R, 41, 82, 94; Tony Tomsic 27, 44B, 46, 60, 65, 78, 87; Corky Trewin 70, 72T, 74; Jim Turner 24, 26, 79, 133, 135; Michael Zagaris 64L, 157. The pictures on pages 55T, 55L, 55R, 56L, 56R, 57 were supplied by courtesy of the Pro Football Hall of Fame.

CONTENTS

INTRODUCTION

Anyone doubting the NFL's commitment to establishing its game in the UK need only think back to our 'traditional' season-opener, the 1987 American Bowl, which was played with all the intensity of a title match. The lead changed hands six times, the last of which gave the Rams a one-point victory over Denver. The Broncos also would figure in the season-ender, Super Bowl XXII, though only for a brief period which saw them open up a ten-point lead before being overwhelmed by Washington. Inbetween those events we had the four-week players' strike.

Looking back over the campaign, it is easy to think of 1982, the year that Channel Four Television embarked on its coverage of American Football. That season, too, experienced its players' strike before being rounded off in fine style by Washington in Super Bowl XVII.

The following year saw the publication of the American Football Book, which, in accord with the superstitious rites of the publishing business, did not carry a volume number. The gods smiled and the project survived to the extent that we have now reached number six. Over the intervening years, the game has evolved from a curiosity, through the cult phase, to its current position, that of being an established part of the British sporting scene. Our domestic organization, newly named The National Gridiron League Ltd, boasts 77 member clubs and claims to be the largest in Europe.

The book, too, has evolved, with the most recent innovations, 'Outstanding Individual Performances' and the charts appearing inside the front and back covers, proving to be popular. As always, I shall welcome any comments, favourable or otherwise, which might lead to its improvement. It continues to be an immense pleasure to share my love of the game.

Left: Rulon Jones, Denver Broncos' defensive end.

Contents page: Washington's Dave Butz and Charles Mann (#71) on the stop against Chicago in the NFC Divisional playoffs.

✩✩✩✩✩✩✩✩ **CHAPTER ONE** ✩✩✩✩✩✩✩✩

A REVIEW OF
THE 1987 SEASON

Prologue

In line with the mini-tradition established by the Los Angeles Raiders and maintained by both San Francisco and Chicago, the New York Football Giants (as they like to be known) had duly won the twenty-first Super Bowl with plenty to spare.

It had been a good season – wouldn't it have to be when a new name is added to the Vince Lombardi Trophy, and especially when that name belongs to one of the outstanding and best respected of America's professional sports organisations?

Lingering in the seats, though, as the contents of the Rose Bowl drained into the streets of Pasadena,

Vinny Testaverde at mini-camp.

the slight shiver came not from the cool of that southern California evening. No, it was in considering the prospects for the 1987 campaign, the NFL's sixty-eighth, when it seemed certain that there would be a players' strike. Still, for every sports fan, access to unlimited optimism comes with the territory. The adversaries might just hammer out an agreement and, in the meantime, we could look forward to the NFL Selection Meeting, known for practical purposes as the 'collegiate draft', which was to be held on April 28.

As anticipated, Tampa Bay made the University of Miami (Florida) quarterback, 1986 Heisman Trophy winner Vinny Testaverde, the first pick overall, well before the appointed date. Having been unable to sign running back Bo Jackson after selecting him with the first option in 1986, this time the Buccaneers were in no mood to take chances and the parties struck a formal deal on April 3.

A club not in need of a quarterback might have chosen outside linebacker Cornelius Bennett, ahead even of Testaverde. Said to make greased lightning look slow, Bennett was gifted with the instincts to match, and the Indianapolis Colts had no hesitation in making him the second player selected. In third place came another University of Miami product, fullback Alonzo Highsmith, who would surely beef up the Oilers' backfield. Again, a player of immense potential, in 1985 Highsmith and Testaverde had combined on a Miami team-record, 88-yard touchdown pass-play.

The case of Oklahoma linebacker Brian Bosworth eventually became unique in league drafting history. With the luxury of being able to choose between remaining in college and entering the draft, Bosworth, who would almost certainly have been one of the first three players selected, did neither. Rather, he opted for entering a supplemental draft in the hope that a club to his liking would engineer a trade to pick him, as, quite legitimately, had the

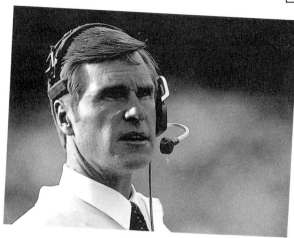

Left: Chiefs new head coach Frank Gansz.

Above: Al Saunders enters his first full season as Chargers head coach.

Cleveland Browns in order to select quarterback Bernie Kosar in a 1985 supplemental draft. Of course, it all meant that Bosworth would, in effect, be selecting his own club. And he was hoping that it would be the Raiders – he even had named his dog 'Raider'. But the league was one move ahead and, for the 'Bosworth' supplemental draft, instead of simply using the normal order of clubs (Tampa Bay would have had the first pick) they opted for a lottery, in which the names of all the clubs went into a hat, with the subtle twist that the chances for each club were weighted in the order of their positions for the normal draft. By this system, the hat contained twenty-eight tickets bearing the name of Tampa Bay, on down to the Giants, who had only one ticket.

His selection by Seattle ended the suspense but not the controversy. Bosworth still had his list of preferred clubs and the Seahawks weren't on it. But after protracted negotiations he signed on the dotted line, for a sum short by not very much of the entire national debt of a banana republic.

Testaverde was to be the cornerstone for the reconstruction of the Buccaneers franchise, and new head coach Ray Perkins would be the builder. A former head coach of the New York Giants (the Giants' resurgence could be traced back to Perkins' tenure which spanned the years 1979 to 1982), he had been the successful head coach at his alma mater, the University of Alabama, for the last four years.

Marion Campbell, who took charge in Atlanta, was another former head coach returning to the firing line. The former head coach of the Philadel-

phia Eagles for all but the final game of the three seasons, 1983 to 1985, Campbell even had coached the same Falcons for twenty-five games spanning the period 1974 to 1976 (he took over for the last six games of the 1974 season and was released after five games of the 1976 season).

The British-born Al Saunders was entering his first full campaign as head coach of the San Diego Chargers, after having succeeded Don Coryell halfway through 1986. Ron Meyer, the former head coach of the Patriots (1982-84), was looking forward to his first full campaign with the Colts, whom he had guided to a 3-0 record on replacing Rod Dowhower. Helped enormously by the strength of Frank Gansz's special teams (they had blocked ten kicks and scored five touchdowns), the Kansas City Chiefs were coming off their first playoff season since 1971. Gansz's reward was the top job in replacement of John Mackovic.

'So who was going to win the Super Bowl?' one wondered. The Giants looked unassailable in the NFC East, but everyone expected both Chicago and San Francisco to be tough, as usual, whilst the Redskins looked good for a wild-card spot. Cleveland, Denver and Seattle were widely regarded as the best of the AFC.

Annually, your writer distinguishes himself by picking losers. In 1987, he came close to breaking that sequence with Chicago, but the soundness of his judgement was once more underlined by his AFC selection, Kansas City, who shared last place with Cincinnati.

WEEK ONE

American Football Conference
Cincinnati 23 at Indianapolis 21
Miami 21 at New England 28
New York Jets 31 at Buffalo 28
San Diego 13 at Kansas City 20
Seattle 17 at Denver 40

National Football Conference
Atlanta 10 at Tampa Bay 48
Dallas 13 at St Louis 24
Detroit 19 at Minnesota 34
New York Giants 19 at Chicago 34
Philadelphia 24 at Washington 34

Interconference Games
Cleveland 21 at New Orleans 28
Los Angeles Raiders 20 at Green Bay 0
Los Angeles Rams 16 at Houston 20
San Francisco 17 at Pittsburgh 30

Interconference Play
AFC 3 – NFC 1

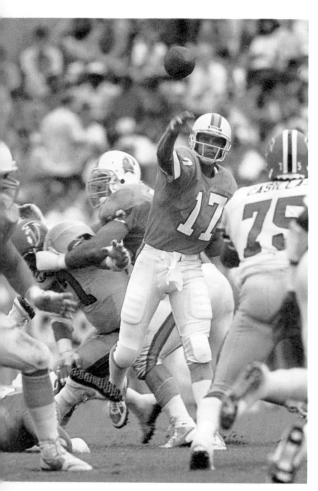

It wouldn't be opening day without its surprise results, and whilst there were no real shockers, Pittsburgh's easy victory at home to San Francisco was unexpected. Again, Houston trailed 13-0 and 16-3 to a Rams team for whom Eric Dickerson gained 149 yards rushing, but they rallied for 17 unanswered points to make a successful start to a campaign which, though they didn't know it, would be their best since 1980. Ray Perkins felt that rookie Vinny Testaverde wasn't quite ready to make his debut, and veteran quarterback Steve DeBerg grasped his opportunity, setting personal and Tampa Bay club records with five touchdown passes against Atlanta. The New Orleans Saints were the only NFC West team to win and they announced their intention to make this 'their best season ever', matching Cleveland blow-for-blow before easing away on seven fourth-quarter points, which included two safeties.

The day's most exciting comeback occurred in St Louis, where, with just under two minutes remaining, the home-team Cardinals still trailed Dallas by the score of 13-3. But wait for it. Quarterback Neil Lomax flipped a brace of touchdown passes to wide receiver Roy Green (Cardinals 17 – Dallas 13), and running back Earl Ferrell ran 15 yards for a touchdown after defensive end Curtis Greer, who registered three sacks, had forced a fumble by Dallas quarterback Danny White. Whew!

Noteworthy victories came for the Chiefs, whose rookie running backs, Christian Okoye and Paul Palmer (he returned a kickoff 95 yards for a touchdown), were prominent in their victory over San Diego, and for the Raiders, who logged the day's only shutout. But for the clash of the titans we had to wait until Monday evening when the Bears, led by reserve quarterback Mike Tomczak who threw touchdown passes of 42 and 56 yards, and helped by a Dennis McKinnon 94-yard punt return for a touchdown, brought the Giants down to earth.

On Sunday, out West, Denver had trailed by ten points before burying the Seahawks with a 33-point avalanche as quarterback John Elway served notice that the Broncos were back in business. In the East, a quarterback came out of obscurity to deliver a similar message, though, at the time, not many people listened. That quarterback was veteran Doug Williams, the Redskins' backup, who, since the 1982 season, had attempted only one pass in the NFL (it fell incomplete). Following an early injury to starter Jay Schroeder, Williams came on to pass for 272 yards and two touchdowns as Washington beat Philadelphia 34-24 . . .

Steve DeBerg threw five touchdown passes.

STANDINGS

AFC East	W	L	T	PF	PA	NFC East	W	L	T	PF	PA
New England	1	0	0	28	21	St Louis	1	0	0	24	13
N.Y. Jets	1	0	0	31	28	Washington	1	0	0	34	24
Buffalo	0	1	0	28	31	Dallas	0	1	0	13	24
Indianapolis	0	1	0	21	23	N.Y. Giants	0	1	0	19	34
Miami	0	1	0	21	28	Philadelphia	0	1	0	24	34
AFC Central						**NFC Central**					
Cincinnati	1	0	0	23	21	Chicago	1	0	0	34	19
Houston	1	0	0	20	16	Minnesota	1	0	0	34	19
Pittsburgh	1	0	0	30	17	Tampa Bay	1	0	0	48	10
Cleveland	0	1	0	21	28	Detroit	0	1	0	19	34
AFC West						Green Bay	0	1	0	0	20
Denver	1	0	0	40	17	**NFC West**					
Kansas City	1	0	0	20	13	New Orleans	1	0	0	28	21
L.A. Raiders	1	0	0	20	0	Atlanta	0	1	0	10	48
San Diego	0	1	0	13	20	L.A. Rams	0	1	0	16	20
Seattle	0	1	0	17	40	San Francisco	0	1	0	17	30

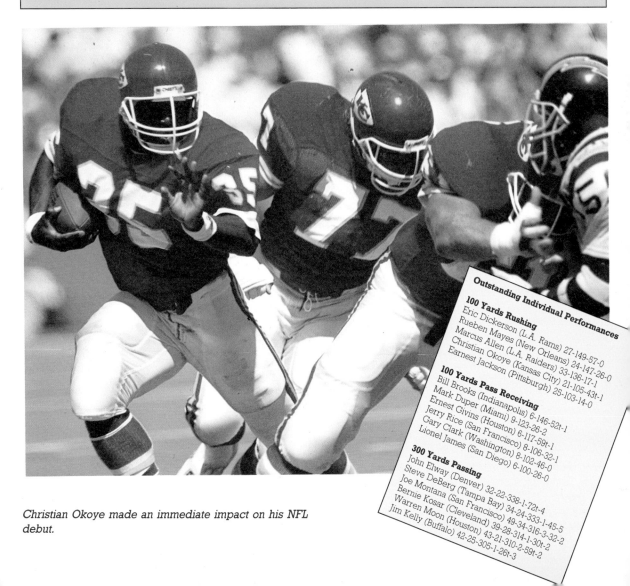

Christian Okoye made an immediate impact on his NFL debut.

Outstanding Individual Performances

100 Yards Rushing
Eric Dickerson (L.A. Rams) 27-149-57-0
Rueben Mayes (New Orleans) 24-147-26-0
Marcus Allen (L.A. Raiders) 33-136-17-1
Christian Okoye (Kansas City) 21-105-43t-1
Earnest Jackson (Pittsburgh) 25-103-14-0

100 Yards Pass Receiving
Bill Brooks (Indianapolis) 6-146-52t-1
Mark Duper (Miami) 9-123-26-2
Ernest Givins (Houston) 6-117-59t-1
Jerry Rice (San Francisco) 8-106-32-1
Gary Clark (Washington) 8-102-46-0
Lionel James (San Diego) 6-100-26-0

300 Yards Passing
John Elway (Denver) 32-22-338-1-72t-4
Steve DeBerg (Tampa Bay) 34-22-333-1-45-5
Joe Montana (San Francisco) 49-34-333-1-45-5
Bernie Kosar (Cleveland) 39-28-314-1-30t-2
Warren Moon (Houston) 43-21-310-2-59t-2
Jim Kelly (Buffalo) 42-25-305-1-26t-3

WEEK TWO

American Football Conference
Houston 30 at Buffalo 34
Kansas City 14 at Seattle 43
Miami 23 at Indianapolis 10
New England 24 at New York Jets 43
Pittsburgh 10 at Cleveland 34

National Football Conference
Dallas 16 at New York Giants 14
Minnesota 21 at Los Angeles Rams 16
New Orleans 17 at Philadelphia 27
Tampa Bay 3 at Chicago 20
Washington 20 at Atlanta 21

Interconference Games
Denver 17 v Green Bay 17 (OT) (at Milwaukee)
Detroit 7 at Los Angeles Raiders 27
St Louis 24 at San Diego 28
San Francisco 27 at Cincinnati 26

Interconference Play
AFC 5 – NFC 2 (1 Tie)

Throughout the spring and summer it had been easy to find reasons for ignoring the approaching players' strike, but now it was almost upon us. That much seemed inevitable, and it was against this background that the teams took to the field on what seemed certain to be our last taste of pro football action for several weeks. Nine clubs took the opportunity to redress the balance as they registered their first victories.

There was drama in Buffalo's victory over Houston, as quarterback Jim Kelly passed ten yards for the winning touchdown to running back Ronnie Harmon with just 57 seconds remaining. In San Diego, the Chargers jumped out to a 28-0 halftime lead but were on the verge of defeat after the Cardinals had stormed back with 24 unanswered points, only to be reprieved when St Louis running back Earl Ferrell dropped a catchable, fourth-down pass at the San Diego one-yard line in the final seconds.

Neither Seattle, who pounded Kansas City, nor Cleveland, who clubbed the Steelers, was in charitable mood. The Broncos, who, arguably, completed the AFC's 'big three', were held to a tie by Green Bay and the elements – they played in a mud-bath.

Atlanta brought off the day's major upset, three times coming from behind to beat the Redskins by the narrowest of margins, whilst the Eagles' victory over New Orleans forced a reappraisal of both clubs. The Cowboys' win against the Giants was flavoured with all the spices for which their traditional rivalry is known, though not even the winning quarterback, Danny White, would remember the

game with much relish. White's passes were intercepted four times, three times by Giants safety Terry Kinard. The Giants' Phil Simms, MVP in Super Bowl XXI, too, was intercepted four times, and left to a chorus of jeers from the home fans. There was something 'normal' about Miami's win over the Colts, in that, being their fourteenth straight in the series stretching back to 1980, the Dolphins extended the NFL's longest winning sequence by one team against another.

It was all deadly serious and yet there really was something comic about Cincinnati's loss to San Francisco – for loss it was. Leading 26-20, in possession and needing to survive the last six seconds, on fourth down the Bengals opted for a sweep instead of punting. The play broke down, leaving San Francisco with two seconds, and that's all it took, with Joe Montana passing 25 yards for the game-tying touchdown to wide receiver Jerry Rice. Ray Wersching's PAT did the rest.

STANDINGS

AFC East	W	L	T	PF	PA
N.Y. Jets	2	0	0	74	52
Buffalo	1	1	0	62	61
Miami	1	1	0	44	38
New England	1	1	0	52	64
Indianapolis	0	2	0	31	46
AFC Central					
Cincinnati	1	1	0	49	48
Cleveland	1	1	0	55	38
Houston	1	1	0	50	50
Pittsburgh	1	1	0	40	51
AFC West					
L.A. Raiders	2	0	0	47	7
Denver	1	0	1	57	34
Kansas City	1	1	0	34	56
San Diego	1	1	0	41	44
Seattle	1	1	0	60	54
NFC East	W	L	T	PF	PA
Dallas	1	1	0	29	38
Philadelphia	1	1	0	51	51
St Louis	1	1	0	48	41
Washington	1	1	0	54	45
N.Y. Giants	0	2	0	33	50
NFC Central					
Chicago	2	0	0	54	22
Minnesota	2	0	0	55	35
Tampa Bay	1	1	0	51	30
Green Bay	0	1	1	17	37
Detroit	0	2	0	26	61
NFC West					
Atlanta	1	1	0	31	68
New Orleans	1	1	0	45	48
San Francisco	1	1	0	44	56
L.A. Rams	0	2	0	32	41

Left: Floyd Dixon helped the Falcons to their upset win.

Below: Jim Kelly beat Houston in a cliffhanger.

WEEK THREE

STRIKE

With the Jets' 43-24 victory over the Patriots in the Monday Night Game, down went the floodlights and up had gone the shutters.

There were essentially six prominent issues in dispute and, of these, four appeared soluble, since, being concerned purely with economics, it seemed a matter merely of finding the point of equilibrium between the opposing positions. These four were concerned with the size of the player roster, a minimum salary level, improved pension payments and guaranteed contracts.

Unlike the background to the 1982 strike, when the NFL owners had signed a lucrative agreement with the television networks, the recently signed TV contract was expected to generate no increase in revenue for the owners. (The contract with the three major networks was for an actual reduction of 3% but the shortfall was made good by selling rights to cable television.) Far from hoarding coffers awash with new money, the owners were counting their pennies.

The NFL roster limit had been set at 45, the players wanted this increased to 52 and the management's negotiating position began at 47. There was an obvious point of contact and you didn't have to be a mathematical genius to arrive somewhere close to 49.

Inevitably, the players were looking for an increase in the salary minimum beyond the current $50,000, a figure exceeded by all but the most modest rookie. Also, on behalf of veterans, they were seeking adjustments to the career incremental scale which would raise the maximum for a 13-year veteran to $320,000. Whilst there was every indication that the owners could live with a $10,000 increase for rookies, their position on modifying the incremental scale was not made clear.

On the subject of pension contributions by the clubs, the players charged that the owners were lagging behind – that there was a deficiency in the fund – and that the owners' contribution should be raised from $12.5 million annually to $25 million. In response, whilst not accepting the existence of a deficiency, the owners proposed a modification to the system to combine severance payments with pensions. It was a new approach. In addition, they offered increases of 16.7% in pension contributions in both 1987 and 1988, followed by increases of 14.3% in 1989, 1990 and 1991.

It was a surprise to many fans that only one in twenty-five players possessed guaranteed contracts. The players were seeking greater job security for the rank and file, and the owners were willing to consider extended guarantees of payment

for veterans of at least four years in the NFL.

In addition to these, however, there were two issues of major significance, namely, those concerned with testing for the use of illegal drugs and, perhaps the greatest stumbling block, the matter of unrestricted free agency for the players.

The widespread social use of illegal drugs is one of the problems which modern democratic societies have yet to solve. Some professional football players use drugs, though, as yet, there exists no reliable estimate as to the extent of the practice. Both the players' union and the club owners agreed on the need for drug testing but their differences lay in its manner and frequency. The players would accept one mandatory test during the preseason, but for any additional tests there would need to be reasonable cause. The owners wanted random testing with no restrictions, and the players regarded this as an unreasonable invasion of privacy.

Most observers saw the issue of free agency as the key area in the entire dispute. Quite simply, on termination of whatever contractual agreement held between player and club, the player was seeking the right to move to a new club of his choice. The freedom of movement – the right to choose one's place of work – they argued, was a fundamental privilege. (Ironically, twelve years earlier, the players had won the right of free agency – it was the outcome of a legal judgement – but they bargained it away in return for an immense package of benefits and conditions.) The rhetoric included references to slavery and the like. And there's no doubt that, in the eyes of many, the players had a case.

In fact, there did exist a form of free agency which allowed a player to change clubs. It went in stages. Once a player became a free agent, he was open to offers. The new club would make an offer but his existing club could retain the player's rights by matching that offer. Should his existing club not wish to match the terms, then the player was free to make the move. It's easy to see that a player could set up his own auction, and that had to be to the player's advantage. (It was a process overlooked by a British press which felt able to sit in judgement of the NFL owners. Not long before then, they had sneered at a sport in which a man could earn $150,000 for kicking a ball half-a-dozen times in a game. 'Not much work for that huge salary!' went the quip. It was the same owners who now were offering even better salaries and benefits.) However, by way of compensation, the player's former club automatically received payment in future draft choices from the player's new club. The players argued that the price in terms of draft choices always would be too high and, in effect, acted as a deterrent to any new club wishing to invoke the system.

In response to those who saw only one side of the argument, the club owners made a very impressive case. They could point to, perhaps, the most successful sports enterprise in history – and the players had enjoyed a full share in that success. They were extremely well paid and had excellent fringe benefits. By careful management, over a sixty-seven-year period, the league had been transformed from a sport with only the barest semblance of organization into a high-tech product which, for a five-month period each year, dominated the attentions of the most demanding public in the western hemisphere – or anywhere else for that matter. Total free agency, which quickly could lead to the few very wealthy clubs garnering all the best talent, might destroy the competitive nature of the NFL as we understood it.

There were no signs of an early settlement. However, for some time there had been circulating rumours that, in an emergency, the club owners were prepared to go out and sign up entirely new squads to fulfil the schedule. They had retained contacts with players who had attended their training camps. Out there somewhere, there were 1,500 men, young and not-so-young, waiting for a phone call.

Atlanta tackle Mike Kenn on picket duty.

WEEK FOUR

American Football Conference
Cleveland 20 at New England 10
Houston 40 at Denver 10
Indianapolis 47 at Buffalo 6
Kansas City 17 at Los Angeles Raiders 35
Miami 20 at Seattle 24
San Diego 10 at Cincinnati 9

National Football Conference
Chicago 35 at Philadelphia 3
Green Bay 23 at Minnesota 16
Los Angeles Rams 10 at New Orleans 37
St Louis 21 at Washington 28
San Francisco 41 at New York Giants 21
Tampa Bay 31 at Detroit 27

Interconference Games
Dallas 38 at New York Jets 24
Pittsburgh 28 at Atlanta 12

Interconference Play
AFC 6 – NFC 3 (1 Tie)

Some people called them 'Scrubs' whilst to those who saw them as the enemies of the working class they were known as 'Scabs'. Their official term was 'Replacement Players'. They might not even have known each others' names, but when the whistle blew they were ready to play. The cast may have changed, then, but after a week's layoff the show was back on the road. For all their technical short-comings, the players lacked nothing in the way of enthusiasm. As might be expected, though, in the early stages there were many mistakes, as in Cincinnati, where three of the first eight plays produced fumbles.

Several veterans opted for crossing the picket lines and, for the offensive players, the uncoordinated defenses presented easy pickings. Against Buffalo, quarterback Gary Hogeboom passed for 259 yards and five touchdowns in the Colts' stroll to a 47-6 victory. Wide receiver Walter Murray, a

Gary Hogeboom made it all look easy against Buffalo.

Outstanding Individual Performances

100 Yards Rushing
Larry Mason (Cleveland) 32-133-22-2
Earnest Jackson (Pittsburgh) 29-104-17-1

100 Yards Pass Receiving
Anthony Allen (Washington) 7-255-88t-3
Walter Murray (Indianapolis) 7-161-43-2
Joey Clinkscales (Pittsburgh) 6-150-57-1
James Brim (Minnesota) 6-144-63t-1
Jimmy Teal (Seattle) 9-137-47-0
J.T. Smith (St Louis) 6-116-38-0

300 Yards Passing
Ed Rubbert (Washington) 24-14-334-1-88t-3
Bruce Mathison (Seattle) 42-20-326-3-47-2

backup in the Colts' regular squad, caught seven passes for 161 yards and two touchdowns. Running back Earnest Jackson rushed for 104 yards in Pittsburgh's 28-12 win at Atlanta. For Dallas, three veteran defensive linemen, starters Ed (Too Tall) Jones and Randy White, and backup Don Smerek overwhelmed a scratch Jets offensive line as the Cowboys sacked quarterback David Norrie eleven times.

In Los Angeles, there surfaced a name from the past as former Bears quarterback Vince Evans donned the 'Silver and Black', passed for 248 yards and two touchdowns, and ran for another, as the replacements kept the Raiders' unbeaten record intact.

Anthony Allen was another player to grab his unexpected opportunity. Allen had played for Atlanta in 1985 and 1986 but was waived in the final preseason roster cut-down. In the Redskins' key victory over divisional rival St Louis, Allen caught seven passes for a club single-game record 255 yards, and scored touchdowns on plays covering 34, 88 and 48 yards.

Before receiving his telephone call, John Fourcade had been warming the bench in Arena Football, but he passed for 222 yards and three touchdowns, including a club-record 82-yarder to tight end Mike Waters, as New Orleans kept the Rams winless on the season.

Two weeks earlier, he'd been watching NFL games on TV as he tended bar, but now quarterback Mike Hohensee passed for three touchdowns in the Bears' win over Philadelphia. After being cut by Tampa Bay, safety Paul Tripoli turned to selling furniture. Recalled for the game against Detroit, he intercepted two passes, tipped a third which was intercepted by Brian Gant, recovered a fumble and made two tackles behind the line of scrimmage. His 15-yard scoring interception brought the Buccaneers back to trail 14-17 in the second quarter of a game which they won by the score of 31-27. Quite suddenly, we had a new collection of heroes.

Above: Earnest Jackson.

Left: Anthony Allen.

STANDINGS					
AFC East	**W**	**L**	**T**	**PF**	**PA**
N.Y. Jets	2	1	0	98	90
Buffalo	1	2	0	68	108
Indianapolis	1	2	0	78	52
Miami	1	2	0	64	62
New England	1	2	0	62	84
AFC Central					
Cleveland	2	1	0	75	48
Houston	2	1	0	90	60
Pittsburgh	2	1	0	68	63
Cincinnati	1	2	0	58	58
AFC West					
L.A. Raiders	3	0	0	82	24
San Deigo	2	1	0	51	53
Seattle	2	1	0	84	74
Denver	1	1	1	67	74
Kansas City	1	2	0	51	91
NFC East	**W**	**L**	**T**	**PF**	**PA**
Dallas	2	1	0	67	62
Washington	2	1	0	82	66
Philadelphia	1	2	0	54	86
St Louis	1	2	0	69	69
N.Y. Giants	0	3	0	54	91
NFC Central					
Chicago	3	0	0	89	25
Minnesota	2	1	0	71	58
Tampa Bay	2	1	0	82	57
Green Bay	1	1	1	40	53
Detroit	0	3	0	53	92
NFC West					
New Orleans	2	1	0	82	58
San Francisco	2	1	0	85	77
Atlanta	1	2	0	43	96
L.A. Rams	0	3	0	42	78

WEEK FIVE

American Football Conference
Buffalo 7 at New England 14
Cincinnati 17 at Seattle 10
Houston 15 at Cleveland 10
Kansas City 0 at Miami 42
Los Angeles Raiders 14 at Denver 30
New York Jets 0 at Indianapolis 6

National Football Conference
Detroit 19 at Green Bay 16 (OT)
Minnesota 7 at Chicago 27
New Orleans 19 at St Louis 24
Philadelphia 22 at Dallas 41
San Francisco 25 at Atlanta 17
Washington 38 at New York Giants 12

Interconference Games
Pittsburgh 21 at Los Angeles Rams 31
San Diego 17 at Tampa Bay 13

Interconference Play
AFC 7– NFC 4 (1 Tie)

Above: Charles White (#33) had his best day as a pro.

By the second round of replacement games, there were those who felt that the results shouldn't count in the final standings. But Bears head coach Mike Ditka made his position clear, fuming, 'I'm sick and tired of hearing about the scab players. The guys that played Sunday were the real Chicago Bears. There were times, if it weren't for the names, I wouldn't have known the difference as to who was playing'.

St Louis head coach Gene Stallings had no difficulties in identifying his players – seventeen of them were regulars and represented the biggest slice of the 150 or so who had eased back into action. When the Cardinals met the Saints, the opening score was 17-11 (regulars who had returned) and the final score 24-19 (points), again in favour of the Cardinals.

Veterans helped the Rams to their first victory of the campaign. Reserve quarterback Steve Dils passed for two touchdowns whilst Charles White had both his career – and the day's – best rushing total with 166 yards. On special-team duty, safety Nolan Cromwell blocked a punt which was recovered for a touchdown by cornerback Kirby Jackson. The Rams' intra-city rivals, the Raiders, had both Howie Long and Bill Pickel back in harness when they travelled to Denver, but they suffered their first defeat of the season thanks mostly to Denver running back Joe Dudek, who rushed for 128 yards and two touchdowns, and the officials, who in error allowed Denver to kick a field goal on fifth down – that's right, fifth down!

The 49ers, with eleven returning veterans including quarterback Joe Montana, had too much fire-power for Atlanta and established a 20-0 halftime lead before coasting the rest of the way. For the second week in a row, a San Diego quarterback came off the bench to rally the team to victory. On Week Four, Mike Kelley had replaced Rick Neuheisel, but against the Buccaneers the roles were reversed. Completing 18 of 22 passes Neuheisel brought the Chargers back from a ten-point, halftime deficit to win by the score of 17-13.

The Giants' demise continued and, after four weeks, the reigning Super Bowl Champion was the only NFL club without a victory. One by one, players were taking potshots and hitting bullseye. Lionel Vital, a nifty little running back, was the latest marksman. Vital had been released by both the Giants and Washington during the 1986 season, but now, wearing the Burgundy and Gold of the Redskins, he rushed for 128 yards and scored one touchdown to earn a double dose of satisfaction.

Below: Michael LeBlanc made the difference for the Patriots in their win over Buffalo.

STANDINGS

AFC East	W	L	T	PF	PA
Indianapolis	2	2	0	84	52
Miami	2	2	0	106	62
New England	2	2	0	76	91
N. Y. Jets	2	2	0	98	96
Buffalo	1	3	0	75	122
AFC Central					
Houston	3	1	0	105	70
Cincinnati	2	2	0	75	68
Cleveland	2	2	0	85	63
Pittsburgh	2	2	0	89	94
AFC West					
L.A. Raiders	3	1	0	96	54
San Diego	3	1	0	68	66
Denver	2	1	1	97	88
Seattle	2	2	0	94	91
Kansas City	1	3	0	51	133
NFC East	**W**	**L**	**T**	**PF**	**PA**
Dallas	3	1	0	108	84
Washington	3	1	0	120	78
St Louis	2	2	0	93	88
Philadelphia	1	3	0	76	127
N.Y. Giants	0	4	0	66	129
NFC Central					
Chicago	4	0	0	116	32
Minnesota	2	2	0	78	85
Tampa Bay	2	2	0	95	74
Green Bay	1	2	1	56	72
Detroit	1	3	0	72	108
NFC West					
San Francisco	3	1	0	110	94
New Orleans	2	2	0	101	82
Atlanta	1	3	0	60	121
L.A. Rams	1	3	0	73	99

Outstanding Individual Performances

100 Yards Rushing
Charles White (L.A. Rams) 33-166-58-1
Chuck Banks (Indianapolis) 25-159-35-0
Michael LeBlanc (New England) 35-146-42-0
Dwight Beverly (New Orleans) 35-139-15-2
Joe Dudek (Denver) 23-128-16-2
Lionel Vital (Washington) 27-128-22t-1
Herman Hunter (Houston) 28-121-21-0
Marc Logan (Cincinnati) 16-103-30-1

100 Yards Pass Receiving
Kevin Bowman (Philadelphia) 5-123-62t-1
Cornell Burbage (Dallas) 3-110-77t-1
Al Williams (San Diego) 5-110-32-0
Leonard Harris (Houston) 6-104-39-0
Eric Martin (New Orleans) 7-101-24-1
Kelvin Edwards (Dallas) 6-100-37-0

300 Yards Passing
Scott Tinsley (Philadelphia) 34-24-338-0-62t-3

WEEK SIX

American Football Conference
Cleveland 34 at Cincinnati 0
Denver 26 at Kansas City 17
Indianapolis 7 at Pittsburgh 21
Miami 31 at New York Jets 37 (OT)
New England 21 at Houston 7
San Diego 23 at Los Angeles Raiders 17

National Football Conference
Los Angeles Rams 20 at Atlanta 24
Minnesota 10 at Tampa Bay 20
New Orleans 19 at Chicago 17
Philadelphia 10 at Green Bay 16 (OT)
St Louis 28 at San Francisco 34
Washington 13 at Dallas 7

Interconference Games
New York Giants 3 at Buffalo 6 (OT)
Seattle 37 at Detroit 14

Interconference Play
AFC 9 – NFC 4 (1 Tie)

Leading up to Week Six it had been clear that the players' strike was on the point of collapse, and by Thursday October 15 it was all over. But the returning veterans hoping to play on Sunday were disappointed, since the NFL owners had established Wednesday, 1 p.m. Eastern Daylight Time, as the deadline for reporting in. With only some 250 regulars on parade, then, Week Six meant that the replacements were given just one more opportunity to stake a claim for a place on the senior roster.

Lionel Vital made his statement, following up his 128 yards rushing of Week Five with a handsome 136 yards, helping Washington to a 13-7 victory over Dallas. And so did Atlanta's rookie free agent quarterback, Erik Kramer. Against the Rams, whose running back, Charles White, was rushing his way to the day's biggest haul for the second week in a row, Kramer passed for three touchdowns as the Falcons rallied from a 17-0 halftime deficit to win by the score of 24-20. Doug Flutie, who had recently arrived after a trade with Chicago, passed for 199 yards and a touchdown, and rushed for 43 yards, in the Patriots' win over Houston.

Elsewhere, big performances by regulars were less surprising. Starting quarterback Joe Montana, and senior reserves Jeff Kemp, Gary Danielson and Pat Ryan, each passed for four touchdowns. The NFL's most prolific, active wide receiver, Seattle's Steve Largent, caught 15 passes for 261 yards and three touchdowns before making a tactful exit – just over five minutes into the second half!

There never has been anything tactful about Elvis Patterson's nickname. The former Giants and now Chargers cornerback, Patterson simply isn't that bad a player, but he was dubbed 'Toast' by the unforgiving press for the number of times he's been 'burned' by wide receivers. By the end of the game against the Raiders, though, he was the 'toast' of San Diego, after having returned a late interception 75 yards for the touchdown which halted a Raiders drive and gave the Chargers a 23-17 win.

Patterson's touchdown meant that the Chargers joined San Francisco and Washington as the only three clubs to sweep the so-called 'replacement' games. Kansas City, Minnesota and Philadelphia were three of the four clubs which lost all three games. The fourth, the New York Giants, remained as the only NFL club without a win on the season.

STANDINGS											
AFC East	W	L	T	PF	PA	**NFC East**	W	L	T	PF	PA
New England	3	2	0	97	98	Washington	4	1	0	133	85
N.Y. Jets	3	2	0	135	127	Dallas	3	2	0	115	97
Buffalo	2	3	0	81	125	St Louis	2	3	0	121	122
Indianapolis	2	3	0	91	73	Philadelphia	1	4	0	86	143
Miami	2	3	0	137	99	N.Y. Giants	0	5	0	69	135
AFC Central						**NFC Central**					
Cleveland	3	2	0	119	63	Chicago	4	1	0	133	51
Houston	3	2	0	112	91	Tampa Bay	3	2	0	115	84
Pittsburgh	3	2	0	110	101	Green Bay	2	2	1	72	82
Cincinnati	2	3	0	75	102	Minnesota	2	3	0	88	105
AFC West						Detroit	1	4	0	86	145
San Diego	4	1	0	91	83	**NFC West**					
Denver	3	1	1	123	105	San Francisco	4	1	0	144	122
L.A. Raiders	3	2	0	113	77	New Orleans	3	2	0	120	99
Seattle	3	2	0	131	105	Atlanta	2	3	0	84	141
Kansas City	1	4	0	68	159	L.A. Rams	1	4	0	93	123

Elvis Patterson returning his key interception against the Raiders.

Outstanding Individual Performances

100 Yards Rushing
Charles White (L.A. Rams) 31-155-17-0
Carl Byrum (Buffalo) 25-139-30-0
Lionel Vital (Washington) 26-136-21-0
Earnest Jackson (Pittsburgh) 24-134-39-0
Derrick McAdoo (St Louis) 23-111-13-3
Kevin Willhite (Green Bay) 16-100-61-0

100 Yards Pass Receiving
Steve Largent (Seattle) 15-261-55-3
Brian Brennan (Cleveland) 10-139-23-1
Otis Grant (Philadelphia) 7-135-41-0
Lee Morris (Green Bay) 6-132-46t-1
Oliver Williams (Houston) 9-124-36t-1
Milton Barney (Atlanta) 6-109-32-1
Craig McEwen (Washington) 7-108-42-0
Steve Holloway (Tampa Bay) 8-107-26-0
Bobby Micho (Denver) 9-105-26t-2
Kelvin Edwards (Dallas) 6-104-38t-1

300 Yards Passing
Jeff Kemp (Seattle) 27-20-344-1-55-4
Erik Kramer (Atlanta) 46-27-335-2-32-3
Joe Montana (San Francisco) 39-31-334-2-35t-4
Pat Ryan (N.Y. Jets) 49-30-301-2-35t-4

WEEK SEVEN

American Football Conference
Buffalo 34 at Miami 31 (OT)
Cincinnati 20 at Pittsburgh 23
Kansas City 21 at San Diego 42
New England 16 at Indianapolis 30
Seattle 35 at Los Angeles Raiders 13

National Football Conference
Chicago 27 at Tampa Bay 26
Dallas 20 at Philadelphia 37
Green Bay 34 at Detroit 33
St Louis 7 at New York Giants 30
San Francisco 24 at New Orleans 22

Interconference Games
Atlanta 33 at Houston 37
Denver 27 at Minnesota 34
Los Angeles Rams 17 at Cleveland 30
New York Jets 16 at Washington 17

Interconference Play
AFC 11 – NFC 6 (1 Tie)

Rueben Mayes was outstanding in a losing cause.

STANDINGS

AFC East	W	L	T	PF	PA
Buffalo	3	3	0	115	156
Indianapolis	3	3	0	121	89
New England	3	3	0	113	128
N.Y. Jets	3	3	0	151	144
Miami	2	4	0	168	133
AFC Central					
Cleveland	4	2	0	149	80
Houston	4	2	0	149	124
Pittsburgh	4	2	0	133	121
Cincinnati	2	4	0	95	125
AFC West					
San Diego	5	1	0	133	104
Seattle	4	2	0	166	118
Denver	3	2	1	150	139
L.A. Raiders	3	3	0	126	112
Kansas City	1	5	0	89	201
NFC East	**W**	**L**	**T**	**PF**	**PA**
Washington	5	1	0	150	101
Dallas	3	3	0	135	134
Philadelphia	2	4	0	123	163
St Louis	2	4	0	128	152
N.Y. Giants	1	5	0	99	142
NFC Central					
Chicago	5	1	0	160	77
Green Bay	3	2	1	106	115
Minnesota	3	3	0	122	132
Tampa Bay	3	3	0	141	111
Detroit	1	5	0	119	179
NFC West					
San Francisco	5	1	0	168	144
New Orleans	3	3	0	142	123
Atlanta	2	4	0	117	178
L.A. Rams	1	5	0	110	153

Outstanding Individual Performances

100 Yards Rushing
Rueben Mayes (New Orleans) 29-144-38-0
Mike Rozier (Houston) 29-144-18-1
Kenneth Davis (Green Bay) 23-129-39t-2
Gerald Riggs (Atlanta) 21-113-26-0
Curt Warner (Seattle) 29-112-9-2

100 Yards Pass Receiving
Carlos Carson (Kansas City) 9-197-63t-2
Walter Stanley (Green Bay) 6-150-70t-1
Chris Burkett (Buffalo) 9-130-33-1
Todd Christensen (L.A. Raiders) 8-124-20-1
Stanley Morgan (New England) 7-102-27t-1
John Stallworth (Pittsburgh) 7-100-45-1

300 Yards Passing
Chuck Long (Detroit) 47-33-362-0-22t-3
Jim Kelly (Buffalo) 39-29-359-0-34-2
Bill Kenney (Kansas City) 38-22-328-1-63t-2
Don Majkowski (Green Bay) 29-19-323-1-70t-1
Boomer Esiason (Cincinnati) 32-20-303-2-43-2
Dan Marino (Miami) 36-24-303-0-25t-4

In future years, serious students of the game may make something of the fact that Week Seven saw the second-highest, single-week total of points in the history of the league – 736 points were scored compared with the highest total of 761 on October 16 and 17 in 1983. The instant analysis was that the defenses weren't ready, and it is true that more than half of the quarterbacks on parade had a field day, each throwing for two or more touchdown passes.

All three of the clubs which had prospered in the strike continued their winning ways, though, in two cases out of three, with some difficulty. The Chargers trampled Kansas City, but the Redskins beat the Jets only after trailing 16-7 with under ten minutes remaining. San Francisco might even have lost to an impressive New Orleans, but the Saints' Morten Andersen failed on a late 52-yard field goal attempt. By way of consolation, with the first of his five successful attempts in that game, Andersen became the NFL's most accurate kicker of all time.

All but Kansas City of the three-game losers ended the sequence, and you didn't need to be a Giants fan to breathe a sigh of relief. The reigning Super Bowl Champions jumped all over the Cardinals, whose only score came with under two minutes left. The unpredictable Eagles recovered three fumbles, blocked a field goal attempt and sacked Danny White five times as they took revenge for an earlier defeat by the Dallas Cowboys. Minnesota quarterback Wade Wilson was one of the few who were not fully back in tune – he threw five interceptions – but the combination of running backs Darrin Nelson (he rushed for 98 yards) and rookie D.J. Dozier, who scored three short-yardage touchdowns, made the difference in the Vikings' 34-27 defeat of Denver.

Elsewhere, a 14-yard touchdown reception by rookie wide receiver Curtis Duncan, with 27 seconds remaining, gave Houston victory over Atlanta, whilst Buffalo quarterback Jim Kelly rallied the Bills from a 21-point deficit for a thrilling overtime win against Miami. Gary Anderson's late, 20-yard field goal brought Pittsburgh victory after they had trailed 20-10 in the fourth quarter. The Bears welcomed back Jim McMahon after an absence stretching back to November 23, 1986, and the expressive quarterback did not disappoint them. Coming on for the second half, he was a little rusty but, with the Bears trailing Tampa Bay by twelve points entering the final quarter, he engineered the two touchdowns which saved a few blushes.

Clyde Simmons (Philadelphia) recovered a fumble and blocked a field goal to set up ten points, and registered two sacks.

WEEK EIGHT

American Football Conference
Cleveland 24 at San Diego 27 (OT)
Houston 31 at Cincinnati 29
Indianapolis 19 at New York Jets 14
Los Angeles Raiders 23 at New England 26
Pittsburgh 24 at Miami 35

National Football Conference
New Orleans 38 at Atlanta 0
New York Giants 24 at Dallas 33
Philadelphia 28 at St Louis 23
San Francisco 31 at Los Angeles Rams 10
Tampa Bay 23 v Green Bay 17 (at Milwaukee)

Interconference Games
Detroit 0 at Denver 34
Kansas City 28 at Chicago 31
Minnesota 17 at Seattle 28
Washington 27 at Buffalo 7

Interconference Play
AFC 13 – NFC 8 (1 Tie)

For some weeks it had been apparent that the Rams and star running back Eric Dickerson did not see eye-to-eye, and the rumours were confirmed when Dickerson was traded to Indianapolis in a complex, three-club arrangement which, in addition, saw the Rams gain running backs Owen Gill (ex-Colts), Greg Bell (ex-Buffalo), three future first-round and three future second-round draft options, whilst Buffalo got outside linebacker Cornelius Bennett, whom the Colts had been unable to sign.

Thus far on the season, the Colts had looked a much-improved team and now, having acquired the man generally regarded as the league's best running back, they became a serious contender. And the threat was underscored when Albert Bentley rushed for 145 yards in their 19-14 defeat of the Jets. Houston was another club to confirm its renaissance, overcoming a 15-point, fourth-quarter deficit to beat Cincinnati and go on top of the AFC Central. In the AFC West, the Chargers were in similar vein, in an overtime victory against Cleveland, whom they had trailed 24-14 entering the final quarter.

The NFC East leader, Washington, had little trouble disposing of the Bills, who were strangely ineffective following their heroics of Week Seven. Behind Washington, the clubs were settling their domestic scores, with Philadelphia beating St Louis on a late touchdown pass from Randall Cunningham to Gregg Garrity, whilst the Cowboys scored 19 fourth-quarter points to overcome a ten-point deficit against the Giants. At 1-6 on the season, all the Giants needed was a minor miracle.

Over in the NFC Central, Jim McMahon was performing another minor miracle to register his 24th consecutive victory as a starter. On four touchdown passes by Chiefs quarterback Bill Kenney, Kansas City established leads of 14-0 and 28-14. Kevin Butler's 27-yard field goal set up the final quarter and McMahon obliged with touchdown passes of 25 and 38 yards to give the Bears yet another nail-biting win. Meanwhile, the Bears' most serious rival in that division, Minnesota, were soundly beaten by a Seahawks club which was finding its touch. Starting quarterback Dave Krieg passed for three touchdowns before leaving with mild concussion, and backup Jeff Kemp added one of 28 yards to wide receiver Ray Butler after the Vikings had drawn to within four points. Following the 49ers' drubbing of the Rams, and the Saints' shutout of Atlanta, the pecking order around the league was becoming established.

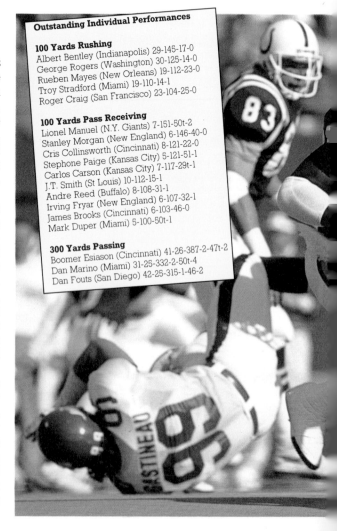

Outstanding Individual Performances

100 Yards Rushing
Albert Bentley (Indianapolis) 29-145-17-0
George Rogers (Washington) 30-125-14-0
Rueben Mayes (New Orleans) 19-112-23-0
Troy Stradford (Miami) 19-110-14-1
Roger Craig (San Francisco) 23-104-25-0

100 Yards Pass Receiving
Lionel Manuel (N.Y. Giants) 7-151-50t-2
Stanley Morgan (New England) 6-146-40-0
Cris Collinsworth (Cincinnati) 8-121-22-0
Stephone Paige (Kansas City) 5-121-51-1
Carlos Carson (Kansas City) 7-117-29t-1
J.T. Smith (St Louis) 10-112-15-1
Andre Reed (Buffalo) 8-108-31-1
Irving Fryar (New England) 6-107-32-1
James Brooks (Cincinnati) 6-103-46-0
Mark Duper (Miami) 5-100-50t-1

300 Yards Passing
Boomer Esiason (Cincinnati) 41-26-387-2-47t-2
Dan Marino (Miami) 31-25-332-2-50t-4
Dan Fouts (San Diego) 42-25-315-1-46-2

STANDINGS

AFC East	W	L	T	PF	PA	NFC East	W	L	T	PF	PA
Indianapolis	4	3	0	140	103	Washington	6	1	0	177	108
New England	4	3	0	139	151	Dallas	4	3	0	168	158
Buffalo	3	4	0	122	183	Philadelphia	3	4	0	151	186
Miami	3	4	0	203	157	St Louis	2	5	0	151	180
N.Y. Jets	3	4	0	165	163	N.Y. Giants	1	6	0	123	175
AFC Central						**NFC Central**					
Houston	5	2	0	180	153	Chicago	6	1	0	191	105
Cleveland	4	3	0	173	107	Tampa Bay	4	3	0	164	128
Pittsburgh	4	3	0	157	156	Green Bay	3	3	1	123	138
Cincinnati	2	5	0	124	156	Minnesota	3	4	0	139	160
AFC West						Detroit	1	6	0	119	213
San Diego	6	1	0	160	128	**NFC West**					
Seattle	5	2	0	194	135	San Francisco	6	1	0	199	154
Denver	4	2	1	184	139	New Orleans	4	3	0	180	123
L.A. Raiders	3	4	0	149	138	Atlanta	2	5	0	117	216
Kansas City	1	6	0	117	232	L.A. Rams	1	6	0	120	184

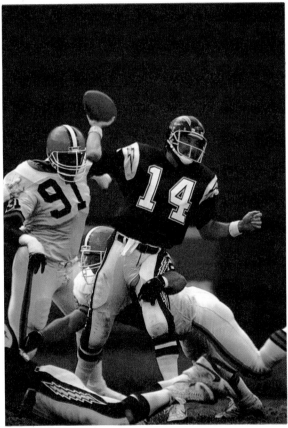

Left: Albert Bentley had his best outing of the season.

Above: Dan Fouts (#14) rallied the Chargers for victory against Cleveland.

WEEK NINE

American Football Conference
Denver 14 at Buffalo 21
Miami 20 at Cincinnati 14
Pittsburgh 17 at Kansas City 16
San Diego 16 at Indianapolis 13
Seattle 14 at New York Jets 30

National Football Conference
Chicago 26 at Green Bay 24
Dallas 17 at Detroit 27
New Orleans 31 at Los Angeles Rams 14
Tampa Bay 28 at St Louis 31
Washington 27 at Philadelphia 31

Interconference Games
Atlanta 3 at Cleveland 38
Houston 20 at San Francisco 27
Los Angeles Raiders 20 at Minnesota 31
New England 10 at New York Giants 17

Interconference Play
AFC 14 – NFC 11 (1 Tie)

Week Nine saw Eric Dickerson rush for 138 yards on his debut as a starter for the Colts, but it was the yardage he didn't gain which cost the club a victory over San Diego. With the scores tied on 13-13 and the Colts at first-and-goal, Dickerson fumbled the ball into the San Diego end zone. With that possession, the Chargers drove 59 yards for Vince Abbott's 39-yard field goal, which came with twelve seconds left. It was the Chargers' seventh straight win, and, with all four of their divisional rivals losing, it left them in a commanding position. Despite outgaining the Vikings in the ratio of two yards to one, the Raiders had slumped to their fifth consecutive loss. In the Monday Night Game, Seattle would be upset by the Jets, and such had been Denver's modest form that it went without much notice when they were defeated by Buffalo to stand at 4-3-1 on the season.

Washington was another team to suffer a surprise defeat as, for the second week in a row, Philadelphia quarterback Randall Cunningham combined with wide receiver Gregg Garrity for the winning touchdown, this time a 40-yarder with 1:06 remaining. At the expense of the Rams, New Orleans continued to roll and San Francisco disposed of Houston, whose loss, coupled with wins by both Cleveland and Pittsburgh, produced a three-way tie on top of the AFC Central. If one felt that the Central was close, a quick glance at the AFC East showed all five teams tied at 4-4! In Miami's 20-14 win over Cincinnati, Dan Marino had thrown a touchdown pass

for the 28th consecutive regular-season game to move into a tie with Seattle's Dave Krieg for the NFL's second-longest sequence (the retired Johnny Unitas is way ahead with 47).

For the third week in a row, Chicago needed to come from behind to win. Troubled by a groin injury, Jim McMahon was not at his best, but he directed the final drive 41 yards, and just four seconds were left when Kevin Butler kicked the 52-yard field goal which gave the Bears a 26-24 win over Green Bay. But on this day, nothing could compare with the Cardinals' comeback against Tampa Bay. Three Steve DeBerg touchdowns had helped the Buccaneers to a 28-3 lead, which lasted until 2:18 inside the final quarter. It was then that rookie tight end Robert Awalt scored the first of four touchdowns, three on passes by quarterback Neil Lomax, as the Cardinals posted the greatest fourth-quarter rally in league history. In addition to registering ten solo tackles, Cardinals linebacker Niko Noga returned a fumble 23 yards for a touchdown.

Outstanding Individual Performances

100 Yards Rushing
Eric Dickerson (Indianapolis) 35-138-13-0
Earnest Jackson (Pittsburgh) 23-125-28-0

100 Yards Pass Receiving
Phil Epps (Green Bay) 6-139-40-1
James Lofton (L.A. Raiders) 4-128-49-1
Robert Awalt (St Louis) 9-124-27-1
Gary Clark (Washington) 5-119-47t-1
Eddie Brown (Cincinnati) 8-105-21-0
Neal Anderson (Chicago) 5-102-59t-1
Drew Hill (Houston) 4-101-48-0
Steve Largent (Seattle) 5-100-30-1

300 Yards Passing
Neil Lomax (St Louis) 36-25-314-1-39-3
Steve DeBerg (Tampa Bay) 37-23-303-0-34t-3

Opposite: JoJo Townsell (Jets) returned a punt 91 yards for a touchdown.

Right: Mike Merriweather (Pittsburgh) intercepted a pass and logged 2.5 sacks against Kansas City.

STANDINGS

AFC East	W	L	T	PF	PA	NFC East	W	L	T	PF	PA
Buffalo	4	4	0	143	197	Washington	6	2	0	204	139
Indianapolis	4	4	0	153	119	Dallas	4	4	0	185	185
Miami	4	4	0	223	171	Philadelphia	4	4	0	182	213
New England	4	4	0	149	168	St Louis	3	5	0	182	208
N.Y. Jets	4	4	0	195	177	N.Y. Giants	2	6	0	140	185
AFC Central						**NFC Central**					
Cleveland	5	3	0	211	110	Chicago	7	1	0	217	129
Houston	5	3	0	200	180	Minnesota	4	4	0	170	180
Pittsburgh	5	3	0	174	172	Tampa Bay	4	4	0	192	159
Cincinnati	2	6	0	138	176	Green Bay	3	4	1	147	164
AFC West						Detroit	2	6	0	146	230
San Diego	7	1	0	176	141	**NFC West**					
Seattle	5	3	0	208	165	San Francisco	7	1	0	226	174
Denver	4	3	1	198	160	New Orleans	5	3	0	211	137
L.A. Raiders	3	5	0	169	169	Atlanta	2	6	0	120	254
Kansas City	1	7	0	133	249	L.A. Rams	1	7	0	134	215

WEEK TEN

American Football Conference
Buffalo 21 at Cleveland 27
Houston 23 at Pittsburgh 3
Indianapolis 40 at Miami 21
Los Angeles Raiders 14 at San Diego 16
New York Jets 16 at Kansas City 9

National Football Conference
Detroit 13 at Washington 20
Los Angeles Rams 27 at St Louis 24
New Orleans 26 at San Francisco 24
New York Giants 20 at Philadelphia 17
Tampa Bay 17 at Minnesota 23

Interconference Games
Chicago 29 at Denver 31
Cincinnati 16 at Atlanta 10
Dallas 23 at New England 17 (OT)
Green Bay 13 at Seattle 24

Interconference Play
AFC 17 – NFC 12 (1 Tie)

*Above: Freeman McNeil was
at his very best against Kansas City.*

*Opposite: Doug Williams
ignited Washington against Detroit.*

Week Ten in the NFL might be renamed the 'Day of the Running Back' as eight men rushed for 100 or more yards and, in seven cases, their teams won. The odd man out was Gerald Riggs. His Atlanta Falcons lost to a late touchdown by Cincinnati running back Larry Kinnebrew, whose two-yard rush gave him an even 100 in the game. Freeman McNeil was in his seventh year as a top-class running back but, following injuries, it appeared that he had lost a step or two of pace, and the Jets had installed Johnny Hector as the senior player. However, following an earlier injury to Hector, McNeil started and tore the Chiefs to shreds with 184 yards, the second-best rushing output of his career. Herschel Walker is in the early stages of what will doubtless be an outstanding NFL career, and it was only on Week Ten that he was named the starting running back ahead of the great veteran, Tony Dorsett. Walker wasted no time earning his spurs, rushing for 173 yards (it

STANDINGS					
AFC East	**W**	**L**	**T**	**PF**	**PA**
Indianapolis	5	4	0	193	140
N.Y. Jets	5	4	0	211	186
Buffalo	4	5	0	164	224
Miami	4	5	0	244	211
New England	4	5	0	166	191
AFC Central					
Cleveland	6	3	0	238	131
Houston	6	3	0	223	183
Pittsburgh	5	4	0	177	195
Cincinnati	3	6	0	154	186
AFC West					
San Diego	8	1	0	192	155
Seattle	6	3	0	232	178
Denver	5	3	1	229	189
L.A. Raiders	3	6	0	183	185
Kansas City	1	8	0	142	265
NFC East	**W**	**L**	**T**	**PF**	**PA**
Washington	7	2	0	224	152
Dallas	5	4	0	208	202
Philadelphia	4	5	0	199	233
N.Y. Giants	3	6	0	160	202
St Louis	3	6	0	206	235
NFC Central					
Chicago	7	2	0	246	160
Minnesota	5	4	0	193	197
Tampa Bay	4	5	0	209	182
Green Bay	3	5	1	160	188
Detroit	2	7	0	159	250
NFC West					
San Francisco	7	2	0	250	200
New Orleans	6	3	0	237	161
Atlanta	2	7	0	130	270
L.A. Rams	2	7	0	161	239

was the fourth-best, single-game total in Dallas history), the last 60 of which came in one chunk as he scored the winning touchdown in overtime against the Patriots.

The truly great rushing performance of the day came from Charles White, in whom the Rams had placed their faith following the trade of Eric Dickerson to the Colts. White gained a career-best 213 yards, leading the Rams to a morale-boosting win over the fast-improving Cardinals. Dickerson was outdone but not totally, as he underlined his value to the Colts with 154 yards rushing in their stunning 40-21 victory over Miami. Following the manner and style of that win, there were few who doubted that Indianapolis now was a genuine contender. Curt Warner showed some of his best form, rushing for 123 yards in Seattle's win over the Packers. The eighth centurion of the day was Darrin Nelson, a running back who has had only few chances to

register big yardage in the Vikings' pass-dominated offenses of recent years. Nelson's 103 yards and three field goals by his namesake, Chuck, kept the Vikings in the hunt for a playoff spot. New Orleans did not have a 100-yard rusher, but in defeating San Francisco 26-24, they passed the credibility test.

Doug Williams came in as a replacement and directed Washington to victory against Detroit. If one could point to a moment when Denver quarterback John Elway earned the unofficial nickname of 'Superman' it was in this game against Chicago. On Monday evening, Elway and Bears quarterback Jim McMahon had their duel, each passing for over 300 yards and three touchdowns. The Bears didn't help themselves by missing two PATs and William Perry fumbled at the Denver goal line. But in the end, they were beaten by a man who, it seemed at the time, didn't know the meaning of defeat.

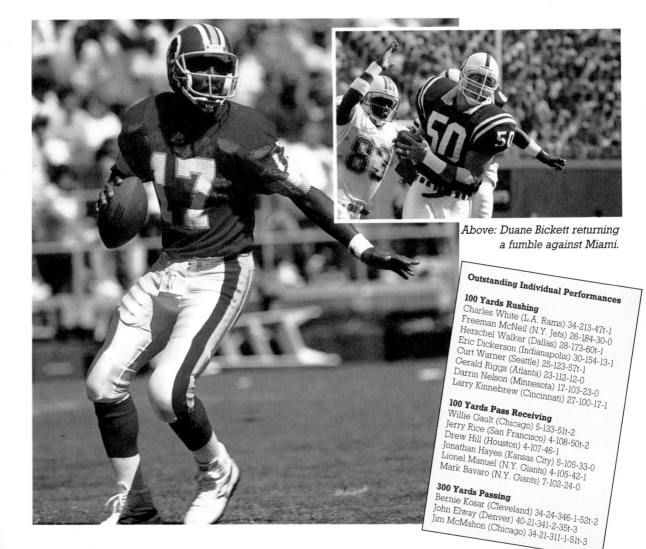

Above: Duane Bickett returning a fumble against Miami.

Outstanding Individual Performances

100 Yards Rushing
Charles White (L.A. Rams) 34-213-47t-1
Freeman McNeil (N.Y. Jets) 26-184-30-0
Herschel Walker (Dallas) 28-173-60t-1
Eric Dickerson (Indianapolis) 30-154-13-1
Curt Warner (Seattle) 25-123-57t-1
Gerald Riggs (Atlanta) 23-112-12-0
Darrin Nelson (Minnesota) 17-103-23-0
Larry Kinnebrew (Cincinnati) 27-100-17-1

100 Yards Pass Receiving
Willie Gault (Chicago) 5-133-51t-2
Jerry Rice (San Francisco) 4-108-50t-2
Drew Hill (Houston) 4-107-46-1
Jonathan Hayes (Kansas City) 5-105-33-0
Lionel Manuel (N.Y. Giants) 4-105-42-1
Mark Bavaro (N.Y. Giants) 7-102-24-0

300 Yards Passing
Bernie Kosar (Cleveland) 34-24-346-1-52t-2
John Elway (Denver) 40-21-341-2-35t-3
Jim McMahon (Chicago) 34-21-311-1-51t-3

WEEK ELEVEN

American Football Conference
Buffalo 17 at New York Jets 14
Cleveland 40 at Houston 7
Denver 23 at Los Angeles Raiders 17
Indianapolis 0 at New England 24
Pittsburgh 30 at Cincinnati 16
San Diego 3 at Seattle 34

National Football Conference
Atlanta 13 at Minnesota 24
Detroit 10 at Chicago 30
Los Angeles Rams 30 at Washington 26
New York Giants 14 at New Orleans 23
St Louis 31 at Philadelphia 19
San Francisco 24 at Tampa Bay 10

Interconference Games
Green Bay 23 at Kansas City 3
Miami 20 at Dallas 14

Interconference Play
AFC 18 – NFC 13 (1 Tie)

Week Eleven might be considered the time when the clubs begin to focus on the playoffs – the divisional races begin to hot up. But for the AFC East teams, it was back to square one since all five ended the day locked in a tie at 5-5. And it was difficult to predict which one would emerge from the pack. Buffalo, whose defense was improving by the game, gained a close victory over the Jets, whilst Miami had just too much offense for Dallas. The Patriots had the most impressive win, scoring 24 points and shutting out the Colts. More than doing themselves a favour, Cleveland also made a point when they overran the second-placed Houston Oilers. Pittsburgh's win over Cincinnati was achieved without too much difficulty and, for all intents and purposes, put the Bengals out of contention. For Pittsburgh, potential superstar rookie defensive back Rod Woodson returned an interception 45 yards for a touchdown. Over in the AFC West, there were the first signs of a changing of the guard as Seattle halted the Chargers' winning sequence at eight. For Seattle, Curt Warner had his second 100-yards-rushing game in a row, whilst quarterback Dave Krieg was particularly sharp, passing for 246 yards and two touchdowns, and rushing for another. John Elway mounted another one-man show (he passed for 298 yards and scored touchdowns by both passing and rushing) in a 23-17 defeat of the Raiders. The Broncos were easing into their finishing burst.

Fresh from their 27-24 win over St Louis, the Rams upset Washington. Taking advantage of turnovers – Mike Wilcher scored on a 35-yard fumble return

and Charles White's touchdown run followed a blocked Washington punt – and with Ron Brown scoring touchdowns on a 95-yard kickoff return and on a 26-yard reception, they led 30-19 after three quarters and allowed only one further score. Even in defeat, though, the Redskins still held a comfortable two-game lead over Dallas. A 31-point scoring burst by St Louis had seen off Philadelphia and lifted them alongside the same Eagles, three games adrift. In the NFC Central, the Bears rebounded from defeat with a solid victory over the modest Detroit Lions, whilst the Vikings, with their third win in a row, and fourth in five games since the strike, had now repaired the damage. In the NFC West, the Saints continued to march and, as expected, the 49ers rebounded from their Week Ten defeat by New Orleans. Also, in San Francisco, there was an interesting sideshow developing. Against Tampa Bay, three touchdown receptions had taken wide receiver Jerry Rice's total on the season to 11. He needed eight more to break the NFL single-season record and there were five games to go.

Opposite: Ron Brown returned to top form against Washington.

Left: Cleveland's Frank Minnifield intercepted three passes.

Outstanding Individual Performances

100 Yards Rushing
Troy Stradford (Miami) 17-169-51-1
Curt Warner (Seattle) 23-119-27-1
Eric Dickerson (Indianapolis) 27-117-16-0
Kevin Mack (Cleveland) 26-114-22-1
Charles White (L.A. Rams) 35-112-10-1
Freeman McNeil (N.Y. Jets) 20-103-16-0

100 Yards Pass Receiving
Tim McGee (Cincinnati) 8-139-49-0
Ernest Givins (Houston) 3-126-83t-1
Vance Johnson (Denver) 5-115-49-1
Jerry Rice (San Francisco) 7-103-42t-3
Stanley Morgan (New England) 5-102-30-0
Stephen Baker (N.Y. Giants) 4-100-46t-1

300 Yards Passing
Boomer Esiason (Cincinnati) 53-30-409-3-49-0
Doug Williams (Washington) 46-24-308-1-60-2
Joe Montana (San Francisco) 45-29-304-1-42t-3

STANDINGS

AFC East	W	L	T	PF	PA	NFC East	W	L	T	PF	PA
Buffalo	5	5	0	181	238	Washington	7	3	0	250	182
Indianapolis	5	5	0	193	164	Dallas	5	5	0	222	222
Miami	5	5	0	264	225	Philadelphia	4	6	0	218	264
New England	5	5	0	190	191	St Louis	4	6	0	237	254
N.Y. Jets	5	5	0	225	203	N.Y. Giants	3	7	0	174	225
AFC Central						**NFC Central**					
Cleveland	7	3	0	278	138	Chicago	8	2	0	276	170
Houston	6	4	0	230	223	Minnesota	6	4	0	217	210
Pittsburgh	6	4	0	207	211	Green Bay	4	5	1	183	191
Cincinnati	3	7	0	170	216	Tampa Bay	4	6	0	219	206
AFC West						Detroit	2	8	0	169	280
San Diego	8	2	0	195	189	**NFC West**					
Seattle	7	3	0	266	181	San Francisco	8	2	0	274	210
Denver	6	3	1	252	206	New Orleans	7	3	0	260	175
L.A. Raiders	3	7	0	200	208	L.A. Rams	3	7	0	191	265
Kansas City	1	9	0	145	288	Atlanta	2	8	0	143	294

WEEK TWELVE

American Football Conference
Cincinnati 20 at New York Jets 27
Denver 31 at San Diego 17
Houston 27 at Indianapolis 51
Los Angeles Raiders 37 at Seattle 14
Miami 0 at Buffalo 27

National Football Conference
Green Bay 10 at Chicago 23
Minnesota 44 at Dallas 38 (OT)
New York Giants 19 at Washington 23
St Louis 34 at Atlanta 21
Tampa Bay 3 at Los Angeles Rams 35

Interconference Games
Cleveland 24 at San Francisco 38
Kansas City 27 at Detroit 20
New Orleans 20 at Pittsburgh 16
Philadelphia 34 at New England 31 (OT)

Interconference Play
AFC 19 – NFC 16 (1 Tie)

Bo Jackson silenced all his critics against the Seahawks.

Way back in April, no-one took much notice when the Raiders expended their seventh-round option to draft running back Bo Jackson. The 1985 Heisman Trophy winner, he'd been picked first in the entire draft in 1986 by Tampa Bay but opted for a career in baseball with the Kansas City Royals. The workings of the system meant that he was again eligible to be drafted and the Raiders felt that a low option was worth the gamble – just on the off-chance that they could persuade him to play for them. It seems that the charms of managing general partner Al Davis proved irresistible since, on completing the baseball season, Jackson joined the Raiders. He was brought along steadily, rushing for 37, 74, 45 and 98 yards after suiting up but not playing on Week Seven against Seattle. On Week Twelve, in the return fixture with Seattle, he rushed for a mammoth 221 yards, the 13th-best total in NFL history, and scored three touchdowns, one on a 91-yard rush which was the equal-eighth longest in NFL history. On one of his touchdown scores, he simply ran over Seahawks inside linebacker Brian Bosworth. The Raiders didn't have a realistic chance of reaching the playoffs, but they might now make life difficult for those who did.

Of the major contenders, Chicago twice had to come from behind to beat Green Bay – Al Harris blocked two Packers field goal attempts – whilst on Thanksgiving Day Minnesota won an overtime spectacular against Dallas. For Minnesota wide receiver Anthony Carter caught eight passes for 184 yards and two touchdowns, but Cowboys veteran wide receiver Mike Renfro countered with 100 yards and three touchdowns, including the 18-yarder which took the game into overtime. Vikings running back Darrin Nelson settled it with a 24-yard touchdown run halfway through the extra period. Cleveland were halted by the 49ers at their efficient best – Jerry Rice caught three touchdown passes – but the Browns retained their one-game lead following losses by both Pittsburgh and Houston, the latter who were beaten badly by the Colts. Buffalo blanked Miami, ending quarterback Dan Marino's consecutive-game, touchdown-passing sequence at 30. But for New England and Cincinnati, two sequences were extended. After missing an opportunity to win the game in regulation time – placekicker Tony Franklin failed on a 31-yard field goal attempt with five seconds remaining – the Patriots eventually lost to the Eagles, extending their record in overtime games to 0-10. Against the Bengals, the Jets turned probable defeat into victory when safety Rich Miano ran 67 yards for the winning touchdown following a blocked 46-yard field goal attempt. For the fourth time in the season, then, Cincinnati was beaten in the final two minutes.

Outstanding Individual Performances

100 Yards Rushing
Bo Jackson (L.A. Raiders) 18-221-91t-2
Charles White (L.A. Rams) 29-137-23-2
Eric Dickerson (Indianapolis) 27-136-29-2
Anthony Toney (Philadelphia) 24-123-36-1
Mike Rozier (Houston) 26-122-18-0
Ronnie Harmon (Buffalo) 23-119-19-0
Darrin Nelson (Minnesota) 16-118-52t-2

100 Yards Pass Receiving
Anthony Carter (Minnesota) 8-184-51-2
Drew Hill (Houston) 7-134-40t-2
Jerry Rice (San Francisco) 7-126-30t-3
Mike Quick (Philadelphia) 5-121-61t-2
Ricky Nattiel (Denver) 4-118-46t-1
Aubrey Matthews (Atlanta) 7-115-32-2
Gary Clark (Washington) 7-112-34t-1
J.T. Smith (St Louis) 10-109-22-0
Tony Collins (New England) 11-100-29-1
Mike Renfro (Dallas) 7-100-19-3

300 Yards Passing
Tom Ramsey (New England) 53-34-402-2-40-3
Neil Lomax (St Louis) 42-25-369-1-49t-2
John Elway (Denver) 32-21-347-1-52-3
Joe Montana (San Francisco) 31-23-342-1-40t-4
Danny White (Dallas) 41-25-341-3-39-4
Jay Schroeder (Washington) 46-28-331-2-34t-3
Warren Moon (Houston) 44-24-327-2-40t-3
Dan Fouts (San Diego) 40-23-322-2-38-0
Randall Cunningham (Philadelphia) 31-18-314-1-61t-2

Elbert Foules (Philadelphia) intercepting a pass in the Eagles' victory over New England.

STANDINGS

AFC East	W	L	T	PF	PA
Buffalo	6	5	0	208	238
Indianapolis	6	5	0	244	191
N.Y. Jets	6	5	0	252	223
Miami	5	6	0	264	252
New England	5	6	0	221	225
AFC Central					
Cleveland	7	4	0	302	176
Houston	6	5	0	257	274
Pittsburgh	6	5	0	223	231
Cincinnati	3	8	0	190	243
AFC West					
San Diego	8	3	0	212	220
Denver	7	3	1	283	223
Seattle	7	4	0	280	218
L.A. Raiders	4	7	0	237	222
Kansas City	2	9	0	172	308
NFC East	**W**	**L**	**T**	**PF**	**PA**
Washington	8	3	0	273	201
Dallas	5	6	0	260	266
Philadelphia	5	6	0	252	295
St Louis	5	6	0	271	275
N.Y. Giants	3	8	0	193	248
NFC Central					
Chicago	9	2	0	299	180
Minnesota	7	4	0	261	248
Green Bay	4	6	1	193	214
Tampa Bay	4	7	0	222	241
Detroit	2	9	0	189	307
NFC West					
San Francisco	9	2	0	312	234
New Orleans	8	3	0	280	191
L.A. Rams	4	7	0	226	268
Atlanta	2	9	0	164	328

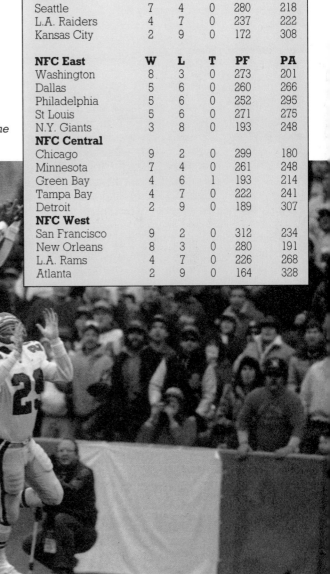

WEEK THIRTEEN

American Football Conference
Buffalo 21 at Los Angeles Raiders 34
Indianapolis 9 at Cleveland 7
Kansas City 27 at Cincinnati 30 (OT)
New England 20 at Denver 31
New York Jets 28 at Miami 37
San Diego 18 at Houston 33
Seattle 9 at Pittsburgh 13

National Football Conference
Atlanta 21 at Dallas 10
Chicago 30 at Minnesota 24
Los Angeles Rams 37 at Detroit 16
Philadelphia 20 at New York Giants 23 (OT)
San Francisco 23 at Green Bay 12
Tampa Bay 34 at New Orleans 44
Washington 34 at St Louis 17

Interconference Play
AFC 19 – NFC 16 (1 Tie)

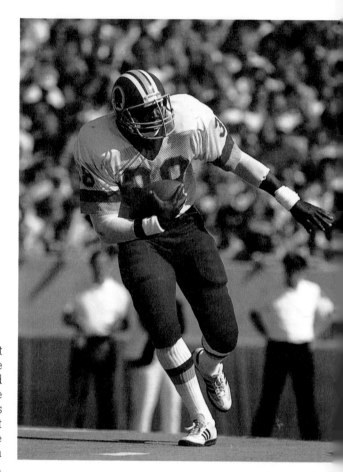

George Rogers (Washington) had the day's best rushing performance.

Where there had been mists there was now almost crystal clarity, at least in the NFC, in which, by the end of Week Thirteen, four teams had clinched spots in the playoffs. Chicago won the title in the NFC Central in a game of high drama. Vikings quarterback Wade Wilson came on in replacement of the injured Tommy Kramer and drilled three touchdown passes to wrest the initiative from a Bears team which had led 13-0 and 20-7. However, with Minnesota leading 24-23 and poised to score what could have been the winning touchdown, the Bears mounted a goal-line stand, prevented a score and snatched a last-minute victory on Dennis Gentry's 38-yard touchdown reception from Mike Tomczak. Sadly, Jim McMahon had suffered yet another injury. By comparison, the Redskins' come-from-behind victory over St Louis was just another day's work, but it was good enough to earn them the title in the NFC East. Over in the West, victories by the 49ers and the Saints earned playoff spots for both clubs, though the title had not yet been decided. The Saints had rushed, passed and tackled just like you'd expect of a club which needed only one win to reach the playoffs for the first time in its history. Whilst their owner danced a 'boogie', however, the players settled for the satisfaction – they knew that there still was a job to be done. In Green Bay, Jerry Rice had to wait until the final quarter for the touchdown reception which both raised his total for the season to 15 and made victory safe for the 49ers.

In the AFC, consecutive victories over Chicago, the Raiders, San Diego and now New England, whom they had overtaken with 14 points in the final quarter, had swept the Broncos to the top of the AFC West. By the margin of the game they'd shared with Green Bay (a tie counts half-a-game won and half-a-game lost), they led from the Chargers and Seattle, each of whom had lost to AFC Central opponents. In handing the Chargers their third straight loss, the Oilers had converted three San Diego fumbles into 16 points, whilst in Pittsburgh, veteran running back Frank Pollard was on his best form as he rushed for a game total of 106 yards, including the fourth-quarter touchdown which sent the Seahawks home disappointed. Indianapolis and Cleveland had one of those old-style contests, dominated by defense. In difficult weather conditions, the Colts' Dean Biasucci kicked field goals of 33, 37 and 41 yards (he had no failures) but he had to share the honours with free safety Mike Prior, who recovered a fumble by Browns running back Earnest Byner on first-and-goal from the Indianapolis five-yard line, to preserve the two-point margin. At last, the Colts were in sole possession of first place in the AFC East.

STANDINGS

AFC East	W	L	T	PF	PA
Indianapolis	7	5	0	253	198
Buffalo	6	6	0	229	272
Miami	6	6	0	301	280
N.Y. Jets	6	6	0	280	260
New England	5	7	0	241	256
AFC Central					
Cleveland	7	5	0	309	185
Houston	7	5	0	290	292
Pittsburgh	7	5	0	236	240
Cincinnati	4	8	0	220	270
AFC West					
Denver	8	3	1	314	243
San Diego	8	4	0	230	253
Seattle	7	5	0	289	231
L.A. Raiders	5	7	0	271	243
Kansas City	2	10	0	199	338

NFC East	W	L	T	PF	PA
Washington†	9	3	0	307	218
Dallas	5	7	0	270	287
Philadelphia	5	7	0	272	318
St Louis	5	7	0	288	309
N.Y. Giants	4	8	0	216	268
NFC Central					
Chicago†	10	2	0	329	204
Minnesota	7	5	0	285	278
Green Bay	4	7	1	205	237
Tampa Bay	4	8	0	256	285
Detroit	2	10	0	205	344
NFC West					
San Francisco*	10	2	0	335	246
New Orleans*	9	3	0	324	225
L.A. Rams	5	7	0	263	284
Atlanta	3	9	0	185	338

† Division Champion
* Clinched Playoff Spot

Above: Karl Mecklenburg (Denver) intercepted two passes
Below: Mark Carrier (Tampa Bay).

Outstanding Individual Performances

100 Yards Rushing
George Rogers (Washington) 29-133-29-1
Troy Stradford (Miami) 30-120-21-3
Gerald Riggs (Atlanta) 30-119-12-0
Frank Pollard (Pittsburgh) 22-106-15-1
Charles White (L.A. Rams) 29-102-14-2
Stump Mitchell (St Louis) 20-101-35-0

100 Yards Pass Receiving
Mark Carrier (Tampa Bay) 8-212-38-1
Henry Ellard (L.A. Rams) 7-171-81t-1
Andre Reed (Buffalo) 7-153-38-0
Wes Chandler (San Diego) 10-140-24-0
Mark Bavaro (N.Y. Giants) 6-133-36-1
James Lofton (L.A. Raiders) 6-132-41t-1
Gary Clark (Washington) 5-130-84t-1
Anthony Carter (Minnesota) 3-106-60t-2
Eric Martin (New Orleans) 2-101-67-0
Al Toon (N.Y. Jets) 5-100-44t-1

300 Yards Passing
Vinny Testaverde (Tampa Bay) 47-22-369-2-38-2
Boomer Esiason (Cincinnati) 44-28-368-0-26-2
Marc Wilson (L.A. Raiders) 32-21-337-0-41t-3
Jim Everett (L.A. Rams) 26-20-324-1-81t-2
Jim Kelly (Buffalo) 36-22-315-0-38-1
Joe Montana (San Francisco) 35-26-308-1-57t-2

WEEK FOURTEEN

American Football Conference
Buffalo 27 at Indianapolis 3
Cincinnati 24 at Cleveland 38
Denver 21 at Seattle 28
Los Angeles Raiders 10 at Kansas City 16
New York Jets 20 at New England 42
Pittsburgh 20 at San Diego 16

National Football Conference
Atlanta 0 at Los Angeles Rams 33
Chicago 0 at San Francisco 41
Dallas 20 at Washington 24
Detroit 20 at Tampa Bay 10
Minnesota 10 v Green Bay 16 (at Milwaukee)
New York Giants 24 at St Louis 27

Interconference Games
Houston 10 at New Orleans 24
Miami 28 at Philadelphia 10

Interconference Play
AFC 20 – NFC 17 (1 Tie)

As the playoff races hotted up elsewhere in the league, San Francisco took a step closer to the title in the NFC West with an astonishing display against Chicago. Quarterback Steve Young came on in the first quarter in replacement of the injured Joe Montana and threw four touchdown passes, three to wide receiver Jerry Rice who thus equalled two of the NFL's better records. His total of 18 touchdown receptions in a single season now matched that of Miami's Mark Clayton (1984), and by catching at least one touchdown pass in eleven consecutive games he equalled the record shared by Elroy (Crazylegs) Hirsch (1950-51) and Buddy Dial (1959-60). By contrast, Chicago reserve quarterback Mike Tomczak threw four interceptions before being replaced by third-stringer Jim Harbaugh. The 49ers' rivals, New Orleans, were not troubled by Houston against whom they took control on touchdown receptions of 54 and seven yards by wide receiver Eric Martin. The team widely expected to gain the one remaining playoff spot in the NFC, Minnesota, tripped up against Green Bay, who drove 72 yards for the winning touchdown, a seven-yard run by Kenneth Davis, which came with slightly more than a minute to play.

Just when it seemed that the Broncos would stroll to the title in the AFC West, they were halted by a rampant Seattle team led by quarterback Dave Krieg, who passed for 238 yards and three touchdowns. Denver's John Elway threw for 335 yards but was sacked five times. The Steelers handed the Chargers their fourth straight loss but they had to overcome a first-quarter, nine-point deficit. With that win they retained a share for the lead with Cleveland in the AFC Central. The Browns had quickly shrugged off their defeat against the Colts and their 38-24 win over Cincinnati was no more than a gentle outing. Browns quarterback Bernie Kosar completed 17 of 26 passes for 241 yards and four touchdowns, whilst running back Kevin Mack blasted for 133 yards. The Colts, on the other hand, could make little headway against Buffalo – they were outgained by 385 net yards to 130 with Eric Dickerson rushing for only 19 yards on 11 carries. For Buffalo, defensive end Bruce Smith, who was the first pick overall in the 1985 draft, had three quarterback sacks. Miami won for the second week in a row, with two third-quarter Mark Clayton touchdown receptions deciding the issue against Philadelphia. But when the dust had settled, it was Buffalo who had emerged as the best-placed team in the AFC East. At this moment, they were one of three teams sharing the lead on top of the division but, because of the intricacies of the tie-breaking system, they needed only to win their final two games to clinch the division title.

Frank Pollard scored a touchdown in Pittsburgh's win over San Diego.

Outstanding Individual Performances

100 Yards Rushing
Charles White (L.A. Rams) 29-159-21t-2
Kevin Mack (Cleveland) 27-133-22t-1
Stump Mitchell (St Louis) 26-111-12-1
Johnny Hector (N.Y. Jets) 22-104-15-1

100 Yards Pass Receiving
Gary Clark (Washington) 9-187-56t-1
Carlos Carson (Kansas City) 4-142-67t-1
Mark Bavaro (N.Y. Giants) 11-137-24-1
Eric Martin (New Orleans) 6-130-54t-2
Webster Slaughter (Cleveland) 5-119-43-2
Tim McGee (Cincinnati) 4-117-44-0
Wes Chandler (San Diego) 7-116-20-0
James Lofton (L.A. Raiders) 5-112-42-0
Al Toon (N.Y. Jets) 8-1/.0-28t-1
Ray Butler (Seattle) 6-107-40t-2
Mark Clayton (Miami) 7-104-21-2
Drew Hill (Houston) 4-102-50-0

300 Yards Passing
Dan Marino (Miami) 39-25-376-1-54-3
Boomer Esiason (Cincinnati) 39-22-361-2-54t-1
Phil Simms (N.Y. Giants) 48-30-359-1-24-2
Danny White (Dallas) 49-27-359-1-33-2
Marc Wilson (L.A. Raiders) 38-22-339-3-42-0
John Elway (Denver) 42-21-335-2-47-1
Dan Fouts (San Diego) 52-29-334-1-30-1

Below right: Vai Sikahema (St Louis) returned a punt 76 yards for a touchdown.

STANDINGS

AFC East	W	L	T	PF	PA
Buffalo	7	6	0	256	275
Indianapolis	7	6	0	256	225
Miami	7	6	0	329	290
New England	6	7	0	283	276
N.Y. Jets	6	7	0	300	302
AFC Central					
Cleveland	8	5	0	347	209
Pittsburgh	8	5	0	256	256
Houston	7	6	0	300	316
Cincinnati	4	9	0	244	308
AFC West					
Denver	8	4	1	335	271
San Diego	8	5	0	246	273
Seattle	8	5	0	317	252
L.A. Raiders	5	8	0	281	259
Kansas City	3	10	0	215	348
NFC East	**W**	**L**	**T**	**PF**	**PA**
Washington†	10	3	0	331	238
St Louis	6	7	0	315	333
Dallas	5	8	0	290	311
Philadelphia	5	8	0	282	346
N.Y. Giants	4	9	0	240	295
NFC Central					
Chicago†	10	3	0	329	245
Minnesota	7	6	0	295	294
Green Bay	5	7	1	221	247
Tampa Bay	4	9	0	266	305
Detroit	3	10	0	225	354
NFC West					
San Francisco*	11	2	0	376	246
New Orleans*	10	3	0	348	235
L.A. Rams	6	7	0	296	284
Atlanta	3	10	0	185	371

† Division Champion
* Clinched Playoff Spot

WEEK FIFTEEN

American Football Conference
Cleveland 24 at Los Angeles Raiders 17
Indianapolis 20 at San Diego 7
Kansas City 17 at Denver 20
New England 13 at Buffalo 7
Pittsburgh 16 at Houston 24

National Football Conference
Atlanta 7 at San Francisco 35
Dallas 29 at Los Angeles Rams 21
Green Bay 10 at New York Giants 20
Minnesota 17 at Detroit 14
St Louis 31 at Tampa Bay 14

Interconference Games
New Orleans 41 at Cincinnati 24
Philadelphia 38 at New York Jets 27
Seattle 34 at Chicago 21
Washington 21 at Miami 23

Interconference Play
AFC 22 – NFC 19 (1 Tie)

San Francisco's Jerry Rice smashed the league single-season record for touchdown receptions, taking his total to 20 with a pair against Atlanta (also, he rushed for a touchdown). Otherwise, with four NFC playoff teams freewheeling towards the finishing line and Minnesota back on the winning trail, the playoff picture in that conference looked set, apart from the fine detail. In the AFC, however, after Week Fifteen, there still were three of the five places open.

Denver became the first AFC club to qualify, but it was only after a few tense moments. Playing the lowly Kansas City Chiefs, Denver swept through the first half to lead 17-3 at the interval, but in the second half it was nearly all Kansas City, as quarterback Bill Kenney began to expose weaknesses in the Broncos' secondary. By the final minute of the game, though still trailing by three points, the Chiefs had driven into Nick Lowery field goal range and seemed on the verge of taking their momentum into overtime. Lowery is one of those kickers on whom you'd stake your life, especially over a distance of 37 yards, but, inexplicably, his field goal attempt drifted wide. It meant that the Broncos had clinched at least a wild card spot in the playoffs. There was no such moment of elation for the Browns, who had beaten the Raiders in Los Angeles but were not sure just where it left them. Even after their officials had spent the flight home trying to unravel the complexities of the tie-breaking system, they still couldn't be certain. However, on arrival in Cleveland, they were told the good news – the NFL had confirmed that

Above: Jeff Donaldson (Houston) had two fourth-quarter pass interceptions.

Opposite: Walter Payton scored his final NFL touchdown in Chicago against Seattle.

they were in the playoffs. Seattle emerged as the next best candidate after beating the Bears with unexpected ease. In what was Walter Payton's final home game at Soldier Field, a third-quarter, 75-yard touchdown reception by Seahawks running back John L. Williams broke a 14-14 deadlock, and from then on the Seahawks were never in danger. Houston appeared as the other obvious candidate after beating Pittsburgh.

With Buffalo's loss to New England, the AFC East was wide open again. From needing only to win the final two games to take the title, the Bills were now eliminated, leaving Indianapolis, Miami and the Patriots to fight out the finish. Dan Marino had passed Miami to an upset win over Washington, and the Colts had dealt the Chargers their fifth consecutive loss – it was becoming painful to say it. It all meant that the Colts were now in charge of their own destiny. A win on the final weekend would bring them the title. The same was true of Cleveland, who needed to beat Pittsburgh for the title in the AFC Central.

Outstanding Individual Performances

100 Yards Rushing
Eric Dickerson (Indianapolis) 23-115-53-0
Herschel Walker (Dallas) 23-108-15-1
Stump Mitchell (St Louis) 23-101-12-1

100 Yards Pass Receiving
Mark Duper (Miami) 6-170-59t-3
Al Toon (N.Y. Jets) 10-168-51t-1
Mike Quick (Philadelphia) 6-148-45t-2
John L. Williams (Seattle) 8-117-75t-1
Gerald Carter (Tampa Bay) 5-116-39-1
Webster Slaughter (Cleveland) 7-115-36-1
Drew Hill (Houston) 4-109-52t-2

300 Yards Passing
Dan Marino (Miami) 50-22-393-1-59t-3
Ken O'Brien (N.Y. Jets) 49-25-301-0-51t-2

STANDINGS

AFC East	W	L	T	PF	PA	NFC East	W	L	T	PF	PA
Indianapolis	8	6	0	276	232	Washington†	10	4	0	352	261
Miami	8	6	0	352	311	St Louis	7	7	0	346	347
Buffalo	7	7	0	263	288	Dallas	6	8	0	319	332
New England	7	7	0	296	283	Philadelphia	6	8	0	320	373
N.Y. Jets	6	8	0	327	340	N.Y. Giants	5	9	0	260	305
AFC Central						**NFC Central**					
Cleveland*	9	5	0	371	226	Chicago†	10	4	0	350	279
Houston	8	6	0	324	332	Minnesota	8	6	0	312	308
Pittsburgh	8	6	0	272	280	Green Bay	5	8	1	231	267
Cincinnati	4	10	0	268	349	Tampa Bay	4	10	0	280	336
AFC West						Detroit	3	11	0	239	371
Denver*	9	4	1	355	288	**NFC West**					
Seattle	9	5	0	351	273	San Francisco*	12	2	0	411	253
San Diego	8	6	0	253	293	New Orleans*	11	3	0	389	259
L.A. Raiders	5	9	0	298	283	L.A. Rams	6	8	0	317	313
Kansas City	3	11	0	232	368	Atlanta	3	11	0	192	406

† Division Champion
* Clinched Playoff Spot

WEEK SIXTEEN

American Football Conference
Cincinnati 17 at Houston 21
Cleveland 19 at Pittsburgh 13
New England 24 at Miami 10
San Diego 0 at Denver 24
Seattle 20 at Kansas City 41

National Football Conference
Detroit 30 at Atlanta 13
Green Bay 24 at New Orleans 33
Los Angeles Rams 0 at San Francisco 48
St Louis 16 at Dallas 21
Washington 27 at Minnesota 24 (OT)

Interconference Games
Buffalo 7 at Philadelphia 17
Chicago 6 at Los Angeles Raiders 3
New York Jets 7 at New York Giants 20
Tampa Bay 6 at Indianapolis 24

Interconference Play
AFC 23 – NFC 22 (1 Tie)

Cornelius Bennett (Buffalo) had 17 tackles, including four sacks, forced three fumbles and deflected a pass.

It wasn't so much that the 49ers saved their best until last – they'd been in a class by themselves for much of the season – but after the eloquence of their 48-0 closing statement against the Rams, there were many who felt that already they had one hand on the Vince Lombardi Trophy. Their super wide receiver, Jerry Rice, took his single-season record for touchdown receptions into another dimension (22) with scoring catches covering 22 and 50 yards from reserve quarterback Steve Young. It meant that for the New Orleans Saints the only prize available was the position of NFC senior wild card. And it duly became theirs, but they had a struggle with Green Bay, whom they beat after trailing 14-3 in the first quarter and 24-19 in the third. Minnesota secured the other playoff berth, or rather, ended up with it. Needing to beat the Redskins to be assured of the second-ranked wild card place, they'd looked well on their way, leading 24-14 with under ten minutes remaining. However, after Ali Haji-Sheikh had kicked a 37-yard field goal, Doug Williams, who earlier had passed 46 yards for a touchdown to wide receiver Ricky Sanders, again found Sanders with a 51-yarder to take the game into overtime. 2:09 into the extra period, Haji-Sheikh's 26-yard field goal settled the issue. The Vikings were left hoping that

St Louis, who now needed only to beat Dallas to secure the final wild card spot, would falter. And they did. The Cardinals simply could not convert their statistical dominance into points and were left to ponder what might have been.

In a Rocky Mountain blizzard, Denver put the Chargers out of their misery and, for themselves, earned the bonus of home-field advantage throughout the AFC playoffs. In the comfort of the Hoosier Dome, Eric Dickerson was at his awesome best, rushing for 196 yards as the Colts strode into the playoffs as division champions for the first time since 1977. The previous day, Saturday, Cleveland had been made to work hard by Pittsburgh but they never trailed and, in the end, won more easily than the 19-13 scoreline would suggest. The Steelers' loss meant that Seattle had secured a playoff spot even before they took to the field. In the event, they were beaten badly by Kansas City, who used the occasion to release a whole season's accumulated frustrations. For Seattle, wide receiver Steve Largent became the NFL all-time leader in receptions (752), going ahead of the retired Charlie Joiner (750), but ace running back Curt Warner went down with a heavily sprained ankle. After suffering a few nervous moments, late in the game against Cincinnati, Houston held on for a four-point victory, securing the AFC's senior wild card place.

Eric Dickerson trampled all over Tampa Bay.

STANDINGS

AFC East	W	L	T	PF	PA
Indianapolis†	9	6	0	300	238
New England	8	7	0	320	293
Miami	8	7	0	362	335
Buffalo	7	8	0	270	305
N.Y. Jets	6	9	0	334	360
AFC Central					
Cleveland†	10	5	0	390	239
Houston*	9	6	0	345	349
Pittsburgh	8	7	0	285	299
Cincinnati	4	11	0	285	370
AFC West					
Denver†	10	4	1	379	288
Seattle*	9	6	0	371	314
San Diego	8	7	0	253	317
L.A. Raiders	5	10	0	301	289
Kansas City	4	11	0	273	388
NFC East	W	L	T	PF	PA
Washington†	11	4	0	379	285
Dallas	7	8	0	340	348
St Louis	7	8	0	362	368
Philadelphia	7	8	0	337	380
N.Y. Giants	6	9	0	280	312
NFC Central					
Chicago†	11	4	0	356	282
Minnesota*	8	7	0	336	335
Green Bay	5	9	1	255	300
Tampa Bay	4	11	0	286	360
Detroit	4	11	0	269	384
NFC West					
San Francisco†	13	2	0	459	253
New Orleans*	12	3	0	422	283
L.A. Rams	6	9	0	317	361
Atlanta	3	12	0	205	436

† Division Champion
* Wild Card

Outstanding Individual Performances

100 Yards Rushing
Eric Dickerson (Indianapolis) 33-196-34t-2
Herschel Walker (Dallas) 25-137-12-2
Joe Morris (N.Y. Giants) 26-132-24-0
Herman Heard (Kansas City) 12-107-37t-1
Mike Rozier (Houston) 20-103-12-0
Keith Byars (Philadelphia) 23-102-22-0

100 Yards Pass Receiving
Ricky Sanders (Washington) 8-164-51t-2
Carlos Carson (Kansas City) 4-120-81t-1
Cris Collinsworth (Cincinnati) 4-119-53-0
Roy Green (St Louis) 7-112-23-0
Mark Bavaro (N.Y. Giants) 6-109-25-1
Drew Hill (Houston) 6-109-27-0
Walter Stanley (Green Bay) 4-109-39t-2
J.T. Smith (St Louis) 11-102-22-1
Stephone Paige (Kansas City) 7-100-46t-1

300 Yards Passing
Bill Kenney (Kansas City) 35-23-320-0-81t-3
Neil Lomax (St Louis) 54-28-314-1-23-1

WEEK SEVENTEEN –
WILD CARD WEEKEND

WEEK SEVENTEEN – WILD CARD WEEKEND

AFC   Seattle 20 at Houston 23 (OT)

Despite dominating the time of possession by more than two thirds to their opponents' one, and moving the ball with some ease, the Houston Oilers needed an overtime field goal to eliminate the brave Seattle Seahawks, who were without their injured star running back, Curt Warner. Seattle drew first blood on wide receiver Steve Largent's 20-yard touchdown reception following a pass interception by cornerback Melvin Jenkins. But with running backs Mike Rozier and rookie Alonzo Highsmith powering the offense towards a game total of 178 net yards rushing, the Oilers went out to a 13-7 lead on field goals by Tony Zendejas either side of Rozier's one-yard touchdown run. A brace of field goals by Norm Johnson brought Seattle level, but Houston appeared to have registered the crucial score on wide receiver Willie Drewrey's third-quarter, 29-yard touchdown reception. Given the opportunity to put the game away on a 29-yard field goal with just 1:47 remaining, Zendejas hit the upright. It offered Seattle a lifeline and they took it, with quarterback Dave Krieg driving them on a wild, ten-play series which culminated in Largent's game-tying, 12-yard touchdown reception. In overtime, the Seahawks felt they'd forced a turnover but an apparent interception by linebacker Fredd Young was ruled an incomplete pass. And when given the chance to redeem himself, later in that drive, Zendejas won the day with a 42-yard field goal.

Above: Tony Zendejas (Houston) won the game in overtime.

Below: Anthony Carter inspired the Vikings to victory.

NFC Minnesota 44 at New Orleans 10

The Saints had ended the regular season with an NFL-best consecutive winning sequence of nine. Their fans massed to see number ten but, by half-time, it was all over. The Saints had conceded 31 points, the last seven coming on a 'Hail Mary' pass after the first half should have been over. Just before then, for the Saints things had looked bad but they were still in contention. In their previous two games, they'd come back from deficits of 21 and nine points to win. They'd reached halftime – an opportunity to regroup – so they thought. But on that fateful last play before the break, the Saints had been caught with twelve men on the field, giving the Vikings one more play from scrimmage. Wade Wilson hurled off a speculative bomb which bounced off the collec-tive grasp of three New Orleans defenders and into the hands of wide receiver Hassan Jones. Earlier, New Orleans had taken advantage of a Tommy Kramer fumble to score the opening touchdown on Eric Martin's 10-yard pass reception. Only 1:23 into the game, it all looked so easy. Chuck Nelson kicked a 42-yard field goal following a Mel Gray fumble at the New Orleans 27, but the spark which catalysed the rout came in the twelfth minute, when Anthony Carter returned a punt 84 yards for a touchdown. It was the first of five touchdowns with a further two Nelson field goals for good measure, as the Vikes booked their trip to San Francisco.

Hassan Jones (#84) 'steals' the prize touchdown.

WEEK EIGHTEEN –
DIVISIONAL PLAYOFFS

American Football Conference

Indianapolis 21 at Cleveland 38

Earnest Byner had been the difference in the regular season, and once again he was a key player as the Browns beat the Colts to move into their second AFC title game in successive years. Back on Week Thirteen, Byner's fumble at the Indianapolis four-yard line probably had cost the Browns some kind of score in a game which they lost 9-7. Now, after seeing his partner, Kevin Mack, leave with an illness early in the contest, Byner took up the slack as he rushed for 122 yards and a touchdown. Also, just under seven minutes into the first quarter, he caught a 10-yard touchdown pass from quarterback Bernie Kosar. With the teams tied at 14-14, early in the second half, the Colts appeared on the verge of taking the lead for the first time after driving from their own 14- to the Browns' 10-yard line. However, Jack Trudeau, who had thrown touchdown passes of 2 and 19 yards, was tackled from behind as he passed and the ball was intercepted. Not until the game was out of reach – they still trailed 31-14 with a little over one minute remaining – did the Colts threaten again.

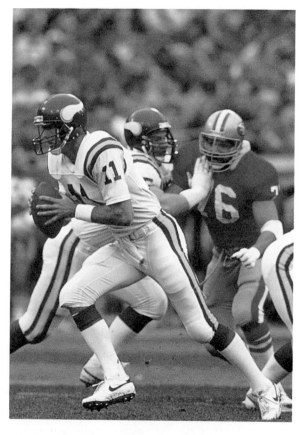

Below: Carl Hairston (#78) blunts the force of Eric Dickerson.

Above: Wade Wilson (Minnesota) sets up another attack against the 49ers.

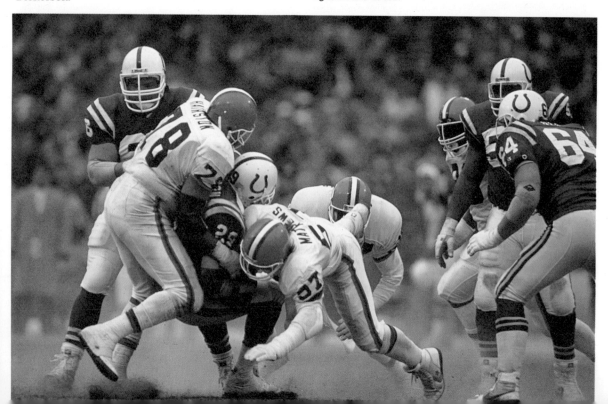

Houston 10 at Denver 34

If the prospect of facing John Elway wasn't enough, the Houston Oilers added to their burdens by, apparently, leaving their composure at home. Following a goal-line fumble by running back Mike Rozier, Denver's Gene Lang scored from the one-yard line. Recovering somewhat, the Oilers drove smoothly into scoring position only to see a Warren Moon pass intercepted by Denver linebacker Karl Mecklenburg on his own ten-yard line. With that possession, Elway directed a 72-yard drive which culminated in his 27-yard touchdown pass to tight end Clarence Kay. Only towards the end of the third quarter did the Oilers regenerate any kind of momentum but, by then, the Broncos were leading 27-3, following a pair of Rich Karlis field goals and Kay's one-yard touchdown reception. The Oilers did find the end zone, on wide receiver Ernest Givins' 19-yard touchdown reception, but Elway countered quickly, driving 49 yards before sneaking the last three himself.

National Football Conference

Washington 21 at Chicago 17

'If Gary Hart can come back so can we,' offered Redskins defensive end Dexter Manley with his team trailing 14-0. Manley was only partially correct – presidential candidate Hart subsequently withdrew – but the Redskins did come back as they repeated their upset of the previous year against the same Chicago Bears. The Bears had been mechanically efficient as they set up a 14-0 lead on touchdowns by Calvin Thomas and wide receiver Ron Morris. But the Redskins fought back and it was on merit when they drew level with touchdown scores by George Rogers and tight end Clint Didier. Darrell Green's touchdown on a 52-yard punt return gave them their first lead. The Bears drew closer on Kevin Butler's 25-yard field goal and seemed on the verge of completing their recovery as Jim McMahon took them down to the Washington 14-yard line. But his pass was intercepted by strong safety Alvin Walton to end what was Chicago's final serious threat.

Minnesota 36 at San Francisco 24

Slowly at first, and then with a momentum as certain as it was unstoppable, the Vikings crept into the game before settling the issue with a display which showed their talents to the full. On offense they had no difficulty moving the ball. On defense they kept a firm control over the NFL leading passer, Joe Montana. At potential crisis points such as early in the second half, after the 49ers had scored with foreboding speed, and later when, under substitute quarterback Steve Young, the 49ers' hopes were

Above: Clarence Kay (Denver) cradles the ball on one of his two touchdown receptions.

rekindled, Minnesota was able to regroup and dismiss each threat as if it never had existed. Quarterback Wade Wilson passed for 298 yards and two touchdowns, and wide receiver Anthony Carter caught ten passes for an NFL-playoff record 227 yards. Incredibly, Carter did not score a touchdown, but his receptions of 63, 40 and 35 yards did establish position for Chuck Nelson field goals, and he ran 30 yards on a reverse to set up Hassan Jones's five-yard touchdown reception. That score was critical, coming as it did after the 49ers' Jeff Fuller had returned an interception 48 yards for the touchdown which reduced the deficit to just ten points early in the second half.

WEEK NINETEEN –
CONFERENCE CHAMPIONSHIPS

American Football Conference

Cleveland 33 at Denver 38

The names were the same; only the venue was different when these two clubs met again in the game to decide the AFC Champion. A year earlier, at the same stage, Denver's John Elway had taken his team on that never-to-be-forgotten, 98-yard drive to bring the Broncos into a tie, late in regulation time, before Rich Karlis kicked the winning field goal in the first period of overtime. Only eight games into the 1987 season, Denver seemed out of contention but, systematically, they leapfrogged their opponents in closing out 6-1. The reward was the home-field advantage for the playoffs, though they'd hardly needed any kind of edge in beating an Oilers club which chose the wrong parts of the field to make its mistakes. Cleveland had come through for its third straight title in what now was considered the tough

AFC Central – not long ago it was considered a weak group. A hard-nosed bunch, theirs was the quest of revenge and, with quarterback Bernie Kosar, the AFC leading passer, at the controls, they had every chance of reaching that goal.

In the event, Kosar and Elway fought out one of the greatest big-game duels in NFL history. At half time, with Denver leading 21-3, as a contest it seemed over. But that merely set up a remarkable rally which saw Cleveland move into a 31-31 tie, 4:12 into the final quarter. However, oblivious of the swing in momentum, Elway needed only five plays, culminating in his 20-yard touchdown pass to running back Sammy Winder, to re-establish a seven-point margin. Back came Cleveland, pressing ever closer to the Denver goal line, only to see running back Earnest Byner have the ball torn from his grasp as he was poised to lunge for the end zone, and recovered by Jeremiah Castille. Denver was off to the Super Bowl for the second year in a row.

Below: John Elway sets play in motion.

National Football Conference

Above: Gary Clark makes one of his three receptions.

Minnesota 10 at Washington 17

If ever there was a team with the hot hand it was the Minnesota Vikings. In successive weeks they'd routed New Orleans, the club with the NFL's second-best regular-season record, and then, in similar fashion, had disposed of San Francisco, the team with the very best regular-season record and one which had closed out the campaign with three wins in which they had outscored their opponents (one of which was the Chicago Bears) by a total of 124 points to 7. For the club whose playoff hopes had rested on the loss of another (St Louis) it had been an astounding transformation. The Redskins had secured the title in the NFC East with time in hand, and yet only rarely had they looked likely to overwhelm anybody. But, in the divisional playoffs for the second year in succession, they'd travelled to Chicago and beaten the Bears fair and square – and

who can argue with that? They had every offensive weapon any team might need and it all pointed to a shoot-out when they entertained the Vikings.

Strangely, the encounter was a restrained affair. After trading touchdowns, the teams entered the second half tied at 7-7. Trailing 10-7, just under five minutes into the fourth quarter, Minnesota had missed an opportunity to go into the lead when they had to settle for a Chuck Nelson field goal after running back D.J. Dozier had been stopped at the Washington one-yard line. Five minutes later, Redskins wide receiver Gary Clark caught a seven-yard touchdown pass. In the dying moments, again the Vikings pressed, only to see running back Darrin Nelson fail to hang on to a straightforward pass from quarterback Wade Wilson at the Washington goal line with 52 seconds remaining.

SUPER BOWL XXII

Washington 42 – Denver 10

Jack Murphy Stadium, San Diego, California, January 31st, 1988

Though many of the names were the same, there were notable absentees from the Denver team which had suffered a crushing defeat at the hands of the Giants in Super Bowl XXI. On defense, gone were linebacker Tom Jackson, cornerback Louis Wright and safety Steve Foley. The playoffs had taken their toll, most significantly with the loss of safety Mike Harden, who broke his arm in the victory over Houston. Retirements and injuries, then, had left the Broncos seriously thin in the defensive secondary. However, there was a ray of hope with the return of safeties Dennis Smith and Randy Robbins, neither of whom could expect to be in the peak of fitness but whose experience would surely be a

welcome boost. On offense, the 1987 Broncos were in much better shape than their predecessors. Also, they had receiving talent in abundance. All three of wide receivers Vance Johnson, Mark Jackson and Ricky Nattiel could produce a big play at any moment, and tight end Clarence Kay was keeping out a player, Orson Mobley, who might start for other clubs around the NFL. At running back, Gerald Willhite was out after suffering a serious leg fracture during the regular season, but the senior player, Sammy Winder, was healthy and would be given solid help by Gene Lang. The offensive line was considered to be rather small but it had helped them reach this stage and no-one was complaining. Without doubt, though, the key player for Denver was John Elway. Such had been the dazzle of his performances, his arm, his rushing, his leadership and

Doug Williams faced his sternest test.

nerve, at times during the regular season, many experts believed he alone could win the Super Bowl – whatever the circumstances. And of the few observers who had not been dazzled, there weren't many who voiced dissent.

Washington presented a completely different picture. A combination of the wisdom of owner Jack Kent Cooke, sound judgement of general manager Bobby Beathard, and the quiet brilliance of head coach Joe Gibbs had produced a third Super Bowl appearance in six years. Balance was the keynote. On defense they rated only 18th in the NFL, but in the playoffs there had been signs that they were coming to the boil. An enormous offensive line was expected to manhandle its way to dominance and create a platform to launch the rushing of George Rogers. And it was perhaps the most telling statistic that a Washington strength, rushing, was ranged up against a Broncos weakness (Denver ranked a poor 20th in the NFL against the rush). In passing, Washington rated even higher than in rushing in the regular season (4th compared with 7th). Veteran wide receiver Art Monk was expected to be available only for light duty, but Gary Clark was in excellent form, as was his probable starting partner, Ricky Sanders. At quarterback, the former Tampa Bay rocket launcher, Doug Williams, had taken over on merit from Jay Schroeder, but there were still those who felt that he had something to prove.

Above: Washington's Dexter Manley puts the 'arm' on John Elway.

Below: Ricky Nattiel stunned the Redskins with this opening touchdown reception over Barry Wilburn.

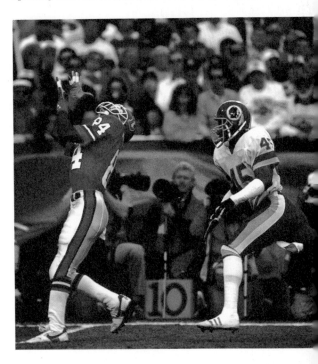

THE GAME

Scoring By Quarters

1st Quarter
Denver: Nattiel, 56-yard pass from Elway; Karlis kick (1:57)
Denver 7 – Washington 0
Denver: Karlis, 24-yard field goal (5:51)
Denver 10 – Washington 0

2nd Quarter
Washington: Sanders, 80-yard pass from Williams; Haji-Sheikh kick (0:53)
Denver 10 – Washington 7
Washington: Clark, 27-yard pass from Williams; Haji-Sheikh kick (4:45)
Denver 10 – Washington 14
Washington: Smith, 58-yard run; Haji-Sheikh kick (8:33)
Denver 10 – Washington 21
Washington: Sanders, 50-yard pass from Williams; Haji-Sheikh kick (11:18)
Denver 10 – Washington 28
Washington: Didier, 8-yard pass from Williams; Haji-Sheikh kick (13:56)
Denver 10 – Washington 35

4th Quarter
Washington: Smith, 4-yard run; Haji-Sheikh kick (1:51)
Denver 10 – Washington 42

Above: Timmy Smith (#36) off and running.

Left: Ricky Sanders coasts in for a touchdown.

Those who had travelled to San Diego to see John Elway preside over the destruction of the Redskins were not disappointed by the start he made, passing 56 yards for a touchdown to wide receiver Ricky Nattiel on the Broncos' first play from scrimmage. Denver's second possession resulted in a Rich Karlis 24-yard field goal and already the Super Bowl had the makings of a rout. On that drive, the Broncos had been stopped at the Washington six-yard line as the offensive line showed its first sign of weakness, but there were few who would have seen it as an omen. It was shortly afterwards that the Redskins made

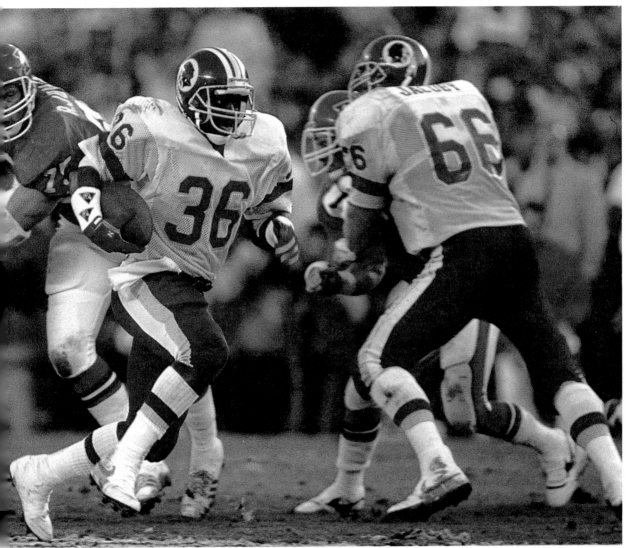

their first serious strike. It came to nothing, but the aplomb with which quarterback Doug Williams combined with wide receiver Art Monk on a 40-yard pass play suggested better things to come. And with the first quarter running out Elway was beginning to look less than super as, apart from a shovel pass, he threw three consecutive incompletions. Furthermore, on one play, he had been sacked for a heavy loss of 18 yards. The Redskins were gathering for the reply.

It came on their first possession of the second quarter. Williams dropped back and, given ample time to set up, he calmly tossed the ball to Ricky Sanders for an 80-yard touchdown. That equalled the Super Bowl record and there were to be more before the final gun.

It had been one of the best-kept secrets that Timmy Smith would start in place of the injured George Rogers, and now the rookie began to motor into the wide open spaces created by the Redskins' 'Counter Gap' play. It was after Smith, and then Kelvin Bryant, had softened up the Broncos defense that Williams passed to Gary Clark for the touchdown which both put Washington ahead to stay and precipitated a frenzy of points. With touchdowns on a run by Smith, and pass receptions by Sanders and Didier, the Redskins accelerated to a Super Bowl-record 35 points in the quarter. Early in the fourth quarter, Smith administered the last rites with his second touchdown.

Amongst the many new records went the one to Smith (most yards rushing – 204), to Ricky Sanders (most yards receiving – 193) and to the game's MVP, Doug Williams (most yards passing – 340). To Williams also went the unofficial prizes for courage and gentlemanly conduct.

ANATOMY OF SUPER BOWL XXII
– QUARTER BY QUARTER –

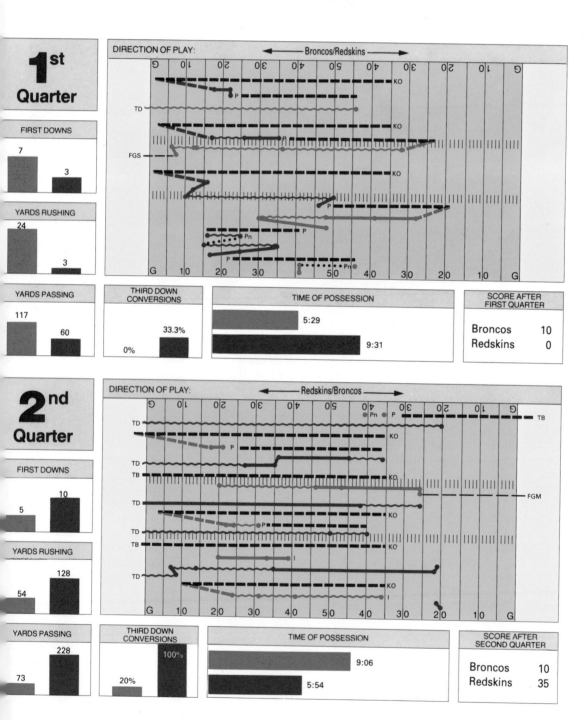

1st Quarter

FIRST DOWNS

7

3

YARDS RUSHING

24

3

YARDS PASSING

117

60

THIRD DOWN CONVERSIONS

33.3%

0%

TIME OF POSSESSION

5:29

9:31

SCORE AFTER FIRST QUARTER

Broncos 10
Redskins 0

2nd Quarter

FIRST DOWNS

5

10

YARDS RUSHING

54

128

YARDS PASSING

73

228

THIRD DOWN CONVERSIONS

100%

20%

TIME OF POSSESSION

9:06

5:54

SCORE AFTER SECOND QUARTER

Broncos 10
Redskins 35

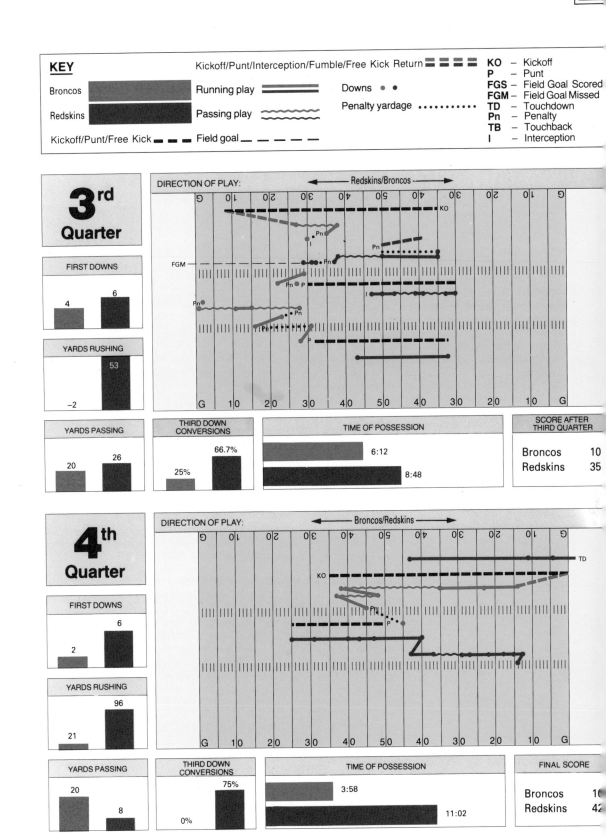

CHAPTER TWO

A HISTORY OF THE WASHINGTON REDSKINS

'This team saw (Slingin') Sammy Baugh, Sonny Jurgensen, (Whiskey) Kilmer.

'Cliff Battles ranged behind its line long before John Riggins did. Frank Filchock passed here. Riley Smith blocked. Bobby Mitchell used to disappear here. Charley Taylor ran long, gorgeous pass routes and plucked the ball from an opponent's ear just as he crossed the goal line. Larry Brown, with a hearing aid in his helmet, crunched lines here. (Bullet Bill) Dudley caught punts here.

'The Washington Redskins are a venerable team steeped in tradition. They're as much a part of Americana as Lee's horse or Sheridan's cavalry. They've got their own song; they were the first to have their own band and cheerleaders.

'They should be "America's Team".'

Jim Murray, *Los Angeles Times*, January 30th, 1983

Later, the same day that Jim Murray's nostalgic reflections appeared in the *Los Angeles Times*, the Washington Redskins mounted a thrilling rally to beat the Miami Dolphins 27-17 in Super Bowl XVII.

50 years had passed since a four-man syndicate, headed by Mr George Preston Marshall, threw in its commitment with that of the owners of the small band of seven clubs which remained, in 1932, as the National Football League went into redoubt. That year saw the low point in league membership, but also it was the time of great optimism. Marshall and his associates, Vincent Bendix, Jay O'Brien and M. Dorland Doyle, needed plenty of that, optimism, when they purchased an NFL franchise for the city of Boston. Their team would be nicknamed 'Braves'.

With all three of rookie running backs Cliff Battles and Jim Musick, and tackle Glen (Turk) Edwards producing immediately, the Braves were competitive right away – they played .500 football in each of their first three campaigns. But there were signs that Boston of the early 1930s simply wasn't a pro football town. The first indication came in the Braves' inaugural year, when the fans didn't turn out in numbers and the partners made an operating loss of $46,000. Only Marshall was prepared to continue the struggle, and he became the sole owner. He decided on a fresh start of sorts, moving the club from Braves Field (it was the home of the National League baseball 'Braves') to Fenway Park (it was the home park of the American League baseball 'Red Sox') and adopting the new nickname of 'Redskins'.

Marshall certainly was not the sort who would let the grass grow under his feet. History would come to regard him as the great innovator – together with George Halas, he sponsored new rules to open up the game, such as the one which allowed a forward pass to be made from any spot behind the line of scrimmage. Also, he was the showman, whose club would have the first marching band, the first fight song (Hail To The Redskins) and the first radio network. In 1950, Washington became one of the first two clubs to have all its games televised. And he knew the value of a dollar. In the early days, when money was tight, he wouldn't hesitate to ask for the return of any ball which sailed into the stands.

'He was way ahead of everybody,' remembered Giants owner Wellington Mara. 'He saw that pro football should be a family game. The wife should demand to go out to the stadium on Sunday. He staged parades. He had an Indian medicine man get out on the field and sprinkle powder in front of the guy who was kicking off. Anything to make a show,' Mara went on.

In 1933 he hired William (Lone Star) Dietz, a full-blooded American Indian, to replace Lud Wray as head coach. On the first day of practice, all the players turned out wearing war paint! Marshall was not averse to interfering in the football side of things, and it may well have been this aspect of his character which led to the Redskins' first losing season, when they went 2-8-1 in 1935 under the club's third head coach and local darling, former Harvard player Eddie Casey. However, when Ray Flaherty became the fourth head coach in just five years, all that sort of thing had to stop.

Flaherty, who had been a three-time all-pro end with the New York Giants, would tolerate no nonsense and, in his first year, he underlined his authority by coaching the Redskins to their first title, the championship of the Eastern Division, which they clinched with a 14-0 defeat of the Giants on the final weekend.

Opposite above: Glen (Turk) Edwards; Far right: Redskins owner George Preston Marshall; Right: Cliff Battles.

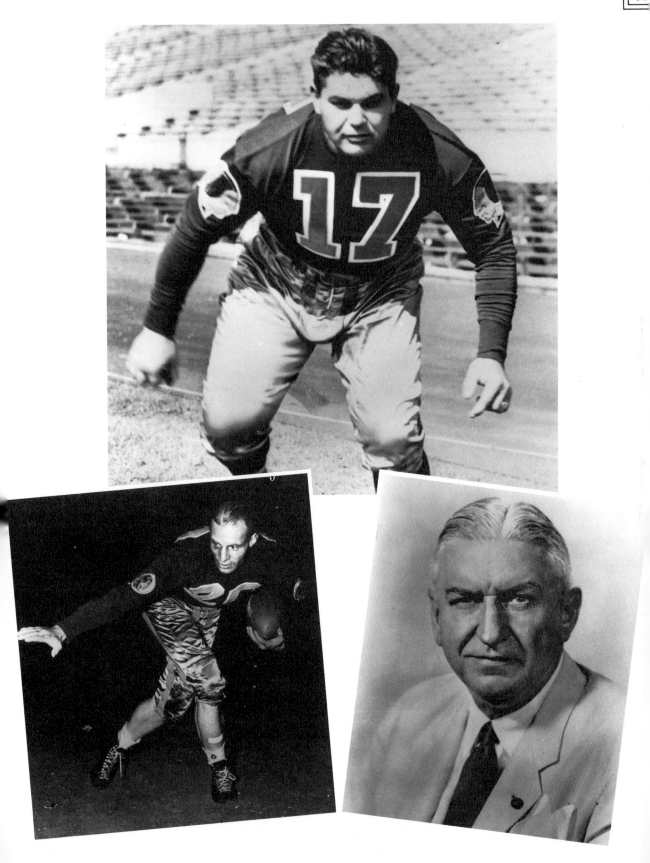

RAY FLAHERTY

had been an All-America single-wing tailback at Texas Christian University. (The single-wing tailback was the forerunner of the modern quarterback.) Teak-tough, raw-boned and rifle-armed, the laconic Baugh was a superstar long before the word had been concocted. It is said that, once, when winding up an explanation of a pass play, his coach concluded, 'Then hit the receiver in the eye.' 'Which eye?' was Baugh's response.

As a rookie, with league-leading rusher Battles as the perfect foil, Baugh was the NFL leading passer. His first victim was the Giants on his debut, when he completed 11 of 16 passes in the 13-3 victory. And he wound up the season by engineering a 28-21 win over the Chicago Bears in the NFL title game. With Washington trailing Chicago 14-7 at half time, Baugh unleashed a furious third-quarter assault which saw him throw touchdown passes of 55, 78 and 35 yards, the first two to end Wayne Millner and the last to wingback Ed Justice. In total, he passed for a then championship-game record 335 yards.

Even now, fifty years on, Baugh's display still is seen as one of the great passing exhibitions of all time. His immediate financial reward was no more than the fair share, $234.26, which went to every player on the winning team.

Left: Redskins head coach Ray Flaherty.

Right: Bill Osmanski on the way to scoring the opening touchdown in the 1940 NFL Championship Game.

Below: Sammy Baugh.

Cocking a snook at the Boston fans, for whom he had developed a disdain, Marshall moved the NFL Championship Game to the Polo Grounds, New York. With an attendance of 29,545 people, the game was a financial success, but the Redskins could not overcome the early loss of Battles (he was injured on the tenth play of the game) and were defeated 21-6 by Green Bay.

'I'm licked,' summarised Marshall, not at the defeat but with the exasperation of a man whose team simply could not fire the stay-at-home citizens of Boston. 'Fans in paying quantities don't seem to want us. Five years of trying and $100,000 in money is enough to spend in one place. We'll stay in the game but it will be somewhere else,' was his conclusion.

That 'somewhere else' turned out to be the city of Washington, D.C., where the fans were indeed prepared to turn out, 19,941 of them on opening day to see the Redskins start with a 13-3 win over the Giants. It was the second beginning.

Already, the Redskins were one year into their first golden period, which would come to a conclusion with the end of the 1945 season. It was a decade in which they never had a net losing campaign; they won six Eastern Division Championships and two NFL Championships. Their first league title came in their very first year in Washington.

From the start, as their playing record confirmed, the Redskins had had a solid squad. But the catalyst which sparked them to greatness arrived in 1937. Selected in the first round of the collegiate draft, (Slingin') Sammy Baugh

The following year, Baugh dislocated a shoulder in the opening game, and he took time to recover his powers. That, coupled with the unavailability of Battles, who quit pro football following a contractual dispute, probably prevented the Redskins from retaining their NFL title. As it was, with a strong backfield of rookies Andy Farkas and Bill Hartman, and veteran Frank Filchock, the latter who had arrived from Pittsburgh in a trade, they were eliminated only in the final game of the regular season, a 36-0 loss to the eventual NFL Champion Giants. Baugh's absence had enabled Filchock to show his paces, and he had made a strong claim for playing time the following year, 1939, as Baugh eased back to full throttle. Flaherty alternated the two, quarter-by-quarter, and Filchock responded by leading the league in touchdown passes, including a 99-yarder to Farkas to establish an unbeatable NFL record. (Subsequently, this has been equalled five times, twice by Washington players.) Again, the Redskins came close to winning the division title, as close as one referee's judgement as to whether or not a field goal was good. In the final regular-season game, with Washington trailing the Giants 9-7 and 45 seconds remaining, Bo Russell's field goal attempt was adjudged to have gone wide to the right. If Mr Marshall was angry or upset, he didn't reveal it, preferring instead to make a grand show of signing Russell to a new contract on the train back to Washington.

By 1940, Baugh was fully fit again. He led the league in passing and set an NFL single-season punting record with an average of 51.4 yards, as he took the Redskins to the Eastern division title and into the NFL Championship

Game, where they would face the Chicago Bears.

On Week Nine of the eleven-game regular season, they'd beaten George Halas's powerhouse by the score of 7-3. When the Bears complained about the officiating, Marshall tore into them, calling them 'quitters' and gibing, 'They're not a second-half team, just a bunch of crybabies.' It's not clear just what effect Marshall's taunts had on the Bears, but in the championship game the Redskins were dealt what still remains as the greatest rout in league history. Bears fullback Bill Osmanski ran 68 yards for a touchdown on the second play of the game. The Bears intercepted eight passes, four by Filchock, and two each by Baugh and Leroy Zimmerman. By the end of the slaughter, the scoreboard showed 73-0 in favour of Chicago.

Two years later, the Redskins avenged the defeat in what was coach Flaherty's last game before he entered the United States Navy. In that 1942 regular season, the Redskins suffered only one defeat, a 14-7 loss to the Giants who, astoundingly, gained only one yard rushing and didn't register a first-down. As champions of the NFL Eastern division, Washington entertained the Bears, who, despite the loss of several players and coach Halas to the armed services, had won all 11 regular-season games. The big game was a bitter struggle. Baugh was kept in check, completing 5 of 13 passes for just 66 yards and one touchdown. He was intercepted twice. But he made one major play when on defense, intercepting a pass to halt a Bears march which had reached the Washington 12-yard line. Following the Redskins' 14-6 win, Baugh remarked, 'I guess this kinda makes up for that thing in 1940, don't it?'

In 1943, for the third time in four years, Washington and Chicago met in the NFL Championship Game and the pendulum was true to its pattern, swinging back in favour of the Bears who won easily, 41-21. That year, the Redskins started out well – they were 6-0-1 – before losing the last three games including two on consecutive weekends to the Giants. The Giants' 31-7 win in the final game brought them into a tie with Washington and forced a playoff for the NFL Eastern division crown. Just when it was needed, the Redskins found some kind of form, with Farkas finishing off three drives with short-yardage touchdown runs and Baugh passing for a touchdown, in the Redskins' 28-0 victory. In the NFL title game, however, Baugh left the field with concussion after taking a severe kick in the head. He returned for the second half, but this championship game would be remembered for another quarterback, the Bears' Sid Luckman, who threw five touchdown passes. It was a sorry performance all round for the Redskins, whose owner, Marshall, was ejected from the playing field (the game was played in Chicago) after trying to gain access to the Redskins' bench. An unrepentant Marshall, who later returned, called the Bears' action 'a first-class, bush-league trick'.

By now, Baugh was one of the league's acknowledged superstars. In 1943, in addition to being the NFL leading passer for the third time, also he led the league in punting (average 45.9 yards) for the fourth consecutive time, and, whilst playing at safety on defense, he intercepted eleven passes to lead the NFL and set the new record. Remarkable though his punting and ball-hawking defense were, even more astonishing was the fact that he was the leading passer whilst still throwing out of the single- and double-wing alignments, formations which had been designed to enhance the rushing game. Around the league, following the Bears' stunning 73-0 victory over the Redskins, there had been a shift towards the T-formation, and in 1944 the Redskins followed suit.

For its installation, they hired Clark Shaughnessy, a coaching wizard, who had worked on the system whilst at Stanford and had been involved with Chicago in their 1940 massacre. Baugh was reluctant to make the change but Filchock loved it. They ended up sharing time in the quarterback position with Filchock faring the better. He was the NFL leading passer, with Baugh in second place. Perhaps it was the indignity of coming second, but Baugh was galvanized into action. In 1945, he immediately tumbled to the effectiveness of the 'new-fangled' system. He shared the title of NFL leading passer with Chicago's Sid Luckman and set a regular-season record with a pass completion percentage of 70.3 – a standard which lasted until Ken Anderson's 70.55% in 1982.

Sadly, the pass which Baugh will remember from that year was the one he attempted from inside his own end zone in the NFL title game against the Cleveland Rams. The ball hit the crossbar and fell to ground inside the end zone for a two-point safety to the Rams (the rule was changed the following year). The Rams went on to win by the score of 15-14.

It is one of pro football's unexplained phenomena that the 1945 title game heralded a 25-year drought, during which time the Redskins would enjoy only four net-win-

ning campaigns. Imagine it. Six division titles and two NFL Championships in ten years. And then, nothing. Of course, though, there were moments. After all, we're speaking of the Washington Redskins and their owner still was the enigmatic Marshall.

Such are the fortunes of pro football that the odd poor decision and a bit of bad luck can have a disproportionate effect. In 1946, Cal Rossi, a UCLA running back, was the Redskins' first-round draftee. But his selection was voided after it was discovered that he had a year of college eligibility remaining. Filchock was traded to the Giants and, as the fates would have it, Baugh suffered an injury. Whilst Filchock led the Giants to the division title, the Redskins dropped to 5-5-1. In 1947, Rossi again was the Redskins' first-round pick but he opted for becoming a schoolmaster in California. That year, though, saw Baugh at the peak of form as he set NFL passing records for attempts (354), completions (210) and yardage (2,938).

In 1948, the former Alabama star, Harry Gilmer, was being groomed as Baugh's successor but the old warrior was not about to step aside. Another fine campaign saw him pass for 2,599 yards and 22 touchdowns. In one game against Boston he passed for an NFL-record 446 yards. Also, rookie safety Dan Sandifer set an NFL record with 13 interceptions. But the Redskins gave up too much on defense and finished second in the division.

1949 saw Baugh's sixth NFL passing title but the Redskins could do no better than a 4-7-1 finish. As Baugh's powers faded and with his heir apparent, Gilmer, unable to take up the slack, the Redskins laboured through three more losing seasons, the last of which saw Baugh's retirement as a player. Later, for two seasons, he coached the AFL's New York Titans (they became known as the Jets), and in 1964 he coached the Houston Oilers. These days, he tends cattle on his ranch down in Texas. And that's where he's happiest.

Earl (Curly) Lambeau had coached the Redskins in 1952, and in 1953, with a powerful defense, he led the team to a net winning campaign. Lambeau retired, leaving a promising nucleus, but it was destroyed when quarterback Eddie LeBaron and end Gene Brito switched to the Canadian Football League, and defensive back Don Doll was traded to the Rams. A porous defense gave up the most points in the league as the Redskins slithered to a 1954 record of 3-9-0.

In 1955 there were real grounds for optimism, with the return of LeBaron and Brito, and the signing of running back Vic Janowicz, the former Ohio State Heisman Trophy winner who had decided to try pro football following a modest career in pro baseball. In a remarkable offensive performance, when they scored 21 points in just 137 seconds of play, the Redskins beat Philadelphia 31-30. Janowicz, who was the NFL second-leading scorer that year with 7 touchdowns, 28 PATS and 6 field goals, was a key player in helping the Redskins to a second-place finish. Tragically, however, Janowicz suffered a severe head injury in a car crash during the club's 1956 training camp, and he never played again. The depression of his loss was a burden throughout that 6-6-0 campaign.

Not until ten seasons on would the Redskins break even. Along the way, they struggled in vain to find a draftee quarterback on whom to base their reconstruction. In 1961 first-round draftee Norm Snead, they found one, though it was not until his second year and following the arrival of one of the league's most exciting dual-purpose backs, Bobby Mitchell, that he began to blossom. For several years, Mr Marshall had been conspicuous for his reluctance to sign black players. In 1962, he broke the ice, only in a roundabout manner. Cleveland was known to covet Ernie Davis, the Syracuse halfback who had won the Heisman Trophy, whilst Washington really liked Mitchell, who, in one game against the Redskins in 1959, had rushed for a mammoth 232 yards on just 14 carries. The Redskins chose Davis with the first pick in the draft and traded him to Cleveland in return for both Mitchell and Cleveland's first-round pick, Leroy Jackson, both of whom were black. (Sadly, Davis fell victim of leukaemia and never did play pro football.)

Mitchell was moved to flanker, where he was brilliant, with an NFL-leading 72 receptions for 1,384 yards and 11 touchdowns. He continued in similar form for the next three years. In 1963 he caught a 99-yard touchdown pass from George Izo en route to leading the NFL in receiving yardage with 1,436. With the drafting of rookie halfback Charley Taylor, and the arrival of quarterback Sonny Jurgensen, who came in a trade which sent Snead to the Eagles, the Redskins assembled a passing offense to

Above: Sonny Jurgensen calls out the signals.

Left: Bobby Mitchell.

equal any in the NFL. For the defense, linebacker Sam Huff was acquired in a trade with the Giants, and they drafted an exciting defensive back, Paul Krause.

Jurgensen, who in his later playing days cut a portly, unathletic-looking cherub of a figure, with a twinkle in his eye, may well be the sweetest passer of all time. And his passes carried a deadly payload. Five times during his career, he passed for more than 400 yards in a game. In 1965, with the Redskins trailing Dallas by the score of 21-0, he rallied the team for a 34-31 win, passing for three touchdowns and a game total of 411 yards. In 1966, his symbioses with Taylor, Mitchell and tight end Jerry Smith produced 72, 58 and 54 receptions respectively. It was in that year that the Redskins established the existing NFL record for the most points in winning a regular-season game, when they beat the Giants by the score of 72-41. Taylor, who eventually retired as the NFL all-time leading receiver, led the league in both 1966 and 1967, the latter in which, astonishingly, Smith came second and Mitchell came fourth.

In 1968, Jurgensen combined with running back Gerry Allen for the third 99-yard touchdown pass-play in Redskins history. Mitchell, Taylor, Jurgensen and Huff are enshrined in the Pro Football Hall of Fame. And Krause, who still holds the NFL record with 81 career pass interceptions, could well join them.

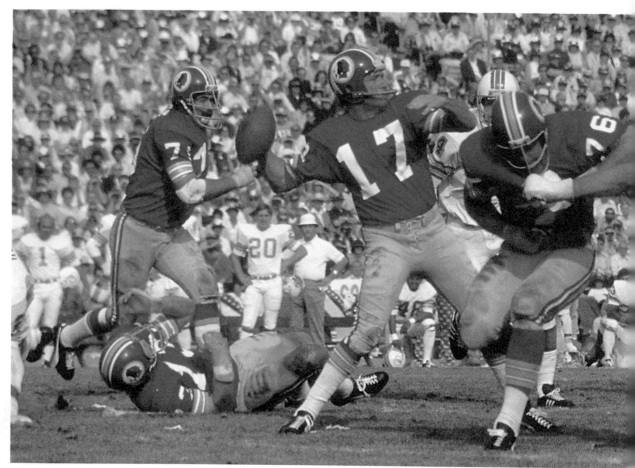

Still, the winning season would not come, but then, in 1969, there arrived perhaps the most charismatic pro football personality of his era. Vince Lombardi was a legend in his own time. Having transformed the Green Bay Packers from a moderate bunch into a superbly-drilled outfit which won five NFL Championships in seven years, including victories in the first two Super Bowls, he was coming to take over in Washington. Given a completely free hand, he made the Redskins a winner by installing a running attack whilst still retaining the expression of Jurgensen's passing game. Jurgensen led the league in passing, with Larry Brown and Charley Harraway forming a solid partnership at running back. Washington went 7-5-2.

However, if 1969 would be remembered for the Redskins' first net-winning campaign since 1955, also, it was the year that Mr Marshall died. Then, the following year, just two weeks before the season opener, Lombardi died of cancer. Even with Brown having an all-pro year, the Redskins slipped to 6-8-0.

Quite by chance, there came available a man, who, though not quite a Lombardi, certainly was a highly-respected NFL head coach and a bit of a character thrown in. He was George Allen, who, over the last five years, had coached the Rams to an overall regular-season record of 49-17-4, including two division titles. He'd been fired on completion of his contract after a dispute with Rams owner

Dan Reeves, and he quickly was snapped up by the Redskins.

Following the death of Marshall, Edward Bennett Williams had taken over the day-to-day running of the club, and, in addition to giving Allen a seven-year contract at $125,000 per annum, together with the odd perk such as a house and a chauffeur-driven limousine, also he gave him a blank cheque. Now it is not that Allen was profligate but, even before the season had begun, Williams remarked wrily, 'I gave George an unlimited budget and he has already exceeded it!'

But Allen was value for money, whatever the amount. Unswerving in his commitment to the value of experience over the potential of youth, he readily traded away future draft options to acquire veterans of known talent. Very quickly, his team was dubbed the 'Over the Hill Gang'. But his methods worked, or only just fell short if winning the Super Bowl Championship is the sole criterion of success.

In his seven-year tenure, Washington never had a losing season. They went to the playoffs five times, four times as the NFC wild card and, in 1972, as champions of the NFC East. In the playoffs of that year, 1972, solid performances brought them victories over Green Bay (16-3) in the divisional playoffs, and over Dallas (26-3) in the NFC Championship Game. But it was their misfortune to come up against Don Shula's Miami Dolphins in Super Bowl VII.

what he was getting when he acquired quarterback Billy Kilmer (ex-New Orleans), wide receiver Roy Jefferson (ex-Baltimore), future Hall of Fame safety Ken Houston (ex-Houston), linebacker Dave Robinson (ex-Green Bay), defensive tackle Diron Talbert and Pardee (both ex-Rams). The price was that in the drafts from 1972 through 1978, the Redskins' first picks were in the 8th, 5th, 6th, 5th, 5th, 4th and 6th rounds. But Allen hadn't spent the entire amount on NFL veterans.

In 1976, he traded his first-round pick to Miami in exchange for the rights to a quarterback whom the Dolphins had drafted in the 1971 fourth round but had been unable to sign. That player had been learning his trade in Canada and his name was Joe Theismann. Also, Allen was prepared to take a chance by signing a free agent running back who, in recent years, had been noted more for his irreverence, contractual disputes and hair style than his rushing. His name, of course, was John Riggins. Wafting a layer of dust off the record book reveals the name of another free agent who came for nothing – defensive tackle Dave Butz. In Butz, Allen's legacy still survives.

In 1978, Allen returned to the Rams. Pardee took over and coached the Redskins to two solid campaigns. In 1979, a dramatic comeback, orchestrated by quarterback Roger Staubach, saw the Cowboys score two late touchdowns in a 35-34 final-week win which robbed the Redskins of both the NFC East title and a spot in the playoffs. After a poor 1980 showing, Pardee was replaced by Joe Gibbs.

Above: Billy Kilmer goes long in Super Bowl VII.

Right: Larry Brown takes on the Detroit Lions.

That 1972 Dolphins club was close to the best that Shula had fashioned, before or since. They were so clinically efficient – they simply executed everything to perfection. Quarterback Bob Griese directed a fine passing offense, but he hardly needed to break a sweat, as running backs Larry Csonka, Jim Kiick and Eugene (Mercury) Morris just went out and pulverised the opposition. Such was the case in a game they won with great certainty, even though by the moderate margin of 14-7. The Redskins' only score, a touchdown by cornerback Mike Bass, came on a 49-yard return following a botched field-goal-cum-pass attempt by Dolphins kicker Garo Yepremian. 'We were never really in the game...and we were never really out of it,' said Redskins linebacker and co-captain Jack Pardee.

It was the closest they came to winning the ultimate prize under Allen, but, building on the platform established by Lombardi, Allen raised the Redskins to heights from which they would descend only rarely to this day. Much has been made of the draft options he traded away, and amongst them there must have been more than a few which could have produced great players. But he knew

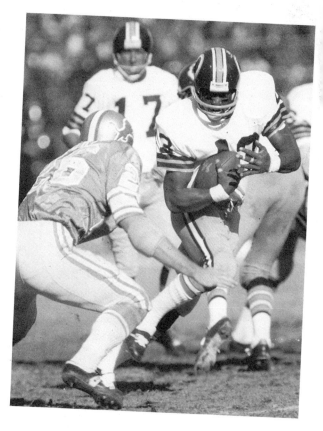

Left: Joe Theismann.

Below: John Riggins.

Gibbs, who had added his own brand of novelty to the lessons he had learned under the tutelage of the former Cardinals and Chargers head coach, Don Coryell, was a risk which paid off. His passing system was daring, requiring as it did the rare combination of intelligence, nerve, vision, powerful arm and authoritative decision making from the quarterback position. Throw in the capacity to talk twenty-to-the-dozen and you have Joe Theismann – the perfect man for the job.

Even with Riggins enthused and wishing to make a point, under the new system of offense the Redskins lost their first five games. And it didn't make too many headlines when they came back to win seven of their final nine. But, very quickly, Theismann had picked up the system, and the Redskins were ready to put it into practice.

The following year, in the strike-shortened nine-game season, Washington could do little wrong as they swept to an NFL-best record of 8-1 (they lost 24-10 to Dallas). If Theismann had been the key during the regular season (he led the NFC in passing), Riggins took over in the playoffs, rushing for 119, 185 and 140 yards in the three games which took Washington to Super Bowl XVII, where they would meet Miami.

Of course, there was a little more to this club which had surprised many 'experts', not least a young and very powerful offensive line, featuring the left side domination of tackle Joe Jacoby and guard Russ Grimm. Who represented the greatest danger? Was it Riggins operating behind that great line, the 'Hogs', or was it Theismann, protected by the same front wall and passing to the 'Smurfs' led by (Downtown) Charlie Brown and playoff sensation Alvin Garrett? In the end, it was Riggins who stole the glory with a Super Bowl-record 166 yards rushing, culminating in a 43-yard touchdown run on fourth-and-one, which gave Washington its first lead with 10:01 remaining in the game. Later, Theismann topped up with a touchdown pass to Brown to make the final score 27-17.

That 1982 squad bore the stamp of a genuine dynasty with, perhaps, a questionable defensive secondary as its only weakness. In the 1983 season, an opening-day defeat by Dallas and an upset to Green Bay in a 48-47 shoot-out apart, the Redskins swept majestically to the NFL's best regular-season record, scoring an all-time, NFL-best 541 points. Riggins rewrote the NFL record book with 24 rushing touchdowns. Theismann threw for 3,714 yards and 29 touchdowns, and Brown caught 78 passes to share first place in the NFC. Along the way, they'd rallied to beat the Raiders 37-35 after having trailed 35-20 halfway through the fourth quarter. In the divisional playoffs, they embarrassed the Rams, Eric Dickerson and all, by the score of 51-7. But San Francisco's Joe Montana exposed a weakness or two in the NFC Championship Game, when he brought the 49ers back into a tie after they had trailed 21-0. Mark Moseley kicked the game-winning, 25-yard field goal inside the final minute.

Unfortunately for the Redskins, in Super Bowl XVIII they met a Raiders club which played up to its reputation and even beyond. They challenged Theismann to throw to wide receivers who were covered one-on-one. He accepted the challenge and lost. Meanwhile, Riggins was held to 64 hard-earned yards on 26 carries. The Raiders' Marcus Allen ran riot, erasing Riggins' name from some parts of the record book, rushing for 191 yards and two touchdowns, one of which covered 74 yards on a broken play. The Raiders murdered them, 38-9.

On reflection, though, it would be quite wrong for the 1983 Redskins to be remembered for a crushing defeat. Rather, perhaps, they should be seen not as a team which failed but one which almost made it two Super Bowl victories in a row. One bad loss did not make them a bad team.

Their status as unquestioned contenders was confirmed in the 1984 season, when they won the title in the NFC East but lost 23-19 to an emerging Chicago powerhouse in the divisional playoffs. In 1985, they ended the regular season tied for the lead in the NFC East with Dallas and the Giants at 10-6, only to be left out in the cold after the application of the tie-breaking procedure.

In 1986, they went 12-4-0 on the regular season to secure the senior wild-card position in the NFC. And in the playoffs, they pulled off a stunning, and yet thoroughly deserved upset of the Bears, 27-13, before falling to the eventual Super Bowl Champion Giants in the NFC title game.

The story of the Redskins' amazing 1987 season is recounted in Chapter One of this book. Perhaps only in the fullness of time will the true value of their achievement be recognised. With both quarterback Doug Williams and running back Timmy Smith likely to be even more effective in the coming season, one dares to imagine that they may even put to rest the so-called Super Bowl jinx. Hail to the Redskins.

BRAVES-REDSKINS RECORD 1932-87

Year	W	L	T	PF	PA
1932	4	4	2	55	79
1933	5	5	2	103	97
1934	6	6	0	107	94
1935	2	8	1	65	123
1936 (a)	7	5	0	149	110
1937 (b)	8	3	0	195	120
1938	6	3	2	148	154
1939	8	2	1	242	94
1940 (a)	9	2	0	245	142
1941	6	5	0	176	174
1942 (b)	10	1	0	227	102
1943 (a)	6	3	1	229	137
1944	6	3	1	169	180
1945 (a)	8	2	0	209	121
1946	5	5	1	171	191
1947	4	8	0	295	367
1948	7	5	0	291	287
1949	4	7	1	268	339
1950	3	9	0	232	326
1951	5	7	0	183	296
1952	4	8	0	240	287
1953	6	5	1	208	215
1954	3	9	0	207	432
1955	8	4	0	246	222
1956	6	6	0	183	225
1957	5	6	1	251	230
1958	4	7	1	214	268
1959	3	9	0	185	350
1960	1	9	2	178	309
1961	1	12	1	174	392
1962	5	7	2	305	376
1963	3	11	0	279	398
1964	6	8	0	307	305
1965	6	8	0	257	301
1966	7	7	0	351	355
1967	5	6	3	347	353
1968	5	9	0	249	358
1969	7	5	2	307	319
1970	6	8	0	297	314
1971 (c)	9	4	1	276	190
1972 (d)	11	3	0	336	218
1973 (c)	10	4	0	325	198
1974 (c)	10	4	0	320	196
1975	8	6	0	325	276
1976 (c)	10	4	0	291	217
1977	9	5	0	196	189
1978	8	8	0	273	283
1979	10	6	0	348	295
1980	6	10	0	261	293
1981	8	8	0	347	349
1982 (e)	8	1	0	190	128
1983 (d)	14	2	0	541	332
1984 (f)	11	5	0	426	310
1985	10	6	0	297	312
1986 (c)	12	4	0	368	296
1987 (e)	11	4	0	379	285

(a) NFL Eastern Division Champion
(b) NFL Champion
(c) NFC Wild Card
(d) NFC Champion
(e) Super Bowl (NFL) Champion
(f) NFC Eastern Division Champion

Braves-Redskins Head Coaches

Coach	Years	Record (incl. playoffs) W	L	T
Lud Wray	1932	4	4	2
William (Lone Star) Dietz	1933-34	11	11	2
Eddie Casey	1935	2	8	1
Ray Flaherty	1936-42	56	23	3
Arthur (Dutch) Bergman	1943	7	4	1
Dudley DeGroot	1944-45	14	6	1
Glen (Turk) Edwards	1946-48	16	18	1
John Whelchel*	1949	3	3	1
Herman Ball†	1949-51	4	16	0
Dick Todd	1951	5	4	0
Earl (Curly) Lambeau	1952-53	10	13	1
Joe Kuharich	1954-58	26	32	2
Mike Nixon	1959-60	4	18	2
Bill McPeak	1961-65	21	46	3
Otto Graham	1966-68	17	22	3
Vince Lombardi	1969	7	5	2
Bill Austin	1970	6	8	0
George Allen	1971-77	69	35	1
Jack Pardee	1978-80	24	24	0
Joe Gibbs	1981-date	85	33	0

* Released after seven games in 1949
† Released after three games in 1951

Left: Joe Gibbs.
Below: Redskins owner Jack Kent Cooke.
Right: Charley Taylor.

Braves-Redskins Personnel in the Pro Football Hall of Fame

Cliff Battles, Halfback (1932-37) 1968*
Sammy Baugh, Halfback-Quarterback (1937-52) 1963*
Bill Dudley, Running Back (1950-51, 1953) 1966*
Glen (Turk) Edwards, Tackle (1932-40) 1969*
Ray Flaherty, Coach (1936-42) 1976*
Otto Graham, Coach (1966-68) 1965*
Ken Houston, Safety (1973-80) 1986*
Sam Huff, Linebacker (1964-67, 1969) 1982*
Christian (Sonny) Jurgensen, Quarterback (1964-74) 1983*
Earl (Curly) Lambeau, Coach (1952-53) 1963*
Vince Lombardi, Coach (1969) 1971*
George Preston Marshall, Founder-Owner (1932-69) 1963*
Wayne Millner, End (1936-41, 1945) 1968*
Bobby Mitchell, Running Back-Wide Receiver (1962-68) 1983*
Charley Taylor, Wide Receiver-Running Back (1964-75, 1977) 1984*

* Indicates year of induction.

CHAPTER THREE

HOW THE SEASON WORKS

The National Football League consists of twenty-eight teams divided into two **Conferences**, the American Football Conference (AFC) and the National Football Conference (NFC). Each conference has fourteen teams, and is subdivided into two five-team **Divisions** and one four-team **Division**. These are essentially based on sensible geographical considerations but also take into account the traditional rivalries which were in existence when the expanded NFL was restructured in 1970. The teams are listed below in order of their final 1987 division standings since this is of importance in arriving at a team's schedule (fixture list) for 1988.

THE SCHEDULE

When considering a team's schedule, it's best to set aside the four teams who each finished the 1987 season in fifth place in their divisions. Looking at the remaining twenty-four, every team plays twelve games against others from its own conference. Again, excluding the four fifth-placed teams, every team will play four games against teams from the rival conference (known as Interconference games), specifically to allow fans in the cities of one conference the opportunity of seeing the star players and teams of the other conference. The structure of a team's schedule depends on whether it plays in a four-team or a five-team division.

AMERICAN FOOTBALL CONFERENCE

Eastern Division

		W	L	T
Indianapolis	AE-1	9	6	0
New England	AE-2	8	7	0
Miami	AE-3	8	7	0
Buffalo	AE-4	7	8	0
N.Y. Jets	AE-5	6	9	0

Central Division

		W	L	T
Cleveland	AC-1	10	5	0
Houston	AC-2	9	6	0
Pittsburgh	AC-3	8	7	0
Cincinnati	AC-4	4	11	0

Western Division

		W	L	T
Denver	AW-1	10	4	1
Seattle	AW-2	9	6	0
San Diego	AW-3	8	7	0
L.A. Raiders	AW-4	5	10	0
Kansas City	AW-5	4	11	0

NATIONAL FOOTBALL CONFERENCE

Eastern Division

		W	L	T
Washington	NE-1	11	4	0
Dallas	NE-2	7	8	0
St Louis	NE-3	7	8	0
Philadelphia	NE-4	7	8	0
N.Y. Giants	NE-5	6	9	0

Central Division

		W	L	T
Chicago	NC-1	11	4	0
Minnesota	NC-2	8	7	0
Green Bay	NC-3	5	9	1
Tampa Bay	NC-4	4	11	0
Detroit	NC-5	4	11	0

Western Division

		W	L	T
San Francisco	NW-1	13	2	0
New Orleans	NW-2	12	3	0
L.A. Rams	NW-3	6	9	0
Atlanta	NW-4	3	12	0

Four-Team Division

A typical schedule, e.g., for the New Orleans Saints, appears below. It is set out, deliberately not in chronological order but to emphasise that the schedule has a quite definite structure.

New Orleans Saints (NFC West)

Atlanta Falcons	NFC West	Home
Atlanta Falcons	NFC West	Away
Los Angeles Rams	NFC West	Home
Los Angeles Rams	NFC West	Away
San Francisco 49ers	NFC West	Home
San Francisco 49ers	NFC West	Away
Detroit Lions	NFC Central	Away
Minnesota Vikings	NFC Central	Away
Tampa Bay Buccaneers	NFC Central	Home
Dallas Cowboys	NFC East	Home
New York Giants	NFC East	Home
Washington Redskins	NFC East	Away
Denver Broncos	AFC West	Home
Los Angeles Raiders	AFC West	Home
San Diego Chargers	AFC West	Away
Seattle Seahawks	AFC West	Away

The Saints will always play their division rivals, Atlanta, the Rams and San Francisco, both home and away. The flavour of intraconference competition is maintained by six games, every year, against teams from outside their division but within their conference. There will always be three games against the NFC East and three against the NFC Central. Again, every year, there will be four games against teams from a particular division of the rival conference, based on a three-year cycle. In 1988, they play against the AFC West; in 1989 they will play teams from the AFC East and in 1990, the AFC Central. For every team in the NFL, a complete list of opponents, other than those within a team's own division, is arrived at by applying the following formula. The letters and numbers refer to Conference, Division and final standing in that division. Thus the Washington Redskins, who are in the National Conference Eastern Division and finished first in that division, are identified as NE-1. Equally, the Cincinnati Bengals, who are in the American Conference Central Division and finished fourth in that division, are labelled AC-4.

AFC EAST-AE

AE-1		AE-2		AE-3		AE-4		AE-5	
H	**A**	**H**	**A**	**H**	**A**	**H**	**A**	**H**	**A**
AC-2	AC-1	AC-4	AC-2	AC-1	AC-3	AC-3	AC-4	AC-2	AC-1
AW-1	AW-3	AW-2	AW-1	AW-3	AW-4	AW-4	AW-2	AC-3	AC-4
NC-1	NC-2	NC-1	NC-2	NC-3	NC-1	NC-2	NC-1	AW-5	AW-5
NC-4	NC-3	NC-4	NC-3	NC-2	NC-4	NC-3	NC-4	NE-5	NC-5

AFC CENTRAL-AC

AC-1		AC-2		AC-3		AC-4	
H	**A**	**H**	**A**	**H**	**A**	**H**	**A**
AE-1	AE-3	AE-2	AE-1	AE-3	AE-4	AE-4	AE-2
AE-5	AW-1	AW-4	AE-5	AW-1	AE-5	AE-5	AW-4
AW-2	AW-5	AW-5	AW-2	AW-5	AW-3	AW-3	AW-5
NE-2	NE-1	NE-1	NE-2	NE-2	NE-1	NE-1	NE-2
NE-4	NE-3	NE-3	NE-4	NE-4	NE-3	NE-3	NE-4

AFC WEST-AW

AW-1		AW-2		AW-3		AW-4		AW-5	
H	**A**	**H**	**A**	**H**	**A**	**H**	**A**	**H**	**A**
AC-1	AC-3	AC-2	AC-1	AC-3	AC-4	AC-4	AC-2	AC-1	AC-2
AE-2	AE-1	AE-4	AE-2	AE-1	AE-3	AE-3	AE-4	AC-4	AC-3
NW-3	NW-1	NW-1	NW-3	NW-1	NW-3	NW-3	NW-1	AE-5	AE-5
NW-4	NW-2	NW-2	NW-4	NW-2	NW-4	NW-4	NW-2	NC-5	NE-5

NFC EAST-NE

NE-1		NE-2		NE-3		NE-4		NE-5	
H	**A**	**H**	**A**	**H**	**A**	**H**	**A**	**H**	**A**
NC-1	NC-3	NC-2	NC-1	NC-3	NC-4	NW-3	NC-2	NC-5	NC-5
NW-2	NW-1	NW-4	NW-2	NW-1	NW-3	NW-4	NC-4	NW-1	NW-2
AC-1	AC-2	AC-2	AC-1	AC-1	AC-2	AC-2	AC-1	NW-3	NW-4
AC-3	AC-4	AC-4	AC-3	AC-3	AC-4	AC-4	AC-3	AW-5	AE-5

NFC CENTRAL-NC

NC-1		NC-2		NC-3		NC-4		NC-5	
H	**A**	**H**	**A**	**H**	**A**	**H**	**A**	**H**	**A**
NE-2	NE-1	NE-4	NE-2	NE-1	NE-3	NE-3	NW-2	NE-5	NE-5
NW-1	NW-3	NW-2	NW-1	NW-3	NW-4	NE-4	NW-4	NW-2	NW-1
AE-3	AE-1	AE-1	AE-3	AE-1	AE-3	AE-3	AE-1	NW-4	NW-3
AE-4	AE-2	AE-2	AE-4	AE-2	AE-4	AE-4	AE-2	AE-5	AW-5

NFC WEST-NW

NW-1		NW-2		NW-3		NW-4	
H	**A**	**H**	**A**	**H**	**A**	**H**	**A**
NC-2	NC-1	NC-4	NC 2	NC-1	NC-3	NC-3	NC-5
NC-5	NE-3	NE-2	NC-5	NC-5	NE-4	NC-4	NE-2
NE-1	NE-5	NE-5	NE-1	NE-3	NE-5	NE-5	NE-4
AW-1	AW-2	AW-1	AW-2	AW-2	AW-1	AW-2	AW-1
AW-4	AW-3	AW-4	AW-3	AW-3	AW-4	AW-3	AW-4

Five-Team Division (Top Four Teams Only)

In the AFC East the schedules for the top four teams have identical structure and include home and away games against the other four teams in the division. Each of the top four teams plays two games against AFC Central teams and two against the AFC West. Also, they play the top four teams in the NFC Central as part of their three-year cycle of interconference games. In 1989, they will play teams from the NFC West and, in 1990, the NFC East. Below is the schedule structure for the Indianapolis Colts.

Indianapolis Colts (AFC East)

Buffalo Bills	AFC East	Home
Buffalo Bills	AFC East	Away
Miami Dolphins	AFC East	Home
Miami Dolphins	AFC East	Away
New England Patriots	AFC East	Home
New England Patriots	AFC East	Away
New York Jets	AFC East	Home
New York Jets	AFC East	Away
Cleveland Browns	AFC Central	Away
Houston Oilers	AFC Central	Home
Denver Broncos	AFC West	Home
San Diego Chargers	AFC West	Away
Chicago Bears	NFC Central	Home
Green Bay Packers	NFC Central	Away
Minnesota Vikings	NFC Central	Away
Tampa Bay Buccaneers	NFC Central	Home

Fifth-Placed Teams

In the AFC, the two fifth-placed teams will each play eight games against teams from their own division and will always play single games against each of the four AFC Central division teams. In the NFC, the two fifth-placed teams each play eight games against teams within their own division and will always play single games against the four NFC West teams. Each of the four fifth-placed teams is guaranteed home and away games against the other fifth-placed team in its own conference, and single games against the two fifth-placed teams from the rival conference. The schedule structures for all four teams are set out as follows:

New York Jets (AFC East)

AFC East		8 games
AFC Central		4 games
Kansas City	(AFC)	Home
Kansas City	(AFC)	Away
New York Giants	(NFC)	Home
Detroit	(NFC)	Away

Kansas City (AFC West)

AFC West		8 games
AFC Central		4 games
New York Jets	(AFC)	Home
New York Jets	(AFC)	Away
Detroit	(NFC)	Home
New York Giants	(NFC)	Away

New York Giants (NFC East)

NFC East		8 games
NFC West		4 games
Detroit	(NFC)	Home
Detroit	(NFC)	Away
Kansas City	(AFC)	Home
New York Jets	(AFC)	Away

Detroit (NFC Central)

NFC Central		8 games
NFC West		4 games
New York Giants	(NFC)	Home
New York Giants	(NFC)	Away
New York Jets	(AFC)	Home
Kansas City	(AFC)	Away

THE PLAYOFFS

On completion of the regular season, each conference holds an elimination competition known as the Playoffs. The teams involved are the three division winners and two Wild Card teams, namely those two, other than the division winners, who have the best won-lost-tied records. The two Wild Card teams play each other to decide which one advances to join the three division winners in the Divisional Playoffs (conference semi-final games). The results of the 1987 National Football Conference playoffs are set out as follows:

Wild Card Game
Minnesota 44 at New Orleans 10

Divisional Playoffs
Minnesota 36 at San Francisco 24
Washington 21 at Chicago 17

NFC Championship Game
Minnesota 10 at Washington 17
Washington advanced to Super Bowl XXII as NFC Champions.

Home-Field Advantage in the Playoffs
For the Wild Card game, the team with the better regular-season record is given the home-field advantage. Again, in the Divisional Playoffs, the home-field advantage goes to the team with the better regular-season record except in so far as the Wild Card winner can never play at home. For the NFC playoffs then, the pecking order was as follows:

	W	L	T
San Francisco*	13	2	0
Chicago*	11	4	0
Washington*	11	4	0
New Orleans†	12	3	0
Minnesota†	8	7	0

* Division Champions
† Wild Card teams

TIE-BREAKING PROCEDURES

Ties are broken by the following list of criteria:

Teams in the same division

A: *Two teams*
1. Head-to-head (best record in games played between the two teams)
2. Best record in games played within the division
3. Best record in games played within the conference
4. Best record in common games
5. Best net points scored in division games (just like goal difference in soccer)
6. Best net points in all games

B: *Three or More Teams* (if two teams remain tied after all other teams are eliminated, the tie-breaking procedure reverts to A:1.)
1. Head-to-head (best record in games played between the teams)
2. Best record in games played within the division
3. Best record in games played within the conference
4. Best record in common games
5. Best net points in division games
6. Best net points in all games

Tie-Breakers for the Wild Card places

(a) If the teams are from the same division, the division tie-breaker is applied.
(b) If the teams are from different divisions, the following procedure is adopted:

C: *Two Teams*
1. Head-to-head (if they have played each other)
2. Best record in games played within the conference
3. Best record in common games (minimum of four)
4. Best average net points in conference games
5. Best net points in all games

D: *Three or More Teams* (If two teams remain tied after all other teams are eliminated, the tie-breaking procedure reverts to A:1, or C:1, whichever is applicable.)
1. Head-to-head sweep (this applies only if one team has either beaten or lost to all the others)
2. Best record in games played within the conference
3. Best record in common games (minimum of four)
4. Best average net points in conference games
5. Best net points in all games

1987 Tie-Breakers

Chicago-Washington (Home-field advantage):
C:2; Chicago (9-2), Washington (9-3)

Houston-Seattle (Home-field advantage):
C:2; Houston (7-4), Seattle (5-6)

THE SUPER BOWL

Though the obvious comparison is with the FA Cup Final, the Super Bowl is best seen as the culmination of an end-of-season knockout competition, involving the champions of six mini leagues together with the Wild Card teams, the latter being considered, perhaps, as potential giant killers. (Only one team, the Oakland Raiders, has won the Super Bowl Championship starting out as a Wild Card.) Unlike for the FA Cup Final, the Super Bowl venue changes from year to year and, since the site is chosen some three years in advance, it is possible for one team to be playing 'at home'. This has never occurred, though both the Los Angeles Rams and the San Francisco 49ers were close to home when they played in Super Bowls XIV and XIX respectively. In selecting the venue, great importance is placed on the likelihood of good weather. Consequently, with the exception of the Pontiac Silverdome (this is a domed stadium), all past Super Bowl stadia have been in the 'sunshine belt', stretching from Florida to California. Super Bowl XXIII will be played at Miami's Joe Robbie Stadium and XXIV at the Louisiana Superdome, New Orleans.

THE PRO BOWL

At the end of the season, the best players from each conference fly off to Hawaii to give the fans out there a treat. The teams are selected by a ballot of head coaches and players in each conference. Each team has two equal votes, those being the head coach's and a consensus of the players' selections. Coaches and players vote only for players in their own conference and may not vote for players from their own teams. Last year, in a low-scoring encounter, the AFC won for the second year in a row, closing to within two of the NFC in the 18-game series.

Pro Bowl MVP Bruce Smith wrestles with Gary Zimmerman (# 65).

AFC-NFC Pro Bowl Results – NFC leads series 10-8

YEAR	DATE	WINNER	LOSER	SITE	ATTENDANCE
1988	Feb. 7	AFC 15	NFC 6	Honolulu	50,113
1987	Feb. 1	AFC 10	NFC 6	Honolulu	50,101
1986	Feb. 2	NFC 28	AFC 24	Honolulu	50,101
1985	Jan. 27	AFC 22	NFC 14	Honolulu	50,385
1984	Jan. 29	NFC 45	AFC 3	Honolulu	50,445
1983	Feb. 6	NFC 20	AFC 19	Honolulu	49,883
1982	Jan. 31	AFC 16	NFC 13	Honolulu	50,402
1981	Feb. 1	NFC 21	AFC 7	Honolulu	50,360
1980	Jan. 27	NFC 37	AFC 27	Honolulu	49,800
1979	Jan. 29	NFC 13	AFC 7	Honolulu	46,281
1978	Jan. 23	NFC 14	AFC 13	Los Angeles	51,337
1977	Jan. 17	AFC 24	NFC 14	Tampa	64,752
1976	Jan. 26	NFC 23	AFC 20	Seattle	30,546
1975	Jan. 20	NFC 17	AFC 10	New Orleans	26,484
1974	Jan. 20	AFC 15	NFC 13	Miami	66,918
1973	Jan. 21	AFC 33	NFC 28	Kansas City	37,091
1972	Jan. 23	AFC 26	NFC 13	Dallas	53,647
1971	Jan. 24	NFC 27	AFC 6	Los Angeles	48,222
				Los Angeles	

PRO BOWL ROSTERS
(Original selections – starters in Capitals)

OFFENSE	AMERICAN FOOTBALL CONFERENCE		NATIONAL FOOTBALL CONFERENCE	
Wide Receivers	AL TOON	N.Y. Jets	JERRY RICE	San Francisco
	STEVE LARGENT	Seattle	MIKE QUICK	Philadelphia
	Carlos Carson	Kansas City	Anthony Carter	Minnesota
	Stanley Morgan	New England	Gary Clark	Washington
Tight Ends	KELLEN WINSLOW	San Diego	MARK BAVARO	N.Y. Giants
	Todd Christensen	L.A. Raiders	Steve Jordan	Minnesota
Tackles	ANTHONY MUNOZ	Cincinnati	JACKIE SLATER	L.A. Rams
	CHRIS HINTON	Indianapolis	GARY ZIMMERMAN	Minnesota
	Cody Risien	Cleveland	Luis Sharpe	St Louis
Guards	KEITH BISHOP	Denver	BILL FRALIC	Atlanta
	MIKE MUNCHAK	Houston	DENNIS HARRAH	L.A. Rams
	Ron Solt	Indianapolis	Brad Edelman	New Orleans
Centers	RAY DONALDSON	Indianapolis	JAY HILGENBERG	Chicago
	Dwight Stephenson	Miami	Doug Smith	L.A. Rams
Quarterbacks	JOHN ELWAY	Denver	JOE MONTANA	San Francisco
	Dan Marino	Miami	Neil Lomax	St Louis
	Bernie Kosar*	Cleveland		
Running Backs	ERIC DICKERSON	Indianapolis	CHARLES WHITE	L.A. Rams
	CURT WARNER	Seattle	RUEBEN MAYES	New Orleans
	Kevin Mack	Cleveland	Herschel Walker	Dallas
	Mike Rozier	Houston	Roger Craig	San Francisco

DEFENSE

Defensive Ends	BRUCE SMITH	Buffalo	REGGIE WHITE	Philadelphia
	JACOB GREEN	Seattle	CHRIS DOLEMAN	Minnesota
	Howie Long	L.A. Raiders	Charles Mann	Washington
Nose Tackles	BILL MAAS	Kansas City	MICHAEL CARTER	San Francisco
	Bob Golic	Cleveland	Steve McMichael	Chicago
Outside Linebackers	ANDRE TIPPETT	New England	CARL BANKS	N.Y. Giants
	DUANE BICKETT	Indianapolis	WILBER MARSHALL	Chicago
	Clay Matthews	Cleveland	Lawrence Taylor	N.Y. Giants
Inside Linebackers	KARL MECKLENBURG	Denver	HARRY CARSON	N.Y. Giants
	FREDD YOUNG	Seattle	MIKE SINGLETARY	Chicago
	John Offerdahl	Miami	Sam Mills	New Orleans
			Scott Studwell*	Minnesota
Cornerbacks	FRANK MINNIFIELD	Cleveland	DARRELL GREEN	Washington
	HANFORD DIXON	Cleveland	JERRY GRAY	L.A. Rams
	Albert Lewis	Kansas City	Dave Waymer	New Orleans
Safeties	DERON CHERRY	Kansas City	JOEY BROWNER	Minnesota
	KENNY EASLEY	Seattle	RONNIE LOTT	San Francisco
	Keith Bostic	Houston	Dave Duerson	Chicago

SPECIAL TEAMS

Placekicker	DEAN BIASUCCI	Indianapolis	MORTEN ANDERSEN	New Orleans
Punter	RALF MOJSIEJENKO	San Diego	JIM ARNOLD	Detroit
Kick Returner	GERALD McNEIL	Cleveland	VAI SIKAHEMA	St Louis
Specialist	STEVE TASKER	Buffalo	RON WOLFLEY	St Louis
Head Coach	MARTY SCHOTTENHEIMER	Cleveland	JERRY BURNS	Minnesota

* Special selection made by head coach

AN ALL-PRO TEAM

Howie Long (# 75) tackles San Francisco's Roger Craig.

Anyone can pick his or her own All-Pro team and just about everyone does. Here's my dream team.

Chicago's Steve McMichael was a force in 1987.

Wide Receivers	Jerry Rice	San Francisco
	Mike Quick	Philadelphia
Tight End	Mark Bavaro	N.Y. Giants
Tackles	Anthony Munoz	Cincinnati
	Gary Zimmerman	Minnesota
Guards	Mike Munchak	Houston
	Bill Fralic	Atlanta
Center	Dwight Stephenson	Miami
Quarterback	Dan Marino	Miami
Running Backs	Eric Dickerson	Indianapolis
	Herschel Walker	Dallas
Defensive Ends	Howie Long	L.A. Raiders
	Reggie White	Philadelphia
Defensive Tackles	Bill Maas	Kansas City
	Steve McMichael	Chicago
Outside Linebackers	Lawrence Taylor	N.Y. Giants
	Carl Banks	N.Y. Giants
Inside Linebackers	Mike Singletary	Chicago
	Fredd Young	Seattle
Safeties	Joey Browner	Minnesota
	Ronnie Lott	San Francisco
Cornerbacks	Darrell Green	Washington
	Raymond Clayborn	New England
Placekicker	Morten Andersen	New Orleans
Punter	Brian Hansen	New Orleans
Punt Returner	Vai Sikahema	Washington
Kickoff Returner	Dennis Gentry	Chicago
Special-team Specialist	Ron Wolfley	St Louis
Head Coach	Chuck Noll	Pittsburgh

CHAMPIONS 1920-1987

National Football League 1920-1969
(Until 1933 based solely on regular-season play)

1920	Akron Pros
1921	Chicago Staleys
1922	Canton Bulldogs
1923	Canton Bulldogs
1924	Cleveland Bulldogs
1925	Chicago Cardinals
1926	Frankford Yellow Jackets
1927	New York Giants
1928	Providence Steam Roller
1929	Green Bay Packers
1930	Green Bay Packers
1931	Green Bay Packers
1932	Chicago Bears 9 – Portsmouth Spartans 0 (Championship Playoff)

NFL Championship Games 1933-69

1933	Chicago Bears 23 – New York Giants 21
1934	New York Giants 30 – Chicago Bears 13
1935	Detroit Lions 26 – New York Giants 7
1936	Green Bay Packers 21 – Boston Redskins 6
1937	Washington Redskins 28 – Chicago Bears 21
1938	New York Giants 23 – Green Bay Packers 17
1939	Green Bay Packers 27 – New York Giants 0
1940	Chicago Bears 73 – Washington Redskins 0
1941	Chicago Bears 37 – New York Giants 9
1942	Washington Redskins 14 – Chicago Bears 6
1943	Chicago Bears 41 – Washington Redskins 21
1944	Green Bay Packers 14 – New York Giants 7
1945	Cleveland Rams 15 – Washington Redskins 14
1946	Chicago Bears 24 – New York Giants 14
1947	Chicago Cardinals 28 – Philadelphia Eagles 21
1948	Philadelphia Eagles 7 – Chicago Cardinals 0
1949	Philadelphia Eagles 14 – Los Angeles Rams 0
1950	Cleveland Browns 30 – Los Angeles Rams 28
1951	Los Angeles Rams 24 – Cleveland Browns 17
1952	Detroit Lions 17 – Cleveland Browns 7
1953	Detroit Lions 17 – Cleveland Browns 16
1954	Cleveland Browns 56 – Detroit Lions 10
1955	Cleveland Browns 38 – Los Angeles Rams 14
1956	New York Giants 47 – Chicago Bears 7
1957	Detroit Lions 59 – Cleveland Browns 14
1958	Baltimore Colts 23 – New York Giants 17 (OT)
1959	Baltimore Colts 31 – New York Giants 16
1960	Philadelphia Eagles 17 – Green Bay Packers 13
1961	Green Bay Packers 37 – New York Giants 0
1962	Green Bay Packers 16 – New York Giants 7
1963	Chicago Bears 14 – New York Giants 10
1964	Cleveland Browns 27 – Baltimore Colts 0
1965	Green Bay Packers 23 – Cleveland Browns 12
1966	Green Bay Packers 34 – Dallas Cowboys 27
1967	Green Bay Packers 21 – Dallas Cowboys 17
1968	Baltimore Colts 34 – Cleveland Browns 0
1969	Minnesota Vikings 27 – Cleveland Browns 7

American Football League Championship Games 1960-1969

1960	Houston Oilers 24 – Los Angeles Chargers 16
1961	Houston Oilers 10 – San Diego Chargers 3
1962	Dallas Texans 20 – Houston Oilers 17 (OT)
1963	San Diego Chargers 51 – Boston Patriots 10
1964	Buffalo Bills 20 – San Diego Chargers 7
1965	Buffalo Bills 23 – San Diego Chargers 0
1966	Kansas City Chiefs 31 – Buffalo Bills 7
1967	Oakland Raiders 40 – Houston Oilers 7
1968	New York Jets 27 – Oakland Raiders 23
1969	Kansas City Chiefs 17 – Oakland Raiders 7

CONFERENCE CHAMPIONSHIP GAMES 1970-1987

NFC

1970	Dallas Cowboys 17 – San Francisco 49ers 10
1971	Dallas Cowboys 14 – San Francisco 49ers 3
1972	Washington Redskins 26 – Dallas Cowboys 3
1973	Minnesota Vikings 27 – Dallas Cowboys 10
1974	Minnesota Vikings 14 – Los Angeles Rams 10
1975	Dallas Cowboys 37 – Los Angeles Rams 7
1976	Minnesota Vikings 24 – Los Angeles Rams 13
1977	Dallas Cowboys 23 – Minnesota Vikings 6
1978	Dallas Cowboys 28 – Los Angeles Rams 0
1979	Los Angeles Rams 9 – Tampa Bay Buccaneers 0
1980	Philadelphia Eagles 20 – Dallas Cowboys 7
1981	San Francisco 49ers 28 – Dallas Cowboys 27
1982	Washington Redskins 31 – Dallas Cowboys 17
1983	Washington Redskins 24 – San Francisco 49ers 21

1984 San Francisco 49ers 23 – Chicago Bears 0
1985 Chicago Bears 24 – Los Angeles Rams 0
1986 New York Giants 17 – Washington Redskins 0
1987 Washington Redskins 17 – Minnesota Vikings 10

AFC
1970 Baltimore Colts 27 – Oakland Raiders 17
1971 Miami Dolphins 21 – Baltimore Colts 0
1972 Miami Dolphins 21 – Pittsburgh Steelers 17
1973 Miami Dolphins 27 – Oakland Raiders 10
1974 Pittsburgh Steelers 24 – Oakland Raiders 13
1975 Pittsburgh Steelers 16 – Oakland Raiders 10
1976 Oakland Raiders 24 – Pittsburgh Steelers 7
1977 Denver Broncos 20 – Oakland Raiders 17
1978 Pittsburgh Steelers 34 – Houston Oilers 5
1979 Pittsburgh Steelers 27 – Houston Oilers 13
1980 Oakland Raiders 34 – San Diego Chargers 27
1981 Cincinnati Bengals 27 – San Diego Chargers 7
1982 Miami Dolphins 14 – New York Jets 0
1983 Los Angeles Raiders 30 – Seattle Seahawks 14
1984 Miami Dolphins 45 – Pittsburgh Steelers 28
1985 New England Patriots 31 – Miami Dolphins 14
1986 Denver Broncos 23 – Cleveland Browns 20 (OT)
1987 Denver Broncos 38 – Cleveland Browns 33

Steve Largent became the all-time leading receiver in 1987.

Super Bowl 1966-1987

Season	SB	Winner		Loser		Stadium	Attendance
1966	I	Green Bay	35	Kansas City	10	Los Angeles Coliseum	61,946
1967	II	Green Bay	33	Oakland	14	Miami Orange Bowl	75,546
1968	III	N.Y. Jets	16	Baltimore	7	Miami Orange Bowl	75,389
1969	IV	Kansas City	23	Minnesota	7	New Orleans Tulane Stadium	80,562
1970	V	Baltimore	16	Dallas	13	Miami Orange Bowl	79,204
1971	VI	Dallas	24	Miami	3	New Orleans Tulane Stadium	81,023
1972	VII	Miami	14	Washington	7	Los Angeles Coliseum	90,182
1973	VIII	Miami	24	Minnesota	7	Houston Rice Stadium	71,882
1974	IX	Pittsburgh	16	Minnesota	6	New Orleans Tulane Stadium	80,997
1975	X	Pittsburgh	21	Dallas	17	Miami Orange Bowl	80,187
1976	XI	Oakland	32	Minnesota	14	Pasadena Rose Bowl	103,438
1977	XII	Dallas	27	Denver	10	New Orleans Superdome	75,583
1978	XIII	Pittsburgh	35	Dallas	31	Miami Orange Bowl	79,484
1979	XIV	Pittsburgh	31	L.A. Rams	19	Pasadena Rose Bowl	103,985
1980	XV	Oakland	27	Philadelphia	10	New Orleans Superdome	76,135
1981	XVI	San Francisco	26	Cincinnati	21	Pontiac Silverdome	81,270
1982	XVII	Washington	27	Miami	17	Pasadena Rose Bowl	103,667
1983	XVIII	L.A. Raiders	38	Washington	9	Tampa Stadium	72,920
1984	XIX	San Francisco	38	Miami	16	Stanford Stadium	84,059
1985	XX	Chicago	46	New England	10	New Orleans Superdome	73,818
1986	XXI	N.Y. Giants	39	Denver	20	Pasadena Rose Bowl	101,063
1987	XXII	Washington	42	Denver	10	San Diego Jack Murphy Stadium	73,302

ALL-TIME INDIVIDUAL RECORDS
(Regular Season only – New Records and Records tied are in bold type)

CAREER BEST

SEASONS PLAYED	26	George Blanda
GAMES PLAYED	340	George Blanda
POINTS	2,002	George Blanda (9-TD, 943-EP, 335-FG)
EXTRA POINTS	943	George Blanda
FIELD GOALS	373	Jan Stenerud
TOUCHDOWNS		
Rushing and Pass Receiving	126	Jim Brown (106-R, 20-P)
Rushing	**110**	**Walter Payton**
Pass Receiving	99	Don Hutson
Passes Thrown	342	Fran Tarkenton
By Interception Return	9	Ken Houston
By Punt Return	8	Jack Christiansen
		Rick Upchurch
By Kickoff Return	6	Ollie Matson
		Gale Sayers
		Travis Williams
By Fumble Recovery Return	4	Billy Thompson
YARDAGE		
Rushing	**16,726**	**Walter Payton**
Pass Receiving	12,146	Charlie Joiner
Passing	47,003	Fran Tarkenton
HOW MANY TIMES		
Pass Receptions	**752**	**Steve Largent**
Passes Completed	3,686	Fran Tarkenton
Interceptions	81	Paul Krause
100-Yard Rushing Games	77	Walter Payton
100-Yard Pass Receiving Games	50	Don Maynard
1,000-Yard Rushing Seasons	10	Walter Payton
MOST SEASONS LEADING LEAGUE		
Points	5	Don Hutson, Green Bay 1940-44
		Gino Cappelletti, Boston 1961, 1963-66
Extra Points	8	George Blanda, Chicago Bears 1956, Houston 1961-62, Oakland 1967-69, 1972, 1974
Field Goals	5	Lou Groza, Cleveland Browns 1950, 1952-54, 1957
Touchdowns	8	Don Hutson, Green Bay 1935-38, 1941-44
Touchdowns, Rushing	5	Jim Brown, Cleveland Browns 1957-59, 1963, 1965
Touchdowns, Pass Receiving	9	Don Hutson, Green Bay 1935-38, 1940-44
Touchdowns, Passes Thrown	4	Johnny Unitas, Baltimore 1957-60
		Len Dawson, Dallas Texans 1962, Kansas City 1963, 1965-66
Yards, Rushing	8	Jim Brown, Cleveland Browns 1957-61, 1963-65
Yards, Pass Receiving	7	Don Hutson, Green Bay 1936, 1938-39, 1941-44
Yards, Passing	5	Sonny Jurgensen, Philadelphia 1961-62, Washington 1966-67, 1969
Pass Receptions	8	Don Hutson, Green Bay 1936-37, 1939, 1941-45
Passes Completed	5	Sammy Baugh, Washington 1937, 1943, 1945, 1947-48
Pass Interceptions	3	Everson Walls, Dallas 1981-82, 1985

SEASON BEST

POINTS	176	Paul Hornung, Green Bay 1960 (15-TD, 41-EP, 15-FG)
EXTRA POINTS	66	Uwe von Schamann, Miami 1984
FIELD GOALS	35	Ali Haji-Sheikh, N.Y. Giants 1983
TOUCHDOWNS		
Rushing and Pass Receiving	24	John Riggins, Washington 1983 (24-R)
Rushing	24	John Riggins, Washington 1983
Pass Receiving	**22**	**Jerry Rice, San Francisco 1987**
Passes Thrown	48	Dan Marino, Miami 1984

By Interception Return	4	Ken Houston, Houston 1971
		Jim Kearney, Kansas City 1972
By Punt Return	4	Jack Christiansen, Detroit 1951
		Rick Upchurch, Denver 1976
By Kickoff Return	4	Travis Williams, Green Bay 1967
		Cecil Turner, Chicago 1970
By Fumble Recovery Return	2	By many players

YARDAGE

Rushing	2,105	Eric Dickerson, L.A. Rams 1984
Pass Receiving	1,746	Charley Hennigan, Houston 1961
Passing	5,084	Dan Marino, Miami 1984

HOW MANY TIMES

Pass Receptions	106	Art Monk, Washington 1984
Passes Completed	378	Dan Marino, Miami 1986
Interceptions	14	Dick 'Night Train' Lane, L.A. Rams 1952

GAME BEST

POINTS	40	Ernie Nevers (6-TD, 4-EP), Chicago Cardinals v Chicago Bears 1929
EXTRA POINTS	9	Pat Harder, Chicago Cardinals v N.Y. Giants 1948
		Bob Waterfield, L.A. Rams v Baltimore 1950
		Charlie Gogolak, Washington v N.Y. Giants 1966
FIELD GOALS	7	Jim Bakken, St Louis v Pittsburgh 1967

TOUCHDOWNS

All methods of scoring	6	Ernie Nevers (6-R), Chicago Cardinals v Chicago Bears 1929
		Dub Jones (4-R, 2-P), Cleveland v Chicago Bears 1951
		Gale Sayers (4-R, 1-P, 1-Ret), Chicago Bears v San Francisco 1965
Rushing	6	Ernie Nevers, Chicago Cardinals v Chicago Bears 1929
Pass Receiving	5	Bob Shaw, Chicago Cardinals v Baltimore 1950
		Kellen Winslow, San Diego v Oakland 1981
Passes Thrown	7	Sid Luckman, Chicago Bears v N.Y. Giants 1943
		Adrian Burk, Philadelphia v Washington 1954
		George Blanda, Houston v N.Y. Titans 1961
		Y.A. Tittle, N.Y. Giants v Washington 1962
		Joe Kapp, Minnesota v Baltimore 1969

YARDAGE

Rushing	275	Walter Payton, Chicago v Minnesota 1977
Pass Receiving	309	Stephone Paige, Kansas City v San Diego 1985
Passing	554	Norm Van Brocklin, L.A. Rams v N.Y. Yanks 1951

HOW MANY TIMES

Rushing Attempts	43	Butch Woolfolk, N.Y. Giants v Philadelphia 1983
		James Wilder, Tampa Bay v Green Bay 1984 (OT)
Pass Receptions	18	Tom Fears, L.A. Rams v Green Bay 1950
Passes Completed	42	Richard Todd, N.Y. Jets v San Francisco 1980
Interceptions	4	By many players

LONGEST

Touchdown Rushing	99 yds	Tony Dorsett, Dallas v Minnesota 1982
Touchdown Pass Receiving	99 yds	Andy Farkas (from Filchock), Washington v Pittsburgh 1939
		Bobby Mitchell (from Izo), Washington v Cleveland 1963
		Pat Studstill (from Sweetan), Detroit v Baltimore 1966
		Gerry Allen (from Jurgensen), Washington v Chicago 1968
		Cliff Branch (from Plunkett), L.A. Raiders v Washington 1983
		Mike Quick (from Jaworski), Philadelphia v Atlanta 1985
Field Goal	63 yds	Tom Dempsey, New Orleans v Detroit 1970
Punt Return (All TDs)	98 yds	Gil LeFebvre, Cincinnati v Brooklyn 1933
		Charlie West, Minnesota v Washington 1968
		Dennis Morgan, Dallas v St Louis 1974
Kickoff Return (All TDs)	106 yds	Al Carmichael, Green Bay v Chicago Bears 1956
		Noland Smith, Kansas City v Denver 1967
		Roy Green, St Louis v Dallas 1979

Interception Return (TD)	**103 yds**	**Vencie Glenn, San Diego v Denver 1987**
Fumble Recovery Return (TD)	104 yds	Jack Tatum, Oakland v Green Bay 1972

TEAM RECORDS

Most Championships	11	Green Bay, 1929-31, 1936, 1939, 1944, 1961-62, 1965-67
	9	Chicago Staleys/Bears, 1921, 1932-33, 1940-41, 1943, 1946, 1963, 1985
	5	N.Y. Giants, 1927, 1934, 1938, 1956, 1986
	4	Detroit, 1935, 1952-53, 1957
		Cleveland Browns, 1950, 1954-55, 1964
		Baltimore, 1958-59, 1968, 1970
		Pittsburgh, 1974-75, 1978-79
		Oakland/L.A. Raiders, 1967, 1976, 1980, 1983
		Washington, 1937, 1942, 1982, 1987
Most Consecutive Games Won (inc. playoffs)	18	Chicago Bears, 1933-34 and 1941-42
		Miami, 1972-73
Most Consecutive Games Won (exc. playoffs)	17	Chicago Bears, 1933-34
Most Consecutive Games Lost	26	Tampa Bay, 1976-77
Most Points in a Season	541	Washington, 1983
Fewest Points in a Season (Since 1932)	37	Cincinnati-St Louis, 1934
Most Points in a Game	72	Washington v N.Y. Giants, 1966
Most Points (Both Teams) in a Game	113	Washington v N.Y. Giants, 1966
Fewest Points (Both Teams) in a Game	0	Many teams; last time N.Y. Giants v Detroit, 1943

ALL-TIME TOP TWENTY
(1987 Active players in capitals)

All-Time Leading Rushers

		Yrs.	Att.	Yards	Ave.	TDs
1.	WALTER PAYTON	13	3,838	16,726	4.4	110
2.	Jim Brown	9	2,359	12,312	5.2	106
3.	Franco Harris	13	2,949	12,120	4.1	91
4.	TONY DORSETT	11	2,755	12,036	4.4	72
5.	John Riggins	14	2,916	11,352	3.9	104
6.	O.J. Simpson	11	2,404	11,236	4.7	61
7.	Earl Campbell	8	2,187	9,407	4.3	74
8.	Jim Taylor	10	1,941	8,597	4.4	83
9.	Joe Perry	14	1,737	8,378	4.8	53
10.	ERIC DICKERSON	5	1,748	8,256	4.7	61
11.	OTTIS ANDERSON	9	1,884	8,086	4.3	47
12.	Larry Csonka	11	1,891	8,081	4.3	64
13.	Mike Pruitt	11	1,844	7,378	4.0	51
14.	Leroy Kelly	10	1,727	7,274	4.2	74
15.	GEORGE ROGERS	7	1,692	7,176	4.2	54
16.	John Henry Johnson	13	1,571	6,803	4.3	48
17.	Wilbert Montgomery	9	1,540	6,789	4.4	45
18.	Chuck Muncie	9	1,561	6,702	4.3	71
19.	Mark van Eeghen	10	1,652	6,650	4.0	37
20.	Lawrence McCutcheon	10	1,521	6,578	4.3	26

All-Time Leading Receivers

		Yrs.	No.	Yards	Ave.	TDs
1.	STEVE LARGENT	12	752	12,041	16.0	95
2.	Charlie Joiner	18	750	12,146	16.2	65
3.	Charley Taylor	13	649	9,110	14.0	79
4.	Don Maynard	15	633	11,834	18.7	88
5.	Raymond Berry	13	631	9,275	14.7	68
6.	Harold Carmichael	14	590	8,985	15.2	79
7.	Fred Biletnikoff	14	589	8,974	15.2	76
8.	Harold Jackson	15	579	10,372	17.9	76
9.	OZZIE NEWSOME	10	575	7,073	12.3	42
10.	JAMES LOFTON	10	571	10,536	18.5	54
11.	Lionel Taylor	10	567	7,195	12.7	45
12.	WES CHANDLER	10	555	8,933	16.1	56
13.	Lance Alworth	11	542	10,266	18.9	85
14.	KELLEN WINSLOW	9	541	6,741	12.5	45
15.	JOHN STALLWORTH	14	537	8,723	16.2	63
16.	Bobby Mitchell	11	521	7,954	15.3	65
17.	Nat Moore	13	510	7,546	14.8	74
18.	DWIGHT CLARK	9	506	6,750	13.3	48
19.	ART MONK	8	504	7,033	14.0	34
20.	Billy Howton	12	503	8,459	16.8	61

All-Time Leading Scorers

		Yrs.	TDs	EPs	FGs	Total
1.	George Blanda	26	9	943	335	2,002
2.	Jan Stenerud	19	0	580	373	1,699
3.	Jim Turner	16	1	521	304	1,439
4.	Mark Moseley	16	0	482	300	1,382
5.	Jim Bakken	17	0	534	282	1,380
6.	Fred Cox	15	0	519	282	1,365
7.	Lou Groza	17	1	641	234	1,349
8.	Gino Cappelletti*	11	42	350	176	1,130
9.	RAY WERSCHING	15	0	456	222	1,122
10.	Don Cockroft	13	0	432	216	1,080
11.	PAT LEAHY	14	0	424	218	1,078
12.	Garo Yepremian	14	0	444	210	1,074
13.	CHRIS BAHR	12	0	424	206	1,042
14.	Bruce Gossett	11	0	374	219	1,031
15.	Sam Baker	15	2	428	179	977
16.	Rafael Septien	10	0	420	180	960
17.	Lou Michaels**	13	1	386	187	955
18.	Roy Gerela	11	0	351	184	903
19.	Bobby Walston	12	46	365	80	881
20.	Pete Gogolak	10	0	344	173	863

* Includes four two-point conversions
** Includes a safety recorded in 1965 when Michaels played as a defensive end.

Kellen Winslow entered the list of leading receivers in 14th place.

All-Time Passer Ratings (Minimum 1,500 attempts)

		Yrs.	Att.	Comp.	Yards	TDs	Int.	Rating
1.	DAN MARINO	5	2,494	1,512	19,422	168	80	94.1
2.	JOE MONTANA	9	3,276	2,084	24,552	172	89	92.5
3.	KEN O'BRIEN	5	1,566	947	11,676	69	43	86.8
4.	DAVE KRIEG	8	2,116	1,224	15,808	130	88	84.6
5.	Roger Staubach	11	2,958	1,685	22,700	153	109	83.4
6.	Len Dawson	19	3,741	2,136	28,711	239	183	82.6
	Sonny Jurgensen	18	4,262	2,433	32,224	255	189	82.6

Ken O'Brien entered the list of leading passers in third place.

		Yrs.	Att.	Comp.	Yards	TDs	Int.	Rating
8.	NEIL LOMAX	7	2,710	1,562	19,376	116	79	82.0
	DANNY WHITE	12	2,908	1,732	21,685	154	129	82.0
10.	Ken Anderson	16	4,475	2,654	32,838	197	160	81.9
11.	Bart Starr	16	3,149	1,808	24,718	152	138	80.5
12.	Fran Tarkenton	18	6,467	3,686	47,003	342	266	80.4
13.	DAN FOUTS	15	5,604	3,297	43,040	254	242	80.2
14.	BILL KENNEY	8	2,316	1,272	16,728	105	81	78.5
15.	Otto Graham	6	1,565	872	13,499	88	94	78.2
	Bert Jones	10	2,551	1,430	18,190	124	101	78.2
	Johnny Unitas	18	5,186	2,830	40,239	290	253	78.2
18.	Frank Ryan	13	2,133	1,090	16,042	149	111	77.6
19.	Joe Theismann	12	3,602	2,044	25,206	160	138	77.4
20.	Bob Griese	14	3,429	1,926	25,092	192	172	77.1

PASSES COMPLETED	No.	YARDS PASSING	Yards	TOUCHDOWN PASSES	No.
1. Fran Tarkenton	3,686	1. Fran Tarkenton	47,003	1. Fran Tarkenton	342
2. DAN FOUTS	3,297	2. DAN FOUTS	43,040	2. Johnny Unitas	290
3. Johnny Unitas	2,830	3. Johnny Unitas	40,239	3. Sonny Jurgensen	255
4. Ken Anderson	2,654	4. Jim Hart	34,665	4. DAN FOUTS	254
5. Jim Hart	2,593	5. John Hadl	33,503	5. John Hadl	244
6. John Brodie	2,469	6. Ken Anderson	32,838	6. Len Dawson	239
7. Sonny Jurgensen	2,433	7. Sonny Jurgensen	32,224	7. George Blanda	236
8. Roman Gabriel	2,366	8. John Brodie	31,548	8. John Brodie	214
9. John Hadl	2,363	9. Norm Snead	30,797	9. Terry Bradshaw	212
10. JOE FERGUSON	2,292	10. Roman Gabriel	29,444	Y.A. Tittle	212
11. Norm Snead	2,276	11. JOE FERGUSON	28,895	11. Jim Hart	209
12. Ken Stabler	2,270	12. Len Dawson	28,711	12. Roman Gabriel	201
13. RON JAWORSKI	2,142	13. Y.A. Tittle	28,339	13. Ken Anderson	197
14. Len Dawson	2,136	14. Terry Bradshaw	27,989	14. Norm Snead	196
15. Y.A. Tittle	2,118	15. Ken Stabler	27,938	Bobby Layne	196
16. JOE MONTANA	2,084	16. Craig Morton	27,908	16. Ken Stabler	194
17. Craig Morton	2,053	17. RON JAWORSKI	27,682	17. Bob Griese	192
18. Joe Theismann	2,044	18. Joe Namath	27,663	18. JOE FERGUSON	190
19. Terry Bradshaw	2,025	19. George Blanda	26,920	19. Sammy Baugh	187
20. Archie Manning	2,011	20. Bobby Layne	26,768	20. Craig Morton	183

INDEX OF RETIRED PLAYERS
LISTED IN THE ALL-TIME STATISTICS

LANE Dick 'Night Train', L.A. Rams (1952-53), Chicago Cardinals (1954-59), Detroit (1960-65)

LAYNE Bobby, Chicago Bears (1948), N.Y. Bulldogs (1949), Detroit (1950-58), Pittsburgh (1958-62)

LeFEBVRE Gil, Cincinnati Reds (1933-34), Detroit (1935)

LUCKMAN Sid, Chicago Bears (1939-50)

MANNING Archie, New Orleans (1971-75 and 1977-82), Houston (1982-83), Minnesota (1983-84)

MATSON Ollie, Chicago Cardinals (1952 and 1954-58), L.A. Rams (1959-62), Detroit (1963), Philadelphia (1964-66)

MAYNARD Don, N.Y. Giants (1958), N.Y. Titans/Jets (1960-72), St Louis (1973)

McCUTCHEON Lawrence, L.A. Rams (1972-79), Denver (1980), Seattle (1980), Buffalo (1981)

MICHAELS Lou, L.A. Rams (1958-60), Pittsburgh (1961-63), Baltimore (1964-69), Green Bay (1971)

MITCHELL Bobby, Cleveland (1958-61), Washington (1962-68)

MONTGOMERY Wilbert, Philadelphia (1977-84), Detroit (1985)

MOORE Nat, Miami (1974-86)

MORGAN Dennis, Dallas (1974), Philadelphia (1975)

MORTON Craig, Dallas (1965-74), N.Y. Giants (1974-76), Denver (1977-82)

MOSELEY Mark, Philadelphia (1970), Houston (1971-72), Washington (1974-86), Cleveland (1986)

MUNCIE Chuck, New Orleans (1976-80), San Diego (1980-84)

NAMATH Joe, N.Y. Jets (1965-76), L.A. Rams (1977)

NEVERS Ernie, Duluth Eskimos (1926-27), Chicago Cardinals (1929-31)

PAYTON Walter, Chicago (1975-87)

PERRY Joe, San Francisco (1948-60 and 1963), Baltimore (1961-62)

PLUNKETT Jim, New England (1971-75), San Francisco (1976-77), Oakland/L.A. Raiders (1978-85)

PRUITT Mike, Cleveland (1976-84), Buffalo (1985) Kansas City (1985-86)

RIGGINS John, N.Y. Jets (1971-75), Washington (1976-79 and 1981-85)

RYAN Frank, L.A. Rams (1958-61), Cleveland (1962-68), Washington (1969-70)

SAYERS Gale, Chicago (1965-71)

SEPTIEN Rafael, L.A. Rams (1977), Dallas (1978-86)

SHAW Bob, Cleveland/L.A. Rams (1945-49), Chicago Cardinals (1950)

SIMPSON O.J., Buffalo (1969-77), San Francisco (1978-79)

SMITH Noland, Kansas City (1967-69), San Francisco (1969)

SNEAD Norm, Washington (1961-63), Philadelphia (1964-70), Minnesota (1971), N.Y. Giants (1972-74 and 1976), San Francisco (1974-75)

STABLER Ken, Oakland (1970-79), Houston (1980-81), New Orleans (1982-84)

STARR Bart, Green Bay (1956-71)

STAUBACH Roger, Dallas (1969-79)

STENERUD Jan, Kansas City (1967-79), Green Bay (1980-83), Minnesota (1984-85)

STUDSTILL Pat, Detroit (1961-62 and 1964-67), L.A. Rams (1968-71), New England (1972)

SWEETAN Karl, Detroit (1966-67), New Orleans (1968), L.A. Rams (1969-70)

TARKENTON Fran, Minnesota (1961-66 and 1972-78), N.Y. Giants (1967-71)

TATUM Jack, Oakland (1971-79), Houston (1980)

TAYLOR Charley, Washington (1964-75 and 1977)

TAYLOR Jim, Green Bay (1958-66), New Orleans (1967)

TAYLOR Lionel, Chicago Bears (1959), Denver (1960-66), Houston (1967-68)

THEISMANN Joe, Washington (1974-85)

THOMPSON Billy, Denver (1969-81)

TITTLE Y.A., Baltimore (1948-50), San Francisco (1951-60), N.Y. Giants (1961-64)

TODD Richard, N.Y. Jets (1976-83), New Orleans (1984-85)

TURNER Cecil, Chicago (1968-73)

TURNER Jim, N.Y. Jets (1964-70), Denver (1971-79)

UNITAS Johnny, Baltimore (1956-72), San Diego (1973)

UPCHURCH Rick, Denver (1975-83)

VAN BROCKLIN Norm, L.A. Rams (1949-57), Philadelphia (1958-60)

van EEGHEN Mark, Oakland (1974-81), New England (1982-83)

von SCHAMANN Uwe, Miami (1979-84)

WALSTON Bobby, Philadelphia (1951-62)

WATERFIELD Bob, Cleveland/L.A. Rams (1945-52)

WEST Charlie, Minnesota (1968-73), Detroit (1974-77), Denver (1978-79)

WILLIAMS Travis, Green Bay (1967-70), L.A. Rams (1971)

YEPREMIAN Garo, Detroit (1966-67), Miami (1970-78), New Orleans (1979), Tampa Bay (1980-81)

CHAPTER FIVE

OUTSTANDING PLAYERS OF 1987

ERIC DICKERSON

Week Eight of the 1987 season saw the opening of another chapter in the life of the NFL's finest active running back. That Sunday saw Eric Dickerson's debut for the Indianapolis Colts, whom he joined in a trade after having spent four years with the Los Angeles Rams, in whose colours he was the NFL Leading Rusher three times. He hardly needed to unveil a new talent but he did anyway, and that was 'adaptability'. No two NFL teams have the same offensive system – plays, moves and timing. Even for veterans, it is felt that the preseason series is critical in the process of gearing up for the regular season. Like prize-fighters they can be ring-rusty. However, following just one cautious first game behind his unfamiliar offensive line, he played as if he'd been a Colt for all his career. San Diego was the first club to be given a bloody nose, when he rushed for 138 yards, though Dickerson will remember that game for his goal-line fumble when on the verge of scoring the touchdown which would have ensured a Colts victory. But all that was forgotten as, with almost indecent haste, he began clocking up 100-yards-rushing games. In the final game of the regular season, with the Colts needing a win to secure the division title, he pulled out all the stops, trampling over the Buccaneers for 196 yards. Though an AFC player for just nine games, he was the only man in that conference to rush for 1,000 yards (these do not include his NFC haul). Already the owner of the NFL single-season rushing record, he needs to rush for 1,000 yards in the 1988 season to equal Franco Harris and Walter Payton, each of whom registered six in a row.

Eric Dickerson.

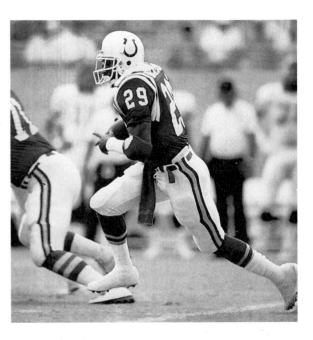

Game by Game – 1987		Rushing		
Opponent	Att	Yds	Lg	TD
at Houston†	27	149	57	0
Minnesota†	26	90	17	0
at New Orleans*				
Pittsburgh*				
at Atlanta*				
at Cleveland†	7	38	27t	1
at N.Y. Jets	10	38	14	0
San Diego	35	138	13	0
at Miami	30	154	13	1
at New England	27	117	16	0
Houston	27	136	29	2
at Cleveland	27	98	9	0
Buffalo	11	19	11	0
at San Diego	23	115	53	0
Tampa Bay	33	196	34t	2
Totals	**283**	**1,288**	**57**	**6**

†L.A. Rams
* Players' Strike – Did not play

HERSCHEL WALKER

One wonders just what Herschel Walker might achieve when the time comes that the Cowboys return to the standards of their illustrious traditions. Even now, he has to be regarded as the most potent dual-purpose backfield player in the NFL. That assertion is confirmed by the 1987 figures which show him to be on top of the entire NFL in combined rushing and receiving yardage with a total of 1,606. Walker's has not been a smooth entry into the league. With the great Tony Dorsett itching for the opportunity to show that he was still the best, the Cowboys had the makings of a running back controversy. And out of that, it often happens that neither player performs up to his best. Walker did not move into the starting tailback spot until Week Ten, but his 173 yards rushing in that game against the Patriots merely confirmed the projections made back in 1982, when, as a junior at Georgia, he won the Heisman Trophy. What no one can have predicted, though, is Walker's effectiveness as a pass receiver. The power, dazzling footwork and world-class speed were all well known, but to these he adds the combination of a sense of timing and super-safe hands. In all probability, the time he lost playing in the USFL probably means that the major NFL career records will remain out of his reach, but Eric Dickerson's single-season rushing record of 2,105 yards is well within his capabilities.

Herschel Walker.

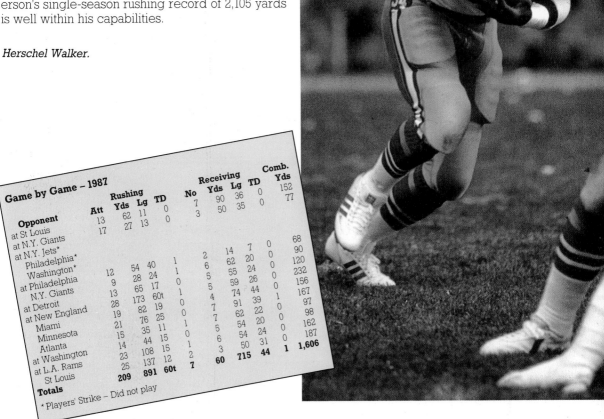

| Game by Game – 1987 | Rushing | | | | Receiving | | | | Comb. |
Opponent	Att	Yds	Lg	TD	No	Yds	Lg	TD	Yds
at St Louis	13	62	11	0	7	90	36	0	152
at N.Y. Giants	17	27	13	0	3	50	35	0	77
at N.Y. Jets*									
Philadelphia*									
Washington*									
at Philadelphia	12	54	40	1	2	14	7	0	68
N.Y. Giants	9	28	24	1	6	62	20	0	90
at Detroit	13	65	17	0	5	55	24	0	120
at New England	28	173	60t	1	5	59	26	0	232
Miami	19	82	19	0	4	74	44	1	156
Minnesota	21	76	25	0	7	91	39	1	167
Atlanta	15	35	11	1	7	62	22	0	97
at Washington	14	44	15	0	5	54	20	0	98
at L.A. Rams	23	108	15	1	6	54	24	0	162
St Louis	25	137	12	2	3	50	31	0	187
Totals	**209**	**891**	**60t**	**7**	**60**	**715**	**44**	**1**	**1,606**

* Players' Strike – Did not play

Game by Game – 1987

Opponent	Att	Rushing Yds	Lg	TD
at Houston	2	−9	−4	0
Minnesota	0	0	0	0
at New Orleans	9	18	4	0
Pittsburgh	33	166	58	1
at Atlanta	31	155	17	0
at Cleveland	13	54	19	1
San Francisco	21	52	11	0
New Orleans	12	213	47t	1
at St Louis	34	112	10	2
at Washington	35	137	23	2
Tampa Bay	29	102	.14	2
at Detroit	29	159	21t	1
Atlanta	26	66	8t	0
Dallas	21	95	18	1
at San Francisco				11
Totals	**324**	**1,374**	**58**	

CHARLES WHITE

It is not only in the children's yarns that everything turns out right, and to the reading list we can now add the unfinished story of Charles White, NFL running back. White's has been that of a nightmare existence, during which he struggled with the horrors of illegal substance abuse. After an outstanding career at the University of Southern California, where, as a senior, he won the Heisman Trophy, he laboured through four seasons with Cleveland (he spent one year on injured reserve) before being discarded. But his former USC mentor, now Rams head coach John Robinson, was still convinced of his ability, and in 1985 he signed White as a free agent. In the first two games of that season, when both Eric Dickerson and Barry Redden were unavailable, White rushed for 83 and 144 yards respectively. He had taken a start along the road back and, following the return of Dickerson, he kept his place on the roster with his exceptional run-blocking and steady kickoff returning. However, late in the 1987 preseason, his problems returned. The patient Robinson decided to extend just one more chance. And after grabbing it, White held on with both hands. The departure of Dickerson for Indianapolis gave White the opportunity to show his undoubted talent, and he used it to the full, rushing for 1,374 yards to lead the NFL and scoring eleven touchdowns. Defenses will be waiting for him in 1988, but it is a challenge that White will now meet head-on.

JERRY RICE

After just three seasons as a pro, Jerry Rice has established himself as the NFL's premier wide receiver. Even before the 1987 campaign began, already he had assembled a first-class curriculum vitae. Coming out of college, he was not noted for his speed, but he quickly silenced the doubters by his performance against the Raiders, when he gave the great Mike Haynes the slip once or twice, and then did the same to Lester Hayes. In his rookie year, he caught 49 passes at an excellent average of 18.9 yards, the best figure amongst the NFC's top twenty receivers. In 1986 he was the NFC leading receiver, with 86 pass receptions, and led the NFL in both the categories of yards (1,570) and touchdowns (15). Last year, he gave a performance unparalleled in NFL annals. Some players just break records – at the limit of their powers they edge into the unknown. Rice took hold of the NFL single-season record for touchdown receptions – Mark Clayton's 18 of the 1984 season – and smashed it to smithereens. Were it not enough that he broke one of the better records, he equalled it in ten games and went two in front in the eleventh game (Clayton's record came in fifteen games). In the twelfth, he lifted it to a new plateau of 22. We have to go back to 1951 for the last time a receiver captured the title of NFL leading scorer, and that was Hall of Famer Elroy (Crazylegs) Hirsch of the Rams. And by catching at least one touchdown pass in thirteen consecutive games (the sequence goes back to the final game of the 1986 season), Rice has a new on-going record, having beaten the previous best (11) shared by Hirsch and Pittsburgh's Buddy Dial.

Game by Game – 1987				
		Receiving		
Opponent	No	Yds	Lg	TD
at Pittsburgh	8	106	32	1
at Cincinnati	4	86	34t	2
at N.Y. Giants*				
at Atlanta*				
St Louis*				
at New Orleans	6	89	39	1
at L.A. Rams	3	70	51t	1
Houston	7	77	21	1
New Orleans	4	108	50t	2
at Tampa Bay	7	103	42t	3
Cleveland	7	126	30t	3
at Green Bay	4	90	57t	1
Chicago	8	75	17	3
Atlanta	4	58	20	2
L.A. Rams	3	90	50t	2
Totals	**65**	**1,078**	**57t**	**22**
* Players' Strike – Did not play				

Opposite: Charles White.

Left: Jerry Rice.

JOE MONTANA

It seems that Joe Montana is destined to end each NFL season, either being dumped unceremoniously on his backside in the playoffs, or receiving the MVP award in the Super Bowl. The latter was the case in Super Bowls XVI and XIX, but his experience of the 49ers' recent playoff exits has been sad. The latest came against a hot Minnesota Vikings club when the 49ers had been strongly fancied to win. But the wonder is that Montana still is in the pro game at all. After injuring his back in the opening game of the 1986 season, an examination revealed a condition of congenital spinal stenosis, associated with acute rupture of a disc. Yet after major surgery to widen his spinal canal and remove the disc, he was back in action on November 9th, when he completed 13 of 19 passes for three touchdowns in the 49ers victory over St Louis. Looking back over the glittering career of this quiet man, whose fabled trigger-finger lost none of its action in the move from Notre Dame to San Francisco, it is equally remarkable that it was only in 1987 that he won the first NFL passing title of his nine-year career. Along the way, he set a new NFL record for consecutive pass completions (22). With his understudy, Steve Young, breathing down his neck, Montana registered a passer rating

of 102.1 to finish almost seven points ahead of the next best, Cleveland's Bernie Kosar. Even after Montana's excellent campaign, though, there still is speculation that Young may be set to pick up his crown. Picking it up is one thing – wearing it is another.

Game by Game – 1987

Opponent	Att	Comp	Passing Yds	Lg	Int	TD
at Pittsburgh	49	34	316	32	3	2
at Cincinnati	37	21	250	38t	0	3
at N.Y. Giants*						
at Atlanta	8	5	63	21	0	1
St Louis	39	31	334	35t	2	4
at New Orleans	32	18	256	39t	0	3
at L.A. Rams	30	21	294	51t	1	3
Houston	46	32	289	23	2	3
New Orleans	29	16	144	29t	2	1
at Tampa Bay	45	29	304	42t	1	3
Cleveland	31	23	342	40t	1	4
at Green Bay	35	26	308	57t	1	2
Chicago	8	4	47	18	0	0
Atlanta	Injured – Did not play					
L.A. Rams	9	6	107	46t	0	2
Totals	**398**	**266**	**3,054**	**57t**	**13**	**31**

* Players' Strike – Did not play

Joe Montana.

BERNIE KOSAR

When he came into the NFL, they said he was perhaps too smart, too sophisticated, and maybe even too aloof. There were questions over his mobility. And the manner of his entry hadn't helped his cause. With eligibility for both the pros and another year in college at his personal disposal, he opted out of the formal draft in order that the Browns could engineer his selection in a later supplemental draft. As a rookie, he was thrown in at the deep end, and he was unable to protect a 21-3 lead in the AFC divisional playoff game against Miami. In 1986, he made excellent progress, starting in all sixteen games and directing Cleveland to the most regular-season victories (12) in its history. In the AFC Championship Game of that season, the Browns were beaten by the individual brilliance of Denver quarterback John Elway. 1987 saw an AFC Championship Game rematch, in Denver, and in a second-half display of consummate authority, Kosar brought the Browns back into a 31-31 tie after they had appeared dead and buried. They lost that game but the vision of that cold-eyed assassin, Kosar, remains. Looking back to the regular season, he won the AFC passing title by a comfortable margin (6.2 points) over Miami's Dan Marino, and whilst it is a little early to make comparisons with the great Otto Graham, who quarterbacked the Browns to championship games in every one of their first ten years in pro football (their first four years were in the AAFC), you do begin to think about it. Let's leave the final words to Graham, who said, 'I believe Kosar is going to be one of the best before he's through. He throws with such accuracy. I liked to throw long and I know he can do that. He's got the size and he moves better than I expected.'

Bernie Kosar.

Game by Game – 1987 Opponent	Att	Comp	Passing Yds	Lg	Int	TD
at New Orleans	39	28	314	30t	1	2
Pittsburgh	29	17	174	37t	1	2
at New England*						
Houston*						
at Cincinnati*						
L.A. Rams	30	19	223	53t	1	2
at San Diego	42	24	298	41t	2	2
Atlanta	23	13	192	54t	0	2
Buffalo	34	24	346	52t	1	1
at Houston	26	15	257	39t	0	1
at San Francisco	37	26	275	37	1	4
Indianapolis	35	16	178	23	0	2
Cincinnati	26	17	241	43	1	1
at L.A. Raiders	32	21	294	36	1	1
at Pittsburgh	36	21	241	26		2
Totals	**389**	**241**	**3,033**	**54t**	**9**	**22**

* Players' Strike – Did not play

J. T. SMITH

John Thomas Smith. 'Who is he? Where did he come from and why has it taken so long?' you might ask. He goes way back, in fact all the way to 1978, when he was signed as a free agent by Washington. After six games with the Redskins, he was signed as a free agent by Kansas City, and that's where the real story begins. In the high-sounding terms of big business, his career profile was excellent as, in his first three years as a wide receiver, he caught 33, 46 and 63 passes for 444, 655 and 852 yards respectively. There, one might think, was a young man going places, especially when also he made the trip to the 1981 AFC-NFC Pro Bowl as the kick returner after returning 40 punts at an average of 14.5 yards and scoring touchdowns covering 75 and 53 yards. Beginning in 1982, however, a series of injuries and the emergence of good young prospects saw his role as a receiver for the Chiefs diminish to that of fifth-stringer. Released by Kansas City before the 1985 season, he was at a loose end. But the Cardinals were in a spot of bother. Signed yet again as a free agent, he was ready to step in when, with starting wide receivers Pat Tilley and Roy Green injured, and the punt returning duties open, the opportunities became available. In 1986, he set the Cardinals'

single-season record for receptions (80), gaining 1,014 yards in the process. In 1987 he caught a new personal-best total of 91 passes to become the NFL leading receiver in both receptions and yards. Professional sport throws up its unlikely heroes, but Smith is not one of those. He was a very likely hero who, somehow, missed his way. Welcome to where you've always belonged, J. T.

Game by Game – 1987		Receiving		
Opponent	No	Yds	Lg	TD
Dallas	5	78	18	0
at San Diego	6	92	23	0
at Washington	6	116	38	0
New Orleans	2	5	6	0
at San Francisco	7	96	26	0
at N.Y. Giants	3	49	20	0
Philadelphia	10	112	15	1
Tampa Bay	8	96	17t	2
L.A. Rams	2	29	19	0
at Philadelphia	5	74	32t	2
at Atlanta	10	109	22	0
Washington	7	65	16	1
N.Y. Giants	4	40	26	0
at Tampa Bay	5	54	15	1
at Dallas	11	102	22	1
Totals	**91**	**1,117**	**38**	**8**

Opposite: J. T. Smith.

Right: Randall Cunningham.

RANDALL CUNNINGHAM

Every now and then, we're reminded of the game's history – the time when a backfield play-maker would either pass or run, according to circumstances. When the good ones ran, they created problems. When the good ones passed well, they'd murder the opposition. Sammy Baugh was that kind of backfield player. Denver's John Elway is another. Inbetween times, there have been a few, and Randall Cunningham is the latest to emerge.

'Elway's got a cannon. I mean a Goose Gossage fastball. The only one I can think of with that kind of arm is that kid in Philadelphia, Randall Cunningham. He's not refined the way Elway is, but he's got a cannon, too. He's got some amazing talent,' said Giants strong safety Kenny Hill.

'Randall Cunningham is just unbelievable. He must shower in vaseline. There's only one Cunningham in the entire NFL and he really gives the Eagles' offense life.' Those words were spoken by the Raiders' former all-pro cornerback, Lester Hayes.

Cunningham has resurrected the dimension of rushing as a viable option to the pass from the quarterback position, and his contribution has been a major factor – perhaps the major factor – as the Eagles have taken on the character of a team that might lose to the weakest one week but could slam the best the following week. Last year, in addition to having his best campaign as a passer, Cunningham also led the Eagles in rushing. It is a potent cocktail which he takes into 1988, and one which may inspire the Eagles to the status of contender.

Game by Game – 1987

Opponent	Passing Att	Comp	Yds	Lg	Int	TD	Rushing Att	Yds	Lg	TD
at Washington	36	21	269	32	2	1	7	39	13	1
New Orleans	34	19	195	25t	1	2	8	32	15	0
Chicago*										
at Dallas*										
at Green Bay*										
Dallas	24	10	127	33	0	2	8	39	14	0
at St Louis	32	17	291	70t	1	3	5	20	9	0
Washington	31	18	268	53	3	3	7	80	45	0
N.Y. Giants	34	17	177	41	1	1	10	71	20	1
St Louis	51	26	272	35	2	2	4	43	22	
at New England	31	18	314	61t	1	2	7	31	24	
at N.Y. Giants	43	20	227	40t	0	2	3	20	14	
Miami	38	22	189	44t	0	1	2	37	31	
at N.Y. Jets	31	19	280	47	0	3	5	47	21	
Buffalo	21	16	177	30	1	1	10	46	23	
Totals	**406**	**223**	**2,786**	**70t**	**12**	**23**	**76**	**505**	**45**	

* Players' Strike – Did not play

☆☆☆☆☆☆☆☆☆ **CHAPTER SIX** ☆☆☆☆☆☆☆☆☆

AMERICAN FOOTBALL CONFERENCE

TEAM RANKINGS

| | OFFENSE | | | | | | DEFENSE | | | | | |
	Total Yds.	Rushing	Passing	Points For	No. Intercepted	No. Sacked	Total Yds.	Rushing	Passing	Points Against	Interceptions	Sacks
Buffalo	8	8	9	13	7 =	10	7	10	6	7	8 =	8 =
Cincinnati	3	2	6	10 =	9 =	7	4	4	8	13	11	4
Cleveland	6	11	3	1	1	4	1	1	5	2	3 =	8 =
Denver	1	6	2	2	7 =	5 =	5	9	4	3	1	10
Houston	5	7	4	5	12 =	5 =	10	8	10	11	3 =	7
Indianapolis	7	4	10	9	3	2	3	6	2	1	6	5
Kansas City	13	9	13	12	4	12	14	14	13	14	14	12 =
L.A. Raiders	4	1	7	8	5 =	13	2	3	1	4	12 =	2
Miami	2	13	1	4	9 =	1	13	12	12	10	10	14
New England	12	10	12	7	5 =	8	6	5	9	5	5	3
N.Y. Jets	10	12	8	6	2	14	11	7	11	12	7	11
Pittsburgh	14	3	14	10 =	14	3	8	2	14	6	2	12 =
San Diego	11	14	5	14	12 =	11	9	11	3	9	12 =	1
Seattle	9	5	11	3	11	9	12	13	7	8	8 =	6

AFC PASSERS

	Att	Comp	% Comp	Yards	Ave Gain	TD	% TD	Long	Int	% Int	Rating Points
Kosar, Bernie, *Clev.*	389	241	62.0	3033	7.80	22	5.7	t54	9	2.3	95.4
Marino, Dan, *Mia.*	444	263	59.2	3245	7.31	26	5.9	t59	13	2.9	89.2
Krieg, Dave, *Sea.*	294	178	60.5	2131	7.25	23	7.8	t75	15	5.1	87.6
Kenney, Bill, *K.C.*	273	154	56.4	2107	7.72	15	5.5	t81	9	3.3	85.8
Hogeboom, Gary, *Ind.*	168	99	58.9	1145	6.82	9	5.4	t72	5	3.0	85.0
Wilson, Marc, *Raiders*	266	152	57.1	2070	7.78	12	4.5	t47	8	3.0	84.6
Kelly, Jim, *Buff.*	419	250	59.7	2798	6.68	19	4.5	47	11	2.6	83.8
Elway, John, *Den.*	410	224	54.6	3198	7.80	19	4.6	t72	12	2.9	83.4
O'Brien, Ken, *Jets*	393	234	59.5	2696	6.86	13	3.3	59	8	2.0	82.8
Grogan, Steve, *N.E.*	161	93	57.8	1183	7.35	10	6.2	40	9	5.6	78.2
Trudeau, Jack, *Ind.*	229	128	55.9	1587	6.93	6	2.6	55	6	2.6	75.4
Moon, Warren, *Hou.*	368	184	50.0	2806	7.63	21	5.7	t83	18	4.9	74.2
Esiason, Boomer, *Cin.*	440	240	54.5	3321	7.55	16	3.6	t61	19	4.3	73.1
Ramsey, Tom, *N.E.*	134	71	53.0	898	6.70	6	4.5	40	6	4.5	70.4
Fouts, Dan, *S.D.*	364	206	56.6	2517	6.91	10	2.7	46	15	4.1	70.0
Malone, Mark, *Pitt.*	336	156	46.4	1896	5.64	6	1.8	63	19	5.7	46.7

Non-qualifiers

	Att	Comp	% Comp	Yards	Ave Gain	TD	% TD	Long	Int	% Int	Rating Points
Danielson, Gary, *Clev.*	33	25	75.8	281	8.52	4	12.1	23	0	0.0	140.3
Kemp, Jeff, *Sea.*	33	23	69.7	396	12.00	5	15.2	55	1	3.0	137.1
Kelley, Mike, *S.D.*	29	17	58.6	305	10.52	1	3.4	67	0	0.0	106.3
Flutie, Doug, *N.E.*	25	15	60.0	199	7.96	1	4.0	30	0	0.0	98.6
Ryan, Pat, *Jets*	53	32	60.4	314	5.92	4	7.5	t35	2	3.8	86.5
Neuheisel, Rick, *S.D.*	59	40	67.8	367	6.22	1	1.7	32	1	1.7	83.1
Bono, Steve, *Pitt.*	74	34	45.9	438	5.92	5	6.8	57	2	2.7	76.3
Karcher, Ken, *Den.*	102	56	54.9	628	6.16	5	4.9	49	4	3.9	73.5
Evans, Vince, *Raiders*	83	39	47.0	630	7.59	5	6.0	47	4	4.8	72.9
Eason, Tony, *N.E.*	79	42	53.2	453	5.73	3	3.8	45	2	2.5	72.4

t = Touchdown

Leader based on rating points, minimum 125 attempts

AFC RECEIVERS – Most Receptions

	No	Yards	Ave	Long	TD
Toon, Al, *Jets*	68	976	14.4	t58	5
Largent, Steve, *Sea.*	58	912	15.7	55	8
Reed, Andre, *Buff.*	57	752	13.2	40	5
Burkett, Chris, *Buff.*	56	765	13.7	47	4
Harmon, Ronnie, *Buff.*	56	477	8.5	42	2
Carson, Carlos, *K.C.*	55	1044	19.0	t81	7
Givins, Ernest, *Hou.*	53	933	17.6	t83	6
Winslow, Kellen, *S.D.*	53	519	9.8	30	3
Byner, Earnest, *Clev.*	52	552	10.6	37	2
Brooks, Bill, *Ind.*	51	722	14.2	t52	3
Allen, Marcus, *Raiders*	51	410	8.0	39	0
Hill, Drew, *Hou.*	49	989	20.2	t52	6
Stradford, Troy, *Mia.*	48	457	9.5	34	1
Slaughter, Webster, *Clev.*	47	806	17.1	t54	7
Christensen, Todd, *Raiders*	47	663	14.1	33	2
Anderson, Gary, *S.D.*	47	503	10.7	38	2
Clayton, Mark, *Mia.*	46	776	16.9	43	7
Brown, Eddie, *Cin.*	44	608	13.8	t47	3
Collins, Tony, *N.E.*	44	347	7.9	29	3
Paige, Stephone, *K.C.*	43	707	16.4	51	4
Brennan, Brian, *Clev.*	43	607	14.1	t53	6
Shuler, Mickey, *Jets*	43	434	10.1	t32	3
Johnson, Vance, *Den.*	42	684	16.3	t59	7
Bouza, Matt, *Ind.*	42	569	13.5	t44	4
Lofton, James, *Raiders*	41	880	21.5	49	5
James, Lionel, *S.D.*	41	593	14.5	46	3
Stallworth, John, *Pitt.*	41	521	12.7	45	2
Morgan, Stanley, *N.E.*	40	672	16.8	45	3
Chandler, Wes, *S.D.*	39	617	15.8	27	2
Williams, John L., *Sea.*	38	420	11.1	t75	3
Jennings, Stanford, *Cin.*	35	277	7.9	24	2
Bentley, Albert, *Ind.*	34	447	13.1	t72	2
Newsome, Ozzie, *Clev.*	34	375	11.0	25	0
Duper, Mark, *Mia.*	33	597	18.1	t59	8

t = Touchdown

AFC RECEIVERS – Most Yards

	Yards	No	Ave	Long	TD
Carson, Carlos, *K.C.*	1044	55	19.0	t81	7
Hill, Drew, *Hou.*	989	49	20.2	t52	6
Toon, Al, *Jets*	976	68	14.4	t58	5
Givins, Ernest, *Hou.*	933	53	17.6	t83	6
Largent, Steve, *Sea.*	912	58	15.7	55	8
Lofton, James, *Raiders*	880	41	21.5	49	5
Slaughter, Webster, *Clev.*	806	47	17.1	t54	7
Clayton, Mark, *Mia.*	776	46	16.9	43	7
Burkett, Chris, *Buff.*	765	56	13.7	47	4
Reed, Andre, *Buff.*	752	57	13.2	40	5
Brooks, Bill, *Ind.*	722	51	14.2	t52	3
Paige, Stephone, *K.C.*	707	43	16.4	51	4
Johnson, Vance, *Den.*	684	42	16.3	t59	7
Morgan, Stanley, *N.E.*	672	40	16.8	45	3
Christensen, Todd, *Raiders*	663	47	14.1	33	2
Nattiel, Ricky, *Den.*	630	31	20.3	54	2
Chandler, Wes, *S.D.*	617	39	15.8	27	2
Brown, Eddie, *Cin.*	608	44	13.8	t47	3
Brennan, Brian, *Clev.*	607	43	14.1	t53	6
Duper, Mark, *Mia.*	597	33	18.1	t59	8
James, Lionel, *S.D.*	593	41	14.5	46	3
Bouza, Matt, *Ind.*	569	42	13.5	t44	4
Byner, Earnest, *Clev.*	552	52	10.6	37	2
Stallworth, John, *Pitt.*	521	41	12.7	45	2
Winslow, Kellen, *S.D.*	519	53	9.8	30	3
Anderson, Gary, *S.D.*	503	47	10.7	38	2
Collinsworth, Cris, *Cin.*	494	31	15.9	53	0
Harmon, Ronnie, *Buff.*	477	56	8.5	42	2
Fryar, Irving, *N.E.*	467	31	15.1	40	5
Butler, Raymond, *Sea.*	465	33	14.1	t40	5
Stradford, Troy, *Mia.*	457	48	9.5	34	1
Bentley, Albert, *Ind.*	447	34	13.1	t72	2
Kay, Clarence, *Den.*	440	31	14.2	30	0
Holman, Rodney, *Cin.*	438	28	15.6	t61	2

t = Touchdown

Carlos Carson was the only AFC player to catch passes for over 1,000 yards.

AFC RUSHERS

	Att	Yards	Ave	Long	TD
Dickerson, Eric, *Rams-Ind.*	283	1288	4.6	57	6
Warner, Curt, *Sea.*	234	985	4.2	t57	8
Rozier, Mike, *Hou.*	229	957	4.2	41	3
Allen, Marcus, *Raiders*	200	754	3.8	44	5
Winder, Sammy, *Den.*	196	741	3.8	19	6
Mack, Kevin, *Clev.*	201	735	3.7	t22	5
Jackson, Earnest, *Pitt.*	180	696	3.9	39	1
Okoye, Christian, *K.C.*	157	660	4.2	t43	3
Bentley, Albert, *Ind.*	142	631	4.4	t17	7
Stradford, Troy, *Mia.*	145	619	4.3	51	6
Kinnebrew, Larry, *Cin.*	145	570	3.9	52	8
Jackson, Bo, *Raiders*	81	554	6.8	t91	4
Pollard, Frank, *Pitt.*	128	536	4.2	33	3
McNeil, Freeman, *Jets*	121	530	4.4	30	0
Williams, John L., *Sea.*	113	500	4.4	48	1
Harmon, Ronnie, *Buff.*	116	485	4.2	21	2
Collins, Tony, *N.E.*	147	474	3.2	19	3
Heard, Herman, *K.C.*	82	466	5.7	t64	3
Abercrombie, Walter, *Pitt.*	123	459	3.7	t28	2
Hector, Johnny, *Jets*	111	435	3.9	t20	11
Byner, Earnest, *Clev.*	105	432	4.1	21	8
Mueller, Jamie, *Buff.*	82	354	4.3	20	2
Adams, Curtis, *S.D.*	90	343	3.8	24	1
Dupard, Reggie, *N.E.*	94	318	3.4	49	3
Jennings, Stanford, *Cin.*	70	314	4.5	18	1
Elway, John, *Den.*	66	304	4.6	29	4
Lang, Gene, *Den.*	89	303	3.4	28	2
Brooks, James, *Cin.*	94	290	3.1	18	1
Hampton, Lorenzo, *Mia.*	75	289	3.9	34	1
Byrum, Carl, *Buff.*	66	280	4.2	30	0
Anderson, Gary, *S.D.*	80	260	3.3	25	3
Vick, Roger, *Jets*	77	257	3.3	14	1
Tatupu, Mosi, *N.E.*	79	248	3.1	19	0
Banks, Chuck, *Ind.*	50	245	4.9	35	0
Esiason, Boomer, *Cin.*	52	241	4.6	19	0
Jackson, Andrew, *Hou.*	60	232	3.9	t16	1
Spencer, Tim, *S.D.*	73	228	3.1	16	0
Riddick, Robb, *Buff.*	59	221	3.7	25	5
Mason, Larry, *Clev.*	56	207	3.7	22	2
Johnson, Bill, *Cin.*	39	205	5.3	20	1
Logan, Marc, *Cin.*	37	203	5.5	51	1
Scott, Ronald, *Mia.*	47	199	4.2	24	3
Perryman, Bob, *N.E.*	41	187	4.6	48	0
Porter, Ricky, *Buff.*	47	177	3.8	13	0
Mueller, Vance, *Raiders*	37	175	4.7	35	1
LeBlanc, Michael, *N.E.*	49	170	3.5	42	1
Malone, Mark, *Pitt.*	34	162	4.8	t42	3
Krieg, Dave, *Sea.*	36	155	4.3	17	2
Palmer, Paul, *K.C.*	24	155	6.5	35	0
Dudek, Joe, *Den.*	35	154	4.4	16	2
Parker, Robert, *K.C.*	47	150	3.2	10	1
Pinkett, Allen, *Hou.*	31	149	4.8	22	2
Evans, Vince, *Raiders*	11	144	13.1	24	1
Hunter, Herman, *Hou.*	34	144	4.2	21	0

t = Touchdown

AFC SCORING – Kickers

	XP	XPA	FG	FGA	PTS
Breech, Jim, *Cin.*	25	27	24	30	97
Biasucci, Dean, *Ind.*	24	24	24	27	96
Zendejas, Tony, *Hou.*	32	33	20	26	92
Karlis, Rich, *Den.*	37	37	18	25	91
Anderson, Gary, *Pitt.*	21	21	22	27	87
Johnson, Norm, *Sea.*	40	40	15	20	85
Leahy, Pat, *Jets*	31	31	18	22	85
Bahr, Chris, *Raiders*	27	28	19	29	84
Lowery, Nick, *K.C.*	26	26	19	23	83
Franklin, Tony, *N.E.*	37	38	15	26	82
Jaeger, Jeff, *Clev.*	33	33	14	22	75
Abbott, Vince, *S.D.*	22	23	13	22	61
Norwood, Scott, *Buff.*	31	31	10	15	61

AFC SCORING – Touchdowns

	TD	TDR	TDP	TDM	PTS
Hector, Johnny, *Jets*	11	11	0	0	66
Byner, Earnest, *Clev.*	10	8	2	0	60
Warner, Curt, *Sea.*	10	8	2	0	60
Bentley, Albert, *Ind.*	9	7	2	0	54
Riddick, Robb, *Buff.*	8	5	3	0	*50
Duper, Mark, *Mia.*	8	0	8	0	48
Kinnebrew, Larry, *Cin.*	8	8	0	0	48
Largent, Steve, *Sea.*	8	0	8	0	48
Carson, Carlos, *K.C.*	7	0	7	0	42
Clayton, Mark, *Mia.*	7	0	7	0	42
Johnson, Vance, *Den.*	7	0	7	0	42
Slaughter, Webster, *Clev.*	7	0	7	0	42
Stradford, Troy, *Mia.*	7	6	1	0	42
Winder, Sammy, *Den.*	7	6	1	0	42

* Includes two points for a safety

AFC KICKOFF RETURNERS

	No	Yards	Ave	Long	TD
Palmer, Paul, *K.C.*	38	923	24.3	t95	2
Young, Glen, *Clev.*	18	412	22.9	44	0
Bentley, Albert, *Ind.*	22	500	22.7	45	0
Mueller, Vance, *Raiders*	27	588	21.8	46	0
Holland, Jamie, *S.D.*	19	410	21.6	46	0
Bell, Ken, *Den.*	15	323	21.5	42	0
Edmonds, Bobby Joe, *Sea.*	27	564	20.9	43	0
Stone, Dwight, *Pitt.*	28	568	20.3	34	0
Humphery, Bobby, *Jets*	18	357	19.8	47	0
Anderson, Gary, *S.D.*	22	433	19.7	31	0
Duncan, Curtis, *Hou.*	28	546	19.5	62	0
Starring, Stephen, *N.E.*	23	445	19.3	43	0
Bussey, Barney, *Cin.*	21	406	19.3	34	0
Hampton, Lorenzo, *Mia.*	16	304	19.0	32	0
Pinkett, Allen, *Hou.*	17	322	18.9	30	0
Stradford, Troy, *Mia.*	14	258	18.4	32	0
McGee, Tim, *Cin.*	15	242	16.1	24	0
Williams, Dokie, *Raiders*	14	221	15.8	27	0

t = Touchdown
Leader based on average return, minimum 14 returns

Above: Mike Rozier – a top-class running back.

Right: Bo Jackson averaged 6.8 yards per carry.

AFC PUNTERS

	No	Yards	Long	Ave	Total Punts	TB	Blk	Opp Ret	Ret Yds	In 20	Net Ave
Mojsiejenko, Ralf, *S.D.*	67	2875	57	42.9	67	12	0	37	392	15	33.5
Newsome, Harry, *Pitt.*	64	2678	57	41.8	65	13	1	36	373	8	31.5
Fulhage, Scott, *Cin.*	52	2168	58	41.7	52	5	0	31	216	10	35.6
Horan, Mike, *Den.*	44	1807	61	41.1	46	5	2	22	186	11	33.1
Goodburn, Kelly, *K.C.*	59	2412	55	40.9	59	5	0	39	403	13	32.4
Talley, Stan, *Raiders*	56	2277	63	40.7	57	5	1	28	207	13	34.6
Gossett, Jeff, *Clev.-Hou.*	44	1777	55	40.4	45	6	1	23	234	4	31.6
Camarillo, Rich, *N.E.*	62	2489	73	40.1	63	8	1	34	333	14	31.7
Rodriguez, Ruben, *Sea.*	47	1880	63	40.0	47	5	0	22	182	17	34.0
Stark, Rohn, *Ind.*	61	2440	63	40.0	63	7	2	33	353	12	30.9
Johnson, Lee, *Hou.-Clev.*	50	1969	66	39.4	50	4	0	25	249	8	32.8
Kidd, John, *Buff.*	64	2495	67	39.0	64	7	0	26	148	20	34.5
Jennings, Dave, *Jets*	64	2444	58	38.2	64	6	0	24	100	12	34.8

Leader based on gross average, minimum 38 punts

AFC SACKERS

	No
Tippett, Andre, *N.E.*	12.5
Smith, Bruce, *Buff.*	12.0
Green, Jacob, *Sea.*	9.5
Young, Fredd, *Sea.*	9.0
Bennett, Cornelius, *Buff.*	8.5
Townsend, Greg, *Raiders*	8.5
Bickett, Duane, *Ind.*	8.0
Hairston, Carl, *Clev.*	8.0
Williams, Lee, *S.D.*	8.0
Jones, Rulon, *Den.*	7.0
Mecklenburg, Karl, *Den.*	7.0
Veris, Garin, *N.E.*	7.0
Bell, Mike, *K.C.*	6.5
Childress, Ray, *Hou.*	6.0
Jones, Sean, *Raiders*	6.0
Maas, Bill, *K.C.*	6.0
Williams, Reggie, *Cin.*	6.0
Merriweather, Mike, *Pitt.*	5.5
Puzzuoli, Dave, *Clev.*	5.5
Still, Art, *K.C.*	5.5
Thompson, Donnell, *Ind.*	5.5
Cooks, Johnie, *Ind.*	5.0
Gordon, Alex, *Jets*	5.0
Phillips, Joe, *S.D.*	5.0
Williams, Brent, *N.E.*	5.0
Gastineau, Mark, *Jets*	4.5
King, Linden, *Raiders*	4.5
Robinson, Jerry, *Raiders*	4.5
Skow, Jim, *Cin.*	4.5
Williams, Toby, *N.E.*	4.5
Bosworth, Brian, *Sea.*	4.0
Bryant, Jeff, *Sea.*	4.0
Edwards, Eddie, *Cin.*	4.0
Fletcher, Simon, *Den.*	4.0
Gary, Keith, *Pitt.*	4.0
King, Emanuel, *Cin.*	4.0
Long, Howie, *Raiders*	4.0
Martin, Charles, *G.B.-Hou.*	4.0
Meads, Johnny, *Hou.*	4.0
Turner, T.J., *Mia.*	4.0
Winter, Blaise, *S.D.*	4.0
Baker, Al, *Clev.*	3.5
Ehin, Chuck, *S.D.*	3.5
Krumrie, Tim, *Cin.*	3.5
Lyons, Marty, *Jets*	3.5
Martin, Rod, *Raiders*	3.5
Nash, Joe, *Sea.*	3.5
Seals, Leon, *Buff.*	3.5
Smith, Doug, *Hou.*	3.5
Sochia, Brian, *Mia.*	3.5

Andre Tippett led the AFC in sacks.

Vencie Glenn returning his pass interception for an NFL-record 103 yards.

AFC PUNT RETURNERS

	No	FC	Yards	Ave	Long	TD
Clark, Kevin, *Den.*	18	1	233	12.9	t71	1
Edmonds, Bobby Joe, *Sea.*	20	4	251	12.6	40	0
James, Lionel, *S.D.*	32	7	400	12.5	t81	1
Townsell, JoJo, *Jets*	32	11	381	11.9	t91	1
McNeil, Gerald, *Clev.*	34	9	386	11.4	40	0
Martin, Mike, *Cin.*	28	5	277	9.9	21	0
Fryar, Irving, *N.E.*	18	12	174	9.7	36	0
Clemons, Michael, *K.C.*	19	4	162	8.5	44	0
Schwedes, Scott, *Mia.*	24	6	203	8.5	31	0
Woodson, Rod, *Pitt.*	16	1	135	8.4	20	0
Johnson, Kenny, *Hou.*	24	5	196	8.2	26	0
Woods, Chris, *Raiders*	26	4	189	7.3	34	0
Pitts, Ron, *Buff.*	23	12	149	6.5	19	0
Brooks, Bill, *Ind.*	22	9	136	6.2	17	0

t = Touchdown
Leader based on average return, minimum 15 returns

AFC INTERCEPTORS

	No	Yards	Ave	Long	TD
Prior, Mike, *Ind.*	6	57	9.5	38	0
Kelso, Mark, *Buff.*	6	25	4.2	12	0
Bostic, Keith, *Hou.*	6	−14	−2.3	7	0
Woodruff, Dwayne, *Pitt.*	5	91	18.2	t33	1
Smith, Billy Ray, *S.D.*	5	28	5.6	12	0
Glenn, Vencie, *S.D.*	4	166	41.5	t103	1
Wright, Felix, *Clev.*	4	152	38.0	68	1
Harden, Mike, *Den.*	4	85	21.3	32	0
Bryant, Domingo, *Hou.*	4	75	18.8	29	0
Marion, Fred, *N.E.*	4	53	13.3	25	0
Easley, Ken, *Sea.*	4	47	11.8	22	0
McElroy, Vann, *Raiders*	4	41	10.3	t35	1
Minnifield, Frank, *Clev.*	4	24	6.0	27	0
Donaldson, Jeff, *Hou.*	4	16	4.0	9	0
Clark, Kevin, *Den.*	3	105	35.0	50	0
Lippett, Ronnie, *N.E.*	3	103	34.3	t45	2
Robinson, Eugene, *Sea.*	3	75	25.0	44	0
Matthews, Clay, *Clev.*	3	62	20.7	36	1
Cherry, Deron, *K.C.*	3	58	19.3	30	0
Jackson, Robert, *Cin.*	3	49	16.3	29	0
Toran, Stacey, *Raiders*	3	48	16.0	t48	1
Jenkins, Mel, *Sea.*	3	46	15.3	34	0
Lankford, Paul, *Mia.*	3	44	14.7	44	0
Ross, Kevin, *K.C.*	3	40	13.3	40	0
Haynes, Mark, *Den.*	3	39	13.0	25	1
Fulcher, David, *Cin.*	3	30	10.0	28	0
Hall, Delton, *Pitt.*	3	29	9.7	t25	1
Howard, Carl, *Jets*	3	29	9.7	29	0
Lilly, Tony, *Den.*	3	29	9.7	24	0
Hamilton, Harry, *Jets*	3	25	8.3	25	0
Miano, Rich, *Jets*	3	24	8.0	21	0
Mecklenburg, Karl, *Den.*	3	23	7.7	16	0
Everett, Thomas, *Pitt.*	3	22	7.3	21	0
Pitts, Ron, *Buff.*	3	19	6.3	12	0
Blackwood, Glenn, *Mia.*	3	17	5.7	17	0
Hinkle, Bryan, *Pitt.*	3	15	5.0	8	0
Robbins, Randy, *Den.*	3	9	3.0	9	0
Ryan, Jim, *Den.*	3	7	2.3	5	0
Dixon, Hanford, *Clev.*	3	5	1.7	6	0

t = Touchdown

BUFFALO BILLS

Address One Bills Drive, Orchard Park, New York 14127.
Stadium Rich Stadium, Orchard Park.
   Capacity 80,290 *Playing Surface* AstroTurf.
Team Colours Royal Blue, Scarlet Red, and White.
Head Coach Marv Levy – third year.
Championships Division 1980; AFL 1964, '65.
History AFL 1960-69, AFC 1970-

Offense

Last year's team report was a little behind schedule. Instead of being 'two or three years away', the Bills entered Week Fifteen needing only to win their last two games to clinch the division title. Beginning the 1988 campaign, they appear to be at least on a par with their domestic competition. The main reason on offense has been the establishment of quarterback Jim Kelly as a player of real class. Kelly, who went to the AFC-NFC Pro Bowl as a replacement for the injured Dan Marino, raised his own club record completion percentage to 59.7 and put together a string of 141 passes without an interception. It is a Bills strength that their passing game is well balanced, with no one receiver as the prime target. It is reflected in the club statistics which show wide receiver Andre Reed as the club leader with 57 catches, one more than both wide receiver Chris Burkett and running back Ronnie Harmon. It was the second year in a row that Reed has led the Bills. Behind Reed and Burkett on the roster, the club has several quality backups, including Trumaine Johnson and a player with deep speed, Walter Broughton. At tight end, Pete Metzelaars continues as the senior player, used mostly for his blocking but on hand for key receptions. The situation at running back is more fluid. Counting 'replacement games', the Bills had five different players start at running back and three at fullback. Despite not yet being a prolific runner, Harmon retains the senior spot ahead of Ricky Porter at running back, though both players may have to step aside if Robb Riddick can return to full fitness after missing the last half of the season with a broken collarbone. Still searching for the kind of sparkle they had with Joe Cribbs and, after him, Greg Bell in the lineup, the Bills drafted Thurman Thomas. And he is everything that Cribbs and Bell were – and maybe more – but he has had knee problems and gained all his yards operating out of the 'I' formation. A late-season push saw rookie Jamie Mueller start the last five games at fullback ahead of Carl Byrum, the latter who entered the season appearing to have a firm hold on the starting spot. Another reason for the Bills' improvement was the solidity of the offensive line, which started intact for almost all the games played by the regulars. Will Wolford and Joe Devlin are the tackles, Jim Ritcher and Tim Vogler the guards, with Kent Hull at center. The backups include former high draft picks Leonard Burton and Mark Traynowicz.

Defense

Head coach Marv Levy wanted outside linebacker Cornelius Bennett and, though he paid a high price in future draft options, he got his man. And Bennett began the repayments immediately. You had to have a particular kind of hardness of heart not to have your fingers crossed that everything would work out, and it was with great relief for everyone that Bennett showed himself to be a superstar right from the start. It wasn't just for his explosive speed, which saw him log 8.5 sacks in only eight games, in the final seven of which he started, but more for the ripple effect he had on the defensive unit as a whole. It meant that another rookie, Shane Conlan, could move to his preferred position of inside linebacker. Conlan, a potential superstar in his own right, led the team in tackles. Inevitably, the other starting linebackers, Scott Radecic and Darryl Talley, were catalysed to their best efforts. The effect was felt on the three-man defensive line, where Bruce Smith had a field day, logging twelve sacks. In the AFC-NFC Pro Bowl, Smith was named MVP. Nose tackle Fred Smerlas and defensive left end Sean McNanie complete a formidable front seven. If there is a problem, it may arise very quickly if one of the starters is injured, for the Bills do not have great depth either for the line or at linebacker. The defensive secondary is considered the weakest area of the unit, but it was a year which saw the introduction of a rookie, right cornerback Nate Odomes, and two second-year players in safeties Mark Kelso and Ron Pitts. Kelso, a former tenth-round draft pick of Philadelphia, saw some action in only three games in 1986, but he came through to start at free safety, from where he led the Bills with six interceptions. Pitts was only a reserve in 1986. The one player of unquestioned class is left cornerback Derrick Burroughs. Opposing quarterbacks don't challenge him often.

1988 SCHEDULE OF GAMES		
September		
4	MINNESOTA	1:00
11	MIAMI	1:00
18	at New England	1:00
25	PITTSBURGH	1:00
October		
2	at Chicago	12:00
9	INDIANAPOLIS	1:00
17	at New York Jets (Mon.)	9:00
23	NEW ENGLAND	1:00
30	GREEN BAY	1:00
November		
6	at Seattle	1:00
14	at Miami (Mon.)	9:00
20	NEW YORK JETS	1:00
27	at Cincinnati	1:00
December		
4	at Tampa Bay	1:00
11	LOS ANGELES RAIDERS	1:00
18	at Indianapolis	1:00

Andre Reed.

Special Teams

Steve Tasker went to the AFC-NFC Pro Bowl as the special-teamer for his all-out effort in a unit which specialised in restricting opponents' kickoff and punt returns. In that context, punter John Kidd's modest gross average of 39.0 yards is acceptable. Ricky Porter may have an increasingly important role to play as a kickoff returner. Placekicker Scott Norwood will be challenged by fifth-round draftee Kirk Roach.

1988 DRAFT

Round	Name	Pos.	Ht.	Wt.	College
2.	Thomas, Thurman	RB	5-9	192	Oklahoma State
3.	Ford, Bernard	WR	5-9	169	Central Florida
5.	Gadson, Ezekial	DB	5-11	207	Pittsburgh
5.	Roach, Kirk	K	6-1	225	Western Carolina
6.	Murray, Dan	LB	6-1	237	East Stroudsburg, Pa.
7.	Borcky, Tim	T	6-7	288	Memphis State
7.	Wright, Bo	RB	5-10	215	Alabama
8.	Hagy, John	DB	6-0	189	Texas
8.	Wright, Jeff	NT	6-2	270	Central Missouri
9.	Bailey, Carlton	NT	6-1	240	North Carolina
10.	Mayhew, Martin	DB	5-8	173	Florida State
11.	Curkendall, Pete	NT	6-2	276	Penn State
12.	Driscoll, John	T	6-5	278	New Hampshire
12.	Erlandson, Tom	LB	6-1	221	Washington

VETERAN ROSTER

No.	Name	Pos.	Ht.	Wt.	NFL Year	College
2	Beecher, Willie	K	5-10	170	2	Utah State
55	Bennett, Cornelius	LB	6-2	235	2	Alabama
50	Bentley, Ray	LB	6-2	245	3	Central Michigan
81	Broughton, Walter	WR	5-10	180	3	Jacksonville State
77	Brown, Tony	T	6-5	285	2	Pittsburgh
85	Burkett, Chris	WR	6-4	210	4	Jackson State
29	Burroughs, Derrick	CB	6-1	180	4	Memphis State
61	Burton, Leonard	T	6-3	275	3	South Carolina
80	Butler, Jerry	WR	6-0	178	8	Clemson
82	Bynum, Reggie	WR	6-1	185	1	Oregon State
35	Byrum, Carl	RB	6-0	235	3	Mississippi Valley St.
69	Christy, Greg	G	6-4	285	2	Pittsburgh
58	Conlan, Shane	LB	6-3	230	2	Penn State
21	Davis, Wayne	CB	5-11	175	4	Indiana State
70	Devlin, Joe	T	6-5	280	12	Iowa
45	Drane, Dwight	S	6-2	205	3	Oklahoma
	Fox, Chas	WR	5-11	190	2	Furman
59	Frerotte, Mitch	G	6-3	280	2	Penn State
53	Furjanic, Tony	LB	6-1	228	3	Notre Dame
99	Garner, Hal	LB	6-4	235	3	Utah State
8	Gelbaugh, Stan	QB	6-3	207	2	Maryland
75	Hamby, Mike	DE	6-4	270	2	Utah State
92	Hammond, Steve	LB	6-4	225	1	Wake Forest
33	Harmon, Ronnie	RB	5-11	192	3	Iowa
71	Hellestrae, Dale	T	6-5	275	4	Southern Methodist
	Howard, Joe	WR	5-9	167	1	Notre Dame
67	Hull, Kent	C	6-4	275	3	Mississippi State
47	Jackson, Kirby	CB	5-10	180	2	Mississippi State
20	Johnson, Flip	WR	5-10	185	1	McNeese State
48	Johnson, Lawrence	S	5-11	202	8	Wisconsin
86	Johnson, Trumaine	WR	6-1	196	4	Grambling State
52	Kaiser, John	LB	6-3	227	5	Arizona
12	Kelly, Jim	QB	6-3	218	3	Miami
38	Kelso, Mark	S	5-11	177	3	William & Mary
4	Kidd, John	P	6-3	208	5	Northwestern
63	Lingner, Adam	C	6-4	260	6	Illinois
54	Marve, Eugene	LB	6-2	240	7	Saginaw Valley State
13	McClure, Brian	QB	6-6	222	1	Bowling Green
84	McKeller, Keith	TE	6-6	230	2	Jacksonville State
95	McNanie, Sean	DE	6-5	270	5	San Diego State
74	Mesner, Bruce	NT	6-5	280	2	Maryland
88	Metzelaars, Pete	TE	6-7	245	7	Wabash
25	Mitchell, Roland	CB	5-11	180	2	Texas Tech
39	Mueller, Jamie	RB	6-1	225	2	Benedictine
11	Norwood, Scott	K	6-0	207	4	James Madison
37	Odomes, Nate	CB	5-9	188	2	Wisconsin
57	Pike, Mark	LB	6-4	257	2	Georgia Tech
27	Pitts, Ron	CB-S-PR	5-10	175	3	UCLA
30	Porter, Kerry	RB	6-1	210	2	Washington State
26	Porter, Ricky	RB	5-10	210	3	Slippery Rock
79	Prater, Dean	DE	6-4	260	7	Oklahoma State
97	Radecic, Scott	LB	6-3	242	5	Penn State
83	Reed, Andre	WR	6-0	190	4	Kutztown, Pa.
14	Reich, Frank	QB	6-4	208	4	Maryland
40	Riddick, Robb	RB-KR	6-0	195	6	Millersville, Pa.
51	Ritcher, Jim	G	6-3	265	9	North Carolina State
87	Rolle, Butch	TE	6-3	242	3	Michigan State
	Sampson, Clint	WR	5-11	183	5	San Diego State
96	Seals, Leon	DE	6-4	265	2	Jackson State
76	Smerlas, Fred	NT	6-3	280	10	Boston College
78	Smith, Bruce	DE	6-4	285	4	Virginia Tech
56	Talley, Darryl	LB	6-4	227	6	West Virginia
89	Tasker, Steve	WR-KR	5-9	185	4	Northwestern
62	Traynowicz, Mark	G-C	6-5	280	4	Nebraska
24	Vital, Lionel	RB	5-9	195	2	Nicholls State
65	Vogler, Tim	G	6-3	285	10	Ohio State
73	Wolford, Will	T	6-5	276	3	Vanderbilt

INDIANAPOLIS COLTS

Address P.O. Box 24100 Indianapolis, Indiana 46224-0100.
Stadium Hoosier Dome, Indianapolis.
   Capacity 60,127 *Playing Surface* AstroTurf.
Team Colours Royal Blue, White, and Silver.
Head Coach Ron Meyer – third year.
Championships Division 1970,'75,'76,'77,'87; Conference
   1970; NFL 1958,'59,'68; Super Bowl 1970.
History NFL 1953-69, AFC 1970-
   (Until 1984, they were known as the Baltimore Colts. A
   team of the same name played in the AAFC, from
   1947 to 1949, and in the NFL in 1950, at the end of
   which they went out of business.)

Offense

The Colts' success story can be traced back to the 1979 draft, when linebacker Barry Krauss and defensive back Nesby Glasgow were selected. In the following years, they continued to draft well without ever looking likely to contend. And then came Eric Dickerson and, quite suddenly, they became a force. There was an extra spring in the step of the offensive linemen, where three of them, left tackle Chris Hinton, right guard Ron Solt and center Ray Donaldson, were selected to the AFC-NFC Pro Bowl. Left guard Ben Utt and right tackle Kevin Call make up a super line which started in every game played by the regulars. In addition, backup guard Randy Dixon is an excellent prospect. And what about that man Dickerson? Almost as soon as he arrived, he began his assault on the Colts' record book. By the end of the season, he had set records for 100-yards-rushing games in a regular season (6), including a new mark with four straight. His 196 yards rushing against Tampa Bay on the final weekend was a club single-game best. Though playing in only nine AFC games, he led that conference with 1,011 yards rushing, increasing his consecutive sequence of 1,000-yards-rushing campaigns to five. Albert Bentley hovers as one of the best backups in the NFL, and, with the likely return of Randy McMillan after injury, one wonders if the Colts might use a two-back system more often. An unsung group of wide receivers, headed by starters Bill Brooks and Matt Bouza, gives the quarterback enough options for variation from the rushing game. Brooks was not the deep threat he was as a rookie – his average per reception went down from 17.4 yards to 14.2 – but he continues to make pleasing progress. Bouza has become a reliable, seasoned veteran. New arrival (Downtown) Charlie Brown was an excellent signing. Behind these three, though, there is little by way of support. Both tight end Pat Beach and H-back Mark Boyer have become respected starters. The emergence of Jack Trudeau as a more prudent operator at quarterback cushioned the effects of injuries which restricted Gary Hogeboom to just six starts. Trudeau, who was 5-3 as the starter in the regular season, played in

seven games when he didn't throw an interception. Sadly, Hogeboom's continuing injury problems, torn ligaments, fractured rib, punctured lung and dislocated shoulder last year alone, may signal a premature end to his career. In relief, the Colts have Sean Salisbury, Mark Herrmann (ex-San Diego) and third-round draftee Chris Chandler.

Defense

Even without Cornelius Bennett, who got away, the Colts ranked sixth in the entire NFL. Donnell Thompson and Jon Hand started at the defensive end positions virtually all year, whilst Byron Darby took over from Jerome Sally at nose tackle for the last four games. Thompson, a 1981 first-round pick, has been helped by the rapid maturing of Hand, a 1986 first-rounder who has started in all but one of his games as a pro. The nose tackle spot is a relative weakness, and the Colts are hoping that former Jets all-pro Joe Klecko can solve the problem and help a defense that ranked 15th in the NFL against the run. There are no worries at linebacker, especially with the return of Barry Krauss, whose recovery from injury has been little short of miraculous. Krauss came back, a healthy, bouncing 269-pounder, and promptly started in the final eleven games played by the regulars. His only non-start came on Week One – perhaps the club couldn't believe his fitness. In his first start, against Miami, he had a team-leading eleven tackles and five assists. Right outside linebacker Duane Bickett led the team with 113 tackles, eight more than left inside linebacker Cliff Odom. Bickett also led the team with eight quarterback sacks, whilst left outside linebacker Johnie Cooks had 5.0. Even for depth, the Colts are well stocked in the likes of Orlando Lowry and Dave Ahrens, the latter who is a fierce tackler. The secondary showed great improvement. Seventh-year veteran Willie Tullis and Mike Prior, who was waived but re-signed as a replacement player, made a strong impact. Ending the season as the starting free safety after an injury to rookie Freddie Robinson, Prior was used mostly as a nickel back

1988 SCHEDULE OF GAMES	September	
	4 HOUSTON	3:00
	11 CHICAGO	12:00
	19 at Cleveland (Mon.)	8:00
	25 MIAMI	12:00
	October	
	2 at New England	1:00
	9 at Buffalo	1:00
	16 TAMPA BAY	12:00
	23 at San Diego	1:00
	31 DENVER (Mon.)	9:00
	November	
	6 NEW YORK JETS	4:00
	13 at Green Bay	12:00
	20 at Minnesota	12:00
	27 NEW ENGLAND	4:00
	December	
	4 at Miami	1:00
	10 at New York Jets (Sat.)	12:30
	18 BUFFALO	1:00

and shared the AFC lead with six interceptions. Tullis started twelve games at left cornerback. Both Glasgow and Eugene Daniel missed only one start at strong safety and right cornerback respectively.

Special Teams

Rohn Stark's lower-than-usual punting average merely reflects the luxury of being able to punt for position rather than sheer distance. Placekicker Dean Biasucci was outstanding and went to his first AFC-NFC Pro Bowl. Bentley leads a solid kickoff return department, but the Colts could use a big-play punt returner, and Billy (White Shoes) Johnson could fill that slot.

1988 DRAFT

Round	Name	Pos.	Ht.	Wt.	College
3.	Chandler, Chris	QB	6-3	212	Washington
4.	Ball, Michael	DB	6-0	209	Southern
5.	Baylor, John	DB	6-0	194	Southern Mississippi
9.	Herrod, Jeff	LB	6-0	236	Mississippi
10.	Alston, O'Brien	LB	6-6	239	Maryland
11.	Dee, Donnie	TE	6-4	240	Tulsa
12.	Kenney, Aatron	WR	5-10	180	Stevens Point, Wis.
12.	Vesling, Tim	K	5-11	179	Syracuse

Center Ray Donaldson earned a repeat trip to the AFC-NFC Pro Bowl.

VETERAN ROSTER

No.	Name	Pos.	Ht.	Wt.	NFL Year	College
57	Ahrens, Dave	LB	6-4	249	8	Wisconsin
79	Armstrong, Harvey	DE	6-3	268	6	Southern Methodist
35	Banks, Chuck	RB	6-1	227	3	West Virginia Tech
45	Banks, Roy	WR	5-10	190	2	Eastern Illinois
81	Beach, Pat	TE	6-4	252	6	Washington State
87	Bellini, Mark	WR	5-11	185	2	Brigham Young
20	Bentley, Albert	RB-KR	5-11	214	4	Miami
4	Biasucci, Dean	K	6-0	191	4	Western Carolina
50	Bickett, Duane	LB	6-5	243	4	Southern California
85	Bouza, Matt	WR	6-3	212	7	California
84	Boyer, Mark	H-B	6-4	242	4	Southern California
88	Brandes, John	TE	6-2	237	2	Cameron, Oklahoma
80	Brooks, Bill	WR-PR	6-0	191	3	Boston University
74	Brotzki, Bob	C	6-5	293	3	Syracuse
68	Broughton, Willie	NT	6-5	281	3	Miami
	Brown, Charlie	WR	5-10	184	7	South Carolina State
71	Call, Kevin	T	6-7	302	5	Colorado State
31	Coleman, Leonard	S	6-2	202	4	Vanderbilt
98	Cooks, Johnie	LB	6-4	252	7	Mississippi State
38	Daniel, Eugene	CB	5-11	178	5	Louisiana State
72	Darby, Byron	DE	6-4	260	6	Southern California
29	Dickerson, Eric	RB	6-3	217	6	Southern Methodist
69	Dixon, Randy	G	6-3	293	2	Pittsburgh
53	Donaldson, Ray	C	6-3	288	9	Georgia
	Ellis, Ray	S	6-1	196	8	Ohio State
73	Gambol, Chris	T	6-6	303	1	Iowa
25	Glasgow, Nesby	S	5-10	184	10	Washington
37	Goode, Chris	CB	6-0	193	2	Alabama
56	Grimsley, Ed	LB	6-0	235	2	Akron
51	Hancock, Kevin	LB	6-2	225	2	Baylor
78	Hand, Jon	DE	6-7	298	3	Alabama
	Herrmann, Mark	QB	6-4	207	8	Purdue
75	Hinton, Chris	T	6-4	295	6	Northwestern
7	Hogeboom, Gary	QB	6-4	208	9	Central Michigan
21	Holt, John	CB	5-10	179	8	West Texas State
58	James, June	LB	6-1	236	3	Texas
	Johnson, Billy	WR-PR	5-9	172	13	Widener
	Johnson, Ezra	DE	6-4	264	12	Morris Brown
94	Kellar, Scott	NT	6-3	279	3	Northern Illinois
	Klecko, Joe	NT	6-3	263	12	Temple
55	Krauss, Barry	LB	6-3	269	10	Alabama
92	Leiding, Jeff	LB	6-3	239	3	Texas
59	Lowry, Orlando	LB	6-4	236	4	Ohio State
49	McCloskey, Mike	H-B	6-5	246	5	Penn State
32	McMillan, Randy	RB	6-0	220	7	Pittsburgh
28	Miller, Chuckie	DB	5-8	173	1	UCLA
52	Moon, Micah	LB	6-0	232	1	North Carolina
86	Murray, Walter	WR	6-4	202	3	Hawaii
93	Odom, Cliff	LB	6-2	245	8	Texas-Arlington
65	Patten, Joel	T	6-7	307	3	Duke
43	Perryman, Jim	S	6-0	187	3	Millikin
39	Prior, Mike	S	6-0	200	3	Illinois State
47	Robinson, Freddie	S	6-1	191	2	Alabama
13	Salisbury, Sean	QB	6-5	215	3	Southern California
76	Sally, Jerome	NT	6-3	270	7	Missouri
83	Sherwin, Tim	TE	6-5	252	8	Boston College
66	Solt, Ron	G	6-3	285	5	Maryland
3	Stark, Rohn	P	6-3	204	7	Florida State
26	Swoope, Craig	S	6-1	200	3	Illinois
99	Thompson, Donnell	DE	6-4	275	8	North Carolina
62	Thorp, Don	NT	6-4	260	3	Illinois
10	Trudeau, Jack	QB	6-3	213	3	Illinois
42	Tullis, Willie	CB-PR	5-11	195	8	Troy State
64	Utt, Ben	G	6-6	286	7	Georgia Tech
	Verdin, Clarence	WR-KR	5-8	160	3	Southwestern Louisiana
34	Wonsley, George	RB	5-10	219	5	Mississippi State
27	Wright, Terry	CB-KR	6-0	195	2	Temple

MIAMI DOLPHINS

DIVISION NINETEEN

Address 4770 Biscayne Boulevard, Suite 1440, Miami, Florida 33137.

Stadium Joe Robbie Stadium, Miami.
Capacity 75,500 *Playing Surface* Grass.

Team Colours Aqua, Coral, and White.

Head Coach Don Shula – nineteenth year.

Championships Division 1971,'72,'73,'74,'79,'81,'83,'84,'85; Conference 1971,'72,'73,'82,'84; Super Bowl 1972,'73.

History AFL 1966-69, AFC 1970-

Offense

The Miami Dolphins did not bounce back and regain the division title they lent to New England in 1986, and that has to be headline news of a club which, always, is expected not only to compete but to dominate. The most obvious explanation is that the rest have caught up with them and they now have a job of work to do. Quarterback Dan Marino was only a little off-song, but, in a highly-competitive conference, he dropped to second place in the AFC list of leading passers. Even so, he continued his march towards ownership of all the NFL passing records with two more four-touchdowns-passing games, bringing his total to 14, three adrift of the record held by Johnny Unitas. Also, Marino remains as the NFL's all-time career-leading passer with a rating of 94.1. As usual, he was well protected by the Dolphins line, but the protection that we take for granted could become increasingly difficult to maintain should all-pro center Dwight Stephenson not regain his full powers following surgery on his left knee. For the moment, the starting line of tackles Jon Giesler and Ronnie Lee, guards Roy Foster and Tom Toth, even with Jeff Dellenbach standing in at center, should be able to provide the platform for Marino to work his magic. Wide receivers Mark Duper and Mark Clayton must still be regarded as one of the best starting pairs in the AFC, and though both players saw their productivity fall a touch, they still caught their passes to good effect, averaging 18.1 and 16.9 yards respectively. Behind them, the slack was taken up by James Pruitt and Jim Jensen, the latter who had the best of his seven years in the pros. The Dolphins have not yet taken the wrapper off last year's second-round pick, Scott Schwedes, who didn't catch a pass all season. It seems that the same old tight ends have been with Miami for ever, but the selection of Ferrell Edmunds in the third round may signal a changing of the guard. But it is not likely to happen with indecent haste – the Dolphins just aren't like that – and Bruce Hardy should continue to start ahead of Dan Johnson. With the rapid emergence of Troy Stradford, the Dolphins' search for a running back seems to be over. Able to catch passes as well, he's a more punchy variety of Tony Nathan. He's just the sort the Dolphins like. With Lorenzo Hampton as Stradford's backup, Ron Davenport could move up to start at fullback ahead of Woody Bennett.

Defense

Top draftees Eric Kumerow and Jarvis Williams cannot solve the Dolphins' defensive problems by themselves, but they must help in the process of rebuilding which has been going on for some time. Throughout the squad, young players are establishing themselves. Starting defensive ends T. J. Turner and John Bosa are entering their third and second years respectively, whilst nose tackle Brian Sochia will be in his sixth. Behind them, rookie Rick Graf took over from Bob Brudzinski at left outside linebacker and second-year right inside linebacker John Offerdahl confirmed his rookie form. Jackie Shipp starts at left inside linebacker with Mark Brown outside on the right. Hugh Green, a former AFC-NFC Pro Bowl outside linebacker, is reported to have rediscovered his sparkle, and that's what the Dolphins were looking for when they picked Kumerow, who is listed as a defensive end but is projected to be a stand-up pass rusher. Looking at the lads who make physical contact, Shipp, Offerdahl and Mark Brown ended as the top three tacklers, with Bosa as the leader on the defensive line. Looking back over the years, there always seems to have been something which hindered the development of the defensive secondary, and for once, in 1987, they were not disrupted by too many injuries. But there were forced changes. Two of Glenn Blackwood's ten starts were at free safety and the rest at strong safety before a knee injury forced him to miss the final two games. Bud Brown, Paul Lankford and Donovan Rose saw action at free safety, where Brown is the senior player. Lankford's preferred position is at left cornerback, where he is the starter. The only player to start in all twelve 'regular' games in the same position was right cornerback William Judson. It may be that Liffort Hobley, who started at strong safety for the last four games, takes over from Blackwood. Second-round draftee Jarvis Williams, who can play both at cornerback and safety, may be given the chance to express his versatility.

1988 SCHEDULE OF GAMES	September	
	4 at Chicago	12:00
	11 at Buffalo	1:00
	18 GREEN BAY	1:00
	25 at Indianapolis	12:00
	October	
	2 MINNESOTA	4:00
	9 at Los Angeles Raiders	1:00
	16 SAN DIEGO	1:00
	23 NEW YORK JETS	4:00
	30 at Tampa Bay	1:00
	November	
	6 at New England	1:00
	14 BUFFALO (Mon.)	9:00
	20 NEW ENGLAND	8:00
	27 at New York Jets	1:00
	December	
	4 INDIANAPOLIS	1:00
	12 CLEVELAND (Mon.)	9:00
	18 at Pittsburgh	1:00

Special Teams

A good punting average by Reggie Roby and steady placekicking by Fuad Reveiz maintained the club's reputation for special teams excellence. As expected, Schwedes did have a role to play as a punt returner, and he averaged a respectable 8.5 yards. Kickoff returns, however, presented a problem, with none of the regulars averaging better than 19.7 yards.

1988 DRAFT

Round	Name	Pos.	Ht.	Wt.	College
1.	Kumerow, Eric	DE	6-6	257	Ohio State
2.	Williams, Jarvis	DB	5-11	192	Florida
3.	Edmunds, Ferrell	TE	6-5	241	Maryland
4.	Johnson, Greg	T	6-4	335	Oklahoma
5.	Thomas, Rodney	DB	5-9	194	Brigham Young
6.	Bratton, Melvin	RB	6-0	223	Miami
6.	Cooper, George	RB	6-0	258	Ohio State
7.	Bell, Kerwin	QB	6-2	208	Florida
8.	Galbreath, Harry	G	6-1	270	Tennessee
8.	Cheek, Louis	T	6-5	270	Texas A&M
9.	Cross, Jeff	DE	6-3	255	Missouri
10.	Jackson, Artis	NT	6-4	305	Texas Tech
11.	Kelleher, Tom	RB	6-0	230	Holy Cross
12.	Kinchen, Brian	TE	6-2	230	Louisiana State

VETERAN ROSTER

No.	Name	Pos.	Ht.	Wt.	NFL Year	College
86	Banks, Fred	WR	5-10	180	3	Liberty University
34	Bennett, Woody	RB	6-2	244	10	Miami
75	Betters, Doug	DE	6-7	265	11	Nevada-Reno
47	Blackwood, Glenn	S	6-0	190	10	Texas
97	Bosa, John	DE	6-4	273	2	Boston College
43	Brown, Bud	S	6-0	194	5	Southern Mississippi
51	Brown, Mark	LB	6-2	235	6	Purdue
	Brown, Tom	RB	6-1	218	1	Pittsburgh
59	Brudzinski, Bob	LB	6-4	235	12	Ohio State
83	Clayton, Mark	WR	5-9	184	6	Louisville
98	Cline, Jackie	NT	6-5	276	2	Alabama
67	Conlin, Chris	C-G	6-3	280	2	Penn State
30	Davenport, Ron	RB	6-2	230	4	Louisville
65	Dellenbach, Jeff	C	6-6	280	4	Wisconsin

No.	Name	Pos.	Ht.	Wt.	Year	College
74	Dennis, Mark	T	6-6	291	2	Illinois
85	Duper, Mark	WR	5-9	187	7	Northwestern St., La.
61	Foster, Roy	G	6-4	275	7	Southern California
53	Frye, David	LB	6-2	227	6	Purdue
79	Giesler, Jon	T	6-5	272	10	Michigan
66	Gilmore, Jim	G	6-5	275	3	Ohio State
58	Graf, Rick	LB	6-5	249	2	Wisconsin
55	Green, Hugh	LB	6-2	225	8	Pittsburgh
71	Gruber, Bob	T	6-5	280	2	Pittsburgh
27	Hampton, Lorenzo	RB	6-0	203	4	Florida
84	Hardy, Bruce	TE	6-5	234	11	Arizona State
29	Hobley, Liffort	S	6-0	199	3	Louisiana State
17	Jaworski, Ron	QB	6-1	205	14	Youngstown State
38	Jenkins, DeShon	CB-S	6-1	198	1	Northwestern St., La.
11	Jensen, Jim	WR	6-4	215	8	Boston University
87	Johnson, Dan	TE	6-3	245	6	Iowa State
49	Judson, William	CB	6-2	190	7	South Carolina State
16	Karsatos, Jim	QB	6-4	230	1	Ohio State
	Kehoe, Scott	T	6-4	275	2	Illinois
54	Kolic, Larry	LB	6-1	238	3	Ohio State
69	Lambrecht, Mike	NT	6-1	271	2	St. Cloud State
44	Lankford, Paul	CB	6-2	184	7	Penn State
72	Lee, Ronnie	T	6-3	275	10	Baylor
99	Little, George	DE-NT	6-4	270	4	Iowa
13	Marino, Dan	QB	6-4	222	6	Pittsburgh
78	Marrone, Doug	G-C	6-5	269	2	Syracuse
28	McNeal, Don	CB	6-0	192	8	Alabama
52	Nicolas, Scott	LB	6-3	226	7	Miami
56	Offerdahl, John	LB	6-2	232	3	Western Michigan
82	Pruitt, James	WR	6-2	199	3	Cal State-Fullerton
7	Reveiz, Fuad	K	5-11	217	4	Tennessee
4	Roby, Reggie	P	6-2	242	6	Iowa
81	Schwedes, Scott	WR-PR	6-0	182	3	Syracuse
50	Shipp, Jackie	LB	6-2	236	5	Oklahoma
25	Smith, Mike	CB	6-0	185	4	Texas-El Paso
70	Sochia, Brian	NT	6-3	274	6	N.W. Oklahoma State
57	Stephenson, Dwight	C	6-2	258	9	Alabama
23	Stradford, Troy	RB	5-9	191	2	Boston College
10	Strock, Don	QB	6-5	225	15	Virginia Tech
24	Thompson, Reyna	CB	5-11	194	3	Baylor
76	Toth, Tom	G	6-5	275	3	Western Michigan
95	Turner, T.J.	DE	6-4	275	3	Houston

Troy Stradford has established himself as the Dolphins' premier threat at running back.

NEW ENGLAND PATRIOTS

Address Sullivan Stadium, Route 1, Foxboro, Mass. 02035.
Stadium Sullivan Stadium, Foxboro.
  Capacity 61,000 *Playing Surface* Super Turf.
Team Colours Red, White, and Blue.
Head Coach Raymond Berry – fifth year.
Championships Division 1978,'86; Conference 1985.
History AFL 1960-69, AFC 1970-
  (Until 1971, they were known as the Boston Patriots.)

Offense

Wins in the final three games were not enough for the Patriots to retain their division title, which duly passed to the Colts. Entering the preseason, veteran quarterback Steve Grogan has been named as the starter, ahead of Tony Eason. Even two years ago, the sight of Grogan on the sidelines, wearing all the communications paraphernalia of an assistant coach, suggested clearly enough the nature of his future with the club. But injuries to Eason brought the wise veteran of thirteen years back to start on occasion, and then for those last three victorious games. 'Never mind the age, how well do they run?' one might ask of old cars and quarterbacks, and Grogan has confirmed his right to occupy centre stage. If Eason is prepared to play second fiddle, he would be an excellent backup, ahead of either Tom Ramsey or Doug Flutie. Coach Berry regards wide receiver as the most exciting area of the team, and even allowing for the fact that Irving Fryar probably will never scale the heights expected of him when he was made the first pick overall in the 1984 draft, the Patriots are loaded. The mercurial Stanley Morgan is the pick of the unit. Despite missing the last four games because of injury, Morgan came second in the club with 40 receptions at a sparkling average of 16.8 yards. Fryar will remain the other starter but will be used more for his running, probably on those end-arounds, which Berry sees as a great asset. Stephen Starring, Cedric Jones, Derwin Williams and Dennis Gadbois, who was a 'replacement' player, are the backups. The Patriots' rushing game did improve from its nadir of the 1986 season, but it still needed the boost which may come with the selection of John Stephens in the first round. Tony Collins led the team in both rushing and pass receptions, but, one understands, for reasons not related to football, he has been released. Craig James is expected to be fit after missing almost the whole of last season, joining a group which contains Reggie Dupard, Mosi Tatupu and Bob Perryman. Tight end Russ Francis returns to his original club to press Lin Dawson for playing time. On the offensive line, rookie tackles Bruce Armstrong and Danny Villa, the latter because of injuries to others, came through to start. Trevor Matich should start at center, with Sean Farrell and Ron Wooten at guard. Other veterans, such as Steve Moore and Art Plunkett, will compete strongly for playing time.

Defense

Defensively, the Patriots slipped a little against the pass but, overall, retained their position, roughly in the middle of the league rankings. Thankfully, all-pro outside linebacker Andre Tippett has been signed to the kind of contract which should ensure that the Patriots will retain his services for the rest of his career. Tippett led the AFC with 12.5 sacks, and, following the retirements of both Steve Nelson and Don Blackmon, every ounce of his experience will be needed. Berry saw Johnny Rembert and Ed Reynolds competing for Nelson's starting spot, but that was before the draft, in which they selected Vincent Brown in the second round. Brown is the sort who likes to mix it and he has the size to play the inside position in the NFL. Ed Williams came through to start in place of Blackmon last season and he impressed enough to hang on to the job. Lawrence McGrew has improved steadily and is fully expected to become a significant force at right inside linebacker. On the defensive line, Toby Williams appears to have settled in at nose tackle, where he has spent the last two seasons after playing three years at defensive end. In his position, 4.5 sacks is a reasonable contribution. The best pass rusher is Garin Veris, who had seven sacks and shared the award of 'lineman of the year' with offensive tackle Armstrong. Encouragingly, but not for Brent Williams, Kenneth Sims regained his starting spot at defensive left end. Sims is particularly effective against the run. As further backups, the Patriots have Milford Hodge and Mike Ruth, who is healthy for the first time in his career. Ronnie Lippett has developed as a really fine cornerback, whilst the senior starter, Raymond Clayborn, will be back after suffering a freak injury. Roland James, too, should return at strong safety, in partnership with free safety Fred Marion, who improves each year and led the team with four interceptions and 103 tackles. Ernest Gibson, Rod McSwain and Jim Bowman are solid backups.

1988 SCHEDULE OF GAMES		
September		
4	NEW YORK JETS	4:00
11	at Minnesota	3:00
18	BUFFALO	1:00
25	at Houston	12:00
October		
2	INDIANAPOLIS	1:00
9	vs. Green Bay at Milwaukee	12:00
16	CINCINNATI	1:00
23	at Buffalo	1:00
30	CHICAGO	1:00
November		
6	MIAMI	1:00
13	at New York Jets	1:00
20	at Miami	8:00
27	at Indianapolis	4:00
December		
4	SEATTLE	1:00
11	TAMPA BAY	1:00
17	at Denver (Sat.)	2:00

Special Teams

Placekicker Tony Franklin is coming off a modest season and will be challenged by draftee Teddy Garcia. Punter Rich Camarillo, the club's all-time leader in both punts and yardage, enjoyed a steady season and appears to be secure. Fryar doubles as a dangerous punt returner but both he and Starring averaged below 20 yards on their kickoff returns.

1988 DRAFT

Round	Name	Pos.	Ht.	Wt.	College
1.	Stephens, John	RB	5-11	215	Northwestern St., La.
2.	Brown, Vincent	LB	6-1	245	Mississippi Valley St.
3.	Rehder, Tom	T	6-6	272	Notre Dame
4.	Goad, Tim	NT	6-2	268	North Carolina
4.	Martin, Sammy	WR	5-10	169	Louisiana State
4.	Garcia, Teddy	K	5-9	175	Northeast Louisiana
5.	Wolkow, Troy	G	6-3	267	Minnesota
6.	Johnson, Steve	TE	6-5	240	Virginia Tech
7.	Usher, Darryl	WR	5-7	178	Illinois
9.	Galbraith, Neil	DB	5-11	172	Central State, Okla.
10.	Lossow, Rodney	C	6-2	270	Wisconsin
11.	Allen, Marvin	RB	5-9	212	Tulane
12.	Nugent, Dave	NT	6-3	270	Boston College

VETERAN ROSTER

No.	Name	Pos.	Ht.	Wt.	NFL Year	College
78	Armstrong, Bruce	T	6-4	284	2	Louisville
25	Beasley, Derrick	S	6-1	205	1	Winston-Salem State
28	Bowman, Jim	S	6-2	210	4	Central Michigan
58	Brock, Pete	C	6-5	275	13	Colorado
3	Camarillo, Rich	P	5-11	185	8	Washington
26	Clayborn, Raymond	CB	6-0	186	12	Texas
40	Davis, Elgin	RB	5-10	192	2	Central Florida
87	Dawson, Lin	TE	6-3	240	7	North Carolina State
21	Dupard, Reggie	RB	5-11	205	3	Southern Methodist
11	Eason, Tony	QB	6-4	212	6	Illinois
66	Fairchild, Paul	C-G	6-4	270	5	Kansas
62	Farrell, Sean	G	6-3	260	7	Penn State
2	Flutie, Doug	QB	5-10	175	3	Boston College
49	Francis, Russ	TE	6-6	242	13	Oregon
1	Franklin, Tony	K	5-8	182	10	Texas A&M
80	Fryar, Irving	WR-PR	6-0	200	5	Nebraska
	Gadbois, Dennis	WR	6-1	185	2	Boston University
43	Gibson, Ernest	CB	5-10	185	5	Furman
99	Gibson, Tom	DE	6-7	250	1	Northern Arizona
14	Grogan, Steve	QB	6-4	210	14	Kansas State
35	Hansen, Bruce	RB	6-1	225	2	Brigham Young
	Heren, Dieter	LB	6-3	225	1	Michigan
97	Hodge, Milford	NT-DE	6-3	278	3	Washington State
41	Holmes, Darryl	S	6-2	190	2	Fort Valley State
32	James, Craig	RB	6-0	215	4	Southern Methodist
38	James, Roland	S	6-2	191	9	Tennessee
83	Jones, Cedric	WR	6-1	184	7	Duke
93	Jordan, Tim	LB	6-3	226	2	Wisconsin
9	Lewis, Walter	QB	6-0	198	1	Alabama
42	Lippett, Ronnie	CB	5-11	180	6	Miami
31	Marion, Fred	S	6-2	191	7	Miami
64	Matich, Trevor	C	6-4	270	4	Brigham Young
48	McCabe, Jerry	LB	6-1	225	2	Holy Cross
50	McGrew, Lawrence	LB	6-5	233	8	Southern California
23	McSwain, Rod	CB	6-1	198	5	Clemson
67	Moore, Steve	T	6-5	305	6	Tennessee State
86	Morgan, Stanley	WR	5-11	181	12	Tennessee
75	Morriss, Guy	C-G	6-4	260	16	Texas Christian
34	Perryman, Bob	RB	6-1	233	2	Michigan
70	Plunkett, Art	T	6-8	282	7	Nevada-Las Vegas
22	Profit, Eugene	CB	5-10	175	3	Yale
12	Ramsey, Tom	QB	6-1	189	4	UCLA
52	Rembert, Johnny	LB	6-3	234	6	Clemson
95	Reynolds, Ed	LB	6-5	242	6	Virginia
65	Ruth, Mike	NT	6-1	266	3	Boston College
88	Scott, Willie	TE	6-4	245	8	South Carolina
94	Sealby, Randy	LB	6-2	225	2	Missouri
77	Sims, Ken	DE	6-5	271	7	Texas
81	Starring, Stephen	WR-KR	5-10	172	6	McNeese State
30	Tatupu, Mosi	RB	6-0	227	11	Southern California
56	Tippett, Andre	LB	6-3	241	7	Iowa
60	Veris, Garin	DE	6-4	255	4	Stanford
73	Villa, Danny	T	6-5	305	2	Arizona State
24	Weathers, Robert	RB	6-2	225	6	Arizona State
	Wilburn, Steve	DE	6-4	266	2	Lincoln College
96	Williams, Brent	DE-NT	6-3	278	3	Toledo
82	Williams, Derwin	WR	6-1	185	4	New Mexico
54	Williams, Ed	LB	6-4	244	5	Texas
90	Williams, Toby	NT	6-4	270	6	Nebraska
61	Wooten, Ron	G	6-4	273	7	North Carolina

Stanley Morgan can still show a clean pair of heels.

NEW YORK JETS

Address 598 Madison Avenue, New York, N.Y. 10022.
Stadium Giants Stadium, East Rutherford, N.J. 07073.
 Capacity 76,891 *Playing Surface* AstroTurf.
Team Colours Kelly Green and White.
Head Coach Joe Walton – sixth year.
Championships AFL 1968; Super Bowl 1968.
History AFL 1960-69, AFC 1970-
 (Until 1963, they were known as the New York Titans.)

Offense

Opening victories over Buffalo and New England gave rise to the feeling that the Jets were going to roll through the campaign. But, after the strike, they never could regain anything like that momentum and ended the season with four straight losses and a last-place finish. The fact remains, however, that the Jets have as much talent as any other team in the AFC East, numbering on their roster a franchise running back, Freemen McNeil, two Pro Bowl wide receivers, Al Toon and Wesley Walker, and a young quarterback, Ken O'Brien, who ranks third in the NFL all-time list of leading passers. The key to their effectiveness lies on a much-maligned offensive line which, only now, may be coming together. Right guard Dan Alexander is the leader of the unit and commands great respect. Reggie McElroy has overcome injuries and is playing something like his former best at right tackle. Former AFC-NFC Pro Bowl center Joe Fields has been released, but Guy Bingham had moved into the starting spot at center anyway. Top draftee Dave Cadigan is pencilled in to start at left tackle with Jim Sweeney, a dedicated pro, expected to start at center, leaving the left guard spot to be filled by Guy Bingham, Ted Banker or the improving Mike Haight. Despite Freeman McNeil's unquestioned ability, his tendency to be injured may encourage the Jets to use him more and more as a shock weapon, leaving Johnny Hector to take the brunt of the starting assignments. Roger Vick appears to have an edge over Nuu Faaola and Marion Barber to start at fullback. O'Brien is a class quarterback but he does go through periods of uncertainty. For two or three games, he'll be accurate to the inch, and then his timing will go astray. He is regarded as superior to Pat Ryan, who, nonetheless, is a tough, gutsy performer who can come in at a second's notice and run the offense. In Mickey Shuler the Jets have one of the most productive tight ends in the league, that is, taking into account his value as a blocker. Wide receivers Toon and Walker, both of whom are in the NFL's top flight, can strike terror in the hearts of any defensive secondary. Walker's rehabilitation from injury, which is said to be progressing well, is crucial to the Jets' title hopes. In Kurt Sohn, they have a sound reserve, but he doesn't yet have Walker's big-play magic.

Defense

Head coach Joe Walton made no secret of his priorities when it came to reinforcing the defense. He used a second- and two third-round options to select defensive backs. It is an area which has given problems for some time. One remembers describing them as the 'walking wounded'. All four of Lester Lyles, Russell Carter, Jerry Holmes and, critically, in Walton's opinion, Kerry Glenn each missed time through injury. Let's hope that the Jets' new recruits are sound. Going into the season, the projections see rookie Terry Williams starting at left cornerback and Carl Howard or Russell Carter at right cornerback. Holmes, the free safety, will be challenged by Rich Miano, whilst Harry Hamilton and Lyles compete to start at strong safety. But it is highly likely that there will be changes. The injury bug did not stop with the defensive backs and the loss of linebacker Lance Mehl may have had the most damaging effect of all. Mehl, a great AFC-NFC Pro Bowler, was the inspirational leader of the defense. He played just three games last year and it is doubtful if he will ever be able to re-scale the heights from which he once dominated. Bob Crable did make a successful comeback after injury to play at the top of his form. Rookie Alex Gordon settled in at left outside linebacker with Troy Benson as his inside partner. Gordon, Benson, Crable and Kevin McArthur are the listed starters, but we must all keep our fingers crossed that Mehl will be fit enough to join the competition. One former great Jets all-pro will not be in the team. That player, Joe Klecko, has been released, though in true fighting spirit, he went out looking for a new club. Also gone is defensive end Barry Bennett, who has been signed by the Raiders. For the defensive line, then, it is even more important that ends Mark Gastineau and Marty Lyons play up to their best. Gastineau, in particular, has been a mere shadow of his former self. Last year, rookie nose tackle Gerald Nichols started the first five games played by the regulars before giving way to Klecko. He is pencilled in as the starter for 1988.

1988 SCHEDULE OF GAMES	September	
	4 at New England	4:00
	11 at Cleveland	4:00
	18 HOUSTON	1:00
	25 at Detroit	1:00
	October	
	2 KANSAS CITY	4:00
	9 at Cincinnati	1:00
	17 BUFFALO (Mon.)	9:00
	23 at Miami	4:00
	30 PITTSBURGH	1:00
	November	
	6 at Indianapolis	4:00
	13 NEW ENGLAND	1:00
	20 at Buffalo	1:00
	27 MIAMI	1:00
	December	
	4 at Kansas City	3:00
	10 INDIANAPOLIS (Sat.)	12:30
	18 NEW YORK GIANTS	1:00

1988 DRAFT

Round	Name	Pos.	Ht.	Wt.	College
1.	Cadigan, Dave	T	6-4	280	Southern California
2.	Williams, Terry	DB	5-10	196	Bethune-Cookman
3.	McMillan, Erik	DB	6-1	193	Missouri
3.	Hasty, James	DB	5-11	198	Washington State
5.	Withycombe, Mike	T	6-5	295	Fresno State
6.	Frase, Paul	DE	6-4	262	Syracuse
7.	Patton, Gary	RB	5-8	180	Eastern Michigan
8.	Neubert, Keith	TE	6-5	242	Nebraska
9.	Tamm, Ralph	G	6-2	265	West Chester, Pa.
10.	Booty, John	DB	5-11	175	Texas Christian
11.	Galvin, John	LB	6-3	220	Boston College
12.	Goss, Albert	NT	6-7	348	Jackson State

VETERAN ROSTER

No.	Name	Pos.	Ht.	Wt.	NFL Year	College
60	Alexander, Dan	T-G	6-4	274	12	Louisiana State
97	Baldwin, Don	DE	6-3	263	2	Purdue
95	Baldwin, Tom	NT	6-4	270	4	Tulsa
63	Banker, Ted	G-C	6-2	275	5	Southeast Missouri
31	Barber, Marion	RB	6-3	228	7	Minnesota
54	Benson, Troy	LB	6-2	235	3	Pittsburgh
64	Bingham, Guy	C-G	6-3	260	9	Montana
23	Bligen, Dennis	RB	5-11	215	5	St. John's
27	Carter, Russell	CB	6-2	195	5	Southern Methodist
59	Clifton, Kyle	LB	6-4	236	5	Texas Christian
50	Crable, Bob	LB	6-3	230	7	Notre Dame
22	Dykes, Sean	CB	5-10	170	2	Bowling Green
52	Elam, Onzy	LB	6-2	225	2	Tennessee State
30	Faaola, Nuu	RB	5-11	210	3	Hawaii
8	Flick, Tom	QB	6-2	190	6	Washington
98	Foster, Jerome	DE	6-2	275	5	Ohio State
99	Gastineau, Mark	DE	6-5	255	10	East Central Okla.
35	Glenn, Kerry	CB	5-9	175	3	Minnesota
55	Gordon, Alex	LB	6-5	246	2	Cincinnati
81	Griggs, Billy	TE	6-3	230	4	Virginia
79	Haight, Mike	G-T	6-4	270	3	Iowa
39	Hamilton, Harry	S	6-0	195	5	Penn State
84	Harper, Michael	WR	5-10	180	3	Southern California
51	Haslett, Jim	LB	6-3	236	9	Indiana, Pa.
34	Hector, Johnny	RB	5-11	200	6	Texas A&M
47	Holmes, Jerry	CB	6-2	175	7	West Virginia
28	Howard, Carl	CB-S	6-2	190	5	Rutgers
48	Humphery, Bobby	CB-KR	5-10	180	5	New Mexico State
89	Klever, Rocky	TE	6-3	230	6	Montana
5	Leahy, Pat	K	6-0	193	15	St. Louis
21	Lewis, Sid	CB	5-11	180	2	Penn State
26	Lyles, Lester	S	6-3	218	4	Virginia
93	Lyons, Marty	DE-NT	6-5	269	10	Alabama
86	Martin, Tracy	WR	6-3	205	2	North Dakota
57	McArthur, Kevin	LB	6-2	245	3	Lamar
68	McElroy, Reggie	T	6-6	275	6	West Texas State
24	McNeil, Freeman	RB	5-11	214	8	UCLA
56	Mehl, Lance	LB	6-3	233	9	Penn State
94	Mersereau, Scott	DE-NT	6-3	278	2	Southern Connecticut
36	Miano, Rich	S	6-0	200	4	Hawaii
58	Monger, Matt	LB	6-1	238	4	Oklahoma State
77	Nichols, Gerald	NT	6-2	261	2	Florida State
7	O'Brien, Ken	QB	6-4	208	6	Cal-Davis
4	O'Connor, Tom	P	6-1	190	2	South Carolina
6	Prokop, Joe	P	6-2	230	3	Cal Poly-Pomona
25	Radachowsky, Geo.	S	5-11	190	4	Boston College
92	Rose, Ken	LB	6-1	215	2	Nevada-Las Vegas
10	Ryan, Pat	QB	6-3	210	11	Tennessee
82	Shuler, Mickey	TE	6-3	231	11	Penn State
87	Sohn, Kurt	WR	5-11	180	7	Fordham
53	Sweeney, Jim	T	6-4	275	5	Pittsburgh
88	Toon, Al	WR	6-4	205	4	Wisconsin
83	Townsell, JoJo	WR-PR	5-9	180	4	UCLA
43	Vick, Roger	RB	6-3	232	2	Texas A&M
85	Walker, Wesley	WR	6-0	182	12	California
38	Zordich, Mike	S	5-11	207	2	Penn State

Special Teams

Placekicker Pat Leahy is coming off a fine season in which one or two long-range field goals might have been enough for all-star recognition. Following the release of Dave Jennings, Tom O'Connor and Joe Prokop will battle for the vacant punting job. Dual-purpose returner JoJo Townsell has that extra special kind of presence when he goes to work. Last season, he returned a punt 91 yards for a touchdown.

Left: Al Toon.

CINCINNATI BENGALS

Address 200 Riverfront Stadium, Cincinnati, Ohio 45202.
Stadium Riverfront Stadium, Cincinnati.
  Capacity 59,754 *Playing Surface* AstroTurf.
Team Colours Black, Orange, and White.
Head Coach Sam Wyche – fifth year.
Championships Division 1970,'73,'81; Conference 1981.
History AFL 1968-69,.AFC 1970-

Offense

The difference between playoff contention and the division cellar is no more than losses by one point (twice), by two, three and by four points. Throw in further defeats by six and seven points and there emerges the picture of a team which, given a bit more luck and a one or two fewer injuries, could have reached the playoffs. Sadly, that seems to have been the saga of the Bengals for much of their history, that is, a story of what might have been. Could this be their year? Another Bengals characteristic is that they always seem to draft well, and this year is no exception. With heavyweight fullback Larry Kinnebrew coming off a modest campaign, the Bengals selected Elbert (Ickey) Woods, who, unexpectedly for a fullback, has a beautifully fluid style of running and fine speed. It looks as if the Bengals will be well off at running back, with Kinnebrew, James Brooks returning to full fitness, Stanford Jennings coming into his own, Bill Johnson better for his experience as a starter and Stanley Wilson back after serving a suspension imposed by Commissioner Rozelle. On his day, Wilson is the best pure rusher the Bengals have. He could make their season. They'll look for a little more consistency from quarterback Boomer Esiason, whose passer rating fell from 87.7 to 73.1. Perhaps the disruption caused by injuries had a greater effect than we realise. At any rate, he is a first-class quarterback and there is no question of his being replaced by backup Turk Schonert. The only real problem at quarterback is the lack of depth. With a complete roster, Cincinnati has as good a set of receivers as any in the league, from wide receivers Eddie Brown, Cris Collinsworth and Tim McGee, through tight end Rodney Holman and on deep into the running backs, where Brooks might be expected to match his rushing output yard for yard. And it is not as if there's a shortage of depth here. Wide receiver Mike Martin has genuine deep speed – last year he averaged 19.7 yards on 20 receptions – and backup tight end Eric Kattus can find the open spaces. One area in which Cincinnati has no worries is the offensive line, where they can be sure of an all-pro performance from left tackle Anthony Munoz. Center Dave Rimington and right guard Max Montoya are not that far below his class, and no-one complains about right tackle Joe Walter when he fades back on pass protection. The two Bruces, Reimers and Kozerski, will battle for the left guard spot.

Defense

It may come as a shock to those who, traditionally, love to criticise Cincinnati defenses, that the 1987 model ranked eighth in the NFL. And who can complain about that? Furthermore, they did it despite little help from two high 1987 draft picks, defensive ends Jason Buck, a first-round selection, and third-rounder Skip McClendon. Again, 1986 third-rounder Mike Hammerstein was unable to break into the starting lineup at nose tackle. That, however, was no disgrace, for the current starter, Tim Krumrie, is a tremendous player. The defensive ends, veteran Eddie Edwards and youngster Jim Skow, were still in place at the end of the campaign. Skow had 4.5 sacks and Edwards had four. The other side of the coin is that those young players who cannot crack the starting lineup represent an outstanding investment for the future. The leading sacker, indeed, the leader of the defense, was right outside linebacker Reggie Williams. He anchors a quartet, again, bristling with youthful talent which has not yet begun to play up to its potential. Both Joe Kelly and Emanuel King were first-round picks and Carl Zander was a second-rounder. 1988 draftee Kevin Walker is an inside specialist who loves physical contact. For quite some time now the Bengals' secondary has had a 'bad press', as they say. It does not have the reputation of being a ball-hawking group but all that could change with the drafting of Rickey Dixon in the 1988 first round. Dixon has the reputation of being one of the best cornerbacks to come out of college in recent years, and he should be an instant replacement for Louis Breeden, who has been released after ten years in the NFL. Lewis Billups hangs onto the job at right cornerback, ahead of Ray Horton, with Eric Thomas hovering as a backup willing to learn: David Fulcher, a really fine strong safety, would rate as the Bengals' best veteran for the secondary, by a nose from free safety Robert Jackson.

1988 SCHEDULE OF GAMES		
September		
4	PHOENIX	1:00
11	at Philadelphia	4:00
18	at Pittsburgh	1:00
25	CLEVELAND	1:00
October		
2	at Los Angeles Raiders	1:00
9	NEW YORK JETS	1:00
16	at New England	1:00
23	HOUSTON	1:00
30	at Cleveland	1:00
November		
6	PITTSBURGH	1:00
13	at Kansas City	12:00
20	at Dallas	12:00
27	BUFFALO	1:00
December		
4	SAN DIEGO	1:00
11	at Houston	12:00
17	WASHINGTON (Sat.)	12:30

Special Teams

The kicking game, the province of punter Scott Fulhage and placekicker Jim Breech, is not a worry. As a punt returner, Martin is better than most, last year averaging 9.9 yards to rank 11th in the NFL, just a blip behind Chicago's Dennis McKinnon. However, for someone willing to travel 'long distances at high speed in the face of obstructions', there would appear to be an opening as a kickoff returner.

1988 DRAFT

Round	Name	Pos.	Ht.	Wt.	College
1.	Dixon, Rickey	DB	5-10	182	Oklahoma
2.	Woods, Ickey	RB	6-0	215	Nevada-Las Vegas
3.	Walker, Kevin	LB	6-2	231	Maryland
4.	Grant, David	NT	6-3	275	West Virginia
5.	Wester, Herb	T	6-7	306	Iowa
6.	Jetton, Paul	G	6-3	291	Texas
7.	Romer, Rich	LB	6-2	212	Union, N.Y.
8.	Maxey, Curtis	NT	6-1	310	Grambling State
9.	Wells, Brandy	DB	5-10	192	Notre Dame
10.	Dillahunt, Ellis	DB	5-10	196	East Carolina
11.	Hickert, Paul	K	6-3	185	Murray State
12.	Parker, Carl	WR	6-2	200	Vanderbilt

VETERAN ROSTER

No.	Name	Pos.	Ht.	Wt.	NFL Year	College
61	Aronson, Doug	G	6-3	290	2	San Diego State
53	Barker, Leo	LB	6-2	227	5	New Mexico State
26	Bell, Leonard	S	5-11	201	1	Indiana
24	Billups, Lewis	CB	5-11	190	3	North Alabama
74	Blados, Brian	T-G	6-5	295	5	North Carolina
55	Brady, Ed	LB	6-2	235	5	Illinois
3	Breech, Jim	K	5-6	161	10	California
21	Brooks, James	RB	5-10	182	8	Auburn
81	Brown, Eddie	WR	6-0	185	4	Miami
99	Buck, Jason	DE	6-5	264	2	Brigham Young
27	Bussey, Barney	S	6-0	195	3	South Carolina State
80	Collinsworth, Cris	WR	6-6	192	8	Florida
93	DeAyala, Kiki	LB	6-1	225	3	Texas
67	Douglas, David	C-G	6-4	280	3	Tennessee
73	Edwards, Eddie	DE	6-5	256	12	Miami
7	Esiason, Boomer	QB	6-4	220	5	Maryland
33	Fulcher, David	S	6-3	228	3	Arizona State
17	Fulhage, Scott	P	5-11	185	2	Kansas State
71	Hammerstein, Mike	NT	6-4	270	3	Michigan
89	Hillary, Ira	WR	5-11	190	2	South Carolina
82	Holman, Rodney	TE	6-3	238	7	Tulane
20	Horton, Ray	CB	5-11	190	6	Washington
92	Inglis, Tim	LB	6-3	241	2	Toledo
37	Jackson, Robert	S	5-10	186	7	Central Michigan
36	Jennings, Stanford	RB	6-1	205	5	Furman
30	Johnson, Bill	RB	6-2	230	4	Arkansas State
84	Kattus, Eric	TE	6-5	235	3	Michigan
58	Kelly, Joe	LB	6-2	227	3	Washington
90	King, Emanuel	LB	6-4	251	4	Alabama
28	Kinnebrew, Larry	RB	6-1	258	6	Tennessee State
64	Kozerski, Bruce	G-C	6-4	275	5	Holy Cross
69	Krumrie, Tim	NT	6-2	262	6	Wisconsin
88	Martin, Mike	WR-PR	5-10	186	6	Illinois
72	McClendon, Skip	DE	6-6	270	2	Arizona State
85	McGee, Tim	WR	5-10	175	3	Tennessee
65	Montoya, Max	G	6-5	275	10	UCLA
78	Munoz, Anthony	T	6-6	278	9	Southern California
12	Norseth, Mike	QB	6-2	200	2	Kansas
75	Reimers, Bruce	G	6-7	280	5	Iowa State
	Reinke, Jeff	DE	6-5	270	1	Mankato State
87	Riggs, Jim	TE	6-5	245	2	Clemson
50	Rimington, Dave	C	6-3	288	6	Nebraska
15	Schonert, Turk	QB	6-1	196	9	Stanford
	Sellers, Lance	LB	6-1	231	2	Boise State
70	Skow, Jim	DE	6-3	250	3	Nebraska
	Thatcher, Chris	G	6-4	275	1	Lafayette
22	Thomas, Eric	CB	5-11	175	2	Tulane
63	Walter, Joe	T	6-6	290	4	Texas Tech
51	White, Leon	LB	6-2	236	3	Brigham Young
41	Wilcots, Solomon	S	5-11	180	2	Colorado
57	Williams, Reggie	LB	6-0	228	13	Dartmouth
32	Wilson, Stanley	RB	5-10	210	3	Oklahoma
49	Wright, Dana	RB	6-1	219	2	Findlay
91	Zander, Carl	LB	6-2	235	4	Tennessee

Boomer Esiason lights the fuses in one of the league's most exciting fireworks displays.

CLEVELAND BROWNS

Address Tower B, Cleveland Stadium, Cleveland, Ohio 44114.

Stadium Cleveland Stadium, Cleveland.
Capacity 80,098 *Playing Surface* Grass.

Team Colours Seal Brown, Orange, and White.

Head Coach Marty Schottenheimer – fifth year.

Championships Division 1971,'80,'85,'86,'87; AAFC 1946,'47,'48,'49; NFL 1950,'54,'55,'64.

History AAFC 1946-49, NFL 1950-69, AFC 1970-

Offense

In the last three campaigns the Browns have won the AFC Central division title. But it is simply not the Browns' way to regard those seasons as successful. They have only one goal, namely, to win the Super Bowl Championship. And each time in the playoffs, they have lost to late scores, twice in the AFC Championship Game. Significantly, though, they have improved steadily, and, if talent in depth and sound organisation are to provide a yardstick, they must be regarded as favourites to represent the AFC in the 'big one'. In 1987, quarterback Bernie Kosar enjoyed his first AFC passing title. Unlike his great rival, Dan Marino, Kosar never quite looks likely to murder the opposition. Rather, his is the style of the ultimate professional; a player able to blank out even the seemingly most hopeless of positions. Furthermore, he has nursed a collection of modest receivers to a level of high efficiency. Six players caught 20 or more passes last year – and at that rate they do not need to be flashy. There is little to choose between Webster Slaughter and Brian Brennan perhaps other than in Slaughter's extra yard of pace. Brennan is a man for the clutch reception whilst the third pure wide receiver, Reggie Langhorne, is a deep threat. Tight end Ozzie Newsome now has caught at least one pass in the last 127 regular season games. With 575 career receptions for 7,073 yards (he is the all-time, NFL-leading tight end in each category) and 42 touchdowns, Newsome is the team's inspirational leader. The bread and butter came from running backs Earnest Byner, with a club-leading 52 receptions, and Kevin Mack, who had 32 catches. Byner can often be seen lining up wide. As pure rushers, in the 1985 campaign, both Mack and Byner rushed for over 1,000 yards, and they gave all the appearance of establishing the NFL's best backfield pair for years to come. However, with the emergence of the passing game, brought about by the arrival of Kosar, the Browns' offense has become more balanced, but it must be of reassurance that, if necessary, head coach Schottenheimer could revert to trench warfare. The starting offensive line, moving from left to right, will consist of Rickey Bolden, Paul Farren, Mike Baab, Dan Fike and Cody Risien. They are really solid and are well backed up by Larry Williams, who started eight games at guard (Farren moved to left tackle) when Bolden was injured, and Gregg Rakoczy.

Defense

Well satisfied with his offense, in the 1988 draft, Schottenheimer took further steps to raise his defense to the levels of the 1986 Giants and perhaps even the 1985 Chicago Bears. The Browns were particularly strong anyway, last year ranking third in the NFL, second against the rush and eighth against the pass. In Bob Golic and backup Dave Puzzuoli, Cleveland may just have the best depth at nose tackle in the conference. Golic could not accept his AFC-NFC Pro Bowl invitation because of an injury, but Puzzuoli stepped in for the playoffs and was a one-man wrecking crew. He may even move ahead of Golic. And there is competition from draftee Michael Dean Perry, whom Schottenheimer feels can make a contribution to the mayhem. Defensive end Carl Hairston is entering his 13th NFL year but is coming off one of his great seasons in which he led the club with eight sacks. Sam Clancy, Reggie Camp, Al Baker and Chris Pike will battle for playing time, both at left end and when giving Hairston a breather. And when the line expands on obvious passing downs, we may see top draftee linebacker Clifford Charlton primed and ready to explode from an outside position. Charlton may start right away in place of Lucius Sanford, who has been released, whilst Clay Matthews, an AFC-NFC Pro Bowler, is a fixture on the other side. Two fierce operators, Mike Johnson and Pro Bowl reserve Eddie Johnson, jam the middle. In addition to solid reserve strength represented by David Grayson, Anthony Griggs and last year's first-round pick, Mike Junkin, there is yet more raw talent in the form of 1988 third-round draftee Van Waiters. The secondary was helped by the drafting of Anthony Blaylock and three safeties, Thane Gash, Danny Copeland and Brian Washington. Last year's starting strong safety, Ray Ellis, has been released, and it is probable that Chris Rockins will step in alongside free safety Felix Wright or Al Gross. Starting cornerbacks Hanford Dixon and Frank Minnifield are regarded as the AFC's best – enough said.

1988 SCHEDULE OF GAMES	September	
	4 at Kansas City	3:00
	11 NEW YORK JETS	4:00
	19 INDIANAPOLIS (Mon.)	8:00
	25 at Cincinnati	1:00
	October	
	2 at Pittsburgh	1:00
	9 SEATTLE	1:00
	16 PHILADELPHIA	1:00
	23 at Phoenix	1:00
	30 CINCINNATI	1:00
	November	
	7 at Houston (Mon.)	8:00
	13 at Denver	2:00
	20 PITTSBURGH	1:00
	27 at Washington	1:00
	December	
	4 DALLAS	1:00
	12 at Miami (Mon.)	9:00
	18 HOUSTON	1:00

Special Teams

Kick returning is a distinct Cleveland strength. Punt returner Gerald (Ice Cube) McNeil is the current AFC Pro Bowler, whilst Glen Young maintained a fine 22.9-yard average on kickoff returns. Either of placekickers Matt Bahr and the young Jeff Jaeger could do the job, but punter Lee Johnson will be challenged in camp.

Earnest Byner.

VETERAN ROSTER

No.	Name	Pos.	Ht.	Wt.	NFL Year	College
61	Baab, Mike	C	6-4	270	7	Texas
9	Bahr, Matt	K	5-10	175	10	Penn State
60	Baker, Al	DE	6-6	270	11	Colorado State
43	Baker, Tony	RB	5-10	175	2	East Carolina
16	Bell, Albert	WR	6-0	170	1	Alabama
77	Bolden, Rickey	T	6-6	280	5	Southern Methodist
36	Braggs, Stephen	CB	5-9	173	2	Texas
86	Brennan, Brian	WR	5-9	178	5	Boston College
97	Bullitt, Steve	LB	6-2	228	1	Texas A&M
44	Byner, Earnest	RB	5-10	215	5	East Carolina
96	Camp, Reggie	DE	6-4	280	6	California
91	Clancy, Sam	DE	6-7	260	5	Pittsburgh
71	Cullity, Dave	T	6-7	275	1	Utah
18	Danielson, Gary	QB	6-2	196	11	Purdue
29	Dixon, Hanford	CB	5-11	186	8	Southern Mississippi
74	Farren, Paul	G-T	6-5	280	6	Boston University
69	Fike, Dan	G	6-7	280	4	Florida
28	Fontenot, Herman	RB	6-0	206	4	Louisiana State
79	Golic, Bob	NT	6-2	270	9	Notre Dame
56	Grayson, David	LB	6-2	229	2	Fresno State
53	Griggs, Anthony	LB	6-3	230	7	Ohio State
27	Gross, Al	S	6-3	195	6	Arizona
78	Hairston, Carl	DE	6-4	260	13	Maryland-East. Shore
65	Haley, Darryl	T	6-4	265	6	Utah
23	Harper, Mark	CB	5-9	174	3	Alcorn State
20	Hill, Will	DB	6-0	197	1	Bishop College
8	Jaeger, Jeff	K	5-11	189	2	Washington
51	Johnson, Eddie	LB	6-1	225	8	Louisville
11	Johnson, Lee	P	6-2	198	4	Brigham Young
59	Johnson, Mike	LB	6-1	228	3	Virginia Tech
95	Jones, Marlon	DE	6-4	260	2	Central State, Okla.
54	Junkin, Mike	LB	6-3	238	2	Duke
19	Kosar, Bernie	QB	6-5	210	4	Miami
88	Langhorne, Reggie	WR	6-2	195	4	Elizabeth City State
25	Logan, Marc	RB	5-11	204	2	Kentucky
34	Mack, Kevin	RB	6-0	225	4	Clemson
42	Manoa, Tim	RB	6-1	227	2	Penn State
57	Matthews, Clay	LB	6-2	235	11	Southern California
89	McNeil, Gerald	WR-PR	5-7	147	3	Baylor
52	Miller, Nick	LB	6-2	238	2	Arkansas
31	Minnifield, Frank	CB	5-9	180	5	Louisville
82	Newsome, Ozzie	TE	6-2	232	11	Alabama
10	Pagel, Mike	QB	6-2	206	7	Arizona State
	Pike, Chris	DE	6-7	291	R	Tulsa
72	Puzzuoli, Dave	NT	6-3	260	6	Pittsburgh
73	Rakoczy, Gregg	C-G	6-6	290	2	Miami
63	Risien, Cody	T	6-7	280	9	Texas A&M
37	Rockins, Chris	S	6-0	195	5	Oklahoma State
40	Sam, Aaron	RB	5-9	196	1	Florida Central
99	Sims, Darryl	DE	6-3	282	4	Wisconsin
84	Slaughter, Webster	WR	6-0	170	3	San Diego State
38	Swarn, George	RB	5-10	205	2	Miami, Ohio
81	Tennell, Derek	TE	6-5	245	2	UCLA
87	Tucker, Travis	TE	6-3	240	4	South Connecticut St.
85	Weathers, Clarence	WR	5-9	170	6	Delaware State
70	Williams, Larry	G	6-5	290	3	Notre Dame
64	Winters, Frank	C	6-3	290	2	Western Illinois
22	Wright, Felix	S	6-2	190	4	Drake
83	Young, Glen	WR-KR	6-2	205	5	Mississippi State

1988 DRAFT

Round	Name	Pos.	Ht.	Wt.	College
1.	Charlton, Clifford	LB	6-2	234	Florida
2.	Perry, Michael Dean	DT	6-0	275	Clemson
3.	Waiters, Van	LB	6-3	235	Indiana
4.	Blaylock, Anthony	DB	5-10	182	Winston-Salem State
7.	Gash, Thane	DB	5-11	192	East Tennessee State
8.	Birden, J.J.	WR	5-9	159	Oregon
9.	Copeland, Danny	DB	6-1	205	Eastern Kentucky
10.	Washington, Brian	DB	6-0	222	Nebraska
11.	Hawkins, Hendley	WR	5-9	183	Nebraska
12.	Slayden, Steve	QB	6-1	186	Duke

HOUSTON OILERS

Address P.O. Box 1516, Houston, Texas 77001.
Stadium Astrodome, Houston.
  Capacity 50,599 *Playing Surface* AstroTurf.
Team Colours Columbia Blue, Scarlet, and White.
Head Coach Jerry Glanville – fourth year.
Championships AFL 1960,'61.
History AFL 1960-69, AFC 1970-

Offense

For the Houston Oilers, 1987 was the year when it all came good, by which is meant that successive drafts and player acquisitions finally produced a contender. And the league is better for it. The building began with the drafting of guard Mike Munchak in 1982 (he is the longest-serving Oilers player). Munchak was the cornerstone of an offensive line which grew stronger with the drafting of guard Bruce Matthews (1983) and tackle Dean Steinkuhler (1984). Center Jay Pennison was an inspired signing from the free agent pool in 1986, and, in 1987, veteran tackle Bruce Davis arrived in a trade with the Raiders. Another major factor has been the emergence of Warren Moon as an authoritative quarterback. It was after the first nine games of the 1986 season that Moon asked to be allowed to try to pass longer more often. His wish was granted, and the Oilers' offense took off. They were 4-3 over the remainder of that season and simply kept on going. Moon is a quarterback just itching to go places, and the partnership of Ernest Givins and Drew Hill at wide receiver is his first-class ticket. Hill, who averaged 20.2 yards on 49 receptions in 1987, was another imaginative acquisition, this time in a trade with the Rams, whilst Givins was even more prolific (he caught 53 passes). Beyond these two, there is the potential talent of the 1987 first-round pick, Haywood Jeffires, whose only problem would be that of inexperience. The Oilers do not expect much by way of pass receptions from the tight end position, but starter Jamie Williams is well respected for his blocking. If the Oilers are sparkling at wide receiver, at running back they look awesome. Former Heisman Trophy winner Mike Rozier has begun to play with presence and certainty, but he may have to yield more ball-carrying time to Alonzo Highsmith, who reminds one of a former Oilers hero, Earl Campbell. Highsmith, a 1987 pick who was known to be an exceptional blocker from his days in college football, signed up only in late October after protracted contractual negotiations. But, towards the end of the campaign, he showed himself to be a player of enormous power and unexpected acceleration. With the drafting of Lorenzo White, an indestructible power runner, to join specialist backs Allen Pinkett, Spencer Tillman and Ray Wallace, the Oilers are extremely well off.

Defense

Last year's defensive line of the third-year players, defensive ends Ray Childress and Richard Byrd, and nose tackle Doug Smith, made tremendous progress even despite Smith's problems with a lingering bout of influenza, Childress's leg troubles and Byrd's back injuries. Also, the coaches felt that Childress and Byrd took time to recover top physical condition after the players' strike. Their effectiveness against the run was not in doubt, but against the pass there were questions, and the Oilers readily sent their first option in round one to the Raiders in exchange for defensive end Sean Jones. The AFC leading sacker in 1986 with 15.5, Jones must help a pass rush in which the leading sacker last year was Childress with a total of six. One does wonder, though, if Jones can be as effective in the Oilers' system. The club has no doubts of his value and they chose not to seek further reinforcement of the pass rush until round nine of the draft, when they selected David Spradlin. They are satisfied at linebacker, too, with Robert Lyles and Johnny Meads on the outsides and John Grimsley paired with Al Smith on the inside. Meads came back well after an injury, whilst Lyles made great progress as a pass defender, even earning a spot in one of the Oilers' 'nickel-back' formations. Grimsley was slowed by an ankle injury for much of the season but he started in every game played by the regulars. Smith was another who played with an injury – he had a problem with his toe – and even though slowed significantly he led the club with 100 tackles. In the secondary, with Bo Eason injured, Jeff Donaldson accepted the opportunity to start at free safety in partnership with Keith Bostic, the latter who led the team with six pass interceptions and went to his first Pro Bowl. Eason saw some action in the last five games and will make a serious bid to regain his old spot. Steve Brown and Patrick Allen form an excellent partnership at cornerback, where reinforcement arrives in the shape of high draftees Quintin Jones and Cris Dishman.

1988 SCHEDULE OF GAMES	September	
	4 at Indianapolis	3:00
	11 LOS ANGELES RAIDERS	3:00
	18 at New York Jets	1:00
	25 NEW ENGLAND	12:00
	October	
	2 at Philadelphia	1:00
	9 KANSAS CITY	12:00
	16 at Pittsburgh	1:00
	23 at Cincinnati	1:00
	30 WASHINGTON	7:00
	November	
	7 CLEVELAND (Mon.)	8:00
	13 at Seattle	1:00
	20 PHOENIX	12:00
	24 at Dallas (Thanksgiving)	3:00
	December	
	4 PITTSBURGH	7:00
	11 CINCINNATI	12:00
	18 at Cleveland	1:00

Special Teams

Tony Zendejas is amongst the NFL's best placekickers, and one imagines that third-round draftee punter Greg Montgomery has an excellent chance of taking over from Jeff Gossett. Returning punts, Kenny Johnson was steady but he may be challenged in camp. Also, Curtis Duncan could use an extra couple of yards on his kickoff return average which was a modest 19.5 yards in 1987.

1988 DRAFT

Round	Name	Pos.	Ht.	Wt.	College
1.	White, Lorenzo	RB	5-10	212	Michigan State
2.	Jones, Quintin	DB	5-11	190	Pittsburgh
3.	Montgomery, Greg	P	6-3	218	Michigan State
5.	Dishman, Cris	DB	6-0	175	Purdue
5.	Verhulst, Chris	TE	6-2	230	Cal State-Chico
6.	Crain, Kurt	LB	6-1	230	Auburn
7.	Eaton, Tracey	DB	6-1	190	Portland State
8.	Viaene, Dave	C	6-5	288	Minnesota-Duluth
9.	Spradlin, David	LB	6-1	228	Texas Christian
10.	Johnson, Marco	WR	5-9	170	Hawaii
11.	Franklin, Jethro	DE	6-1	250	Fresno State
12.	Brantley, John	LB	6-1	223	Georgia

VETERAN ROSTER

No.	Name	Pos.	Ht.	Wt.	NFL Year	College
29	Allen, Patrick	CB	5-10	180	5	Utah State
97	Banks, Robert	DE	6-5	254	1	Notre Dame
36	Birdsong, Craig	S	6-2	217	2	North Texas State
25	Bostic, Keith	S	6-1	223	6	Michigan
24	Brown, Steve	CB	5-11	187	6	Oregon
38	Bryant, Domingo	S	6-4	175	2	Texas A&M
71	Byrd, Richard	DE	6-4	265	4	Southern Mississippi
14	Carlson, Cody	QB	6-3	203	2	Baylor
56	Caston, Toby	LB	6-1	235	2	Louisiana State
79	Childress, Ray	DE	6-6	276	4	Texas A&M
98	Cooks, Rayford	DE	6-3	245	2	North Texas State
77	Davis, Bruce	T	6-6	280	10	UCLA
73	Davis, John	T-G	6-4	304	2	Georgia Tech
31	Donaldson, Jeff	S	6-0	194	5	Colorado
82	Drewery, Willie	WR-PR	5-7	164	4	West Virginia
80	Duncan, Curtis	WR-KR	5-11	184	2	Northwestern
58	Dusbabek, Mark	LB	6-3	232	1	Minnesota
21	Eason, Bo	S	6-2	205	5	Cal-Davis
51	Fairs, Eric	LB	6-3	238	3	Memphis State
95	Fuller, William	DE	6-3	260	3	North Carolina
81	Givins, Ernest	WR	5-9	172	3	Louisville
8	Gossett, Jeff	P	6-2	200	7	Eastern Illinois
59	Grimsley, John	LB	6-2	236	5	Kentucky
83	Harris, Leonard	WR	5-8	165	3	Texas Tech
32	Highsmith, Alonzo	RB	6-1	235	2	Miami
85	Hill, Drew	WR	5-9	170	9	Georgia Tech
49	James, Arrike	TE	6-4	238	2	Delta State
84	Jeffires, Haywood	WR	6-2	198	2	North Carolina State
22	Johnson, Kenny	S-PR	5-10	175	9	Mississippi State
23	Johnson, Richard	CB	6-1	190	4	Wisconsin
57	Johnson, Walter	LB	6-0	241	2	Louisiana Tech
	Jones, Sean	DE	6-7	265	5	Northeastern
93	Lyles, Robert	LB	6-1	223	5	Texas Christian
78	Maggs, Don	T-G	6-5	277	3	Tulane
94	Martin, Charles	NT	6-4	280	5	Livingston
74	Matthews, Bruce	G-C	6-5	280	6	Southern California
26	McMillian, Audrey	CB	6-0	190	4	Houston
91	Meads, Johnny	LB	6-2	230	5	Nicholls State
1	Moon, Warren	QB	6-3	210	5	Washington
63	Munchak, Mike	G	6-3	280	7	Penn State
89	Parks, Jeff	TE	6-4	240	3	Auburn
10	Pease, Brent	QB	6-2	200	2	Montana
52	Pennison, Jay	C	6-1	275	3	Nicholls State
20	Pinkett, Allen	RB-KR	5-9	185	3	Notre Dame
30	Rozier, Mike	RB	5-10	211	4	Nebraska
53	Seale, Eugene	LB	5-10	250	2	Lamar
54	Smith, Al	LB	6-1	230	2	Utah State
99	Smith, Doug	NT	6-5	282	4	Auburn
70	Steinkuhler, Dean	T	6-3	278	5	Nebraska
33	Tillman, Spencer	RB	5-11	206	2	Oklahoma
45	Valentine, Ira	RB	6-0	212	2	Texas A&M
35	Wallace, Ray	RB	6-0	220	3	Purdue
69	Williams, Doug	T	6-5	288	3	Texas A&M
87	Williams, Jamie	TE	6-4	245	6	Nebraska
7	Zendejas, Tony	K	5-8	165	4	Nevada-Reno

Quarterback Warren Moon threw a personal-best 21 touchdown passes in the 1987 campaign.

PITTSBURGH STEELERS

Address Three Rivers Stadium, 300 Stadium Circle,
Pittsburgh, Pa. 15212.

Stadium Three Rivers Stadium, Pittsburgh.
Capacity 59,000 *Playing Surface* AstroTurf.

Team Colours Black and Gold.

Head Coach Chuck Noll – twentieth year.

Championships Division 1972,'74,'75,'76,'77,'78,'79,'83,'84;
Conference 1974,'75,'78,'79; Super Bowl 1974,'75,'78,'79.

History NFL 1933-69, AFC 1970-
(Until 1940, they were known as the Pittsburgh Pirates.)

Offense

As was anticipated, the Steelers did improve in 1987 – they had their first net-winning campaign since 1984 – despite increased competition from Cleveland and the emerging Houston Oilers. Even so, with the philosophy still in favour of building the defense, it may be that 1988 will see a holding operation – a pause for consolidation of gains. The area in most obvious need, namely, at quarterback, may not have been helped by much more than a cosmetic treatment. Mark Malone, who spent eight modest years with the club, has been traded to San Diego, whilst Todd Blackledge arrived via a trade with Kansas City. Blackledge, who owns the dubious distinction of being the only quarterback from that vintage 1983 first-round crop not to make an impact at some time or other, has had an unhappy time with the Chiefs. Occasionally, he would be the coach's favourite but, mostly, he will remember the controversy with Bill Kenney, who, in truth, always looked more likely to run that Chiefs offense. Firstly, though, he'll have to beat out Bubby Brister. Of his wide receivers, Louis Lipps is the target which counts as bullseye, with Charles Lockett as the other likely starter by a nose ahead of the angular Weegie Thompson. From the tight end position, the Steelers look for solid blocking, and, in this respect, Preston Gothard has the edge over Danzell Lee. The Steelers' rushing game requires reliable backs who can exploit the club's particular expertise in blocking systems, which always seems to generate gaps in the most impenetrable of defensive lines. Frank Pollard and Earnest Jackson handle the fullback role whilst Walter Abercrombie is the man they expect to break free for the big gain. In this respect, breakaway speed, Dwight Stone may be ready to show what he can do. Rich Erenberg's status is questionable following reconstructive knee surgery. As always, the offensive line will be excellent. The starters will emerge from tackles Buddy Aydelette and Tunch Ilkin, and guards Craig Wolfley and Terry Long, with John Rienstra as the wild card providing he has overcome his stomach problems. The great center, Mike Webster, is entering his 15th NFL year. Draftees Dermontti Dawson and Chuck Lanza will compete for the honour of being his successor. Elsewhere, Mark Behning and Brian Blankenship are fine backups.

Defense

1987 was the year that the old physical, reckless style of play – Steelers style – resurfaced, and it led to a ranking of 13th overall in the NFL. The Steelers led all other NFL defenses in scoring, producing seven touchdowns, two on fumble returns and five on interception returns. However, a dramatic fall-off in sacks (down to 26 in 15 games from 43 the previous year) must be a worry. There's not much wrong with the starting three-man line of ends Keith Willis and Edmund Nelson, and nose tackle Gary Dunn. Keith Gary was a useful fourth man, chipping in at defensive end in times of need. However, head coach Chuck Noll felt that he needed help and he made defensive end Aaron Jones his first selection. It was a major surprise, since, in many scouting notebooks, Jones was some way down the list and a full dimension below the likes of Neil Smith and Chad Hennings. The Steelers feel that he has good size and super speed. Furthermore, he's an 'every-down' player, durable, and you have the feeling that the Steelers might have picked a 'sleeper'. Looking further down the draft list, the speedy Darin Jordan could be a factor in rebuilding a pass rush. The existing quartet at linebacker did not need any help. On the outsides, Mike Merriweather (1986) and Bryan Hinkle (1987) each has been voted the club's MVP. Merriweather, the blitzer, is always likely to log three sacks in a game. On the inside, David Little is coming off his best year in the pros. Robin Cole, a great Steelers veteran, is beginning to slow and will share increasing time with Gregg Carr and Hardy Nickerson. The secondary is in the early stages of becoming one of the NFL's all-time great quartets. Out of a host of contenders, Dwayne Woodruff, Delton Hall and Rod Woodson will compete for the cornerback positions, whilst Cornell Gowdy and Larry Griffin will battle to start alongside free safety Thomas Everett.

1988 SCHEDULE OF GAMES		
September		
4	DALLAS	1:00
11	at Washington	1:00
18	CINCINNATI	1:00
25	at Buffalo	1:00
October		
2	CLEVELAND	1:00
9	at Phoenix	1:00
16	HOUSTON	1:00
23	DENVER	1:00
30	at New York Jets	1:00
November		
6	at Cincinnati	1:00
13	PHILADELPHIA	1:00
20	at Cleveland	1:00
27	KANSAS CITY	1:00
December		
4	at Houston	7:00
11	at San Diego	1:00
18	MIAMI	1:00

Special Teams

On special teams, Woodson and Stone have enough class to handle kickoff returns, with the speedy Woodson remaining as the most obvious punt returner. Gary Anderson is a Pro Bowl-quality placekicker. And even though punter Harry Newsome is coming off a moderate year, he should be retained.

1988 DRAFT

Round	Name	Pos.	Ht.	Wt.	College
1.	Jones, Aaron	DE	6-4	248	Eastern Kentucky
2.	Dawson, Dermontti	G	6-2	267	Kentucky
3.	Lanza, Chuck	C	6-2	270	Notre Dame
5.	Jordan, Darin	LB	6-1	242	Northeastern
5.	Reese, Jerry	NT	6-1	270	Kentucky
6.	Williams, Warren	RB	5-11	204	Miami
7.	Zeno, Marc	WR	6-2	205	Tulane
8.	Nichols, Mark	NT	6-1	252	Michigan State
8.	Hinnant, Mike	TE	6-2	247	Temple
9.	Lockbaum, Gordie	RB	5-10	195	Holy Cross
10.	Jackson, John	T	6-6	280	Eastern Kentucky
11.	Dawson, Bobby	DB	5-11	210	Illinois
12.	Earle, James	LB	6-4	224	Clemson

VETERAN ROSTER

No.	Name	Pos.	Ht.	Wt.	NFL Year	College
34	Abercrombie, Walt.	RB	6-0	210	7	Baylor
81	Alston, Lyneal	WR	6-1	205	2	Southern Mississippi
1	Anderson, Gary	K	5-11	170	7	Syracuse
72	Aydelette, Buddy	T-C	6-4	262	3	Alabama
66	Behning, Mark	T	6-6	277	2	Nebraska
14	Blackledge, Todd	QB	6-3	219	6	Penn State
60	Blankenship, Brian	G-C	6-1	281	2	Nebraska
15	Bono, Steve	QB	6-4	215	4	UCLA
6	Brister, Bubby	QB	6-3	200	3	Northeast Louisiana
91	Carr, Gregg	LB	6-2	224	4	Auburn
44	Carter, Rodney	RB	6-0	212	2	Purdue
88	Clinkscales, Joey	WR	6-0	204	2	Tennessee
56	Cole, Robin	LB	6-2	225	12	New Mexico
67	Dunn, Gary	NT	6-3	278	12	Miami

No.	Name	Pos.	Ht.	Wt.	Year	College
24	Erenberg, Rich	RB	5-10	205	4	Colgate
27	Everett, Thomas	S-PR	5-9	179	2	Baylor
68	Freeman, Lorenzo	NT	6-5	270	2	Pittsburgh
92	Gary, Keith	DE	6-3	260	6	Oklahoma
86	Gothard, Preston	TE	6-4	242	4	Alabama
29	Gowdy, Cornell	CB-S	6-1	195	3	Morgan State
22	Griffin, Larry	CB	6-0	199	3	North Carolina
35	Hall, Delton	CB	6-1	205	2	Clemson
96	Henton, Anthony	LB	6-1	234	2	Troy State
53	Hinkle, Bryan	LB	6-2	215	7	Oregon
33	Hoge, Merril	RB	6-2	212	2	Idaho State
62	Ilkin, Tunch	T	6-3	265	9	Indiana State
43	Jackson, Earnest	RB	5-9	219	6	Texas A&M
78	Johnson, Tim	DE	6-3	260	2	Penn State
84	Lee, Danzell	TE	6-2	229	2	Lamar
83	Lipps, Louis	WR	5-10	190	5	Southern Mississippi
50	Little, David	LB	6-1	230	8	Florida
95	Lloyd, Greg	LB	6-2	227	1	Fort Valley State
89	Lockett, Charles	WR	6-0	179	2	Cal State-Long Beach
74	Long, Terry	G	5-11	275	5	East Carolina
57	Merriweather, Mike	LB	6-2	221	7	Pacific
	Minter, Mike	DT	6-3	275	2	North Texas State
64	Nelson, Edmund	DE	6-3	266	7	Auburn
18	Newsome, Harry	P	6-0	189	4	Wake Forest
54	Nickerson, Hardy	LB	6-2	224	2	California
30	Pollard, Frank	RB	5-10	230	9	Baylor
76	Quick, Jerry	G	6-5	273	2	Wichita State
79	Rienstra, John	G	6-5	269	3	Temple
47	Riley, Cameron	DB	6-1	195	2	Missouri
28	Sanchez, Lupe	S	5-10	195	3	UCLA
20	Stone, Dwight	RB-KR	6-0	188	2	Middle Tennessee St.
90	Stowe, Tyronne	LB	6-1	232	2	Rutgers
87	Thompson, Weegie	WR	6-6	210	5	Florida State
52	Webster, Mike	C	6-2	254	15	Wisconsin
98	Williams, Gerald	DE-NT	6-3	270	3	Auburn
93	Willis, Keith	DE	6-1	260	7	Northeastern
73	Wolfley, Craig	G-T	6-1	272	9	Syracuse
49	Woodruff, Dwayne	CB	6-0	198	9	Louisville
26	Woodson, Rod	CB-KR	6-0	202	2	Purdue
80	Young, Theo	TE	6-2	237	2	Arkansas

Rod Woodson is a player of great presence.

DENVER BRONCOS

Address 5700 Logan Street, Denver, Colorado 80216.
Stadium Denver Mile High Stadium.
   Capacity 76,274
   Playing Surface Grass (Prescription Athletic Turf).
Team Colours Orange, Royal Blue, and White.
Head Coach Dan Reeves – eighth year.
Championships Division 1977,'78,'84,'86,'87;
   Conference 1977,'86,'87.
History AFL 1960-69, AFC 1970-

Offense

For the second successive year the Broncos are faced with the task of regrouping after suffering a major defeat in the Super Bowl. And, if anything, they are in even better shape to do it than last year. They took a big step towards beefing up the offensive line by drafting tackle Gerald Perry, whose 300-plus pounds will bolster what was considered to be a lightweight outfit. The strength of the line lies on the left side in Dave Studdard and Keith Bishop. Jim Juriga returns from injury and may even challenge Studdard, whose knee injury in the Super Bowl has required surgery. Again, Billy Bryan would provide a boost at center were he to return from injury. Otherwise, Mike Freeman will continue, with the pairing of Stefan Humphries and Ken Lanier on his right. The key to maintaining the Broncos' momentum is, of course, the play of quarterback John Elway. On his day he is 'Superman', but there are those who felt that, last year, at times he was just too much of a one-man show. With a fully-fit squad, the club does provide him with a high-quality, if not superstar supporting cast. Sammy Winder is the model of reliability at halfback, and fullback Gene Lang did enough in short bursts to suggest that he might become a big factor. Thus far, the long-striding Steve Sewell, scything through the line or flaring out to catch passes, has given only a taste of what he could achieve. Joe Dudek, who helped out in the replacement games, might secure a place on the roster if Gerald Willhite cannot return after suffering that dreadful leg injury in late October. At wide receiver there is an embarrassment of talent, led by 'The Three Amigos', Vance Johnson, Mark Jackson and Ricky Nattiel. All three have tremendous deep speed. Sam Graddy is even faster but he has yet to show that he can hang onto the ball. Former starter Steve Watson has no trouble in the latter respect, but he may lose out in the scramble for playing time. Happily, as he demonstrated last year, tight end Clarence Kay has overcome the attitude problems which stifled his talents, and his blossoming came at a time when backup Orson Mobley underlined his class. Mobley, a player of terrific size for a tight end, appears to be only the opportunity away from becoming another Mark Bavaro.

Defense

It was one of the surprises last year when the Denver defense became ordinary, for want of a better word. Perhaps that should have been expected following the retirements of Louis Wright and Steve Foley in particular. And they were ravaged by injuries to key players, amongst which were Dennis Smith, Randy Robbins and, in the playoffs, Mike Harden. Almost everywhere, including the pass rush, they were modest, when judged by their own high standards. They must hope that defensive end Rulon Jones and linebacker Karl Mecklenburg, both of whom came to life only in the playoffs, can maintain that form. They did have a problem at nose tackle, where the preseason injury to Tony Colorito left Greg Kragen unchallenged. First-round pick Ted Gregory could be the long-term answer, but even the best draftee linemen always seem to need time to gear up to the sheer physical requirements of the pros. Andrew Provence, who was obtained in an offseason trade with Atlanta, will challenge Andre Townsend for playing time in partnership with Jones. The linebacking quartet was not reinforced in the draft and we must expect Simon Fletcher, Ricky Hunley and Jim Ryan to line up alongside Mecklenburg, with Michael Brooks, Marc Munford and Rick Dennison as the senior backups. The defensive secondary could leap right back with the rehabilitation of Harden and with Dennis Smith back to full fitness. Harden would start at free safety with Smith at strong safety. In the terminology of professional soccer, both men 'can make things happen', picking off passes, causing fumbles, charging down kicks and the like. Elsewhere, though, on the existing veteran roster, there was a shortage of sharpness and authority, and it was a gap which the Broncos recognised when they drafted Kevin Guidry and Corris Ervin. Randy Robbins and Tony Lilly give modest depth at safety, whilst Jeremiah Castille will battle with Mark Haynes and Steve Wilson to start on the corners.

1988 SCHEDULE OF GAMES	September	
	4 SEATTLE	2:00
	11 SAN DIEGO	2:00
	18 at Kansas City	12:00
	26 LOS ANGELES RAIDERS (Mon.)	6:00
	October	
	2 at San Diego	1:00
	9 at San Francisco	1:00
	16 ATLANTA	2:00
	23 at Pittsburgh	1:00
	31 at Indianapolis (Mon.)	9:00
	November	
	6 KANSAS CITY	2:00
	13 CLEVELAND	2:00
	20 at New Orleans	12:00
	27 LOS ANGELES RAMS	2:00
	December	
	4 at Los Angeles Raiders	1:00
	11 at Seattle	5:00
	17 NEW ENGLAND (Sat.)	2:00

Special Teams

Placekicker Rich Karlis now looks settled for a long career with the Broncos and Mike Horan is one of the better punters. K. C. Clark showed unexpected elusiveness returning punts at an average of 12.9 yards, especially on his 71-yard multi-sidestep ramble for a touchdown. Ken Bell and Vance Johnson take care of the kickoff returns at a respectable standard.

1988 DRAFT

Round	Name	Pos.	Ht.	Wt.	College
1.	Gregory, Ted	NT	6-1	262	Syracuse
2.	Perry, Gerald	T	6-5	308	Southern
3.	Guidry, Kevin	DB	6-0	178	Louisiana State
5.	Ervin, Corris	DB	5-11	175	Central Florida
7.	Kelly, Pat	TE	6-6	236	Syracuse
7.	Frank, Garry	G	6-2	288	Mississippi State
9.	Farr, Mel	RB	6-0	215	UCLA
10.	Williams, Channing	RB	5-9	220	Arizona State
11.	Calvin, Richard	RB	6-0	205	Washington State
12.	Carter, Johnny	NT	6-2	288	Grambling State

VETERAN ROSTER

No.	Name	Pos.	Ht.	Wt.	NFL Year	College
86	Andrews, Mitch	TE	6-2	239	2	Louisiana State
53	Baran, Dave	T	6-6	275	1	UCLA
35	Bell, Ken	RB-KR	5-10	190	3	Boston College
54	Bishop, Keith	G	6-3	265	8	Baylor
24	Boddie, Tony	RB	5-11	198	2	Montana State
65	Bowyer, Walt	DE	6-4	260	5	Arizona State
34	Braxton, Tyrone	S	5-11	174	2	North Dakota State
56	Brooks, Michael	LB	6-1	235	2	Louisiana State
64	Bryan, Billy	C	6-2	255	11	Duke
95	Bryan, Steve	NT	6-2	256	2	Oklahoma
28	Castille, Jeremiah	CB	5-10	175	6	Alabama
27	Clark, K.C.	S-PR	5-10	185	2	San Jose State
69	Colorito, Tony	DE	6-5	260	2	Southern California
42	Demerritt, James	RB	6-0	215	1	Jackson State
55	Dennison, Rick	LB	6-3	220	7	Colorado State
	Dorsett, Tony	RB	5-11	188	12	Pittsburgh
32	Dudek, Joe	RB	6-0	181	2	Plymouth State
7	Elway, John	QB	6-3	210	6	Stanford
73	Fletcher, Simon	LB	6-5	240	4	Houston
62	Freeman, Mike	C	6-3	256	4	Arizona
90	Gilbert, Freddie	DE	6-4	275	3	Georgia
83	Graddy, Sam	WR	5-10	165	2	Tennessee
31	Harden, Mike	S	6-1	192	9	Michigan
36	Haynes, Mark	CB	5-11	195	9	Colorado
78	Hood, Winford	G	6-3	265	5	Georgia
2	Horan, Mike	P	5-11	190	5	Cal State-Long Beach
60	Howard, Paul	G	6-3	260	14	Brigham Young
79	Humphries, Stefan	G	6-3	268	5	Michigan
98	Hunley, Ricky	LB	6-2	238	5	Arizona
80	Jackson, Mark	WR	5-9	174	3	Purdue
82	Johnson, Vance	WR	5-11	174	4	Arizona
20	Jones, Daryl	CB	6-0	193	2	Georgia
75	Jones, Rulon	DE	6-6	260	9	Utah State
66	Juriga, Jim	T	6-6	269	1	Illinois
12	Karcher, Ken	QB	6-3	205	2	Tulane
3	Karlis, Rich	K	6-0	180	7	Cincinnati
72	Kartz, Keith	T	6-4	270	2	California
88	Kay, Clarence	TE	6-2	237	5	Georgia
97	Klostermann, Bruce	LB	6-4	225	2	South Dakota State
71	Kragen, Greg	NT	6-3	245	4	Utah State
8	Kubiak, Gary	QB	6-0	192	6	Texas A&M
33	Lang, Gene	RB-KR	5-10	196	5	Louisiana State
76	Lanier, Ken	T	6-3	269	8	Florida State
68	Lee, Larry	C-G	6-2	263	8	UCLA
22	Lilly, Tony	S	6-0	199	5	Florida
59	Lucas, Tim	LB	6-3	230	2	California
29	Marshall, Warren	RB	6-0	216	2	James Madison
85	Massie, Rick	WR	6-1	190	2	Kentucky
77	Mecklenburg, Karl	LB	6-3	230	6	Minnesota
46	Micho, Bobby	RB-TE	6-3	240	4	Texas
89	Mobley, Orson	TE	6-5	256	3	Salem College
51	Munford, Marc	LB	6-2	231	2	Nebraska
84	Nattiel, Ricky	WR	5-9	180	2	Florida
38	Plummer, Bruce	S-CB	6-1	197	2	Mississippi State
	Provence, Andrew	DE	6-3	267	6	South Carolina
93	Reed, Richard	DE	6-3	260	1	Oklahoma
74	Remsberg, Dan	T	6-6	275	3	Abilene Christian
48	Robbins, Randy	S	6-2	189	5	Arizona
50	Ryan, Jim	LB	6-1	225	10	William & Mary
30	Sewell, Steve	RB	6-3	210	4	Oklahoma
49	Smith, Dennis	S	6-3	200	8	Southern California
70	Studdard, Dave	T	6-4	260	10	Texas
61	Townsend, Andre	DE	6-3	265	5	Mississippi
81	Watson, Steve	WR	6-4	195	10	Temple
58	Wilkinson, Rafe	LB	6-3	235	1	Richmond
47	Willhite, Gerald	RB	5-10	200	7	San Jose State
45	Wilson, Steve	CB	5-10	195	10	Howard
23	Winder, Sammy	RB	5-11	203	7	Southern Mississippi

John Elway is the beating heart of the Broncos offense.

KANSAS CITY CHIEFS

Address One Arrowhead Drive, Kansas City, Missouri
64129.
Stadium Arrowhead Stadium, Kansas City.
Capacity 78,067 *Playing Surface* AstroTurf-8.
Team Colours Red, Gold, and White.
Head Coach Frank Gansz – second year.
Championships Division 1971; AFL 1962,'66,'69;
Super Bowl 1969.
History AFL 1960-69, AFC 1970-
(Until 1963, they were known as the Dallas Texans.)

Offense

Kansas City's collapse was one of the least explicable aspects of the 1987 season. Even allowing for a weakness on defense, which probably was overstated by head coach Frank Gansz, it is easy to imagine their contending for honours even though they play in the difficult AFC West. During the offseason, they traded Todd Blackledge to Pittsburgh, solving what had been a difficulty at quarterback in the sense that, as long as he was there, a controversy always was possible. For a brief period, then, Bill Kenney was the undisputed starter, ahead of Frank Seurer. And Kenney, whose experience and standing is such that he calls his own plays, could certainly take the Chiefs to the playoffs, given any kind of luck. However, subsequently, the Chiefs signed former 49ers, Broncos and Buccaneers quarterback Steve DeBerg, who is not only as good as any other backup in the NFL, but is good enough to start. It all suggests another potential controversy, and that would be a pity. The Chiefs' wide receivers are excellent. Led by AFC-NFC Pro Bowler Carlos Carson and Stephone Paige, they can strike from any point on the field. Henry Marshall is one of the best backups around and could so easily revert to the role of starter should the need arise. They didn't have quite the depth of recent years, but the selection of J. R. Ambrose in the fourth round of the draft should solve that problem. At tight end, Jonathan Hayes should continue as the starter. At last the Chiefs have the makings of a rushing game. Rookie Christian Okoye didn't have quite the effect we were all hoping for, but he represented a raw threat every time he took a handoff. And Herman Heard, a much underrated player, made good progress to become Okoye's established starting partner. Paul Palmer sparkled on his limited opportunities and it may be that the club is now willing to expose him to a little more physical contact. The only problem on the offensive line seems to be that of finding the right formula from a crowd consisting of three or four genuine starters and several of near-starter class. Guard Mark Adickes and tackle Irv Eatman will probably start on the right side, with tackle John Alt and guard Brad Budde on the left. Tom Baugh may have an edge over Rick Donnalley at center. In David Lutz, Brian Jozwiak and Rich Baldinger, there is talented and experienced depth.

Defense

What was expected to become a dominant force, the defense, never emerged and Gansz sought immediate remedial treatment by selecting defensive end Neil Smith in the first round of the draft. He wanted Smith so badly that he was prepared to pay the price of the 29th option (it was traded to Detroit) in the draft simply to move up to a position of certainty. Let's hope that Smith invigorates a pass rush which logged only 26 sacks in fifteen games last year. The existing three-man line of defensive ends Mike Bell and Art Still, and nose tackle Bill Maas, is outstanding, at least on its form before last year's hiccup. And it would not make sense to use Smith instead of either Still or Bell. One imagines the Chiefs using more four-man fronts on second down, especially if, say, they've held the opposition to a short gain on first down. Linebacking has been a relative weakness for some time, but there are signs of improvement with inside linebacker Dino Hackett as the focal point and Aaron Pearson performing well enough in Hackett's shadow. However, they could use a greater contribution from outside linebackers Tim Cofield and Louis Cooper, who were no better than par in 1987 and, at one stage, saw their starting roles in jeopardy. Once more, though, Smith's involvement, in any capacity, should help out. Jack Del Rio and Todd Howard are versatile reserves. The secondary could easily bounce back to its former status as, on its day, the league's most dangerous. All of safeties Lloyd Burruss and Deron Cherry, and cornerback Albert Lewis are current or former AFC-NFC Pro Bowlers. There really could not be any complaints over the play of right cornerback Kevin Ross, who has started in every game of his pro career. Also, there is excellent depth in Sherman Cocroft and J. C. Pearson, and third-round draftee Kevin Porter was an excellent investment.

1988 SCHEDULE OF GAMES		
September		
4 CLEVELAND		3:00
11 at Seattle		1:00
18 DENVER		12:00
25 SAN DIEGO		3:00
October		
2 at New York Jets		4:00
9 at Houston		12:00
16 LOS ANGELES RAIDERS		12:00
23 DETROIT		12:00
30 at Los Angeles Raiders		1:00
November		
6 at Denver		2:00
13 CINCINNATI		12:00
20 SEATTLE		12:00
27 at Pittsburgh		1:00
December		
4 NEW YORK JETS		3:00
11 at New York Giants		1:00
18 at San Diego		1:00

Dino Hackett is a major force at inside linebacker.

Special Teams

Twice the special team sprung rookie Paul Palmer for touchdowns on kickoff returns, whilst Jitter Fields scored on a punt return. Palmer must be respected every time he touches the ball, and regular punt returner Michael Clemons did well enough, averaging 8.5 yards. Placekicker Nick Lowery could get a job anywhere, but for the punting role there will be a fair old duel between Lewis Colbert and Kelly Goodburn in camp.

1988 DRAFT

Round	Name	Pos.	Ht.	Wt.	College
1.	Smith, Neil	DE	6-4	260	Nebraska
3.	Porter, Kevin	DB	5-10	209	Auburn
4.	Ambrose, J.R.	WR	6-0	186	Mississippi
6.	Saxon, James	RB	5-11	197	San Jose State
7.	Stedman, Troy	LB	6-2	233	Washburn
8.	Roberts, Alfredo	TE	6-3	244	Miami
9.	Abdur-Ra'oof, Azizuddin	WR	6-0	197	Maryland
10.	Gamble, Kenny	RB	5-10	190	Colgate
11.	McManus, Danny	QB	5-11	200	Florida State

VETERAN ROSTER

No.	Name	Pos.	Ht.	Wt.	NFL Year	College
61	Adickes, Mark	G	6-4	270	3	Baylor
76	Alt, John	T	6-7	290	5	Iowa
87	Arnold, Walt	TE	6-3	228	9	New Mexico
91	Baldinger, Gary	DE	6-3	265	3	Wake Forest
77	Baldinger, Rich	G-T	6-4	285	6	Wake Forest
58	Baugh, Tom	C-G	6-3	274	3	Southern Illinois
99	Bell, Mike	DE	6-4	260	8	Colorado State
71	Budde, Brad	G	6-4	271	8	Southern California
34	Burruss, Lloyd	S	6-0	209	8	Maryland
88	Carson, Carlos	WR	5-11	180	9	Louisiana State
20	Cherry, Deron	S	5-11	193	8	Rutgers
46	Clemons, Michael	RB-PR	5-5	166	2	William & Mary
22	Cocroft, Sherman	S-CB	6-1	192	4	San Jose State
54	Cofield, Tim	LB	6-2	245	3	Elizabeth City State
81	Colbert, Darrell	WR	5-10	174	2	Texas Southern
5	Colbert, Lewis	P	5-11	179	3	Auburn
55	Cooper, Louis	LB	6-2	240	4	Western Carolina

No.	Name	Pos.	Ht.	Wt.	Year	College
	DeBerg, Steve	QB	6-3	210	11	San Jose State
50	Del Rio, Jack	LB	6-4	238	4	Southern California
51	Donnalley, Rick	C	6-2	260	7	North Carolina
75	Eatman, Irv	T	6-7	293	3	UCLA
40	Fields, Jitter	CB-PR	5-9	180	3	Texas
48	Garron, Andre	RB	5-11	193	1	New Hampshire
2	Goodburn, Kelly	P	6-2	195	2	Emporia State
98	Griffin, Leonard	DE	6-4	258	3	Grambling State
56	Hackett, Dino	LB	6-3	228	3	Appalachian State
57	Harrell, James	LB	6-2	240	9	Florida
86	Harry, Emile	WR	5-11	175	2	Stanford
85	Hayes, Jonathan	TE	6-5	240	4	Iowa
44	Heard, Herman	RB	5-10	182	5	Southern Colorado
93	Holle, Eric	NT	6-5	265	5	Texas
53	Howard, Todd	LB	6-2	235	2	Texas A&M
11	Hudson, Doug	QB	6-2	201	2	Nicholls State
52	Hyde, Glenn	C	6-3	255	11	Pittsburgh
60	Ingram, Byron	C-G	6-2	270	2	Eastern Kentucky
45	Johnson, Sidney	CB	5-9	170	1	California
73	Jozwiak, Brian	G	6-5	310	3	West Virginia
80	Keel, Mark	TE	6-4	228	2	Arizona
9	Kenney, Bill	QB	6-4	207	10	Northern Colorado
74	Koch, Pete	DT	6-6	265	5	Maryland
29	Lewis, Albert	CB	6-2	192	6	Grambling State
8	Lowery, Nick	K	6-4	189	9	Dartmouth
72	Lutz, David	T	6-6	290	6	Georgia Tech
63	Maas, Bill	NT	6-5	268	5	Pittsburgh
89	Marshall, Henry	WR	6-2	216	13	Missouri
94	McAlister, Ken	LB	6-5	230	7	San Francisco
32	Moriarty, Larry	RB	6-1	237	6	Notre Dame
35	Okoye, Christian	RB	6-1	253	2	Azusa Pacific
83	Paige, Stephone	WR	6-2	185	6	Fresno State
26	Palmer, Paul	RB-KR	5-9	184	2	Temple
96	Pearson, Aaron	LB	6-0	240	3	Mississippi State
24	Pearson, J.C.	CB	5-11	183	3	Washington
31	Ross, Kevin	CB	5-9	182	5	Temple
65	Rourke, Jim	G-T	6-5	263	8	Boston College
10	Seurer, Frank	QB	6-1	195	3	Kansas
	Snipes, Angelo	LB	6-0	229	3	West Georgia
59	Spani, Gary	LB	6-2	229	10	Kansas State
67	Still, Art	DE	6-7	255	11	Kentucky
	Taylor, Kitrick	WR-KR	5-10	183	1	Washington State
	Woodard, Ray	DE	6-6	290	2	Texas

LOS ANGELES RAIDERS

Address 332 Center Street, El Segundo, California 90245.
Stadium Los Angeles Memorial Coliseum.
 Capacity 92,516 *Playing Surface* Grass.
Team Colours Silver and Black.
Head Coach Mike Shanahan – first year.
Championships Division 1970,'72,'73,'74,'75,'76,'83,'85;
 Conference 1976,'80,'83; AFL 1967;
 Super Bowl 1976,'80,'83.
History AFL 1960-69, AFC 1970-
 (Until 1982, they were known as the Oakland Raiders.)

Offense

With three selections in the first round of the draft, clearly there are going to be changes in the near future if not right away. But the most significant aspect of the offseason may well have been the implicit confirmation of Marc Wilson as the starting quarterback. Rumour upon rumour had the Raiders going after Philadelphia's Randall Cunningham, and then the target, it was said, was Redskins backup Jay Schroeder. Then someone remembered that Wilson wasn't that bad after all, indeed, he's healthy, he's brave and there's nothing wrong with his arm. Rusty Hilger would not be regarded as the best backup in the NFL but, at a time when the Raiders look thin in more than one area, he'll have to do, with Steve Beuerlein as a long-term project. So much of Wilson's fortunes rest on the play of others, not least the offensive line and at running back. Of course, Bo Jackson's early appearance would be a major boost, but it seems likely that he will remain in pro baseball until the termination of the Royals' involvement in the chase for honours. Jackson alone would give the club an offense and it is because of his very brilliance that the many talents of Marcus Allen are overlooked. Just a return to something like his efficient best would be enough for any club. Allen's probable starting partner will be one of Frank Hawkins, Steve Strachan and Steve Smith, with Vance Mueller as the reserve halfback. The offensive line did make progress and it can enter the 1988 campaign with some optimism. Increasingly, center Don Mosebar looks like emulating his great Raiders predecessors. Elsewhere on the line, tackle John Clay is expected to make an impact and another 1987 rookie, Bruce Wilkerson, could start, either at tackle or guard, such was his demonstrated versatility last year. Bill Lewis made the transition from center to guard without too much difficulty. Of the older veterans, an in-form Brian Holloway could make a major contribution, say, in the key area of left tackle, whilst Charley Hannah still has a part to play at guard. The receivers are excellent. Just imagine the superb James Lofton homing in on a long ball, top draftee Tim Brown curling over the middle and Jessie Hester trying to outdo the pair of them. Todd Christensen will be straining to re-establish his status as the NFL's most prolific tight end whilst Allen can always steal the show.

Defense

They may not strike quite the fear in the opposition, and there are one or two grey hairs showing, but the 1988 defense will be no more generous than the 1987 unit which, in league terms, ranked fifth overall, seventh against the rush and second against the pass. Defensive end Sean Jones has been traded to Houston, but there's no shortage of talent, even though in two first-round picks, Bob Buczkowski (1986) and rookie Scott Davis, as yet it is latent. Defensive end Howie Long still rates double-teaming, a fact of life for the opposition which is obliged to leave the other defensive end in single coverage. In that sense, Long and his good mate, nose tackle Bill Pickel, could make a hero out of anybody lining up in the other end position. Greg Townsend is a fine pass rusher – last year he led the club with 8.5 quarterback sacks – and it is healthy that Malcolm Taylor will apply more pressure on Pickel. Tim Rother, a fourth-round draftee, assures the club's strength for the future. Behind the line, the quality does begin to fall off, slowly at linebacker before making a dip in the secondary. Perhaps that may be too unkind a judgement, particularly in the secondary, but it is a fact that the defense can no longer take for granted the Raiders' certainty of dominating in one-on-one coverage. Cornerback Mike Haynes used to represent the state of the art but he has slowed. Neither of Ron Fellows and Lionel Washington would be regarded as of normal Raiders standing. No one has yet replaced former starting strong safety Mike Davis – although Stacey Toran is improving. However, free safety Vann McElroy is every inch a true Raider – he's lethal – and first-round draftee cornerback Terry McDaniel may just come through to start. At linebacker there is still a solid core on the inside, where Matt Millen and Reggie McKenzie jam the run, but, on the outside, Rod Martin is slowing and Jerry Robinson has never really established his role as pass rusher or pass defender. Linden King, Jamie Kimmel and Jeff Barnes are steady backups.

1988 SCHEDULE OF GAMES

September		
4 SAN DIEGO		1:00
11 at Houston		3:00
18 LOS ANGELES RAMS		1:00
26 at Denver (Mon.)		6:00
October		
2 CINCINNATI		1:00
9 MIAMI		1:00
16 at Kansas City		12:00
23 at New Orleans		12:00
30 KANSAS CITY		1:00
November		
6 at San Diego		5:00
13 at San Francisco		1:00
20 ATLANTA		1:00
28 at Seattle (Mon.)		6:00
December		
4 DENVER		1:00
11 at Buffalo		1:00
18 SEATTLE		1:00

Special Teams

'Steady without being spectacular' would be a fair description of the kicking game which is in the care of placekicker Chris Bahr and punter Stan Talley. Curiously, the Raiders don't usually feature an expressive returner, though it might be as a punt returner that Brown earns his first headline. Mueller is a much underrated kickoff returner.

1988 DRAFT

Round	Name	Pos.	Ht.	Wt.	College
1.	Brown, Tim	WR	5-11	194	Notre Dame
1.	McDaniel, Terry	DB	5-10	174	Tennessee
1.	Davis, Scott	DE	6-7	265	Illinois
4.	Rother, Tim	DT	6-7	270	Nebraska
5.	Price, Dennis	DB	6-1	170	UCLA
6.	Grabisna, Erwin	LB	6-2	243	Case Western
7.	Crudup, Derrick	DB	6-2	212	Oklahoma
8.	Alexander, Mike	WR	6-2	202	Penn State
9.	Ware, Reggie	RB	6-1	240	Auburn
9.	Tabor, Scott	P	6-2	192	California
10.	Harrell, Newt	T	6-5	295	West Texas State
11.	Weber, David	QB	6-3	200	Carroll, Wis.
12.	Kunkel, Greg	G	6-4	282	Kentucky

VETERAN ROSTER

No.	Name	Pos.	Ht.	Wt.	NFL Year	College
44	Adams, Stefon	S-PR	5-10	190	3	East Carolina
32	Allen, Marcus	RB	6-2	205	7	Southern California
33	Anderson, Eddie	S	6-1	200	3	Fort Valley State
10	Bahr, Chris	K	5-10	170	13	Penn State
56	Barnes, Jeff	LB	6-2	230	12	California
	Bennett, Barry	DE	6-4	260	11	Concordia, Minn.
	Beuerlein, Steve	QB	6-2	205	1	Notre Dame
95	Buczkowski, Bob	DE	6-5	265	2	Pittsburgh
46	Christensen, Todd	TE	6-3	230	10	Brigham Young
78	Clay, John	T	6-5	295	2	Missouri
92	Cormier, Joe	LB	6-6	225	2	Southern California
45	Davis, James	S	6-0	200	7	Southern
11	Evans, Vince	QB	6-2	205	9	Southern California
21	Fellows, Ron	CB	6-0	175	8	Missouri
86	Fernandez, Mervyn	WR	6-3	200	2	San Jose State
63	Gesek, John	C	6-5	275	1	Cal State-Sacramento
73	Hannah, Charley	G	6-5	270	12	Alabama
27	Hawkins, Frank	RB	5-9	210	8	Nevada-Reno
37	Hayes, Lester	CB	6-0	200	11	Texas A&M
22	Haynes, Mike	CB	6-2	190	13	Arizona State
84	Hester, Jessie	WR	5-11	170	4	Florida State
12	Hilger, Rusty	QB	6-4	205	4	Oklahoma State
76	Holloway, Brian	T	6-7	285	8	Stanford
34	Jackson, Bo	RB	6-1	230	2	Auburn
74	Jordan, Shelby	T	6-7	280	12	Washington, Mo.
87	Junkin, Trey	TE	6-2	230	6	Louisiana Tech
59	Kimmel, Jamie	LB	6-3	235	3	Syracuse
52	King, Linden	LB	6-4	245	11	Colorado State
51	Lewis, Bill	G	6-7	275	3	Nebraska
80	Lofton, James	WR	6-3	190	11	Stanford
75	Long, Howie	DE	6-5	265	8	Villanova
60	Marsh, Curt	G	6-5	275	5	Washington
53	Martin, Rod	LB	6-2	225	12	Southern California
65	Marvin, Mickey	G	6-4	265	11	Tennessee
	McCallum, Nap.	RB	6-2	215	2	Navy
26	McElroy, Vann	S	6-2	195	7	Baylor
54	McKenzie, Reggie	LB	6-1	235	4	Tennessee
20	McLemore, Chris	RB	6-1	225	2	Arizona
55	Millen, Matt	LB	6-2	245	9	Penn State
64	Miraldi, Dean	G-T	6-5	280	5	Utah
72	Mosebar, Don	C	6-6	275	6	Southern California
42	Mueller, Vance	RB	6-0	210	3	Occidental
81	Parker, Andy	TE	6-5	245	5	Utah
71	Pickel, Bill	NT	6-5	260	6	Rutgers
16	Plunkett, Jim	QB	6-2	220	17	Stanford
	Riehm, Chris	G	6-6	275	3	Ohio State
57	Robinson, Jerry	LB	6-2	225	10	UCLA
43	Seale, Sam	CB	5-9	185	5	Western State, Colo.
35	Smith, Steve	RB	6-1	235	2	Penn State
39	Strachan, Steve	RB	6-1	215	4	Boston College
5	Talley, Stan	P	6-5	220	2	Texas Christian
96	Taylor, Malcolm	NT	6-6	280	5	Tennessee State
30	Toran, Stacey	S	6-2	200	5	Notre Dame
93	Townsend, Greg	DE	6-3	250	6	Texas Christian
	Tubbs, Brad	WR	6-4	200	1	St. Mary's, California
48	Washington, Lionel	CB	6-0	185	6	Tulane
91	Washington, Ronnie	LB	6-1	245	3	Northeast Louisiana
67	Wheeler, Dwight	G	6-3	285	8	Tennessee State
68	Wilkerson, Bruce	G	6-5	280	2	Tennessee
98	Willis, Mitch	NT	6-8	280	4	Southern Methodist
6	Wilson, Marc	QB	6-6	205	9	Brigham Young
90	Wise, Mike	DE	6-6	260	2	Cal-Davis
88	Woods, Chris	WR-PR	5-11	185	2	Auburn
66	Wright, Steve	T	6-6	275	6	Northern Iowa

James Lofton maintained the Raiders' tradition as a deep-threat wide receiver.

SAN DIEGO CHARGERS

Address San Diego Jack Murphy Stadium, P.O. Box 20666, San Diego, California 92120.

Stadium San Diego Jack Murphy Stadium. *Capacity* 60,750 *Playing Surface* Grass.

Team Colours Blue, White, and Gold.

Head Coach Al Saunders – third year.

Championships Division 1979,'80,'81; AFL 1963.

History AFL 1960-69, AFC 1970-

(For 1960 only, they were known as the Los Angeles Chargers.)

Offense

1987 saw a dramatic change in the character of a team whose offense, in the past, always promised to be the most expressive in the NFL. The philosophy shifted from passing to rushing, and, whilst the passing game was indeed more conservative, the rushing game never developed as a force. The Chargers enter the 1988 season without the services of their great quarterback, Dan Fouts, whose retirement breaks the final link with the early days under Don Coryell, when their reputation was established. In the search for a quarterback to propel the club into the new era, the Chargers have signed veterans Mark Malone (ex-Steelers) and Steve Fuller (ex-Chiefs and Bears), who join second-year player Mark Vlasic. For the lucky starter, it will be no easy task. But it is not as if the Chargers are lacking in talent. Tight end Kellen Winslow is almost back to the kind of form which, before he suffered a serious knee injury in 1984, made him an almost automatic all-pro selection. Eleventh-year wide receiver Wes Chandler still has a major role to play, even though he may be slowing a little. Entering training camp, Lionel James is projected as the other starter. If either of the two rookies, Anthony Miller and Quinn Early, can make the adjustment to pro football, there ought to be no problems catching passes. Furthermore, the club can expect continued productivity from running back Gary Anderson, whose 47 receptions in 1987 gave him second place on the team behind Winslow (53). When it comes to rushing, however, it is a telling statement that not one of the running backs averaged as high as four yards per carry in 1987. Anderson should continue to start, if only for reasons of his versatility, but the club must be hoping that the former Rams running back, Barry Redden, can reproduce his best. A potential 1,000-yard rusher – and he'd rip them off in great style – Redden could make the club a serious contender. Encouragingly, James FitzPatrick came through to start at left guard, and the signs are that he could form a partnership with left tackle Jim Lachey good enough to take the club well into the 1990s. Center Don Macek is very solid. Dennis McKnight will start at right guard but there will be a competition involving Broderick Thompson and Gary Kowalski for the right tackle spot. Fourth-round draftees Stacy Searels and David Richards enrich a backup pool which includes Sam Claphan and Curtis Rouse.

Defense

Despite a modest performance by the offense, the Chargers enjoyed their first net-winning season since 1982 and, for this, great credit must go to the defense. The unit improved from 23rd to 15th overall in the NFL, 24th against the run and 4th against the pass. Astonishingly, the ranking against the pass represents the Chargers' best position since the NFL was realigned in 1970. Without doubt, the arrival of former Cleveland all-pro outside linebacker Chip Banks was a tremendous boost. Itching to make a point, Banks turned up early for practice and kept the same attitude throughout the campaign. More importantly, he spurred the other outside linebacker, Billy Ray Smith, to a performance which saw him lead the team in both tackles (88) and pass interceptions (5), and register three sacks. At inside linebacker, they're not so well off. Gary Plummer and Thomas Benson are the likely starters, with Steve Busick, Randy Kirk and draftee Cedric Figaro as backups. Defensive end Lee Williams apart, the defensive line, too, could use a little sparkle. Even though attracting multiple coverage, Williams led the team with eight quarterback sacks. The other end, Joe Phillips, and nose tackle Chuck Ehin are a pair of hard-working battlers but no more than that. The Chargers really need the return of defensive end Leslie O'Neal, who was outstanding before suffering a serious knee injury in the 1986 season. In what was his rookie season, O'Neal was the Chargers' leading sacker with 12.5 before going down with the injury on Week Thirteen. The defensive secondary should have Gill Byrd starting at right cornerback, with Vencie Glenn at free safety. Jeff Dale returns from injury and should displace Martin Bayless at strong safety. Elvis Patterson and Louis Brock dispute the left cornerback position. Daniel Hunter, Danny Walters and former Raider Mike Davis are the backups.

1988 SCHEDULE OF GAMES	September	
	4 at Los Angeles Raiders	1:00
	11 at Denver	2:00
	18 SEATTLE	1:00
	25 at Kansas City	3:00
	October	
	2 DENVER	1:00
	9 NEW ORLEANS	1:00
	16 at Miami	1:00
	23 INDIANAPOLIS	1:00
	30 at Seattle	1:00
	November	
	6 LOS ANGELES RAIDERS	5:00
	13 at Atlanta	1:00
	20 at Los Angeles Rams	1:00
	27 SAN FRANCISCO	1:00
	December	
	4 at Cincinnati	1:00
	11 PITTSBURGH	1:00
	18 KANSAS CITY	1:00

Unusually for a linebacker, Billy Ray Smith led the Chargers in interceptions.

Special Teams

Punter Ralf Mojsiejenko is the current AFC-NFC Pro Bowler, and whilst at times the British-born Vince Abbott appears to lack power, he seems likely to continue as the placekicker. Lionel James is a really elusive punt returner – one of the league's best – but the Chargers need a consistent kickoff returner.

VETERAN ROSTER

No.	Name	Pos.	Ht.	Wt.	NFL Year	College
10	Abbott, Vince	K	5-11	206	2	Cal State-Fullerton
42	Adams, Curtis	RB	5-11	194	3	Central Michigan
40	Anderson, Gary	RB-KR	6-0	181	4	Arkansas
96	Baldwin, Keith	DE	6-4	270	6	Texas A&M
56	Banks, Chip	LB	6-4	236	7	Southern California
44	Bayless, Martin	S	6-2	200	5	Bowling Green
57	Benson, Thomas	LB	6-2	235	5	Oklahoma
82	Bernstine, Rod	TE	6-3	235	2	Texas A&M
58	Brandon, David	LB	6-4	225	2	Memphis State
38	Brock, Lou	CB	5-10	175	2	Southern California
	Browner, Keith	LB	6-6	245	5	Southern California
55	Busick, Steve	LB	6-4	227	8	Southern California
22	Byrd, Gill	CB-S	5-11	196	6	San Jose State
28	Caldwell, Ralph	LB	6-2	242	2	Indiana
89	Chandler, Wes	WR	6-0	188	11	Florida
71	Charles, Mike	NT	6-4	287	6	Syracuse
77	Claphan, Sam	T-G	6-6	288	8	Oklahoma
37	Dale, Jeff	S	6-3	213	3	Louisiana State
61	Dallafior, Ken	C	6-4	278	4	Minnesota
36	Davis, Mike	S	6-3	205	10	Colorado
76	Ehin, Chuck	NT	6-4	265	6	Brigham Young
45	Faucette, Chuck	LB	6-3	238	1	Maryland
70	FitzPatrick, James	G	6-7	286	3	Southern California
	Fuller, Steve	QB	6-4	195	9	Clemson
25	Glenn, Vencie	S	6-0	187	3	Indiana State
92	Hardison, Dee	NT-DE	6-4	291	11	North Carolina
86	Holland, Jamie	WR	6-1	186	2	Ohio State
27	Hunter, Daniel	CB	5-11	178	4	Henderson, Ark.
52	Jackson, Jeffrey	LB	6-1	230	4	Auburn
26	James, Lionel	WR-PR	5-6	170	5	Auburn
21	Jones, Nelson	CB	6-1	190	1	North Carolina State
94	Kirk, Randy	LB	6-2	235	2	San Diego State
68	Kowalski, Gary	T	6-6	273	5	Boston College
74	Lachey, Jim	T	6-6	289	4	Ohio State
51	Lowe, Woodrow	LB	6-0	229	12	Alabama
62	Macek, Don	C	6-2	270	13	Boston College
73	MacEsker, Joe	T	6-7	305	1	Texas-El Paso
	Malone, Mark	QB	6-4	224	9	Arizona State
60	McKnight, Dennis	G	6-3	270	7	Drake
69	Miller, Les	DE	6-7	285	2	Fort Hays State
2	Mojsiejenko, Ralf	P	6-3	212	4	Michigan State
91	O'Neal, Leslie	DE	6-4	255	2	Oklahoma State
34	Patterson, Elvis	CB	5-11	198	5	Kansas
75	Phillips, Joe	DE	6-5	275	3	Southern Methodist
50	Plummer, Gary	LB	6-2	240	3	California
20	Redden, Barry	RB	5-10	219	7	Richmond
66	Rosado, Dan	G-T	6-3	280	2	Northern Illinois
79	Rouse, Curtis	G-T	6-3	340	7	Tennessee-Chatt.
24	Scott, Kevin	RB	5-9	181	1	Stanford
85	Sievers, Eric	TE	6-4	230	8	Maryland
54	Smith, Billy Ray	LB	6-3	236	6	Arkansas
43	Spencer, Tim	RB	6-1	227	4	Ohio State
59	Taylor, John	LB	6-4	235	3	Hawaii
76	Thompson, Broderick	G	6-4	290	3	Kansas
98	Unrein, Terry	DE	6-5	280	3	Colorado State
13	Vlasic, Mark	QB	6-3	206	2	Iowa
23	Walters, Danny	CB	6-1	200	5	Arkansas
81	Ware, Timmie	WR	5-10	170	3	Southern California
84	Williams, Al	WR	5-10	180	2	Nevada-Reno
99	Williams, Lee	DE	6-5	263	5	Bethune-Cookman
72	Wilson, Karl	DE	6-4	268	2	Louisiana State
80	Winslow, Kellen	TE	6-5	251	10	Missouri

1988 DRAFT

Round	Name	Pos.	Ht.	Wt.	College
1.	Miller, Anthony	WR	5-10	175	Tennessee
3.	Early, Quinn	WR	5-11	180	Iowa
4.	Campbell, Joe	DE	6-3	228	New Mexico State
4.	Searels, Stacy	T	6-4	272	Auburn
4.	Richards, David	T	6-4	305	UCLA
6.	Figaro, Cedric	LB	6-1	248	Notre Dame
9.	Howard, Joey	T	6-5	280	Tennessee
11.	Miller, Ed	C	6-2	255	Pittsburgh
11.	Hinkle, George	NT	6-5	270	Arizona
12.	Phillips, Wendell	DB	5-11	198	North Alabama

SEATTLE SEAHAWKS

Address 11220 N.E. 53rd Street, Kirkland, Washington
98033.
Stadium Kingdome, Seattle.
Capacity 64,984 *Playing Surface* AstroTurf.
Team Colours Blue, Green, and Silver.
Head Coach Chuck Knox – sixth year.
Championships None.
History NFC 1976, AFC 1977–

Offense

The Seahawks enter the 1988 season as one of the best-balanced clubs in the league, and it is ironic that their only problem on offense may arise out of a wish to try to strengthen the squad. The move came only hours before the draft, when they traded for the right to negotiate with quarterback Kelly Stouffer, whom the Cardinals had drafted in the 1987 first round but had been unable to sign. It was no secret that the Seahawks weren't completely happy with Dave Krieg but he was a proven starter, and in Jeff Kemp they had a first-class backup. Stouffer, then, throws his raw talent into a stew which, already, had the flavour of controversy. At wide receiver, Steve Largent returns for a 13th year with one NFL career record (752 catches) in the bag and two more, for most yards receiving (he needs another 106 yards) and touchdown receptions (he needs five more), just waiting to be picked up. In the early going, Largent's starting partner will probably be Ray Butler, who has made a new career with the Seahawks after almost six full seasons with the Colts. The speedy Daryl Turner, 36 of whose 101 career receptions have been for touchdowns, was the third receiver ahead of Byron Franklin and Paul Skansi, but a double-barrelled challenge will come from top draftees Brian Blades and Tommy Kane. At running back, Seattle has the perfect combination in Curt Warner and John L. Williams. Warner has all the speed, moves and overall presence of a franchise running back, whilst Williams is becoming the model fullback. In addition, Williams has developed into a really useful pass receiver. Behind the starters, though, the Seahawks were rather thin, and the drafting of Kevin Harmon will help. Tight end Mike Tice is a good blocker but has never been a prolific receiver, and it may be that draftee Robert Tyler, who was selected for his skills as a receiver, may see a fair amount of action on third-and-long. The offensive line is a solid group, with left tackle Ron Mattes, in particular, emerging as a player of class. Right tackle Mike Wilson has been respected ever since his early days with the Bengals. Guards Edwin Bailey and Bryan Millard, and center Blair Bush complete a line which is entering its third campaign as the starting unit. The backups include Jon Borchardt, Grant Feasel and a top-quality tackle, Ron Heller, a four-year starter for Tampa Bay who came in an offseason trade.

Defense

Surprisingly, for a club with so much talent for the front seven positions, the Seahawks' defense ranked a poor 22nd in the league last year. Against the run, they were particularly weak (26th), and with only 37 quarterback sacks they registered their lowest total in the tenure of head coach Chuck Knox. Only in the sixth round did they select for the defense, and it is not likely that the draftee, Roy Hart, will have an immediate impact. For the seventh time in his eight-year career, defensive end Jacob Green led the team in sacks (9.5). Green is the NFL's third-leading career sacker (since records first were kept in 1982) with 67, behind the Giants' Lawrence Taylor (73.5) and Washington's Dexter Manley (73). Jeff Bryant is the other starting defensive end and Joe Nash continues at nose tackle. Probably unfairly, much of the blame for the weakness against the run fell on Nash, but he is not likely to be displaced by either of the backups, Roland Barbay and Lester Williams. The list at linebacker reads like a pro football Who's Who. Once the clatter of camera shutters which greeted his arrival had died down, inside linebacker Brian Bosworth settled in quickly and played in the style one would expect of a future superstar laying the foundation for his career. At this stage, though, left inside linebacker Fredd Young is the better of the two. Young, a lightning-quick, ferocious tackler, has been selected to the AFC-NFC Pro Bowl in all four of his NFL years (he was picked twice as a special-teamer). Outside linebackers Greg Gaines and Bruce Scholtz keep out another former high draftee, 1987 first-rounder Tony Woods. Knox is concerned that his defensive secondary had difficulty against the long pass, and he will miss strong safety Kenny Easley, who has a medical problem. However, Paul Moyer is an excellent replacement and combines well with free safety Eugene Robinson. Terry Taylor and Patrick Hunter are the starting cornerbacks ahead of Kerry Justin, Melvin Jenkins and David Hollis.

1988 SCHEDULE OF GAMES	September	
	4 at Denver	2:00
	11 KANSAS CITY	1:00
	18 at San Diego	1:00
	25 SAN FRANCISCO	1:00
	October	
	2 at Atlanta	1:00
	9 at Cleveland	1:00
	16 NEW ORLEANS	1:00
	23 at Los Angeles Rams	1:00
	30 SAN DIEGO	1:00
	November	
	6 BUFFALO	1:00
	13 HOUSTON	1:00
	20 at Kansas City	12:00
	28 LOS ANGELES RAIDERS (Mon.)	6:00
	December	
	4 at New England	1:00
	11 DENVER	5:00
	18 at Los Angeles Raiders	1:00

Special Teams

The club is well satisfied with both placekicker Norm Johnson and punter Ruben Rodriguez, the latter who improved throughout what was his rookie year. Bobby Joe Edmonds returns punts as his speciality and kickoffs because there was no one else. However, after averaging 26.3 yards on ten kickoff returns in 1987, Hollis may be used more often.

Linebacker Brian Bosworth is a future superstar.

VETERAN ROSTER

No.	Name	Pos.	Ht.	Wt.	NFL Year	College
33	Agee, Tommie	RB	6-0	220	1	Auburn
65	Bailey, Edwin	G	6-4	276	8	South Carolina State
62	Barbay, Roland	NT	6-4	260	2	Louisiana State
76	Borchardt, Jon	T	6-5	272	10	Montana State
55	Bosworth, Brian	LB	6-2	248	2	Oklahoma
77	Bryant, Jeff	DE	6-5	272	7	Clemson
34	Burse, Tony	RB	6-0	220	2	Middle Tennessee St.
59	Bush, Blair	C	6-3	272	11	Washington
53	Butler, Keith	LB	6-4	239	11	Memphis State
83	Butler, Ray	WR	6-3	206	9	Southern California
84	Clark, Louis	WR	6-0	206	2	Mississippi State
64	Dove, Wes	DE	6-7	270	1	Syracuse
45	Easley, Kenny	S	6-3	198	8	UCLA
30	Edmonds, Bobby Joe	RB-KR	5-11	186	3	Arkansas
66	Eisenhooth, Stan	C	6-6	300	1	Towson State
54	Feasel, Grant	C	6-7	280	4	Abilene Christian
88	Franklin, Byron	WR	6-1	183	7	Auburn
56	Gaines, Greg	LB	6-3	222	7	Tennessee
79	Green, Jacob	DE	6-3	252	9	Texas A&M
46	Hairston, Ray	LB	6-2	235	1	Illinois
	Heller, Ron	T	6-6	280	5	Penn State
25	Hollis, David	CB	5-11	175	2	Nevada-Las Vegas
23	Hunter, Patrick	CB	5-11	185	3	Nevada-Reno
24	Jenkins, Melvin	CB	5-10	170	2	Cincinnati
52	Johnson, M.L.	LB	6-3	225	2	Hawaii
9	Johnson, Norm	K	6-2	198	7	UCLA
26	Justin, Kerry	CB	5-11	185	9	Oregon State
15	Kemp, Jeff	QB	6-0	201	8	Dartmouth
17	Krieg, Dave	QB	6-1	196	9	Milton
37	Lane, Eric	RB	6-0	201	8	Brigham Young
80	Largent, Steve	WR	5-11	184	13	Tulsa
11	Mathison, Bruce	QB	6-3	205	5	Nebraska
70	Mattes, Ron	T	6-6	306	3	Virginia
51	Merriman, Sam	LB	6-3	232	6	Idaho
71	Millard, Bryan	G	6-5	282	5	Texas
61	Mitz, Alonzo	DE	6-3	273	3	Florida
99	Mokofisi, Filipo	LB	6-1	230	1	Utah
35	Moore, Mark	S	6-0	194	2	Oklahoma State
43	Morris, Randall	RB	6-0	200	5	Tennessee
21	Moyer, Paul	S	6-1	201	6	Arizona State
72	Nash, Joe	NT	6-2	257	7	Boston College
73	Powell, Alvin	G	6-5	296	2	Winston-Salem State
41	Robinson, Eugene	S	6-0	186	4	Colgate
5	Rodriguez, Ruben	P	6-2	220	2	Arizona
27	Romes, Charles	CB	6-1	190	12	North Carolina Central
58	Scholtz, Bruce	LB	6-6	242	7	Texas
74	Singer, Curt	T	6-5	279	2	Tennessee
82	Skansi, Paul	WR	5-11	183	6	Washington
	Stouffer, Kelly	QB	6-3	210	R	Colorado State
87	Strozier, Wilbur	TE	6-4	255	2	Georgia
20	Taylor, Terry	CB	5-10	191	5	Southern Illinois
85	Teal, Jimmy	WR	5-11	175	4	Texas A&M
86	Tice, Mike	TE	6-7	247	8	Maryland
81	Turner, Daryl	WR	6-3	194	5	Michigan State
28	Warner, Curt	RB	5-11	205	5	Penn State
89	Williams, Bob	TE	6-3	235	2	Penn State
32	Williams, John L.	RB	5-11	226	3	Florida
91	Williams, Lester	NT	6-3	290	7	Miami
75	Wilson, Mike	T	6-5	280	11	Georgia
57	Woods, Tony	LB	6-4	244	2	Pittsburgh
92	Wyman, David	LB	6-2	229	2	Stanford
50	Young, Fredd	LB	6-1	233	5	New Mexico State

1988 DRAFT

Round	Name	Pos.	Ht.	Wt.	College
2.	Blades, Brian	WR	5-11	180	Miami
3.	Kane, Tommy	WR	5-11	176	Syracuse
4.	Harmon, Kevin	RB	5-11	194	Iowa
6.	Hart, Roy	NT	6-0	270	South Carolina
7.	Jackson, Ray	DB	5-11	190	Ohio State
8.	Tyler, Robert	TE	6-5	250	South Carolina State
9.	Wise, Deatrich	NT	6-4	275	Jackson State
10.	Jones, Derwin	DE	6-3	280	Miami
11.	McLeod, Rick	T	6-5	265	Washington
11.	Harper, Dwayne	DB	5-10	168	South Carolina State
12.	Des Rochers, Dave	T	6-6	272	San Diego State

CHAPTER SEVEN

NATIONAL FOOTBALL CONFERENCE

TEAM RANKINGS

	OFFENSE						DEFENSE					
	Total Yds.	Rushing	Passing	Points For	No. Intercepted	No. Sacked	Total Yds.	Rushing	Passing	Points Against	Interceptions	Sacks
Atlanta	14	14	12	14	14	8	14	14	8	14	12	14
Chicago	6	7	6	5	12	9	2	1	3	2	14	1
Dallas	5	9	5	6	9	10 =	9	4	13	4 =	8	5
Detroit	12	12	9	12	13	2	12	13	9	13	8	7
Green Bay	11	10	13	13	5 =	7	6	10	6	5	9	13
L.A. Rams	10	4	14	9	7 =	1	10	8	12	10	10 =	11
Minnesota	8	6	10	8	11	10 =	5	7	7	7	2	8 =
New Orleans	7	2	11	2	1	4 =	3	2	2	3	1	6
N.Y. Giants	9	11	4	11	10	13	4	9	4	6	7	3
Philadelphia	4	5	7	7	4	14	11	5	14	12	6	2
St Louis	3	8	3	4	3	12	13	11	11	11	13	8 =
San Francisco	1	1	1	1	2	4 =	1	3	1	1	3	12
Tampa Bay	13	13	8	10	5 =	6	7	12	5	9	10 =	10
Washington	2	3	2	3	7 =	3	8	6	10	4	4 =	4

NFC PASSERS

	Att	Comp	% Comp	Yards	Ave Gain	TD	% TD	Long	Int	% Int	Rating Points
Montana, Joe, *S.F.*	398	266	66.8	3054	7.67	31	7.8	t57	13	3.3	102.1
Williams, Doug, *Wash.*	143	81	56.6	1156	8.08	11	7.7	62	5	3.5	94.0
Simms, Phil, *Giants*	282	163	57.8	2230	7.91	17	6.0	t50	9	3.2	90.0
Lomax, Neil, *St L.*	463	275	59.4	3387	7.32	24	5.2	57	12	2.6	88.5
McMahon, Jim, *Chi.*	210	125	59.5	1639	7.80	12	5.7	t59	8	3.8	87.4
DeBerg, Steve, *T.B.*	275	159	57.8	1891	6.88	14	5.1	t64	7	2.5	85.3
Cunningham, Randall, *Phil.*	406	223	54.9	2786	6.86	23	5.7	t70	12	3.0	83.0
Hebert, Bobby, *N.O.*	294	164	55.8	2119	7.21	15	5.1	67	9	3.1	82.9
Wilson, Wade, *Minn.*	264	140	53.0	2106	7.98	14	5.3	t73	13	4.9	76.7
White, Danny, *Dall.*	362	215	59.4	2617	7.23	12	3.3	43	17	4.7	73.2
Schroeder, Jay, *Wash.*	267	129	48.3	1878	7.03	12	4.5	t84	10	3.7	71.0
Majkowski, Don, *G.B.*	127	55	43.3	875	6.89	5	3.9	t70	3	2.4	70.2
Everett, Jim, *Rams*	302	162	53.6	2064	6.83	10	3.3	t81	13	4.3	68.4
Campbell, Scott, *Atl.*	260	136	52.3	1728	6.65	11	4.2	t44	14	5.4	65.0
Long, Chuck, *Det.*	416	232	55.8	2598	6.25	11	2.6	53	20	4.8	63.4
Tomczak, Mike, *Chi.*	178	97	54.5	1220	6.85	5	2.8	t56	10	5.6	62.0
Wright, Randy, *G.B.*	247	132	53.4	1507	6.10	6	2.4	66	11	4.5	61.6
Testaverde, Vinny, *T.B.*	165	71	43.0	1081	6.55	5	3.0	40	6	3.6	60.2
Rutledge, Jeff, *Giants*	155	79	51.0	1048	6.76	5	3.2	50	11	7.1	53.9
Non-qualifiers											
Young, Steve, *S.F.*	69	37	53.6	570	8.26	10	14.5	t50	0	0.0	120.8
Wilson, Dave, *N.O.*	24	13	54.2	243	10.13	2	8.3	38	0	0.0	117.2
Sweeney, Kevin, *Dall.*	28	14	50.0	291	10.39	4	14.3	t77	1	3.6	111.8
Rubbert, Ed, *Wash.*	49	26	53.1	532	10.86	4	8.2	t88	1	2.0	110.2
Hohensee, Mike, *Chi.*	52	28	53.8	343	6.60	4	7.7	28	1	1.9	92.1

t = Touchdown
Leader based on rating points, minimum 125 attempts

Neal Anderson led the Bears with 47 receptions.

NFC RECEIVERS – Most Receptions

	No	Yards	Ave	Long	TD
Smith, J.T., *St L.*	91	1117	12.3	38	8
Craig, Roger, *S.F.*	66	492	7.5	t35	1
Rice, Jerry, *S.F.*	65	1078	16.6	t57	22
Walker, Herschel, *Dall.*	60	715	11.9	44	1
Mandley, Pete, *Det.*	58	720	12.4	41	7
Clark, Gary, *Wash.*	56	1066	19.0	t84	7
Bavaro, Mark, *Giants*	55	867	15.8	38	8
Ellard, Henry, *Rams*	51	799	15.7	t81	3
Anderson, Neal, *Chi.*	47	467	9.9	t59	3
Quick, Mike, *Phil.*	46	790	17.2	t61	11
Renfro, Mike, *Dall.*	46	662	14.4	43	4
Mitchell, Stump, *St L.*	45	397	8.8	39	2
Martin, Eric, *N.O.*	44	778	17.7	67	7
Green, Roy, *St L.*	43	731	17.0	57	4
Bryant, Kelvin, *Wash.*	43	490	11.4	39	5
Awalt, Robert, *St L.*	42	526	12.5	35	6
Wilder, James, *T.B.*	40	328	8.2	32	1
Toney, Anthony, *Phil.*	39	341	8.7	33	1
Carter, Anthony, *Minn.*	38	922	24.3	t73	7
Stanley, Walter, *G.B.*	38	672	17.7	t70	3
Carter, Gerald, *T.B.*	38	586	15.4	57	5
Monk, Art, *Wash.*	38	483	12.7	62	6
Sanders, Ricky, *Wash.*	37	630	17.0	57	3
Dixon, Floyd, *Atl.*	36	600	16.7	t51	5
Cosbie, Doug, *Dall.*	36	421	11.7	30	3
Neal, Frankie, *G.B.*	36	420	11.7	38	3
Spagnola, John, *Phil.*	36	350	9.7	22	2
Gault, Willie, *Chi.*	35	705	20.1	t56	7
Jordan, Steve, *Minn.*	35	490	14.0	38	2
Adams, George, *Giants*	35	298	8.5	25	1
Edwards, Kelvin, *Dall.*	34	521	15.3	t38	3
Epps, Phillip, *G.B.*	34	516	15.2	40	2
Magee, Calvin, *T.B.*	34	424	12.5	37	3
Newsome, Tim, *Dall.*	34	274	8.1	30	2
Jones, James, *Det.*	34	262	7.7	35	0

t = Touchdown

NFC RECEIVERS – Most Yards

	Yards	No	Ave	Long	TD
Smith, J.T., *St L.*	1117	91	12.3	38	8
Rice, Jerry, *S.F.*	1078	65	16.6	t57	22
Clark, Gary, *Wash.*	1066	56	19.0	t84	7
Carter, Anthony, *Minn.*	922	38	24.3	t73	7
Bavaro, Mark, *Giants*	867	55	15.8	38	8
Ellard, Henry, *Rams*	799	51	15.7	t81	3
Quick, Mike, *Phil.*	790	46	17.2	t61	11
Martin, Eric, *N.O.*	778	44	17.7	67	7
Green, Roy, *St L.*	731	43	17.0	57	4
Mandley, Pete, *Det.*	720	58	12.4	41	7
Walker, Herschel, *Dall.*	715	60	11.9	44	1
Gault, Willie, *Chi.*	705	35	20.1	t56	7
Stanley, Walter, *G.B.*	672	38	17.7	t70	3
Renfro, Mike, *Dall.*	662	46	14.4	43	4
Sanders, Ricky, *Wash.*	630	37	17.0	57	3
Dixon, Floyd, *Atl.*	600	36	16.7	t51	5
Carter, Gerald, *T.B.*	586	38	15.4	57	5
Manuel, Lionel, *Giants*	545	30	18.2	t50	6
Matthews, Aubrey, *Atl.*	537	32	16.8	57	3
Awalt, Robert, *St L.*	526	42	12.5	35	6
Brown, Ron, *Rams*	521	26	20.0	52	2
Edwards, Kelvin, *Dall.*	521	34	15.3	t38	3
Epps, Phillip, *G.B.*	516	34	15.2	40	2
Craig, Roger, *S.F.*	492	66	7.5	t35	1
Bryant, Kelvin, *Wash.*	490	43	11.4	39	5
Jordan, Steve, *Minn.*	490	35	14.0	38	2
Monk, Art, *Wash.*	483	38	12.7	62	6
Jackson, Kenny, *Phil.*	471	21	22.4	t70	3
Anderson, Neal, *Chi.*	467	47	9.9	t59	3
Wilson, Mike, *S.F.*	450	29	15.5	t46	5

t = Touchdown

NFC RUSHERS

	Att	Yards	Ave	Long	TD
White, Charles, *Rams*	324	1374	4.2	58	11
Mayes, Rueben, *N.O.*	243	917	3.8	38	5
Walker, Herschel, *Dall.*	209	891	4.3	t60	7
Riggs, Gerald, *Atl.*	203	875	4.3	44	2
Craig, Roger, *S.F.*	215	815	3.8	25	3
Mitchell, Stump, *St L.*	203	781	3.8	42	3
Morris, Joe, *Giants*	193	658	3.4	34	3
Nelson, Darrin, *Minn.*	131	642	4.9	72	2
Rogers, George, *Wash.*	163	613	3.8	29	6
Anderson, Neal, *Chi.*	129	586	4.5	t38	3
Payton, Walter, *Chi.*	146	533	3.7	17	4
Ferrell, Earl, *St L.*	113	512	4.5	t35	7
Hilliard, Dalton, *N.O.*	123	508	4.1	t30	7
Cunningham, Randall, *Phil.*	76	505	6.6	45	3
Wilder, James, *T.B.*	106	488	4.6	21	0
Toney, Anthony, *Phil.*	127	473	3.7	36	5
Dorsett, Tony, *Dall.*	130	456	3.5	24	1
Byars, Keith, *Phil.*	116	426	3.7	30	3
Davis, Kenneth, *G.B.*	109	413	3.8	t39	3
Bryant, Kelvin, *Wash.*	77	406	5.3	28	1
Vital, Lionel, *Wash.*	80	346	4.3	t22	2
Jones, James, *Det.*	96	342	3.6	19	0
Anderson, Alfred, *Minn.*	68	319	4.7	27	2
Smith, Jeff, *T.B.*	100	309	3.1	46	2
Cribbs, Joe, *S.F.*	70	300	4.3	20	1
Fullwood, Brent, *G.B.*	84	274	3.3	18	5
James, Garry, *Det.*	82	270	3.3	17	4
Wilson, Wade, *Minn.*	41	263	6.4	38	5
Dozier, D.J., *Minn.*	69	257	3.7	19	5
Rathman, Tom, *S.F.*	62	257	4.1	35	1
Willhite, Kevin, *G.B.*	53	251	4.7	61	0
Griffin, Keith, *Wash.*	62	242	3.9	13	0
McAdoo, Derrick, *St L.*	53	230	4.3	17	3
Beverly, Dwight, *N.O.*	62	217	3.5	25	2
Clark, Jessie, *G.B.*	56	211	3.8	57	0
Hunter, Eddie, *Jets-T.B.*	56	210	3.8	23	0
Ellerson, Gary, *Det.*	47	196	4.2	33	3
Carruth, Paul Ott, *G.B.*	64	192	3.0	23	3
Young, Steve, *S.F.*	26	190	7.3	t29	1
Bernard, Karl, *Det.*	45	187	4.2	14	2
Fenney, Rick, *Minn.*	42	174	4.1	12	2
Adams, George, *Giants*	61	169	2.8	14	1
Haddix, Michael, *Phil.*	59	165	2.8	11	0
Rouson, Lee, *Giants*	41	155	3.8	14	0
Pelluer, Steve, *Dall.*	25	142	5.7	21	1
Montana, Joe, *S.F.*	35	141	4.0	20	1
Francis, Jon, *Rams*	35	138	3.9	23	0
Brown, Reggie, *Phil.*	39	136	3.5	23	0
Fourcade, John, *N.O.*	19	134	7.1	18	0
Word, Barry, *N.O.*	36	133	3.7	20	2
Rice, Allen, *Minn.*	51	131	2.6	13	1
Heimuli, Lakei, *Chi.*	34	128	3.8	12	0
Majkowski, Don, *G.B.*	15	127	8.5	33	0
Smith, Timmy, *Wash.*	29	126	4.3	15	0
Blount, Alvin, *Dall.*	46	125	2.7	15	3
Sydney, Harry, *S.F.*	29	125	4.3	15	0
Sanders, Thomas, *Chi.*	23	122	5.3	17	1
Newsome, Tim, *Dall.*	25	121	4.8	t24	2
Schroeder, Jay, *Wash.*	26	120	4.6	31	3

t = Touchdown

NFC SCORING – Kickers

	XP	XPA	FG	FGA	PTS
Andersen, Morten, *N.O.*	37	37	28	36	121
Ruzek, Roger, *Dall.*	26	26	22	25	92
Lansford, Mike, *Rams*	36	38	17	21	87
Butler, Kevin, *Chi.*	28	30	19	28	85
McFadden, Paul, *Phil.*	36	36	16	26	84
Wersching, Ray, *S.F.*	44	46	13	17	83
Murray, Ed, *Det.*	21	21	20	32	81
Allegre, Raul, *Giants*	25	26	17	27	76
Nelson, Chuck, *Minn.*	36	37	13	24	75
Haji-Sheikh, Ali, *Wash.*	29	32	13	19	68
Igwebuike, Donald, *T.B.*	24	26	14	18	66
Zendejas, Max, *G.B.*	13	15	16	19	61
Gallery, Jim, *St L.*	30	31	9	19	57
Del Greco, Al, *G.B.-St L.*	19	20	9	15	46
Luckhurst, Mick, *Atl.*	17	17	9	13	44

NFC SCORING – Touchdowns

	TD	TDR	TDP	TDM	PTS
Rice, Jerry, *S.F.*	23	1	22	0	138
Quick, Mike, *Phil.*	11	0	11	0	66
White, Charles, *Rams*	11	11	0	0	66
Bavaro, Mark, *Giants*	8	0	8	0	48
Hilliard, Dalton, *N.O.*	8	7	1	0	48
Smith, J.T., *St L.*	8	0	8	0	48
Walker, Herschel, *Dall.*	8	7	1	0	48
Carter, Anthony, *Minn.*	7	0	7	0	42
Clark, Gary, *Wash.*	7	0	7	0	42
Dozier, D.J., *Minn.*	7	5	2	0	42
Ferrell, Earl, *St L.*	7	7	0	0	42
Gault, Willie, *Chi.*	7	0	7	0	42
Mandley, Pete, *Det.*	7	0	7	0	42
Martin, Eric, *N.O.*	7	0	7	0	42

NFC KICKOFF RETURNERS

	No	Yards	Ave	Long	TD
Stamps, Sylvester, *Atl.*	24	660	27.5	t97	1
Gentry, Dennis, *Chi.*	25	621	24.8	t88	1
Rouson, Lee, *Giants*	22	497	22.6	49	0
Lee, Gary, *Det.*	32	719	22.5	50	0
Guggemos, Neal, *Minn.*	36	808	22.4	42	0
Sikahema, Vai, *St L.*	34	761	22.4	50	0
Clack, Darryl, *Dall.*	29	635	21.9	48	0
Brown, Ron, *Rams*	27	581	21.5	t95	1
Fullwood, Brent, *G.B.*	24	510	21.3	46	0
Gray, Mel, *N.O.*	30	636	21.2	43	0
Rodgers, Del, *S.F.*	17	358	21.1	50	0
Emery, Larry, *Atl.*	21	440	21.0	66	0
Futrell, Bobby, *T.B.*	31	609	19.6	40	0
McAdoo, Derrick, *St L.*	23	444	19.3	30	0
Griffin, Keith, *Wash.*	25	478	19.1	54	0
Sanders, Thomas, *Chi.*	20	349	17.5	42	0
Morse, Bobby, *Phil.*	24	386	16.1	28	0

t = Touchdown
Leader based on average return, minimum 14 returns

Atlanta's Sylvester (Zip Code) Stamps was the NFL leader in kickoff return average.

NFC PUNTERS

	No	Yards	Long	Ave	Total Punts	TB	Blk	Opp Ret	Ret Yds	In 20	Net Ave
Donnelly, Rick, *Atl.*	61	2686	62	44.0	63	8	2	38	501	9	32.1
Arnold, Jim, *Det.*	46	2007	60	43.6	46	4	0	22	104	17	39.6
Landeta, Sean, *Giants*	65	2773	64	42.7	66	6	1	38	606	13	31.0
Hatcher, Dale, *Rams*	76	3140	62	41.3	77	4	1	43	317	19	35.6
Bracken, Don, *G.B.*	72	2947	65	40.9	73	5	1	45	354	13	34.2
Cox, Steve, *Wash.*	63	2571	77	40.8	64	7	1	29	193	14	35.0
Hansen, Brian, *N.O.*	52	2104	60	40.5	52	6	0	23	135	19	35.6
Horne, Greg, *Cin.-St L.*	43	1730	57	40.2	43	7	0	25	237	6	31.5
Coleman, Greg, *Minn.*	45	1786	54	39.7	46	3	1	30	323	5	30.5
Saxon, Mike, *Dall.*	68	2685	63	39.5	68	5	0	36	260	20	34.2
Runager, Max, *S.F.*	55	2157	56	39.2	56	7	1	23	167	13	33.0
Garcia, Frank, *T.B.*	62	2409	58	38.9	62	5	0	38	553	12	28.3
Teltschik, John, *Phil.*	82	3131	60	38.2	83	4	1	47	399	13	32.0
Cater, Greg, *St L.*	39	1470	68	37.7	40	2	1	17	204	10	30.7

Leader based on gross average, minimum 38 punts

NFC SACKERS

	No
White, Reggie, *Phil.*	21.0
Dent, Richard, *Chi.*	12.5
Taylor, Lawrence, *Giants*	12.0
Doleman, Chris, *Minn.*	11.0
Nunn, Freddie Joe, *St L.*	11.0
Swilling, Pat, *N.O.*	10.5
Jones, Ed L., *Dall.*	10.0
Jackson, Rickey, *N.O.*	9.5
Mann, Charles, *Wash.*	9.5
Banks, Carl, *Giants*	9.0
Martin, Doug, *Minn.*	9.0
Cofer, Mike, *Det.*	8.5
Manley, Dexter, *Wash.*	8.5
Holmes, Ron, *T.B.*	8.0
Marshall, Leonard, *Giants*	8.0
Harris, Timothy, *G.B.*	7.0
Jeter, Gary, *Rams*	7.0
Mays, Stafford, *Minn.*	7.0
McMichael, Steve, *Chi.*	7.0
Greene, Kevin, *Rams*	6.5
Haley, Charles, *S.F.*	6.5
McInerney, Sean, *Chi.*	6.5
Washington, Chris, *T.B.*	6.5
Wilson, Otis, *Chi.*	6.5
Ferguson, Keith, *Det.*	6.0
Greer, Curtis, *St L.*	6.0
Miller, Shawn, *Rams*	6.0
Simmons, Clyde, *Phil.*	6.0
Warren, Frank, *N.O.*	6.0
White, Randy, *Dall.*	6.0
Howard, Erik, *Giants*	5.5
Wilks, Jim, *N.O.*	5.5
Jeffcoat, Jim, *Dall.*	5.0
Marshall, Wilber, *Chi.*	5.0
Martin, George, *Giants*	5.0
Martin, Steve, *Wash.*	5.0
Wilcher, Mike, *Rams*	5.0
Clark, Bruce, *N.O.*	4.5
Clasby, Bob, *St L.*	4.5
Kugler, Pete, *S.F.*	4.5
Anderson, John, *G.B.*	4.0
Brown, Jerome, *Phil.*	4.0
Carreker, Alphonso, *G.B.*	4.0
Coleman, Monte, *Wash.*	4.0
Joyner, Seth, *Phil.*	4.0
Moor, Buddy, *Atl.*	4.0
Novell, Jay, *Chi.*	4.0
Rohrer, Jeff, *Dall.*	4.0
Williams, Jimmy, *Det.*	4.0

Mel Gray led the NFL in punt return average.

Barry Wilburn led the NFL in pass interceptions by the margin of three.

NFC PUNT RETURNERS

	No	FC	Yards	Ave	Long	TD
Gray, Mel, *N.O.*	24	5	352	14.7	80	0
McLemore, Dana, *S.F.*	21	7	265	12.6	t83	1
Lewis, Leo, *Minn.*	22	7	275	12.5	t78	1
Sikahema, Vai, *St L.*	44	7	550	12.5	t76	1
Mandley, Pete, *Det.*	23	6	250	10.9	54	0
McKinnon, Dennis, *Chi.*	40	4	405	10.1	t94	2
Martin, Kelvin, *Dall.*	22	2	216	9.8	38	0
McConkey, Phil, *Giants*	42	14	394	9.4	37	0
Futrell, Bobby, *T.B.*	24	6	213	8.9	22	0
Johnson, Billy, *Atl.*	21	6	168	8.0	45	0
Yarber, Eric, *Wash.*	37	9	273	7.4	33	0
Ellard, Henry, *Rams*	15	6	107	7.1	29	0
Stanley, Walter, *G.B.*	28	4	173	6.2	48	0
Morse, Bobby, *Phil.*	20	13	121	6.1	23	0

t = Touchdown
Leader based on average return, minimum 15 returns

NFC INTERCEPTORS

	No	Yards	Ave	Long	TD
Wilburn, Barry, *Wash.*	9	135	15.0	t100	1
Griffin, James, *Det.*	6	130	21.7	29	0
Browner, Joey, *Minn.*	6	67	11.2	23	0
Kinard, Terry, *Giants*	5	163	32.6	t70	1
Waymer, Dave, *N.O.*	5	78	15.6	35	0
Sutton, Reggie, *N.O.*	5	68	13.6	26	0
Curtis, Travis, *St L.*	5	65	13.0	31	0
Lott, Ronnie, *S.F.*	5	62	12.4	34	0
Walls, Everson, *Dall.*	5	38	7.6	30	0
Griffin, Don, *S.F.*	5	1	0.2	1	0
Downs, Michael, *Dall.*	4	56	14.0	27	0
Butler, Bobby, *Atl.*	4	48	12.0	31	0
Henderson, Wymon, *Minn.*	4	33	8.3	17	0
Mack, Milton, *N.O.*	4	32	8.0	26	0
Bowles, Todd, *Wash.*	4	24	6.0	24	0
Foules, Elbert, *Phil.*	4	6	1.5	6	0
Morris, Jim Bob, *G.B.*	3	135	45.0	73	0
Green, Darrell, *Wash.*	3	65	21.7	56	0
Waters, Andre, *Phil.*	3	63	21.0	63	0
Lee, Carl, *Minn.*	3	53	17.7	36	0
Galloway, Duane, *Det.*	3	46	15.3	30	0
Jakes, Van, *N.O.*	3	32	10.7	27	0
Bates, Bill, *Dall.*	3	28	9.3	28	0
Walton, Alvin, *Wash.*	3	28	9.3	24	0
Harris, John, *Minn.*	3	20	6.7	14	0
McNorton, Bruce, *Det.*	3	20	6.7	20	0
Maxie, Brett, *N.O.*	3	17	5.7	10	0
Tripoli, Paul, *T.B.*	3	17	5.7	t15	1
Brown, Dave, *G.B.*	3	16	5.3	11	0
Taylor, Lawrence, *Giants*	3	16	5.3	15	0
Atkins, Gene, *N.O.*	3	12	4.0	8	0
Haynes, Tommy, *Dall.*	3	7	2.3	7	0
Duerson, Dave, *Chi.*	3	0	0.0	0	0

t = Touchdown

DALLAS COWBOYS

Address Cowboys Center, One Cowboys Parkway, Irving, Texas 75063.

Stadium Texas Stadium, Irving.
Capacity 63,855 *Playing Surface* Texas Turf.

Team Colours Royal Blue, Metallic Silver Blue, and White.

Head Coach Tom Landry – twenty-ninth year.

Championships Division 1970,'71,'73,'76,'77,'78,'79,'81,'85; Conference 1970,'71,'75,'77,'78; Super Bowl 1971,'77.

History NFL 1960-69, NFC 1970-

Offense

After suffering back-to-back losing seasons for the first time since 1963-64, the Cowboys approach their 29th year in the NFL with renewed optimism. Almost the entire offense either has been rebuilt or is nearing the completion of reconstruction. On the interior offensive line, only center Tom Rafferty remains of the unit which started for the 1985 division championship team, and even he now plays only on passing and kicking downs, taking over in those circumstances from George Lilja. Two hefty rookie tackles, Kevin Gogan and Daryle Smith, developed much more quickly than expected, whilst Nate Newton and Crawford Ker ended the season as the starting guards. With former starting left tackle Mark Tuinei returning after injury to join 316-pound guard Jeff Zimmerman and draftees Mark Hutson and Dave Widell in the competition for places, the Cowboys begin to look very solid. Doug Cosbie has lost some of his sharpness but he remains a steady, dual-purpose tight end and should hold off the challenge of Thornton Chandler. At running back, a potentially damaging controversy has been averted by the club naming Herschel Walker as the starting tailback, ahead of the great veteran, Tony Dorsett. Subsequently, Dorsett was traded to the Denver Broncos. Allowing for Walker's ability as a pass receiver, the Cowboys probably now have the single most potent running back in the league. Timmy Newsome is the likely starter at fullback, ahead of Todd Fowler. 1988 may be the year that Steve Pelluer takes over from Danny White as the starting quarterback. White did not recover his full powers following the wrist fracture he suffered midway through the 1986 campaign. Pelluer has come through some sticky patches but he is young, powerful and decidedly fast when he tucks the ball under his arm and sets off into open field. In the scramble for the remaining spot, Paul McDonald and last year's rookie, Kevin Sweeney, are joined by this year's sixth-round pick, Scott Secules, who made excellent progress in his senior year and could well land the job. Given a little good fortune, the Cowboys could have wide receiver Mike Sherrard back in harness at sometime in the coming season. Sherrard, who is recovering from having broken the same leg twice, could form one of those dream partnerships with this year's top pick, Michael Irvin. Entering the campaign, though, Mike Renfro and Kelvin Edwards are the probable starters.

Defense

The rebuilding has continued on defense with equal promise. Indeed, the Cowboys are easing in their new players while still retaining their valued veterans. One such veteran is former all-pro defensive tackle Randy White, who, following the emergence of former first-round picks Kevin Brooks and Danny Noonan, may shift to the role of standup defensive end. However, at least one familiar name, that of Ed (Too Tall) Jones, remains in the role which, apart from a one-year foray into professional boxing, he has dominated ever since 1975. Last year, Jones led the team with ten sacks and is under no pressure to retain his starting spot at defensive left end. Jim Jeffcoat is the starter at right end, with Mark Walen and Don Smerek the principal backups at tackle and end respectively. Curiously, the ageing veteran, White, and last year's impressive free-agent rookie, Ron Burton, could play major roles. Burton was excellent in replacement of injured starting middle linebacker Eugene Lockhart, so much so that he may now be given an extended opportunity to challenge for playing time at outside linebacker, where Mike Hegman and Jeff Rohrer have started for the past three seasons. Hegman, a twelve-year veteran, missed the last three games of the 1987 season with a broken leg. Steve DeOssie, Jesse Penn and Garth Jax are fine backups, but the real lift at linebacking comes with the arrival of second-round draftee Ken Norton, a genuine value-for-money player who can wreak havoc. The secondary looks secure and should improve with the development of last year's second-round steal, right cornerback Ron Francis. At left cornerback, four-time AFC-NFC Pro Bowler Everson Walls would be expected to intercept half-a-dozen passes. Safeties Bill Bates and Michael Downs may have to work to hold off challenges from Vince Albritton and Victor Scott.

1988 SCHEDULE OF GAMES	September	
	4 at Pittsburgh	1:00
	12 at Phoenix (Mon.)	6:00
	18 NEW YORK GIANTS	3:00
	25 ATLANTA	12:00
	October	
	3 at New Orleans (Mon.)	8:00
	9 WASHINGTON	12:00
	16 at Chicago	12:00
	23 at Philadelphia	1:00
	30 PHOENIX	12:00
	November	
	6 at New York Giants	1:00
	13 MINNESOTA	7:00
	20 CINCINNATI	12:00
	24 HOUSTON (Thanksgiving)	3:00
	December	
	4 at Cleveland	1:00
	11 at Washington	1:00
	18 PHILADELPHIA	12:00

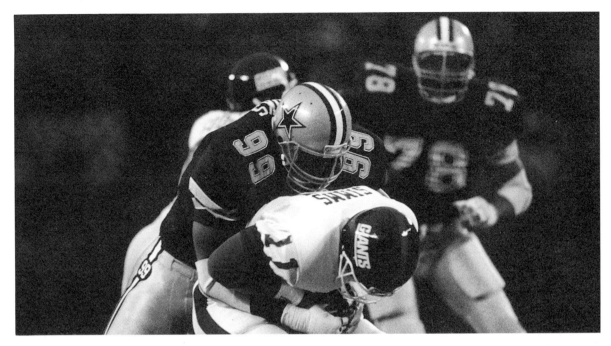

Special Teams

First-year placekicker Roger Ruzek is coming off a fine season, when he set the club record for field goal accuracy (.880), and Mike Saxon has become an accurate, medium-range punter. Kelvin Martin is likely to continue giving good service as a punt returner, whilst Darryl Clack's kickoff returning should enhance his chances of retaining a roster spot.

Kevin Brooks (# 99) is set to become a major force at defensive tackle.

1988 DRAFT

Round	Name	Pos.	Ht.	Wt.	College
1.	Irvin, Michael	WR	6-2	200	Miami
2.	Norton, Ken	LB	6-2	227	UCLA
3.	Hutson, Mark	G	6-3	291	Oklahoma
4.	Widell, Dave	T	6-6	282	Boston College
6.	Secules, Scott	QB	6-2	215	Virginia
7.	Hooven, Owen	T	6-8	305	Oregon State
8.	Higgs, Mark	RB	5-6	185	Kentucky
9.	Bedford, Brian	WR	6-3	210	California
10.	Owens, Billy	DB	6-0	195	Pittsburgh
11.	Hennings, Chad	DE	6-5	250	Air Force
12.	Hummel, Ben	LB	6-4	232	UCLA

VETERAN ROSTER

No.	Name	Pos.	Ht.	Wt.	NFL Year	College
36	Albritton, Vince	S	6-2	217	5	Washington
2	Alexander, Ray	WR	6-4	196	2	Florida A&M
87	Banks, Gordon	WR	5-10	170	6	Stanford
80	Barksdale, Rod	WR	6-0	193	3	Arizona
40	Bates, Bill	S	6-1	199	6	Tennessee
99	Brooks, Kevin	DT	6-6	278	4	Michigan
57	Burton, Ron	LB	6-1	245	2	North Carolina
89	Chandler, Thornton	TE	6-5	242	3	Alabama
70	Cisowski, Steve	T	6-5	275	2	Santa Clara
42	Clack, Darryl	RB-KR	5-10	220	3	Arizona State
84	Cosbie, Doug	TE	6-6	241	10	Santa Clara
55	DeOssie, Steve	LB	6-2	249	5	Boston College
26	Downs, Michael	S	6-3	212	8	Rice
81	Edwards, Kelvin	WR-PR	6-2	205	3	Liberty University
85	Folsom, Steve	TE	6-5	236	3	Utah
46	Fowler, Todd	RB	6-3	222	4	Stephen F. Austin
38	Francis, Ron	CB	5-9	199	2	Baylor

No.	Name	Pos.	Ht.	Wt.	Year	College
	Gay, Everett	WR	6-2	204	1	Texas
66	Gogan, Kevin	T	6-7	310	2	Washington
58	Hegman, Mike	LB	6-1	225	13	Tennessee State
45	Hendrix, Manuel	CB	5-11	181	3	Utah
52	Hurd, Jeff	LB	6-2	245	2	Kansas State
53	Jax, Garth	LB	6-2	222	3	Florida State
77	Jeffcoat, Jim	DE	6-5	263	6	Arizona State
72	Jones, Ed	DE	6-9	275	14	Tennessee State
68	Ker, Crawford	G	6-3	283	4	Florida
67	Lilja, George	C	6-4	282	7	Michigan
56	Lockhart, Eugene	LB	6-2	230	5	Houston
83	Martin, Kelvin	WR-PR	5-9	163	2	Boston College
14	McDonald, Paul	QB	6-2	182	9	Southern California
30	Newsome, Tim	RB	6-1	235	9	Winston-Salem State
61	Newton, Nate	G	6-3	315	3	Florida A&M
73	Noonan, Danny	DT	6-4	270	2	Nebraska
16	Pelluer, Steve	QB	6-4	208	5	Washington
59	Penn, Jesse	LB	6-3	224	4	Virginia Tech
64	Rafferty, Tom	C	6-3	263	13	Penn State
82	Renfro, Mike	WR	6-0	184	11	Texas Christian
50	Rohrer, Jeff	LB	6-2	222	7	Yale
9	Ruzek, Roger	K	6-2	190	2	Weber State
4	Saxon, Mike	P	6-3	193	4	San Diego State
22	Scott, Victor	S	6-0	203	5	Colorado
86	Sherrard, Mike	WR	6-2	194	2	UCLA
60	Smerek, Don	DT	6-7	266	7	Nevada-Reno
79	Smith, Daryle	T	6-5	278	2	Tennessee
97	Smith, Robert	DE	6-7	267	1	Grambling State
19	Sweeney, Kevin	QB	6-0	193	2	Fresno State
63	Titensor, Glen	G	6-4	275	7	Brigham Young
71	Tuinei, Mark	T	6-5	282	6	Hawaii
95	Walen, Mark	DT	6-5	262	2	UCLA
34	Walker, Herschel	RB	6-1	225	3	Georgia
24	Walls, Everson	CB	6-1	192	8	Grambling State
94	Watts, Randy	DE	6-6	305	2	Catawba
65	White, Bob	G-C	6-5	267	2	Rhode Island
11	White, Danny	QB	6-3	198	13	Arizona State
54	White, Randy	DT	6-4	263	14	Maryland
23	Williams, Robert	CB	5-10	190	2	Baylor
76	Zimmerman, Jeff	G	6-3	316	2	Florida

NEW YORK GIANTS

Address Giants Stadium, East Rutherford, New Jersey 07073.

Stadium Giants Stadium, East Rutherford.
Capacity 76,891 *Playing Surface* AstroTurf.

Team Colours Blue, Red, and White.

Head Coach Bill Parcells – sixth year.

Championships Division 1986; Conference 1986; NFL 1927,'34,'38,'56; Super Bowl 1986.

History NFL 1925-69, NFC 1970-

Offense

Even after the event, it still is amazing that the Giants, a team with so much talent that they hardly needed a draft, finished in the NFC East cellar. Looking at it a little more positively, in games played by the regulars they were 6-6. Coming into the 1988 season, they will be without left tackle Brad Benson, who has retired, and, probably, former starting right tackle Karl Nelson, who missed the whole of last season and may not have recovered fully from the combined effects of organic illness and surgery for an arthritic shoulder. (Thankfully, his progress following radiotherapy for the organic illness is excellent.) Last year, in Nelson's absence, William Roberts came in and, over the final weeks, made good progress and looked much more like the 1984 first-round pick who started as a rookie but missed the entire 1985 season with an injury. Roberts may shift back to left tackle, making way for the winner of a competition which will include the top draftees, Eric Moore and John Elliott. The other likely starters are guards Chris Godfrey and Bill Ard, and center Bart Oates. The line is anchored by all-pro tight end Mark Bavaro, a punishing blocker who also led the club in pass receptions. Bavaro is backed up by the reliable Zeke Mowatt, who could start for some NFL clubs. One reason for the Giants' failure to challenge last year was the lack of a threat at running back, where Joe Morris, in particular, was much below par, averaging only 3.4 yards per carry and with a longest gain of 34 yards. In George Adams, who caught 35 passes to rank second in the club, and Lee Rouson, the Giants have two young horses straining at the reins. Behind the blocking of fullback Maurice Carthon, either man could explode to league-wide prominence. Surprisingly, in a modest season for the club, quarterback Phil Simms had the best campaign of his career and must now be regarded amongst the NFL's finest at his position. His major problem last year was the lack of a hot wide receiver. In support of Simms, Jeff Rutledge should continue as the senior reserve whilst the drafting of Mike Perez presents exciting possibilities for the future. The 1987 first-round pick, wide receiver Mark Ingram, did not come through as quickly as the club had hoped, but both third-round pick Stephen Baker and fourth-round pick Odessa Turner showed fine speed and promise. No one is writing off Ingram's prospects but, for the moment, Lionel Manuel and Baker are expected to resume as the starters.

Defense

The Giants' inability to dominate defensively in 1987, despite being knee-deep in all-star performers, probably will never be explained satisfactorily. Certainly, nose tackle Jim Burt was fit to start in only eight games, but his replacement, Erik Howard, did extremely well, logging 5.5 sacks. With the development of both Howard and former first-round pick defensive end Eric Dorsey, the Giants begin to look ominously powerful. Dorsey may see more time as a starter, ahead of George Martin, with Pro Bowler Leonard Marshall at defensive right end. Linebacking continues to be of a quality way off the scale, at the high end, with Carl Banks now having established himself the equal of the magnificent Lawrence Taylor. Banks, who often keys on the running back and goes for the backfield tackle, came second in the club with nine quarterback sacks, one more than Marshall, behind Taylor's 12. Inside linebacker Harry Carson is another perennial Pro Bowler, and he shows few signs of losing his edge, even after twelve years in the world's most inhospitable trenches. Increasingly though, Thomas (Pepper) Johnson, a former second-round draftee, is becoming a factor. In addition, Gary Reasons will be seeking to re-establish himself after a season during which he could not regain his starting spot following a contractual holdout. Head coach Parcells is spoiled for choice. The secondary is less strong and both starting safeties, Kenny Hill (ankle) and Terry Kinard (shoulder), are coming off post-season surgery. They are expected to continue as the starters, allowing more time for former second-round picks Greg Lasker and Adrian White to develop. Encouragingly, cornerback Mark Collins came through his second season with good marks, not least for his tackling in which he led the secondary and came fourth in the club. Perry Williams completes the starting quartet, with Herb Welch, Wayne Haddix and draftee Sheldon White as backups.

1988 SCHEDULE OF GAMES		
September		
5	WASHINGTON (Mon.)	9:00
11	SAN FRANCISCO	1:00
18	at Dallas	3:00
25	LOS ANGELES RAMS	4:00
October		
2	at Washington	1:00
10	at Philadelphia (Mon.)	9:00
16	DETROIT	1:00
23	at Atlanta	1:00
30	at Detroit	1:00
November		
6	DALLAS	1:00
13	at Phoenix	2:00
20	PHILADELPHIA	4:00
27	at New Orleans	7:00
December		
4	PHOENIX	1:00
11	KANSAS CITY	1:00
18	at New York Jets	1:00

Special Teams

Punter Sean Landeta is the pick of the special teams which, otherwise, could use an impact player. Phil McConkey (punts) and Rouson (kickoffs) are expected to continue as the senior returners. Placekicker Raul Allegre is not under threat but he is coming off a moderate year in which he was successful on only three of nine attempts in the range, 40-49 yards.

VETERAN ROSTER

No.	Name	Pos.	Ht.	Wt.	NFL Year	College
	Abraham, Robert	LB	6-1	236	6	North Carolina State
33	Adams, George	RB	6-1	225	3	Kentucky
2	Allegre, Raul	K	5-10	167	6	Texas
24	Anderson, Ottis	RB	6-2	225	10	Miami
67	Ard, Bill	G	6-3	270	8	Wake Forest
85	Baker, Stephen	WR	5-8	160	2	Fresno State
58	Banks, Carl	LB	6-4	235	5	Michigan State
89	Bavaro, Mark	TE	6-4	245	4	Notre Dame
79	Berthusen, Bill	NT	6-5	285	2	Iowa State
69	Black, Mike	T	6-4	280	3	Cal State-Sacramento
64	Burt, Jim	NT	6-1	260	8	Miami
	Byrd, Boris	DB	6-0	210	2	Austin Peay
53	Carson, Harry	LB	6-2	240	13	South Carolina State
44	Carthon, Maurice	RB	6-1	225	4	Arkansas State
21	Clayton, Harvey	CB	5-9	186	6	Florida State
25	Collins, Mark	CB	5-10	190	3	Cal State-Fullerton
77	Dorsey, Eric	DE	6-5	280	3	Notre Dame
28	Flynn, Tom	S	6-0	195	5	Pittsburgh
30	Galbreath, Tony	RB	6-0	228	13	Missouri
61	Godfrey, Chris	G	6-3	265	6	Michigan
37	Haddix, Wayne	CB	6-1	203	2	Liberty University
54	Headen, Andy	LB	6-5	242	6	Clemson
48	Hill, Kenny	S	6-0	195	8	Yale
15	Hostetler, Jeff	QB	6-3	212	5	West Virginia
74	Howard, Erik	NT-DE	6-4	268	3	Washington State
57	Hunt, Byron	LB	6-5	242	8	Southern Methodist
82	Ingram, Mark	WR	5-10	188	2	Michigan State
68	Johnson, Damian	G	6-5	290	3	Kansas State
52	Johnson, Thomas	LB	6-3	248	3	Ohio State
59	Johnston, Brian	C	6-3	275	3	North Carolina
43	Kinard, Terry	S	6-1	200	6	Clemson
5	Landeta, Sean	P	6-0	200	4	Towson State
46	Lasker, Greg	S	6-0	200	3	Arkansas
86	Manuel, Lionel	WR	5-11	180	5	Pacific
70	Marshall, Leonard	DE	6-3	285	6	Louisiana State
75	Martin, George	DE	6-4	255	14	Oregon
80	McConkey, Phil	WR-KR	5-10	170	5	Navy
	Morgan, Dan	G	6-6	285	3	Penn State
20	Morris, Joe	RB	5-7	195	7	Syracuse
84	Mowatt, Zeke	TE	6-3	240	5	Florida State
63	Nelson, Karl	T	6-6	285	4	Iowa State
65	Oates, Bart	C	6-3	265	4	Brigham Young
55	Reasons, Gary	LB	6-4	234	5	Northwestern St., La.
26	Richardson, Tim	RB	6-0	215	1	Pacific
72	Riesenberg, Doug	T	6-5	275	2	California
66	Roberts, William	T	6-5	280	4	Ohio State
81	Robinson, Stacy	WR	5-11	186	4	North Dakota State
22	Rouson, Lee	RB	6-1	222	4	Colorado
17	Rutledge, Jeff	QB	6-1	195	10	Alabama
11	Simms, Phil	QB	6-3	214	9	Morehead State
56	Taylor, Lawrence	LB	6-3	243	8	North Carolina
83	Turner, Odessa	WR	6-3	205	2	Northwestern St., La.
34	Varajon, Michael	RB	6-1	232	2	Toledo
73	Washington, John	DE	6-4	275	3	Oklahoma State
27	Welch, Herb	CB	5-11	180	4	UCLA
36	White, Adrian	S	6-0	200	2	Florida
23	Williams, Perry	CB	6-2	203	5	North Carolina State

1988 DRAFT

Round	Name	Pos.	Ht.	Wt.	College
1.	Moore, Eric	T	6-5	285	Indiana
2.	Elliott, John	T	6-6	305	Michigan
3.	White, Sheldon	DB	5-11	190	Miami, Ohio
4.	Shaw, Ricky	LB	6-4	235	Oklahoma State
5.	Carter, Jon	DE	6-3	261	Pittsburgh
6.	Houle, David	G	6-4	270	Michigan State
7.	Perez, Mike	QB	6-1	208	San Jose State
7.	Whitaker, Danta	TE	6-3	245	Mississippi Valley St.
8.	Lilly, Sammy	DB	5-9	170	Georgia Tech
10.	Hickerson, Eric	DB	6-1	212	Indiana
10.	Wilkes, Steve	TE	6-4	252	Appalachian State
11.	Harris, Greg	WR	5-9	160	Troy State
12.	Futrell, David	NT	6-1	262	Brigham Young
12.	McCormack, Brendan	DT	6-6	275	South Carolina

Phil Simms is coming off his best year in the pros.

PHILADELPHIA EAGLES

Address Veterans Stadium, Broad St. and Pattison Ave., Philadelphia, Pa. 19148.

Stadium Veterans Stadium, Philadelphia.
Capacity 66,592 *Playing Surface* AstroTurf.

Team Colours Kelly Green, Silver, and White.

Head Coach Buddy Ryan – third year.

Championships Division 1980; Conference 1980; NFL 1948,'49,'60.

History NFL 1933-69, NFC 1970-

Offense

The Eagles have just enjoyed a season of great improvement and, after a sound draft, they are ready to challenge, even in this competitive division. They made progress on the offensive line, plugging a few of the gaps which led to an alarmingly high number of quarterback sacks in 1986. By comparison, just 50 sacks conceded in the twelve games played by the regulars is quite acceptable. Head coach Buddy Ryan projects left guard Ben Tamburello (ahead of Adam Schreiber) and right tackle Reggie Singletary (ahead of Joe Conwell) to move in as starters in company with center Gerry Feehery, left tackle Matt Darwin and right guard Ron Baker. Twelve months ago they looked to be in a spot of bother but now, with third-round draftee tackle Matt Patchan having arrived, they have some depth. Quarterback Randall Cunningham has become a one-man show. Not only did he develop as one of the league's better passers but, also, he led the Eagles in rushing, in that capacity scoring three touchdowns. Steadily, the talent spotters have assembled for him an array of exciting targets. Already they have the great all-pro wide receiver, Mike Quick and the sure-handed Gregg Garrity. The 1987 supplemental draftee, Cris Carter, has genuine starter class and is expected to make a serious challenge to take the place of Kenny Jackson, who has retired. In the recent draft, the Eagles used their first option to pick tight end Keith Jackson, whose breathtaking skills as a receiver could enable the passing offense to take the step into a higher dimension. First, though, he'll have to beat out John Spagnola, a really solid veteran of eight years. If, however, the Eagles are to win a title, they must establish a rushing game, and that would mean Keith Byars playing up to his potential. Byars' two-year career has been hampered by injuries, fractured bones in each of his feet, which have prevented his taking part in either of the two preseason training camps. He has been training throughout the offseason and, for the first time, he should be ready to get after the opposition. It is a prospect which your writer has been savouring since Byars' days at Ohio State. Fullback Anthony Toney is well respected, both as a rusher and as a pass receiver, each category in which he ranked second in the club. But it is his blocking which could unlock the final door and launch Byars into the distance. Michael Haddix also has developed as a solid blocker, whilst Junior Tautalatasi is on hand as a shock trooper.

Defense

It has been Ryan's main priority to gather talent for the defensive line and now he has it in abundance. Defensive ends Reggie White and Clyde Simmons, and defensive tackles Mike Pitts and Jerome Brown may just form the best quartet in pro football. After leading the league with 21 sacks, one fewer than the NFL single-season record even though playing in only twelve games, White was a unanimous all-pro choice. Clearly Simmons derived benefit from the presence of White, but he made excellent progress to start all twelve games in his second pro season. Brown matured quickly as a rookie and started in eight games. Mike Pitts fitted in well after arriving via a trade with Atlanta, and he was confirmed as the senior left tackle when Ken Clarke was released in April. At linebacker, it looks as if only Seth Joyner is certain of his starting spot, and it has to be healthy that solid players are battling for the remaining two places. Mike Reichenbach would have expected to start but Byron Evans, who played in the final three games when Reichenbach was injured, may get the nod. Dwayne Jiles and Ty Allert will battle for the right outside position. Garry Cobb, a smart, tenth-year veteran, will back up in all three positions. The secondary is the least secure area, and though safeties Terry Hoage and Andre Waters are effective against the rush, the quartet did have difficulty defending against the pass. They would receive an enormous boost were former Pro Bowl safety Wes Hopkins to recover from the serious knee injury which has kept him out since the fourth game of the 1986 season. Roynell Young holds down the left cornerback position, but there is a great opportunity for all of the four draftee defensive backs, led by Eric Allen, to win a job on the right corner. Also involved in that preseason competition will be the returning veterans, Elbert Foules, Cedrick Brown and William Frizzell.

1988 SCHEDULE OF GAMES		
September		
4	at Tampa Bay	1:00
11	CINCINNATI	4:00
18	at Washington	1:00
25	at Minnesota	12:00
October		
2	HOUSTON	1:00
10	NEW YORK GIANTS (Mon.)	9:00
16	at Cleveland	1:00
23	DALLAS	1:00
30	ATLANTA	1:00
November		
6	LOS ANGELES RAMS	1:00
13	at Pittsburgh	1:00
20	at New York Giants	4:00
27	PHOENIX	1:00
December		
4	WASHINGTON	1:00
10	at Phoenix (Sat.)	2:00
18	at Dallas	12:00

NFC EASTERN DIVISION

Special Teams

Both placekicker Paul McFadden and punter John Teltschik are coming off modest seasons. Teltschik's gross average went down by 3.4 yards for no obvious tactical reason, and McFadden faces a stern challenge from Canadian free agent Dean Dorsey. Kick returning also is an area in need of improvement. Here, Carter has all the required talents and it may be his major contribution if he can not crack the starting lineup as a wide receiver.

1988 DRAFT

Round	Name	Pos.	Ht.	Wt.	College
1.	Jackson, Keith	TE	6-2	241	Oklahoma
2.	Allen, Eric	DB	5-9	184	Arizona State
3.	Patchan, Matt	T	6-3	275	Miami
5.	Everett, Eric	DB	5-10	160	Texas Tech
6.	McPherson, Don	QB	6-0	180	Syracuse
6.	Sterling, Rob	DB	5-11	190	Maine
7.	White, Todd	WR	5-11	185	Cal State-Fullerton
8.	Smith, David	RB	6-1	222	Western Kentucky
10.	Schuster, Joe	DT	6-5	270	Iowa
11.	Jenkins, Izel	DB	5-9	185	North Carolina State
12.	Kaufusi, Steve	DE	6-4	272	Brigham Young

VETERAN ROSTER

No.	Name	Pos.	Ht.	Wt.	NFL Year	College
72	Alexander, David	T	6-3	275	2	Tulsa
58	Allert, Ty	LB	6-2	233	3	Texas
87	Bailey, Eric	TE	6-5	240	2	Kansas State
63	Baker, Ron	G	6-4	274	11	Oklahoma State
16	Booker, Martin	WR	6-1	191	1	Villanova
23	Brown, Cedrick	CB	5-10	182	2	Washington State
99	Brown, Jerome	DT	6-2	288	2	Miami
41	Byars, Keith	RB	6-1	238	3	Ohio State
80	Carter, Cris	WR	6-3	194	2	Ohio State
6	Cavanaugh, Matt	QB	6-2	210	11	Pittsburgh
27	Clemons, Topper	RB	5-11	205	2	Wake Forest
50	Cobb, Garry	LB	6-2	230	10	Southern California
79	Conwell, Joe	T	6-5	286	3	North Carolina
21	Cooper, Evan	S	5-11	194	5	Michigan
45	Crawford, Charles	RB	6-2	243	2	Oklahoma State
12	Cunningham, Randall	QB	6-4	201	4	Nevada-Las Vegas
78	Darwin, Matt	T	6-4	275	3	Texas A&M
2	Dorsey, Dean	K	5-11	190	1	Toronto
93	Dumbauld, Jon	DT	6-4	259	3	Kentucky
56	Evans, Byron	LB	6-2	225	2	Arizona
67	Feehery, Gerry	C	6-2	270	6	Syracuse
29	Foules, Elbert	CB	5-11	193	6	Alcorn State
33	Frizzell, William	CB-S	6-3	205	5	North Carolina Central
86	Garrity, Gregg	WR-PR	5-10	169	6	Penn State
38	Gary, Russell	S	5-11	200	8	Nebraska
83	Giles, Jimmie	TE	6-3	240	12	Alcorn State
90	Golic, Mike	NT	6-5	275	3	Notre Dame
26	Haddix, Michael	RB	6-2	227	6	Mississippi State
34	Hoage, Terry	S	6-3	201	5	Georgia
22	Hoggard, D.D.	CB	6-0	188	3	North Carolina State
48	Hopkins, Wes	S	6-1	212	5	Southern Methodist
53	Jiles, Dwayne	LB	6-4	250	4	Texas Tech
54	Johnson, Alonzo	LB	6-3	222	3	Florida
85	Johnson, Ron	WR	6-3	186	4	Cal State-Long Beach
59	Joyner, Seth	LB	6-2	248	3	Texas-El Paso
64	Kelley, Mike	G-C	6-5	280	4	Notre Dame
97	Klingel, John	DE	6-3	267	2	Eastern Kentucky
9	Lambiotte, Ken	QB	6-3	191	1	William & Mary
65	Landsee, Bob	G-C	6-4	275	3	Wisconsin
89	Little, Dave	TE	6-2	226	5	Middle Tennessee St.
8	McFadden, Paul	K	5-11	166	5	Youngstown State
36	Morse, Bobby	RB-KR	5-10	213	2	Michigan State
57	Moten, Ron	LB	6-1	230	1	Florida
74	Pitts, Mike	DE-DT	6-5	277	6	Alabama
82	Quick, Mike	WR	6-2	190	7	North Carolina State
66	Reeves, Ken	T	6-5	270	4	Texas A&M
55	Reichenbach, Mike	LB	6-2	230	5	East Stroudsburg, Pa.
24	Reid, Alan	RB	5-8	197	2	Minnesota
76	Schreiber, Adam	G-C	6-4	277	5	Texas
95	Schulz, Jody	LB	6-3	235	5	East Carolina
96	Simmons, Clyde	DE	6-6	276	3	Western Carolina
68	Singletary, Reggie	G	6-3	280	3	North Carolina State
88	Spagnola, John	TE	6-4	242	9	Yale
61	Tamburello, Ben	G-C	6-3	278	1	Auburn
37	Tautalatasi, Junior	RB	5-10	210	3	Washington State
10	Teltschik, John	P	6-2	209	3	Texas
25	Toney, Anthony	RB	6-0	227	3	Texas A&M
20	Waters, Andre	S	5-11	199	5	Cheyney, Pa.
92	White, Reggie	DE	6-5	285	4	Tennessee
43	Young, Roynell	CB	6-1	185	9	Alcorn State

Fullback Anthony Toney is the key to springing Keith Byars.

PHOENIX CARDINALS

Address P.O. Box 888, Phoenix, Arizona, 85001.
Stadium Sun Devil Stadium, Tempe, Arizona.
Capacity 70,021 *Playing Surface* Grass.
Team Colours Cardinal Red, Black, and White.
Head Coach Gene Stallings – third year.
Championships Division 1974,'75; NFL 1925,'47.
History NFL 1920-69, NFC 1970-
(They were known as the Chicago Cardinals until 1960, when they moved to St Louis. In 1988, the franchise, still under the same ownership, was transferred to Phoenix.)

Offense

Over their twenty-seven-year stay in the city of St Louis, the Cardinals neither won a playoff game nor earned the right to a home playoff game. It is, however, very easy to see their competing right from the start in their new home of Phoenix. A year ago, it was well known that Neil Lomax was available to be traded, and yet he enters the 1988 season fully in command and rated highly in the league. Lomax was at the hub of an offense which almost doubled its points per game, up from an NFL-worst average of 13.6 in 1986. His personal reward was a second selection to the AFC-NFC Pro Bowl. Some of the credit for the revival must go to an offensive line which played far better than expected. Starting in the key position of left tackle, Luis Sharpe had his best year to date, and the line has a settled look, with guard Joe Bostic returning after injury to reclaim his spot at left guard, where the rookie, Todd Peat, did well as a replacement. Elsewhere, the starters will be Derek Kennard at center, Lance Smith at right guard and Tootie Robbins at right tackle. Again, playing his full part in a rejuvenated offense was tenth-year veteran wide receiver J. T. Smith, who caught a Cardinals club-record 91 passes and led the entire NFL. At an age when most receivers would be fading gracefully, Smith is at the peak of his form and raring to go. That may not be true of his probable starting partner, Roy Green, who, because of injuries, has slipped from the lofty heights of the 1983 and 1984 seasons, over which period he caught 156 passes for 2,782 yards and 26 touchdowns. Down the sideline he used to be sensational, and over the middle he was deadly. Last year, that middle area quickly became the province of rookie Robert Awalt, who may be the best young pass receiving tight end prospect since the arrival of San Diego's Kellen Winslow. At a stroke, Awalt represented an extra facet in an area of the diamond which had lost some of its sparkle. Stump Mitchell confirmed his status as a solid running back but, in truth, he never looked to be in top gear, whereas Earl Ferrell did show class before a late-season injury. Mitchell is worth his starting spot for his role as a pass receiver, but that the offensive backfield is an area in need of help was indicated by the drafting of Tony Jeffery in the second round.

Defense

It may be the fall in effectiveness of the Cardinals' defense which kept them out of the playoffs. They slipped from fourth in the NFL in 1986 all the way down to 25th. Defense against the pass dropped off alarmingly, though there were mitigating circumstances, not least the unavailability of defensive tackle David Galloway until December and the loss of their best pass rusher, defensive end Curtis Greer, for the final three games. Statistically, defensive end Freddie Joe Nunn was the pick of the line, registering 11 quarterback sacks, and he looked the part after making the transition from outside linebacker over just the one campaign. It is anticipated that one of Bob Clasby, Mark Duda and Steve Alvord will occupy the remaining spot open at defensive tackle. At outside linebacker, in Anthony Bell and E. J. Junior, the Cardinals field two former first-round picks, but in a year considered to offer a good rookie crop, wisely they selected Ken Harvey with their first option. In truth, neither Bell nor Junior played consistently up to his best and this is an area in which improvement is required. Harvey is on the light side – he might have trouble if the opposition runs at him – but he is an outstanding prospect for development as a third-down pass-coverage specialist. The hard-tackling Niko Noga has made the middle linebacker position his own. The secondary had trouble all year, and this is reflected in the 30 touchdown passes scored by the opposition (it was the second-highest total in the NFL). However, this did come as a surprise, for there certainly would not appear to be a weakness at safety, where the starters are Leonard Smith and Lonnie Young, backed up by last year's second-round draftee, Tim McDonald. Rookie safety Travis Curtis came in as a nickel back and led the club with five interceptions. There is a concern at cornerback, where neither of starters Cedric Mack and Carl Carter is dominant. Draftee Michael Brim is from a small college but he has good speed and could see action.

1988 SCHEDULE OF GAMES	September	
	4 at Cincinnati	1:00
	12 DALLAS (Mon.)	6:00
	18 at Tampa Bay	1:00
	25 WASHINGTON	1:00
	October	
	2 at Los Angeles Rams	1:00
	9 PITTSBURGH	1:00
	16 at Washington	1:00
	23 CLEVELAND	1:00
	30 at Dallas	12:00
	November	
	6 SAN FRANCISCO	2:00
	13 NEW YORK GIANTS	2:00
	20 at Houston	12:00
	27 at Philadelphia	1:00
	December	
	4 at New York Giants	1:00
	10 PHILADELPHIA (Sat.)	2:00
	18 GREEN BAY	2:00

Tight end Robert Awalt will challenge for a Pro Bowl spot.

Special Teams

The Cardinals' kickoff coverage teams are excellent, as is their own kickoff and punt returning, with Pro Bowler Vai Sikahema doing both jobs. Placekicking has been a Cardinals headache for some years now. Al Del Greco and Jim Gallery will battle for the job. There's hope for the punting department with the drafting of dual-purpose quarterback-punter Tom Tupa in the third round.

1988 DRAFT

Round	Name	Pos.	Ht.	Wt.	College
1.	Harvey, Ken	LB	6-2	222	California
2.	Jeffery, Tony	RB	5-11	204	Texas Christian
3.	Tupa, Tom	P-QB	6-4	212	Ohio State
4.	Brim, Michael	DB	6-0	185	Virginia Union
5.	Gaines, Chris	LB	6-0	230	Vanderbilt
5.	Jordan, Tony	RB	6-2	219	Kansas State
6.	Phillips, Jon	G	6-3	270	Oklahoma
7.	Jones, Ernie	WR	5-11	185	Indiana
8.	Moore, Tim	LB	6-2	220	Michigan State
9.	Dill, Scott	G	6-4	270	Memphis State
10.	Schillinger, Andy	WR	5-11	180	Miami, Ohio
11.	McCoy, Keith	DB	5-11	172	Fresno State
12.	Carrier, Chris	DB	6-4	212	Louisiana State

VETERAN ROSTER

No.	Name	Pos.	Ht.	Wt.	NFL Year	College
60	Alvord, Steve	DT	6-4	272	2	Washington
80	Awalt, Robert	TE	6-5	248	2	San Diego State
52	Baker, Charlie	LB	6-2	234	9	New Mexico
55	Bell, Anthony	LB	6-3	231	3	Michigan State
71	Bostic, Joe	G	6-3	268	10	Clemson
62	Brown, Ray	G-T	6-5	280	3	Arkansas State
82	Brown, Ron	WR	5-10	186	2	Colorado
41	Carter, Carl	CB	5-11	180	3	Texas Tech
74	Chilton, Gene	T-C	6-3	271	3	Texas
79	Clasby, Bob	DT	6-5	260	3	Notre Dame
20	Curtis, Travis	S	5-10	180	2	West Virginia
53	Davis, Wayne	LB	6-1	213	2	Alabama
17	Del Greco, Al	K	5-10	191	5	Auburn
73	Duda, Mark	DT	6-3	279	6	Maryland
31	Ferrell, Earl	RB	6-0	224	7	East Tennessee State
13	Gallery, Jim	K	6-1	190	2	Minnesota
65	Galloway, David	DT	6-3	279	7	Florida
76	Garalczyk, Mark	DT	6-5	272	2	Western Michigan
10	Garza, Sammy	QB	6-1	184	2	Texas-El Paso
81	Green, Roy	WR	6-0	195	10	Henderson, Ark.
75	Greer, Curtis	DE	6-4	258	8	Michigan
89	Harris, William	TE	6-4	243	2	Bishop College
83	Holmes, Don	WR	5-10	180	2	Mesa, Colorado
11	Horne, Greg	P	6-0	188	2	Arkansas
21	Jackson, Mark	CB	5-9	180	2	Abilene Christian
50	Jarostchuk, Ilia	LB	6-3	231	2	New Hampshire
27	Johnson, Greggory	S	6-1	197	6	Oklahoma State
87	Johnson, Troy	WR	6-1	175	3	Southern
54	Junior, E.J.	LB	6-3	235	8	Alabama
70	Kennard, Derek	C	6-3	285	3	Nevada-Reno
15	Lomax, Neil	QB	6-3	215	8	Portland State
47	Mack, Cedric	CB	6-0	194	6	Baylor
33	McAdoo, Derrick	RB	5-10	198	2	Baylor
46	McDonald, Tim	S	6-2	207	2	Southern California
30	Mitchell, Stump	RB	5-9	188	8	Citadel
68	Morris, Michael	T	6-5	275	2	Northeast Missouri St.
57	Noga, Niko	LB	6-1	235	5	Hawaii
85	Novacek, Jay	TE	6-4	235	4	Wyoming
78	Nunn, Freddie Joe	DE	6-4	255	4	Mississippi
64	Peat, Todd	G	6-2	294	2	Northern Illinois
26	Peoples, Tim	DB	6-0	200	2	Washington
63	Robbins, Tootie	T	6-5	302	7	East Carolina
51	Ruether, Mike	C	6-4	275	3	Texas
72	Saddler, Rod	DE	6-5	276	2	Texas A&M
39	Sargent, Broderick	RB	5-10	215	3	Baylor
69	Scotts, Colin	DT-DE	6-5	263	2	Hawaii
67	Sharpe, Luis	T	6-4	260	7	UCLA
36	Sikahema, Vai	RB-KR	5-9	191	3	Brigham Young
84	Smith, J.T.	WR	6-2	185	11	North Texas State
61	Smith, Lance	G	6-2	262	4	Louisiana State
45	Smith, Leonard	S	5-11	202	6	McNeese State
18	Stoudt, Cliff	QB	6-4	215	10	Youngstown State
	Vatterott, Charles	G-T	6-4	263	1	Southwest Texas State
66	Welter, Tom	T	6-5	280	1	Nebraska
24	Wolfley, Ron	RB	6-0	222	4	West Virginia
43	Young, Lonnie	S	6-1	182	4	Michigan State

WASHINGTON REDSKINS

Address Redskin Park, P.O. Box 17247, Dulles
International Airport, Washington, D.C. 20041.
Stadium Robert F. Kennedy Stadium, Washington.
Capacity 55,750
Playing Surface Grass (Prescription Athletic Turf).
Team Colours Burgundy and Gold.
Head Coach Joe Gibbs – eighth year.
Championships Division 1972,'83,'84,'87;
Conference 1972,'82,'83,'87;
NFL 1937,'42; Super Bowl 1982,'87.
History NFL 1932-69, NFC 1970-
(Originally named the Boston Braves for the 1932
season only, they were renamed the Boston Redskins
until, in 1937, they moved to Washington.)

Offense

Surveying the entire offense, there are no signs of a weakness, even down amongst the backups, where the likes of wide receiver Anthony Allen, quarterback Jay Schroeder and running back Keith Griffin are capable of big performances. Turning to the starters, though, pride of place must go to quarterback Doug Williams, whom one remembers as the young Tampa Bay rifleman but who now has added great poise to his armoury. Whether gunning the ball or feathering it out, Williams is a master of his craft. By comparison, backup Schroeder is unpolished, but he played a major role in keeping the Redskins in contention following the injury which brought a sudden end to the career of Joe Theismann in 1985. Ordinarily, one would have expected to see Gary Clark and Art Monk as the starting wide receivers, and whilst the elusive Clark should continue in that role, it may be that Monk has to share increasing time with Ricky Sanders, who ravaged the Broncos' secondary for 193 yards and two touchdowns on nine receptions in the Super Bowl. Monk presents a combination of graceful, deceptive speed, excellent hands and coolness under pressure. At running back, the starting role has been transferred from George Rogers (he has been released) to last year's fifth-round draftee and Super Bowl hero, Timmy Smith. A year ago, one imagined Kelvin Bryant easing into Rogers' place, but he now can be retained for his dual-purpose value – he averaged an excellent 5.3 yards per rush and a fine 11.4 yards on 43 pass receptions. Smith is not what one would call a franchise back. He certainly is not the fastest around. But he is a disciplined runner. He goes where he is told, through those yawning gaps created by that super offensive line. Russ Grimm moved from left guard to solve what was felt to be a weakness at center. Following his knee injury and a return to form by Jeff Bostic, Grimm couldn't regain his former place from Raleigh McKenzie, who looked a natural – as if they didn't have enough talent. Left tackle Joe Jacoby would be a popular pick as the NFC's best,

whilst, on the right side, Mark May and R. C. Thielemann are very tough. There is nothing at all wrong with tight ends Don Warren, the blocker, and Clint Didier, who is now to be regarded as a key receiver.

Defense

The glamour of the Redskins defense lies at defensive end, where Charles Mann and Dexter Manley form a terrifying partnership. They came first and second in the club with 9.5 and 8.5 sacks respectively. What isn't logged officially is the number of times they almost get their man, meaning that the quarterback is hurried into a hasty pass. With 73 career sacks since official records first were kept in 1982, Manley is the leading defensive lineman in the NFL and ranks second only to Giants linebacker Lawrence Taylor. Defensive tackle Dave Butz goes on and on – he is entering his fifteenth season – dominant against the run and always a potential threat to bat down a pass. The other starter, Darryl Grant, is as solid as a rock. Steve Hamilton and Markus Koch are the backups at defensive end whilst Dean Hamel is the reserve at tackle. For some time the Redskins have been really solid at linebacker, where Mel Kaufman, Neal Olkewicz and Monte Coleman were the nominal starters, with Rich Milot seeing a great deal of action as the senior backup. Following the acquisition of former Chicago and current all-pro, Wilber Marshall, who was signed after his contract had expired, Milot was released. The Redskins' pass rush was good anyway but now, with Marshall firing in from one of the outside positions, it could be the best in pro football. Entering the campaign, the defensive secondary was seen as a relative weakness, but the unit responded with a fine showing. Cornerback Barry Wilburn must regard himself as unfortunate not to be selected to the AFC-NFC Pro Bowl after having led the entire NFL with nine pass interceptions. On the other corner, Darrell Green is becoming an automatic choice as a Pro Bowl starter. At safety, two players came through to establish themselves as starters. Alvin Walton

1988 SCHEDULE OF GAMES	September	
	5 at New York Giants (Mon.)	9:00
	11 PITTSBURGH	1:00
	18 PHILADELPHIA	1:00
	25 at Phoenix	1:00
	October	
	2 NEW YORK GIANTS	1:00
	9 at Dallas	12:00
	16 PHOENIX	1:00
	23 vs. Green Bay at Milwaukee	12:00
	30 at Houston	7:00
	November	
	6 NEW ORLEANS	4:00
	13 CHICAGO	1:00
	21 at San Francisco (Mon.)	6:00
	27 CLEVELAND	1:00
	December	
	4 at Philadelphia	1:00
	11 DALLAS	1:00
	17 at Cincinnati (Sat.)	12:30

uses the direct approach – he just flattens people – whilst Todd Bowles showed a subtle awareness of the complexities of playing the free safety position. Clarence Vaughn is the senior backup at safety with Dennis Woodberry and 1987 second-round pick Brian Davis giving depth on the corners.

Special Teams

Following the rapid decline of Ali Haji-Sheikh, it is almost certain that the job of placekicker will go either to Jess Atkinson or top draftee Chip Lohmiller. Steve Cox is a valuable punter and occasional long-range field goal specialist. There are, however, opportunities in both the kick and punt return departments.

1988 DRAFT

Round	Name	Pos.	Ht.	Wt.	College
2.	Lohmiller, Chip	K	6-2	202	Minnesota
3.	Oliphant, Mike	KR	5-9	175	Puget Sound
4.	Morris, Jamie	RB	5-7	180	Michigan
5.	Mims, Carl	DB	5-9	182	Sam Houston State
6.	Humphries, Stan	QB	6-2	220	Northeast Louisiana
7.	Hicks, Harold	DB	5-11	197	San Diego State
8.	McGill, Darryl	RB	5-9	210	Wake Forest
9.	Peterson, Blake	LB	6-4	245	Mesa, Colo.
10.	Brown, Henry	T	6-4	270	Ohio State
11.	Koch, Curt	DE	6-7	270	Colorado
12.	Ross, Wayne	P	6-3	215	San Diego State

VETERAN ROSTER

No.	Name	Pos.	Ht.	Wt.	NFL Year	College
89	Allen, Anthony	WR	5-11	182	4	Washington
4	Atkinson, Jess	K	5-9	168	3	Maryland
95	Benish, Dan	DT	6-5	275	6	Clemson
53	Bostic, Jeff	C	6-2	260	9	Clemson
23	Bowles, Todd	S	6-2	203	3	Temple
29	Branch, Reggie	RB	5-11	235	4	East Carolina
	Brilz, Darrick	G	6-3	264	2	Oregon State
24	Bryant, Kelvin	RB	6-2	195	3	North Carolina
65	Butz, Dave	DT	6-7	295	15	Purdue
50	Caldwell, Ravin	LB	6-3	229	2	Arkansas
88	Caravello, Joe	TE	6-3	270	2	Tulane
	Carlson, Mark	T	6-6	284	2	South Connecticut St.
84	Clark, Gary	WR	5-9	173	4	James Madison
51	Coleman, Monte	LB	6-2	230	10	Central Arkansas
56	Copeland, Anthony	LB	6-2	250	2	Louisville
12	Cox, Steve	P-K	6-4	195	8	Arkansas
	Coyle, Eric	C	6-3	260	2	Colorado
34	Davis, Brian	CB	6-2	190	2	Nebraska
86	Didier, Clint	TE	6-5	240	7	Portland State
48	Gage, Steve	S	6-3	210	2	Tulsa
54	Gouveia, Kurt	LB	6-1	227	2	Brigham Young
77	Grant, Darryl	DT	6-1	275	8	Rice
28	Green, Darrell	CB-PR	5-8	170	6	Texas A&I
35	Griffin, Keith	RB	5-8	185	5	Miami
68	Grimm, Russ	C	6-3	275	8	Pittsburgh
6	Haji-Sheikh, Ali	K	6-0	172	5	Michigan
78	Hamel, Dean	DT	6-3	290	4	Tulsa
64	Hamilton, Steve	DE-DT	6-4	270	4	East Carolina
	Hitchcock, Ray	C	6-2	289	2	Minnesota
66	Jacoby, Joe	T	6-7	305	8	Louisville
21	Jessie, Tim	RB	5-11	190	2	Auburn
82	Jones, Anthony	TE	6-3	248	5	Wichita State
55	Kaufman, Mel	LB	6-2	230	7	Cal Poly-SLO
61	Kehr, Rick	G-T	6-3	285	2	Carthage
79	Kleine, Wally	T	6-9	320	1	Notre Dame
74	Koch, Markus	DE	6-5	275	3	Boise State
72	Manley, Dexter	DE	6-3	257	8	Oklahoma State
71	Mann, Charles	DE	6-6	270	6	Nevada-Reno
58	Marshall, Wilber	LB	6-1	225	5	Florida
73	May, Mark	T	6-6	295	8	Pittsburgh
	McEwen, Craig	TE	6-1	220	1	Utah

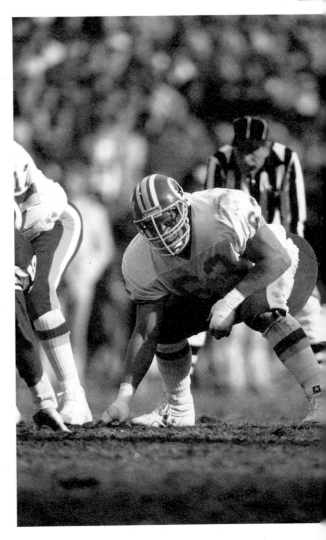

Raleigh McKenzie has become one of the league's outstanding guards.

No.	Name	Pos.	Ht.	Wt.	Year	College
63	McKenzie, Raleigh	G	6-2	275	4	Tennessee
81	Monk, Art	WR	6-3	209	9	Syracuse
52	Olkewicz, Neal	LB	6-0	233	10	Maryland
87	Orr, Terry	TE	6-3	227	3	Texas
	Reese, Albert	TE	6-4	245	1	Southern Methodist
	Robinson, Kenneth	LB	6-1	234	1	South Carolina
11	Rypien, Mark	QB	6-4	234	2	Washington State
83	Sanders, Ricky	WR-KR	5-11	180	3	Southwest Texas State
10	Schroeder, Jay	QB	6-4	215	5	UCLA
76	Simmons, Ed	T	6-5	280	2	Eastern Washington
36	Smith, Timmy	RB-KR	5-11	216	2	Texas Tech
69	Thielemann, R.C.	G	6-4	272	12	Arkansas
47	Thomas, Johnny	CB	5-9	190	1	Baylor
31	Vaughn, Clarence	S	6-0	202	2	Northern Illinois
40	Walton, Alvin	S	6-0	180	3	Kansas
85	Warren, Don	TE	6-4	242	10	San Diego State
45	Wilburn, Barry	CB	6-3	186	4	Mississippi
17	Williams, Doug	QB	6-4	220	8	Grambling State
	Wilson, Wayne	RB	6-3	220	10	Shepherd
46	Woodberry, Dennis	CB	5-10	183	3	Southern Arkansas
80	Yarber, Eric	WR-PR	5-8	156	3	Idaho

CHICAGO BEARS

Address Halas Hall, 250 N. Washington, Lake Forest, Illinois 60045.

Stadium Soldier Field, Chicago.
Capacity 66,030 *Playing Surface* Grass.

Team Colours Navy Blue, Orange, and White.

Head Coach Mike Ditka – seventh year.

Championships Division 1984,'85,'86,'87; Conference 1985; NFL 1921,'32,'33,'40,'41,'43,'46,'63; Super Bowl 1985.

History NFL 1920-69, NFC 1970-
(Before 1922, they were known as firstly the Decatur Staleys and then the Chicago Staleys.)

Offense

Head coach Mike Ditka was elected to the Hall of Fame, Walter Payton will join him in five years' time following his retirement with ten NFL career records in his pocket, the Bears won their fourth straight Central division title and Jim McMahon was healthy for the playoffs. It was all set up for a second Super Bowl Championship, but it never came. For the second successive year, the Bears could not protect their lead over Washington. Entering the 1988 campaign, though, the Bears still appear to have the best all-round talent. The offensive line is still youthful and yet has no superior in the league. Anchored by Jay Hilgenberg at center, with Mark Bortz and Tom Thayer at guard and the pairing of Jim Covert and Keith Van Horne at tackle, they should have little trouble paving a way for Neal Anderson, who now is the Bears' premier running back. He led the club in both rushing and pass receptions last year but, as long as Payton was still suited up, Walter still was the senior player. Matt Suhey may soon be retiring but the club is well off for fullbacks with Calvin Thomas and Thomas Sanders on call. However, they used their first pick in the draft to acquire Brad Muster, a 6-3, 222-pound blaster, and now seem set for the remainder of the decade and beyond. Jim McMahon has had yet more surgery on his right (passing) shoulder. He promises to be at his most healthy since the club's NFL title year, and it is easy to imagine his embarking on another sequence of winning starts – his latest run was halted at 25 by John Elway and the Broncos. In reserve, the Bears have Mike Tomczak and the 1987 first-round draftee, Jim Harbaugh. The Bears, then, are comfortable at quarterback and could even retain their title without McMahon. But to win the ultimate prize, they do need his unique brand of aggression. The Bears have excellent receivers, indeed, Ditka is spoiled for choice in pairing any one of Dennis McKinnon, Dennis Gentry, Ron Morris and even Keith Ortego with Willie Gault. Adding further depth, the Bears picked Wendell Davis, a precise pattern runner possessing safe hands, with the second of their two first-round options. Emery Moorehead is the senior tight end and, with the release of Tim Wrightman, Cap Boso appears to have found a permanent home.

Defense

On defense, the Bears were not quite the force of their NFL title year and there was the odd personality conflict between head coach Ditka and some of his players. Not connected with this, during the offseason, linebacker Wilber Marshall signed for the Redskins. Ron Rivera is not the equal of the great Marshall, but he is a genuine starter and should really develop, given an extended opportunity to fit into the system. That system, Vince Tobin's modification of the style created by Buddy Ryan, still will see the Bears blitzing on three out of every ten downs. It is a method which worked well last year even though three quarters of the passing touchdowns which they gave up came in the face of the blitz. At middle linebacker, perennial Pro Bowler Mike Singletary is the emotional leader of the entire defense, whilst Otis Wilson is a first-class operator at left linebacker. The defensive line was hampered by a nagging injury to Dan Hampton, and it may be that the former all-pro does not reproduce his best form. But Steve McMichael is coming off a tremendous year and, in common with the club's 1987 sack leader, defensive end Richard Dent, has been selected to two AFC-NFC Pro Bowls. William Perry, on the other hand, may be in danger of fading out of the picture. A superb athlete, Perry simply can not control his appetite. His demotion created an opportunity for Al Harris, which he took and should establish himself at defensive left end. To the amazement of your writer, the defensive secondary still gives rise for doubts amongst the media 'experts'. Dave Duerson, an AFC-NFC Pro Bowler, is the strong safety, but there's a position open at free safety following the surprise release of Todd Bell. At cornerback, Maurice Douglass and Vestee Jackson have confirmed their seniority over Reggie Phillips and Mike Richardson, who rate as first-class backups. The erudite Gary Fencik, who used to lead the Bears in both tackles and (jokingly please) complete sentences, has retired.

1988 SCHEDULE OF GAMES	September	
	4 MIAMI	12:00
	11 at Indianapolis	12:00
	18 MINNESOTA	12:00
	25 at Green Bay	12:00
	October	
	2 BUFFALO	12:00
	9 at Detroit	1:00
	16 DALLAS	12:00
	24 SAN FRANCISCO (Mon.)	8:00
	30 at New England	1:00
	November	
	6 TAMPA BAY	12:00
	13 at Washington	1:00
	20 at Tampa Bay	1:00
	27 GREEN BAY	12:00
	December	
	5 at Los Angeles Rams (Mon.)	6:00
	11 DETROIT	12:00
	19 at Minnesota (Mon.)	8:00

Special Teams

McKinnon was the only NFL player to return two punts for touchdowns in 1987, whilst Gentry is now established amongst the NFL's very best kickoff returners. Place-kicker Kevin Butler remains as a reliable, medium-range operator. It is probable that punter Bryan Wagner will regain the job he lost, because of injury, to Tommy Barnhardt.

1988 DRAFT

Round	Name	Pos.	Ht.	Wt.	College
1.	Muster, Brad	RB	6-3	222	Stanford
1.	Davis, Wendell	WR	5-11	190	Louisiana State
2.	Jones, Dante	LB	6-1	228	Oklahoma
3.	Jarvis, Ralph	DE	6-5	260	Temple
4.	Thornton, Jim	TE	6-2	244	Cal State-Fullerton
5.	Johnson, Troy	LB	6-1	225	Oklahoma
6.	Stinson, Lemuel	DB	5-9	160	Texas Tech
7.	Rentie, Caesar	T	6-2	288	Oklahoma
8.	Tate, David	DB	6-0	180	Colorado
8.	Reed, Harvey	RB	5-10	178	Howard
9.	Magee, Rogie	WR	6-2	208	Louisiana State
10.	Porter, Joel	G	6-3	272	Baylor
11.	Forch, Steve	LB	6-1	240	Nebraska
12.	Clark, Greg	LB	6-1	235	Arizona State

VETERAN ROSTER

No.	Name	Pos.	Ht.	Wt.	NFL Year	College
54	Adickes, John	C	6-3	264	2	Baylor
47	Allen, Egypt	S	6-0	203	2	Texas Christian
70	Althoff, Jim	DT	6-3	278	2	Winona State
35	Anderson, Neal	RB	5-11	210	3	Florida
81	Barnes, Lew	WR	5-8	160	2	Oregon
17	Barnhardt, Tommy	P	6-3	205	2	North Carolina
79	Becker, Kurt	G	6-5	280	7	Michigan
68	Blair, Paul	T	6-4	295	3	Oklahoma State
62	Bortz, Mark	G	6-6	275	6	Iowa
86	Boso, Cap	TE	6-3	224	2	Illinois
6	Butler, Kevin	K	6-1	204	4	Georgia
94	Chapura, Dick	DT	6-3	280	2	Missouri
74	Covert, Jim	T	6-4	275	6	Pittsburgh
95	Dent, Richard	DE	6-5	263	6	Tennessee State
37	Douglass, Maurice	CB	5-11	200	3	Kentucky
22	Duerson, Dave	S	6-1	210	6	Notre Dame
83	Gault, Willie	WR	6-1	183	6	Tennessee
23	Gayle, Shaun	S	5-11	193	5	Ohio State
29	Gentry, Dennis	WR-KR	5-8	180	7	Baylor
99	Hampton, Dan	DE-DT	6-5	267	10	Arkansas
4	Harbaugh, Jim	QB	6-3	202	2	Michigan
90	Harris, Al	DE	6-5	270	9	Arizona State
63	Hilgenberg, Jay	C	6-3	260	8	Iowa
24	Jackson, Vestee	CB	6-0	186	3	Washington
93	Johnson, Will	LB	6-4	245	2	Northeast Louisiana
88	Kozlowski, Glen	WR	6-1	190	2	Brigham Young
43	Lynch, Lorenzo	DB	5-9	197	2	Cal State-Sacramento
85	McKinnon, Dennis	WR-PR	6-1	185	5	Florida State
9	McMahon, Jim	QB	6-1	190	7	Brigham Young
76	McMichael, Steve	DT	6-2	265	9	Texas
87	Moorehead, Emery	TE	6-2	225	12	Colorado
84	Morris, Ron	WR	6-1	187	2	Southern Methodist
51	Morrissey, Jim	LB	6-3	222	4	Michigan State
46	Mosley, Anthony	RB	5-9	204	2	Fresno State
91	Norvell, Jay	LB	6-2	232	2	Iowa
89	Ortego, Keith	WR	6-0	182	4	McNeese State
	Patterson, Votie	WR	5-11	185	1	West Texas State
72	Perry, William	DT	6-2	315	4	Clemson
48	Phillips, Reggie	CB	5-10	170	4	Southern Methodist
27	Richardson, Mike	CB	6-0	188	6	Arizona State
59	Rivera, Ron	LB	6-3	235	5	California
53	Rodenhauser, Mark	C	6-5	260	2	Illinois State
52	Rubens, Larry	C	6-2	262	4	Montana State
20	Sanders, Thomas	RB-KR	5-11	203	4	Texas A&M
50	Singletary, Mike	LB	6-0	235	8	Baylor
60	Smith, Keith	DE-TE	6-5	240	2	Texas-El Paso
97	Smith, Sean	DT-DE	6-4	275	2	Grambling State
26	Suhey, Matt	RB	5-11	216	9	Penn State
57	Thayer, Tom	G	6-4	280	4	Notre Dame
33	Thomas, Calvin	RB	5-11	245	7	Illinois
18	Tomczak, Mike	QB	6-1	195	4	Ohio State
78	Van Horne, Keith	T	6-6	285	8	Southern California
15	Wagner, Bryan	P	6-2	195	2	Cal State-Northridge
55	Wilson, Otis	LB	6-2	227	9	Louisville
73	Wojciechowski, John	G	6-4	262	2	Michigan State

Willie Gault now is the Bears' senior starter at wide receiver.

DETROIT LIONS

Address Pontiac Silverdome, 1200 Featherstone Road –
Box 4200, Pontiac, Michigan 48057.
Stadium Pontiac Silverdome.
Capacity 80,638 *Playing Surface* AstroTurf.
Team Colours Honolulu Blue and Silver.
Head Coach Darryl Rogers – fourth year.
Championships Division 1983; NFL 1935,'52,'53,'57.
History NFL 1930-69, NFC 1970-
(Until 1934, they were known as the Portsmouth (Ohio)
Spartans.)

Offense

There are two ends to a stick and, for too long, the Lions
have been holding the part that nobody wants. They may
just be ready to pass it on. Certainly, the Lions finished
with the NFL's second-worst record (actually, they were
tied at 4-11 with three other teams but came bottom of that
group after application of the strength-of-schedule rule),
but, in years to come, 1987 could well be seen as a period
of establishment. With Eric Hipple injured, it made sense
to throw – no puns intended – young quarterback Chuck
Long in at the deep end. And though he'll not regard it as
the most enjoyable season of his football career, he stayed
afloat. Not the sort to burst into tears, he'll have learned
from every sack, and every pass interception. He will be
better in 1988. He has a good offensive line – it is a Lions
strength – and one which can improve. The starting
tackles will be Lomas Brown and Harvey Salem, with Keith
Dorney and one of Joe Milinichik and Kevin Glover at
guard. Steve Mott anchors the line at center. As a unit, they
were excellent on pass protection, allowing only 17
quarterback sacks in the 12 games played by the regular
squad. If they do not get rave notices for their run blocking, it may be more a reflection of the lack of escape veloc-
ity in the backfield, where neither of James Jones and
Garry James showed much bounce. Again, though, it
would be wrong to judge two players who, given different
circumstances, could bring vivid colour to an otherwise
monochromatic and, often, ponderous offense. The combination which might just spark the entire unit could be the
backups, Karl Bernard, a 1987 free-agent signing, and
Packers castoff Gary Ellerson. At wide receiver, the Lions
will persist with last year's group which was led in content
by the composed Pete Mandley but in style by the 1987
12th-round pick, Gary Lee, who averaged 16.2 yards on 19
receptions. You have to like Jeff Chadwick, who still would
appear to be the man most likely to catch passes for the
magic four figures. With Long still establishing himself,
though, look for Jones to continue picking up the short-
range passes. For some time the Lions have been seeking
a tight end, and the most recent candidate is second-
round draftee Pat Carter. He's a big healthy lad who
comes with a reputation for being able to block and catch
a few passes. And that's a combination which could earn
him a starting spot.

Defense

Looking at the defense it is easy to be optimistic, after seeing the Lions use their top two draft picks for this unit. Ben-
nie Blades, who can play any role at defensive back,
would have been a very high pick in any year and he
represents immediate relief for a defense which ranked
19th in the league against the pass. Again, there's help in
the shape of Devon Mitchell, who as a rookie, starred in
the 1986 season but missed the whole of 1987 with an
injury. He'll be the free safety, with Blades probably occu-
pying the strong spot. The starting cornerbacks will be the
experienced veterans, Bruce McNorton and Bobby Wat-
kins. With their second pick, the Lions took Chris Spielman, an inside linebacker with impeccable credentials
for entry into the NFL. A star at Ohio State University,
Spielman is a fierce competitor and must help to stem the
flow of enemy running backs. He could start right away,
teaming up with last year's rookie surprise, Dennis Gibson. Any kind of authority on the inside will give greater
freedom to Mike Cofer and Jimmy Williams, two outside
linebackers of genuine class but who have been forced to
operate under trying circumstances. With Vernon Max-
well and Shelton Robinson in reserve, this unit begins to
appear deep. Last year the defensive line received help,
not from the expected source, defensive end Reggie Rogers, but rather from rookie nose tackle Jerry Ball, who did
well as a starter in all the twelve games played by the
regulars. Rogers, who was the Lions' first-round selection
and the seventh pick overall, was a disappointment. In
questionable physical condition, he also battled with
personal and emotional problems. He was never a factor
and it remains to be seen if he can handle the pressures of
life at the top. Eric Williams shifted over from nose tackle
to left defensive end and Keith Ferguson continued on the
right side, from where he registered six quarterback
sacks. William Gay and Curtis Green, two former starters,
are the reserves in a unit which needs a little luck.

1988 SCHEDULE OF GAMES		
September		
4	ATLANTA	1:00
11	at Los Angeles Rams	1:00
18	NEW ORLEANS	1:00
25	NEW YORK JETS	1:00
October		
2	at San Francisco	1:00
9	CHICAGO	1:00
16	at New York Giants	1:00
23	at Kansas City	12:00
30	NEW YORK GIANTS	1:00
November		
6	at Minnesota	12:00
13	TAMPA BAY	1:00
20	vs. Green Bay at Milwaukee	12:00
24	MINNESOTA	
	(Thanksgiving)	12:30
December		
4	GREEN BAY	1:00
11	at Chicago	12:00
18	at Tampa Bay	1:00

Punter Jim Arnold.
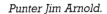

Special Teams

The kicking game is healthy, with Ed Murray as reliable as ever and punter Jim Arnold blossoming to Pro Bowl status. Remarkably, Arnold recovered his starting job only after a Week-One injury to Russell Erxleben. Mandley is one of the NFL's better punt returners, whilst Lee came fourth in the NFC for kickoff return average.

1988 DRAFT

Round	Name	Pos.	Ht.	Wt.	College
1.	Blades, Bennie	DB	6-0	212	Miami
2.	Spielman, Chris	LB	6-1	235	Ohio State
2.	Carter, Pat	TE	6-4	261	Florida State
3.	Roundtree, Ray	WR	6-0	180	Penn State
4.	White, William	DB	5-9	190	Ohio State
5.	Andolsek, Eric	G	6-1	278	Louisiana State
6.	Painter, Carl	RB	5-9	181	Hampton Institute
7.	James, Jeff	WR	5-10	180	Stanford
8.	Hadd, Gary	DE	6-3	260	Minnesota
9.	Corrington, Kip	DB	5-11	174	Texas A&M
9.	Irvin, Todd	T	6-5	285	Mississippi
10.	Craig, Paco	WR	5-10	168	UCLA
11.	McCoin, Danny	QB	6-2	200	Cincinnati

VETERAN ROSTER

No.	Name	Pos.	Ht.	Wt.	NFL Year	College
6	Arnold, Jim	P	6-3	211	6	Vanderbilt
68	Baack, Steve	G	6-4	265	5	Oregon
93	Ball, Jerry	NT	6-1	283	2	Southern Methodist
61	Barrows, Scott	C-G	6-2	278	3	West Virginia
25	Bernard, Karl	RB	5-11	205	2	Southwest Louisiana
80	Bland, Carl	WR	5-11	182	5	Virginia Union
75	Brown, Lomas	T	6-4	282	4	Florida
96	Butcher, Paul	LB	6-0	219	3	Wayne State
89	Chadwick, Jeff	WR	6-3	190	6	Grand Valley State
45	Cherry, Raphel	S	6-0	194	3	Hawaii
55	Cofer, Mike	LB	6-5	245	6	Tennessee
70	Dorney, Keith	G	6-5	285	10	Penn State
42	Ellerson, Gary	RB	5-11	220	4	Wisconsin
77	Ferguson, Keith	DE	6-5	260	8	Ohio State
40	Galloway, Duane	CB	5-8	181	3	Arizona State
79	Gay, William	DE	6-5	260	11	Southern California
98	Gibson, Dennis	LB	6-2	240	2	Iowa State
53	Glover, Kevin	C	6-2	267	4	Maryland
62	Green, Curtis	NT-DE	6-3	265	8	Alabama State
34	Griffin, James	S	6-2	197	6	Middle Tennessee St.
17	Hipple, Eric	QB	6-2	198	8	Utah State
33	James, Garry	RB	5-10	214	3	Louisiana State
58	Jamison, George	LB	6-1	226	2	Cincinnati
30	Jones, James	RB	6-2	229	6	Florida
87	Kab, Vyto	TE	6-5	240	6	Penn State
83	Lee, Gary	WR	6-1	202	2	Georgia Tech
81	Lewis, Mark	TE	6-2	250	4	Texas A&M
50	Lockett, Danny	LB	6-2	228	2	Arizona
16	Long, Chuck	QB	6-4	211	3	Iowa
82	Mandley, Pete	WR-PR	5-10	191	5	Northern Arizona
57	Maxwell, Vernon	LB	6-2	235	6	Arizona State
29	McNorton, Bruce	CB	5-11	175	7	Georgetown, Ken.
74	Milinichik, Joe	G	6-5	275	2	North Carolina State
31	Mitchell, Devon	S	6-1	194	2	Iowa
52	Mott, Steve	C	6-3	270	6	Alabama
3	Murray, Ed	K	5-10	175	9	Tulane
86	Nichols, Mark	WR	6-2	208	7	San Jose State
49	Paige, Tony	RB	5-10	225	5	Virginia Tech
51	Robinson, Shelton	LB	6-2	236	7	North Carolina
60	Rogers, Reggie	DE	6-6	272	2	Washington
84	Rubick, Rob	TE	6-3	234	7	Grand Valley State
97	Saleaumua, Dan	NT	6-0	285	2	Arizona State
73	Salem, Harvey	G-T	6-6	285	6	California
11	Saltz, Lee	QB	6-1	195	1	Temple
64	Sanders, Eric	T-G	6-7	280	8	Nevada-Reno
28	Sheffield, Chris	CB	6-1	188	3	Albany State
41	Smith, Ricky	CB	6-1	188	5	Alabama State
27	Watkins, Bobby	CB	5-10	186	7	Southwest Texas State
76	Williams, Eric	DE	6-4	280	5	Washington State
59	Williams, Jimmy	LB	6-3	230	7	Nebraska
38	Williams, Scott	RB	6-2	234	3	Georgia
21	Woolfolk, Butch	RB-KR	6-1	212	7	Michigan

GREEN BAY PACKERS

Address 1265 Lombardi Avenue, Green Bay, Wisconsin
54307-0628.
Stadia Lambeau Field, Green Bay, and Milwaukee
County Stadium, Milwaukee.
Capacity (Lambeau Field) 57,091, (Milwaukee County
Stadium) 56,051. *Playing Surfaces* Grass, both stadia.
Team Colours Dark Green, Gold, and White.
Head Coach Lindy Infante – first year.
Championships Division 1972;
NFL 1929,'30,'31,'36,'39,'44,'61,'62,'65,'66,'67;
Super Bowl 1966,'67.
History NFL 1921-69, NFC 1970-

Offense

Watching the Packers become more competitive was one
of the most pleasing aspects of last season, and it is a trend
which they should continue under new head coach Lindy
Infante. The line has become the most solid area of the
offense, and it is reassuring that last year's starting quintet
returns intact. Ken Ruettgers and Keith Uecker are the
tackles, with Rich Moran and Ron Hallstrom at guard
flanking center Mark Cannon. Ruettgers is the pick of a
group which is well supported by Tom Neville, Alan Vein-
grad, Bill Cherry and the mammoth Steve Collier. 1987
third-round draftee tackle Dave Croston returns from
injury. It is far from certain however, just which one of
Randy Wright and Don Majkowski they'll be protecting as
the starting quarterback. In Infante's words, 'It's the area
that has the biggest question mark attached to it.' Entering
his fifth pro year, Wright ought to be peaking, but Majkowski has looked to have the better talent albeit in short
spells. Spicing the mixture, Robbie Bosco, who missed his
first two NFL years with arm problems, has looked really
good in early workouts. At running back, Kenneth Davis
has emerged as the spearhead with Jessie Clark a touch in
front of Paul Ott Carruth to start at fullback. Last year's first-
round pick, Brent Fullwood, did not develop as quickly as
anticipated, but he was troubled with hamstring problems. They are strengthened further by the drafting of
Keith Woodside. Following the 1987 trade of former all-
pro James Lofton to the Raiders, the Packers did look
alarmingly thin at wide receiver. But Walter Stanley came
through to lead by example and Phillip Epps continued his
climb up the Packers all-time receiving list – he now ranks
tenth. Before the draft, Stanley and Epps were regarded
as the starters, ahead of last year's rookie find, Frankie
Neal, Lee Morris, Keith Paskett and Patrick Scott. However, in the first round they picked Sterling Sharpe, who
could turn out to be the best of what is considered the
finest crop of wide receivers ever to enter the NFL.
Sharpe bears the stamp of a future all-pro. Gifted with all
the necessary speed and pass-catching skills, Sharpe also
is a highly-disciplined young man, professional in his
training habits and an avid viewer of game films. At tight

end, an area which could use a little more variety, Ed
West and backup Joey Hackett are used more for their
blocking than their pass receiving.

Defense

Only four teams in the NFC, all of which went to the
playoffs, gave up fewer points than a Packers defense
which has become a hustling, spoiling unit. All three of last
year's starters, ends Alphonso Carreker and Robert
Brown, and nose tackle Jerry Boyarsky will return, backed
up by former Bengal Ross Browner and now joined by
second-round draftee defensive tackle Shawn Patterson.
The starting trio logged only nine sacks between them,
and though they establish solid pressure, Infante makes
no secret of the fact that he is expecting one of his linemen
to emerge as a more effective pass rusher. The strength of
the defense lies at linebacker, where the elder statesman,
John Anderson, is going into his 11th NFL year. With 65
solo tackles, Anderson came second in the club behind
left inside linebacker Brian Noble, who had 76. Right
inside linebacker Johnny Holland was voted the club's
'Rookie of the Year' after starting in all twelve games
played by the regulars. The real impact player who may
rise to even greater heights under Infante's direction is
Tim Harris, who, in his combination role as outside line-
backer-defensive end, led the team with seven quarterback sacks. The backups include John Dorsey, Scott Stephen and Clayton Weishuhn, a former Patriots player who
could make a really classy contribution were he to stay
clear of the injuries which have dogged his career. The
defensive secondary is well stocked with experience in
right cornerback Dave Brown, who is the NFL leading
active interceptor with 53, and ninth-year player Mark
Lee at left cornerback. Strong safety Mark Murphy
returned to his best form after spending 1986 on injured
reserve. Free safety Ken Stills, entering his fourth season,

1988 SCHEDULE OF GAMES	September	
	4 LOS ANGELES RAMS	12:00
	11 TAMPA BAY	12:00
	18 at Miami	1:00
	25 CHICAGO	12:00
	October	
	2 at Tampa Bay	1:00
	9 NEW ENGLAND at Milwaukee	12:00
	16 at Minnesota	12:00
	23 WASHINGTON at Milwaukee	12:00
	30 at Buffalo	1:00
	November	
	6 at Atlanta	1:00
	13 INDIANAPOLIS	12:00
	20 DETROIT at Milwaukee	12:00
	27 at Chicago	12:00
	December	
	4 at Detroit	1:00
	11 MINNESOTA	12:00
	18 at Phoenix	2:00

is the junior member of the quartet, but he lacks nothing by way of intensity. (He was labelled a 'heat-seeking missile' by former head coach Forrest Gregg.) Depth for the secondary comes from the versatile George (Tiger) Greene, and a quartet of developing young players, Chris Mandeville, Jim Bob Morris, Norman Jefferson and Ken Johnson.

VETERAN ROSTER

No.	Name	Pos.	Ht.	Wt.	NFL Year	College
59	Anderson, John	LB	6-3	229	11	Michigan
6	Bosco, Robbie	QB	6-2	198	1	Brigham Young
61	Boyarsky, Jerry	NT	6-3	290	8	Pittsburgh
17	Bracken, Don	P	6-0	211	4	Michigan
32	Brown, Dave	CB	6-1	197	14	Michigan
93	Brown, Robert	DE	6-2	267	7	Virginia Tech
79	Browner, Ross	DE	6-3	265	11	Notre Dame
58	Cannon, Mark	C	6-3	258	5	Texas-Arlington
76	Carreker, Alphonso	DE-NT	6-6	271	5	Florida State
30	Carruth, Paul Ott	RB	6-1	220	3	Alabama
69	Cherry, Bill	C	6-4	277	3	Middle Tennessee St.
33	Clark, Jessie	RB	6-0	228	6	Arkansas
64	Collier, Steve	T	6-7	342	2	Bethune-Cookman
20	Cook, Kelly	RB	5-10	225	2	Oklahoma State
60	Croston, Dave	T	6-5	280	1	Iowa
36	Davis, Kenneth	RB	5-10	209	3	Texas Christian
56	Dent, Burnell	LB	6-1	236	3	Tulane
99	Dorsey, John	LB	6-3	243	5	Connecticut
71	Drost, Jeff	DT	6-5	286	1	Iowa
27	Elliott, Tony	DB	5-10	195	1	Central Michigan
85	Epps, Phillip	WR	5-10	165	6	Texas Christian
84	Fitzgerald, Patrick	WR	6-3	197	1	Boise State
21	Fullwood, Brent	RB-KR	5-11	209	2	Auburn
23	Greene, Tiger	S	6-0	194	4	Western Carolina
89	Hackett, Joey	TE	6-5	267	3	Elon College
65	Hallstrom, Ron	G	6-6	290	7	Iowa
63	Harris, Gregg	G	6-4	279	1	Wake Forest
97	Harris, Tim	LB	6-5	235	3	Memphis State
50	Holland, Johnny	LB	6-2	221	2	Texas A&M
38	Jefferson, Norman	CB	5-10	183	2	Louisiana State
39	Johnson, Kenneth	CB	6-0	185	2	Mississippi State
41	King, Don	DB	5-11	200	1	Southern Methodist
22	Lee, Mark	CB	5-11	189	9	Washington
7	Majkowski, Don	QB	6-2	197	2	Virginia
44	Mandeville, Chris	S	6-1	213	2	Cal-Davis
88	Marshall, Willie	WR	6-1	190	1	Temple
98	Moore, Brent	LB	6-5	242	2	Southern California
57	Moran, Rich	G	6-2	275	4	San Diego State
47	Morris, Jim Bob	S	6-3	211	2	Kansas State
81	Morris, Lee	WR	5-10	180	2	Oklahoma
37	Murphy, Mark	S	6-2	201	7	West Liberty, W.Va.
80	Neal, Frankie	WR	6-1	202	2	Fort Hays State
72	Neville, Tom	G	6-5	306	3	Fresno State
91	Noble, Brian	LB	6-3	252	4	Arizona State
82	Paskett, Keith	WR	5-11	180	2	Western Kentucky
	Powe, Karl	WR	6-2	185	2	Alabama State
77	Robison, Tom	G	6-4	290	2	Texas A&M
75	Ruettgers, Ken	T	6-5	280	4	Southern California
83	Scott, Patrick	WR	5-10	170	2	Grambling State
87	Stanley, Walter	WR-PR	5-9	179	4	Mesa, Colorado
54	Stephen, Scott	LB	6-2	232	2	Arizona State
29	Stills, Ken	S	5-10	186	4	Wisconsin
48	Summers, Don	TE	6-4	235	4	Boise State
92	Thomas, Ben	DE-NT	6-4	275	3	Auburn
45	Thomas, Lavale	RB	6-0	205	1	Fresno State
70	Uecker, Keith	T	6-5	284	6	Auburn
73	Veingrad, Alan	T	6-5	277	3	East Texas State
28	Watts, Elbert	CB	6-1	205	2	Southern California
52	Weddington, Mike	LB	6-4	245	3	Oklahoma
51	Weishuhn, Clayton	LB	6-1	218	5	Angelo State
86	West, Ed	TE	6-1	243	5	Auburn
35	Willhite, Kevin	RB	5-11	208	2	Oregon
	Winter, Blaise	DE	6-3	274	4	Syracuse
16	Wright, Randy	QB	6-2	203	5	Wisconsin
8	Zendejas, Max	K	5-11	184	3	Arizona

Special Teams

Successful on 16 of 19 field goal attempts, Max Zendejas looks to have landed a permanent job, though punter Don Bracken may be challenged in camp. Rookie Sharpe may see early action in the kickoff and punt return department, where his demonstrated skills could improve on the yields from kickoff returner Fullwood (avg. 21.3 yards) and punt returner Stanley (avg. 6.2 yards).

1988 DRAFT

Round	Name	Pos.	Ht.	Wt.	College
1.	Sharpe, Sterling	WR	5-11	195	South Carolina
2.	Patterson, Shawn	DT	6-5	261	Arizona State
3.	Woodside, Keith	RB	5-11	202	Texas A&M
4.	Putzier, Rollin	DT	6-4	282	Oregon
4.	Cecil, Chuck	DB	6-0	186	Arizona
5.	Reed, Darrell	LB	6-1	220	Oklahoma
6.	Hill, Nate	DE	6-3	266	Auburn
7.	Richard, Gary	DB	5-9	167	Pittsburgh
8.	Collins, Patrick	RB	5-9	175	Oklahoma
9.	Wilkinson, Neal	TE	6-4	234	James Madison
10.	Keyes, Bud	QB	6-3	210	Wisconsin
12.	Bolton, Scott	WR	5-11	187	Auburn

Walter Stanley led the Packers in pass receptions.

MINNESOTA VIKINGS

Address 9520 Viking Drive, Eden Prairie, Minnesota 55344.
Stadium Hubert H. Humphrey Metrodome, Minneapolis.
  Capacity 63,000 *Playing Surface* AstroTurf.
Team Colours Purple, Gold, and White.
Head Coach Jerry Burns – third year.
Championships Division 1970,'71,'73,'74,'75,'76,'77,'78,'80;
  Conference 1973,'74,'76; NFL 1969.
History NFL 1961-69, NFC 1970-

Offense

They shrugged off an 0-3 legacy from the 'replacement' players, entered the playoffs, heads down and via the tradesmen's entrance, promptly knocked off the two teams with the best regular-season records and came within a dropped goal-line pass of taking the eventual Super Bowl Champion Redskins into overtime in the NFC title game. Assuming that it was the real Minnesota Vikings which stood up in the playoffs, you might say that they are back. The offensive line features Pro Bowler Gary Zimmerman in the key position of left tackle. Zimmerman's arrival two years ago marked the beginning of an improvement which has a little further to go. The other starters are tackle Tim Irwin, center Kirk Lowdermilk, and guards David Huffman and most probably Terry Tausch, the latter who returns from injury and should relegate Greg Koch to reserve status. In the draft, the unit received a major injection with the selection of the Arizona State guards Randall McDaniel and Todd Kalis. Head coach Jerry Burns has the lovely problem of choosing between Tommy Kramer and Wade Wilson as his starting quarterback, and whilst Kramer has just a little more polish than his younger rival, one feels that Wilson's raw talent may be enough to win him the job. Behind them is Rich Gannon, a player of immense natural athletic ability. Turning good field position into points was a Vikings weakness in 1987, but the problem may be more one of tactics than personnel. Running back Darrin Nelson averaged a sprightly 4.9 yards per carry whilst fullback Alfred Anderson logged a smart 4.7. Rookie D. J. Dozier did not have a major impact until he was near the goal line, from where he punched into the end zone for five touchdowns. Dozier should improve after a learning year, but he will be challenged for playing time by another 1987 rookie, Rick Fenney, who proved to be an eighth-round bargain. Another reason for the Vikings' emergence was their increased willingness to involve wide receiver Anthony Carter. A player with fine hands and mercurial speed, Carter averaged 24.3 yards (it was the best of all the major wide receivers) on 38 pass receptions and scored seven touchdowns. Leo Lewis, a scrappy little competitor, is his starting partner, with Hassan Jones, Jim Gustafson and Greg Richardson as backups. Tight end Steve Jordan confirmed his dramatic 1986 entry into the top bracket.

Defense

In Minneapolis, they are beginning to talk of the old 'Purple People Eaters', the four-man defensive line which established an awesome reputation in the days when the Vikings ruled the NFC Central division. The modern version, featuring defensive ends Chris Doleman and Doug Martin, with Keith Millard and Henry Thomas at tackle, is developing into a fearsome group. Doleman was moved up to defensive end for his strength and explosive speed, and he led the team with eleven sacks ahead of Martin's nine. Also, Doleman's six forced fumbles ranks second only to Alan Page's seven of the 1975 season. Millard, an expressive player, and rookie surprise Thomas take the brunt of the run. Including postseason, the Vikings have gone 26 straight games in which no opposing running back has rushed for 100 yards. And the line is not simply starter deep. Former Cardinals player Stafford Mays received a new lease of life and played a valuable role with seven sacks. Tim Newton is a former starter whilst Gerald Robinson was a 1986 first-round pick. Young outside linebacker Jesse Solomon led the club with 92 solo tackles as he showed great progress. On the left outside, David Howard improved steadily throughout his third year as a pro. The middle area still is the domain of Scott Studwell, the teak-tough veteran of eleven years. Walker Lee Ashley has recovered from his injuries two years ago and is ready to step in should Studwell begin to lose his edge. 1987 second-round draftee Ray Berry and Chris Martin are the backups on the outsides. In selecting four defensive backs in the recent draft, the Vikings recognise a weakness in the secondary, though it is not as if they have gaping holes to fill. Strong safety Joey Browner led the club with six pass interceptions and went to his third straight AFC-NFC Pro Bowl. Free safety John Harris is a wise veteran. Carl Lee is another solid performer, whilst the other cornerback, Issiac Holt, can be sensational but does tend to lose concentration.

1988 SCHEDULE OF GAMES	September	
	4 at Buffalo	1:00
	11 NEW ENGLAND	3:00
	18 at Chicago	12:00
	25 PHILADELPHIA	12:00
	October	
	2 at Miami	4:00
	9 TAMPA BAY	12:00
	16 GREEN BAY	12:00
	23 at Tampa Bay	1:00
	30 at San Francisco	1:00
	November	
	6 DETROIT	12:00
	13 at Dallas	7:00
	20 INDIANAPOLIS	12:00
	24 at Detroit (Thanksgiving)	12:30
	December	
	4 NEW ORLEANS	12:00
	11 at Green Bay	12:00
	19 CHICAGO (Mon.)	8:00

Special Teams

Both punt returner Leo Lewis and kickoff returner Neal Guggemos are excellent, averaging 12.5 and 22.4 yards respectively. However, placekicker Chuck Nelson suffered a loss of form and faces a challenge in camp. Also, there will be a competition between 12th-year veteran Greg Coleman and fourth-year player Bucky Scribner.

1988 DRAFT

Round	Name	Pos.	Ht.	Wt.	College
1.	McDaniel, Randall	G	6-3	260	Arizona State
2.	Edwards, Brad	DB	6-1	200	South Carolina
3.	Noga, Al	DT	6-1	250	Hawaii
4.	Kalis, Todd	G	6-6	275	Arizona State
5.	Fullington, Darrell	DB	6-1	187	Miami
6.	White, Derrick	DB	5-8	185	Oklahoma
7.	Beckman, Brad	TE	6-2	230	Nebraska-Omaha
8.	Cain, Joe	LB	6-1	225	Oregon Tech
9.	McGowan, Paul	LB	6-0	227	Florida State
10.	Habib, Brian	DT	6-5	274	Washington
11.	Floyd, Norman	DB	5-11	190	South Carolina

VETERAN ROSTER

No.	Name	Pos.	Ht.	Wt.	NFL Year	College
46	Anderson, Alfred	RB	6-1	217	5	Baylor
53	Anno, Sam	LB	6-2	230	2	Southern California
58	Ashley, Walker Lee	LB	6-0	232	5	Penn State
50	Berry, Ray	LB	6-2	230	2	Baylor
19	Brim, James	WR	6-3	187	2	Wake Forest
47	Browner, Joey	S	6-2	210	6	Southern California
81	Carter, Anthony	WR	5-11	174	4	Michigan
8	Coleman, Greg	P	6-0	185	12	Florida A&M
56	Doleman, Chris	DE	6-5	262	4	Pittsburgh
42	Dozier, D.J.	RB-KR	6-0	198	2	Penn State
31	Fenney, Rick	RB	6-1	240	2	Washington
62	Foote, Chris	C	6-4	265	7	Southern California
22	Freeman, Steve	S	5-11	185	14	Mississippi State
16	Gannon, Rich	QB	6-3	197	2	Delaware
41	Guggemos, Neal	S-KR	6-0	190	3	St. Thomas, Minnesota
80	Gustafson, Jim	WR	6-1	178	3	St. Thomas, Minnesota

No.	Name	Pos.	Ht.	Wt.	Year	College
44	Harris, John	S	6-2	197	11	Arizona State
24	Henderson, Wymon	CB	5-10	186	2	Nevada-Las Vegas
82	Hilton, Carl	TE	6-3	236	3	Houston
30	Holt, Issiac	CB	6-2	199	4	Alcorn State
51	Howard, David	LB	6-2	234	4	Cal State-Long Beach
72	Huffman, David	G-T-C	6-6	285	9	Notre Dame
76	Irwin, Tim	T	6-7	290	8	Tennessee
84	Jones, Hassan	WR	6-0	198	3	Florida State
83	Jordan, Steve	TE-T	6-3	235	7	Brown
68	Koch, Greg	G-T	6-4	276	12	Arkansas
9	Kramer, Tommy	QB	6-2	192	12	Rice
39	Lee, Carl	CB	5-11	188	6	Marshall
87	Lewis, Leo	WR-PR	5-8	167	8	Missouri
23	Love, Terry	S	6-2	205	1	Murray State
63	Lowdermilk, Kirk	C	6-3	264	4	Ohio State
71	MacDonald, Mark	G	6-4	265	4	Boston College
57	Martin, Chris	LB	6-2	231	6	Auburn
79	Martin, Doug	DE	6-3	258	9	Washington
73	Mays, Stafford	DE-DT	6-2	264	9	Washington
75	Millard, Keith	DT	6-5	264	4	Washington State
86	Mularkey, Mike	TE	6-4	236	6	Florida
77	Mullaney, Mark	DE	6-6	242	13	Colorado State
1	Nelson, Chuck	K	5-1	175	5	Washington
20	Nelson, Darrin	RB	5-9	185	7	Stanford
96	Newton, Tim	DT	6-0	297	4	Florida
52	Rasmussen, Randy	G	6-1	254	5	Minnesota
36	Rice, Allen	RB	5-10	206	5	Baylor
89	Richardson, Greg	WR-PR	5-7	172	2	Alabama
95	Robinson, Gerald	DE	6-3	261	3	Auburn
48	Rutland, Reggie	CB	6-1	195	2	Georgia Tech
13	Scribner, Bucky	P	6-0	205	4	Kansas
40	Smith, Wayne	CB	6-0	170	9	Purdue
54	Solomon, Jesse	LB	6-0	236	3	Florida State
55	Studwell, Scott	LB	6-2	229	12	Illinois
67	Swilley, Dennis	C	6-3	265	11	Texas A&M
66	Tausch, Terry	G	6-5	276	7	Texas
97	Thomas, Henry	DT	6-2	268	2	Louisiana State
11	Wilson, Wade	QB	6-3	206	8	East Texas State
65	Zimmerman, Gary	T	6-6	284	3	Oregon

Darrin Nelson gives sparkle to the Vikings' offensive backfield.

TAMPA BAY BUCCANEERS

Address One Buccaneer Place, Tampa, Florida 33607.
Stadium Tampa Stadium, Tampa.
  Capacity 74,315 *Playing Surface* Grass.
Team Colours Florida Orange, White, and Red.
Head Coach Ray Perkins – second year.
Championships Division 1979,'81.
History AFC 1976, NFC 1977-

Offense

Head coach Ray Perkins doesn't believe in messing around, and he might well have been thinking of that adage 'the future is now' when he traded veteran quarterback Steve DeBerg. Veteran Joe Ferguson has been acquired in a trade, but DeBerg's departure means that Vinny Testaverde, the strong-armed giant who was the first pick overall in 1987, simply will have to do the job. His prospects do look better than they were a year ago, for the Buccaneers have taken significant steps, both to protect the man on whose performance their prosperity rests and to develop the kind of rushing game which will complement his talents. First-round draftee Paul Gruber could have an immediate impact in both respects, run blocking and on pass protection. The team's best veteran offensive lineman, center Randy Grimes, is right at the heart of things, but there will be a competition involving Dan Turk, Rick Mallory, George Yarno and fourth-round draftee John Bruhin for the guard positions. Ron Heller, the starting right tackle since his rookie season, has been traded to Seattle. Gruber should start at left tackle with Rob Taylor moving to right tackle. Running back James Wilder has been carrying a heavy load with great honour for so long that it still surprises one to note that he is entering only his eighth year. He still has a lot of yards in him, both as a rusher and a receiver, the latter which he confirmed by leading the club for the fifth time in the past six seasons. But it made sense to take the opportunity of drafting Lars Tate, who, though no frail thing, is an action-packed, smaller version. With Wilder having settled down nicely after his switch to fullback (interestingly, he had the best rushing average of his career), Tate will share time with the former Chiefs player, Jeff Smith, at tailback. The 1987 second-round pick, Don Smith, spent the year on injured reserve and could provide much-needed explosive speed. Whereas the Buccaneers were weak at wide receiver, the rapid development of rookie Mark Carrier and the progress of tight end Calvin Magee brought the best out of the eight-year veteran, Gerald Carter, who led the team in receiving yardage. Rookie Bruce Hill showed himself to be an exciting prospect over the final four games, with a lowest haul of 73 yards receiving on a total of 17 catches. With both Magee and 1987 fourth-round pick Ron Hall at tight end, the Bucs have two men who can catch passes and handle themselves at the line of scrimmage.

Defense

When it came to stopping the opposition, the Bucs made significant improvement, with defensive end Ron Holmes outstanding as he registered eight sacks in ten games. John Cannon started at defensive left end whilst Kevin Kellin was on standby duty. Nose tackle Mike Stensrud has been released, leaving a vacant spot to be filled by either Dan Sileo, whom the Bucs obtained in a supplemental draft, or Curt Jarvis. If one had to point to a Tampa Bay weakness, however, it would be the defensive line, on which they could use another of Holmes's quality. Curiously, linebacking always seems to have been a strength, even when the Bucs were going through the really difficult years. They have a collection of big meanies, the lightest of whom weighs in at 230 pounds. Ervin Randle has emerged as a run-stuffing inside linebacker, whilst Jeff Davis and Scot Brantley share the other inside spot. The club is even better off at outside linebacker, where, currently, Chris Washington ranks as the best, ahead of the pairing of Jackie Walker and Winston Moss, either of whom could easily start full time. It is a measure of their great depth that Kevin Murphy ranks only fourth. It is probably true, but the Bucs aren't saying it, that their quality at linebacker shores up the defensive line and enables the club to build elsewhere. There is every reason for optimism about the defensive secondary, where young cornerbacks Ricky Reynolds and Rod Jones worked well as a pair. The situation at safety is less certain but probably will still have former Bengal Bobby Kemp at strong safety, with Ray Isom and Paul Tripoli sharing the free safety position. By normal NFL dimensions, there's not much to Isom, who weighs only 190 pounds, but he showed tenacity and powers of leadership on entering the fray in midseason, after being activated from injured reserve. Bobby Futrell is the nickel back.

1988 SCHEDULE OF GAMES		
September		
4	PHILADELPHIA	1:00
11	at Green Bay	12:00
18	PHOENIX	1:00
25	at New Orleans	12:00
October		
2	GREEN BAY	1:00
9	at Minnesota	12:00
16	at Indianapolis	12:00
23	MINNESOTA	1:00
30	MIAMI	1:00
November		
6	at Chicago	12:00
13	at Detroit	1:00
20	CHICAGO	1:00
27	at Atlanta	1:00
December		
4	BUFFALO	1:00
11	at New England	1:00
18	DETROIT	1:00

Tight end Calvin Magee is a key part of the Bucs' offense.

Special Teams

Placekicker Donald Igwebuike maintained his three-year record of not having missed a field goal from less than 34 yards out, but the Bucs are looking for a new punter. Dual-purpose returner Futrell is not spectacular but Perkins is not complaining, and that means that Futrell is satisfying the man who matters.

1988 DRAFT

Round	Name	Pos.	Ht.	Wt.	College
1.	Gruber, Paul	T	6-4	295	Wisconsin
2.	Tate, Lars	RB	6-1	210	Georgia
4.	Goff, Robert	DT	6-3	260	Auburn
4.	Bruhin, John	G	6-3	275	Tennessee State
4.	Robbins, Monte	P	6-3	202	Michigan
5.	Howard, William	RB	6-0	240	Tennessee
6.	Lee, Shawn	DT	6-3	265	North Alabama
7.	Goode, Kerry	RB	5-11	200	Alabama
8.	Simpson, Anthony	RB	5-9	240	East Carolina
9.	Davis, Reuben	DT	6-3	278	North Carolina
11.	Pillow, Frank	WR	5-11	180	Tennessee State
12.	Jones, Victor	LB	6-1	234	Virginia Tech

VETERAN ROSTER

No.	Name	Pos.	Ht.	Wt.	NFL Year	College
39	Austin, Cliff	RB	6-0	190	6	Clemson
52	Brantley, Scot	LB	6-1	230	9	Florida
	Brophy, Jay	LB	6-3	232	4	Miami
78	Cannon, John	DE	6-5	260	7	William & Mary
89	Carrier, Mark	WR	6-0	182	2	Nicholls State
87	Carter, Gerald	WR	6-1	190	9	Texas A&M
71	Cooper, Mark	T	6-5	270	6	Miami
58	Davis, Jeff	LB	6-0	230	7	Clemson
	Edwards, Randy	DE-NT	6-4	267	5	Alabama
	Elder, Donnie	CB	5-9	175	3	Memphis State
38	Evans, James	RB	6-0	220	2	Southern
	Ferguson, Joe	QB	6-1	195	16	Arkansas
81	Freeman, Phil	WR	5-11	185	4	Arizona
36	Futrell, Bobby	CB-KR	5-11	190	3	Elizabeth City Stat
91	Gant, Brian	LB	6-0	235	2	Illinois State
	Gill, Owen	RB	6-1	240	4	Iowa
31	Gordon, Sonny	S	5-11	192	2	Ohio State
53	Graham, Don	LB	6-2	244	2	Penn State
60	Grimes, Randy	C	6-4	270	6	Baylor
82	Hall, Ron	TE	6-4	238	2	Hawaii
84	Hill, Bruce	WR	6-0	175	2	Arizona State
90	Holmes, Ron	DE	6-4	255	4	Washington
25	Howard, Bobby	RB	6-0	210	3	Indiana
37	Hunter, Eddie	RB	5-10	195	2	Virginia Tech
1	Igwebuike, Donald	K	5-9	185	4	Clemson
28	Isom, Ray	DB	5-9	190	2	Penn State
95	Jarvis, Curt	DE	6-2	266	2	Alabama
22	Jones, Rod	CB	6-0	175	3	Southern Methodist
75	Kellin, Kevin	DE	6-5	250	3	Minnesota
33	Kemp, Bobby	S	6-0	190	8	Cal State-Fullerton
77	Maarleveld, J.D.	T	6-6	300	3	Maryland
86	Magee, Calvin	TE	6-3	239	4	Southern
68	Mallory, Rick	G	6-2	265	4	Washington
99	McHale, Tom	DE	6-4	275	2	Cornell
98	McInerney, Sean	DE	6-3	260	2	Frostburg State
83	Miller, Solomon	WR	6-1	185	3	Utah State
57	Moss, Winston	LB	6-3	235	2	Miami
59	Murphy, Kevin	LB	6-2	230	3	Oklahoma
54	Randle, Ervin	LB	6-1	250	4	Baylor
29	Reynolds, Ricky	CB	5-11	182	2	Washington State
30	Robinson, Mark	S	5-11	202	5	Penn State
55	Rolling, Henry	LB	6-2	210	1	Nevada-Reno
93	Sileo, Dan	NT	6-2	282	2	Miami
62	Simmonds, Mike	G	6-4	281	1	Indiana State
47	Smith, Don	RB	5-11	199	1	Mississippi State
35	Smith, Jeff	RB	5-9	204	4	Nebraska
70	Swayne, Harry	DE	6-5	268	2	Rutgers
85	Taylor, Gene	WR	6-2	189	2	Fresno State
72	Taylor, Rob	T	6-6	285	3	Northwestern
14	Testaverde, Vinny	QB	6-5	220	2	Miami
64	Thomas, Kevin	C	6-2	268	1	Arizona State
24	Tripoli, Paul	S	6-0	197	2	Alabama
50	Turk, Dan	C-G	6-4	260	3	Wisconsin
56	Walker, Jackie	LB	6-5	245	3	Jackson State
51	Washington, Chris	LB	6-4	230	5	Iowa State
32	Wilder, James	RB	6-3	225	8	Missouri
3	Williams, Keith	RB	5-10	173	2	Southwest Missouri
34	Wright, Adrian	RB	6-1	230	2	Virginia Union
66	Yarno, George	G	6-2	265	9	Washington State

ATLANTA FALCONS

Address Suwanee Road at I-85, Suwanee, Georgia 30174.
Stadium Atlanta-Fulton County Stadium.
   Capacity 59,643 *Playing Surface* Grass.
Team Colours Red, Black, White, and Silver.
Head Coach Marion Campbell – second year.
Championships Division 1980.
History NFL 1966-69, NFC 1970-

Offense

It wasn't all gloom and doom for the Falcons – wins over Dallas and the subsequent Super Bowl Champion Redskins, in games played by the regulars, must count for something. But there can be no doubts that the Falcons need help in quite a few areas. Looking at the twenty major categories of team offensive statistics, the Falcons came last in the NFL in no fewer than nine. One area in which they weren't quite so bad was in quarterback protection, and here the offensive line of tackles Mike Kenn and Leonard Mitchell, guards John Scully and Bill Fralic, and center Wayne Radloff did a reasonable job. Fralic is a superstar, and if Kenn could regenerate the form which earned him five straight AFC-NFC Pro Bowl selections (1981-85), this line could create more than a few opportunities. Waiting to exploit them is running back Gerald Riggs, who put that angled, slashing style of his to good use to earn his third straight AFC-NFC Pro Bowl appearance and logged four 100-yards-rushing games as he rose to 26th place the NFL's all-time list of leading rushers. Riggs will be given a boost if last year's rookie, Kenny Flowers, a potential franchise back in his own right, can come through to offer a second major threat. With only James Primus arriving from the draft, a great deal depends on these two. The same is true of young quarterback Chris Miller, who must feel a little more secure following the release of former starter David Archer. With the Falcons looking to the future, Miller has an edge over the former Steeler, Scott Campbell, and it may even be that Campbell is pressed by third-stringer Erik Kramer, who was sensational in rallying the Falcons to victory against the Rams on Week Six. At wide receiver, the Falcons can field three genuine starters, Stacey Bailey, Floyd Dixon and Aubrey Matthews, all with deep speed as each man confirmed by averaging 16.3 yards or better last year. Bailey was starting before suffering a shoulder injury in mid-November, and he should regain that role, probably at the expense of Matthews. In only his second year, Dixon led the team in both receptions and yards receiving, and is an excellent prospect. The positions of tight end and H-back are of crucial importance in the Falcons' system. Of the veterans, Ken Whisenhunt is the best receiver. They are reinforced by the aggressive Alex Higdon, who was the first offensive player selected by the club in the draft.

Defense

The first time that the Falcons had the first pick overall in the draft, they selected middle linebacker Tommy Nobis, who, as a pro, was the equal of the great Chicago Bears player, Dick Butkus. Aundray Bruce, whom the Falcons made the first pick overall in this year's draft, need not be that good to have a major impact in an area which has been very modest in recent years. On his own, he could exceed the total of sacks, six, gained by Atlanta linebackers (regulars) over the past two seasons. Let's wish him luck. Bruce should start right away, probably at right outside linebacker, though the defensive formation has not yet been declared. The club's preseason depth chart gives nothing away – it shows three defensive linemen and three linebackers – but one imagines that second-round pick Marcus Cotton needs only to play up to his collegiate reputation to earn the starting spot on the other side, ahead even of former first-round pick Tim Green. Starting middle/inside linebacker John Rade was the leading tackler by a considerable margin ahead of strong safety Robert Moore. It won't look quite the same defense without inside linebacker Buddy Curry, who was the leading tackler for seven straight seasons but has been released. Another former first-rounder, Tony Casillas, has settled down to be an effective nose tackle, flanked by two first-class defensive ends in Rick Bryan and Mike Gann. The trio has suffered by having only modest support from the linebackers and, given greater help, it is easy to see their developing into one of the league's more-respected units. The defensive secondary will be given a boost by the return of former starting free safety Bret Clark, who played in only one game before breaking his fibula. An all-action type, he catalyses the unit. Robert Moore strengthened his hold at strong safety. Bobby Butler, the team leader with four interceptions, and Scott Case are the starting cornerbacks, supported by James Britt and David Croudip.

1988 SCHEDULE OF GAMES	September	
	4 at Detroit	1:00
	11 NEW ORLEANS	1:00
	18 at San Francisco	1:00
	25 at Dallas	12:00
	October	
	2 SEATTLE	1:00
	9 LOS ANGELES RAMS	1:00
	16 at Denver	2:00
	23 NEW YORK GIANTS	1:00
	30 at Philadelphia	1:00
	November	
	6 GREEN BAY	1:00
	13 SAN DIEGO	1:00
	20 at Los Angeles Raiders	1:00
	27 TAMPA BAY	1:00
	December	
	4 SAN FRANCISCO	1:00
	11 at Los Angeles Rams	1:00
	18 at New Orleans	12:00

Special Teams

Mick Luckhurst has become one of the NFL's best kickers and must be close to all-star selection. Punter Rick Donnelly led the entire NFL with a gross average of 44 yards. Adding to a fine special-teams effort, Sylvester Stamps enjoyed an outstanding season, in which he was the NFL leading kickoff returner. Matthews may take over as the punt returner.

Gerald Riggs remains as the essential spearhead of the Falcons' offense.

1988 DRAFT

Round	Name	Pos.	Ht.	Wt.	College
1.	Bruce, Aundray	LB	6-5	237	Auburn
2.	Cotton, Marcus	LB	6-3	210	Southern California
3.	Higdon, Alex	TE	6-5	251	Ohio State
5.	Dimry, Charles	DB	6-0	165	Nevada-Las Vegas
6.	Thomas, George	WR	5-9	165	Nevada-Las Vegas
6.	Hoover, Houston	G	6-2	262	Jackson State
7.	Haynes, Michael	WR	5-11	180	Northern Arizona
8.	Brown, Phillip	LB	6-3	228	Alabama
9.	Primus, James	RB	5-10	190	UCLA
10.	Clayton, Stan	T	6-2	275	Penn State
11.	Milling, James	WR	5-9	160	Maryland
12.	Wiley, Carter	DB	6-2	215	Virginia Tech

VETERAN ROSTER

No.	Name	Pos.	Ht.	Wt.	NFL Year	College
82	Bailey, Stacey	WR	6-1	157	7	San Jose State
53	Barnett, Doug	C	6-4	260	4	Azusa Pacific
26	Britt, James	CB	6-0	185	5	Louisiana State
98	Brown, Greg	DE-NT	6-5	265	8	Kansas State
77	Bryan, Rick	DE	6-4	265	5	Oklahoma
23	Butler, Bobby	CB	5-11	175	8	Florida State
10	Campbell, Scott	QB	6-0	195	5	Purdue
25	Case, Scott	CB	6-0	178	5	Oklahoma
75	Casillas, Tony	NT	6-3	280	3	Oklahoma
20	Cason, Wendell	S	5-11	192	4	Oregon
28	Clark, Bret	S	6-3	198	2	Nebraska
56	Costello, Joe	LB	6-3	244	5	Central State, Conn.
30	Croudip, David	CB	5-8	183	5	San Diego State
86	Dixon, Floyd	WR	5-9	170	3	Stephen F. Austin
3	Donnelly, Rick	P	6-0	190	4	Wyoming
64	Dukes, Jamie	G-C	6-1	278	3	Florida State
24	Emery, Larry	RB	5-9	195	2	Wisconsin
39	Everett, Major	RB	5-10	218	6	Mississippi College
48	Flowers, Kenny	RB	6-0	210	2	Clemson
79	Fralic, Bill	G	6-5	280	4	Pittsburgh
76	Gann, Mike	DE	6-5	275	4	Notre Dame
41	Gordon, Tim	S	6-0	188	2	Tulsa
99	Green, Tim	LB	6-2	245	3	Syracuse
68	Harrison, Dennis	DE	6-8	280	11	Vanderbilt
66	Hinson, Billy	G	6-1	278	2	Florida
84	Jones, Joey	WR	5-8	165	2	Alabama
78	Kenn, Mike	T	6-7	277	11	Michigan
14	Kramer, Erik	QB	6-0	192	2	North Carolina State
52	Kraynak, Rich	LB	6-1	230	6	Pittsburgh
93	Laughlin, Jim	LB	6-1	222	8	Ohio State
	Lavette, Robert	RB	5-11	190	4	Georgia Tech
18	Luckhurst, Mick	K	6-2	183	8	California
83	Matthews, Aubrey	WR	5-7	165	3	Delta State
40	Meyers, Eddie	RB	5-9	210	1	Navy
87	Middleton, Ron	TE	6-2	252	3	Auburn
62	Miller, Brett	T	6-7	300	6	Iowa
12	Miller, Chris	QB	6-2	195	2	Oregon
73	Mitchell, Leonard	T	6-7	295	8	Houston
34	Moore, Robert	S	5-11	190	3	Northwestern St., La.
67	Mraz, Mark	DE	6-4	255	2	Utah State
59	Rade, John	LB	6-1	240	6	Boise State
55	Radloff, Wayne	C-G	6-5	277	4	Georgia
95	Reid, Michael	LB	6-2	226	2	Wisconsin
42	Riggs, Gerald	RB	6-1	232	7	Arizona State
61	Scully, John	G	6-6	270	8	Notre Dame
44	Settle, John	RB	5-9	207	2	Appalachian State
80	Sharp, Dan	TE	6-2	235	2	Texas Christian
37	Shelley, Elbert	S	5-11	180	2	Arkansas State
29	Stamps, Sylvester	RB-KR	5-7	171	4	Jackson State
58	Tuggle, Jessie	LB	5-11	225	2	Valdosta State
45	Whisenhunt, Ken	TE	6-3	240	4	Georgia Tech
51	Wilkes, Reggie	LB	6-4	242	11	Georgia Tech
54	Williams, Joel	LB	6-1	227	10	Wisconsin-LaCrosse

LOS ANGELES RAMS

Address 2327 West Lincoln Avenue, Anaheim, California 92801.

Stadium Anaheim Stadium, Anaheim.
Capacity 69,007 *Playing Surface* Grass.

Team Colours Royal Blue, Gold, and White.

Head Coach John Robinson – sixth year.

Championships Division 1973,'74,'75,'76,'77,'78,'79,'85;
Conference 1979; NFL 1945,'51.

History NFL 1937-69, NFC 1970-
(Until 1946, they were known as the Cleveland Rams.)

Offense

A magnificent individual performance by running back Charles White apart, the Rams have just laboured through an eminently forgettable campaign which ended when they suffered the worst loss in the history of the franchise, a 48-0 drubbing at the hands of the 49ers. But by the third week in April, when the draft took place, the trade of superstar running back Eric Dickerson to the Colts didn't look quite so bad a deal. After all, he didn't want to play for them anymore and now the second of three major installments was being paid. The first payment brought them Greg Bell, a first-class running back who had done excellent things for the Bills but felt unsettled. Injury brought an early end to his impact but he will be ready to line up in the backfield by the preseason opener. From the draft, they obtained the UCLA running back, Gaston Green, who was probably the most exciting available at his position. Thus far, he has not shown himself to be durable but then the Rams also have White, and the likes of Mike Guman and Tim Tyrrell to do the blocking. Quarterback Jim Everett did not develop as quickly as the Rams would have liked, but he didn't exactly fall apart and there are few who doubt that he will make a fine pro. Steve Dils is the senior backup but he'll have to keep an eye on Hugh Millen, who spent most of the campaign on injured reserve after looking good in brief spells during the preseason. Again, the Rams used the draft to find outstanding talent at wide receiver in the form of Aaron Cox and Willie Anderson. Following the retirement of Ron Brown, who wishes to concentrate on athletics, and with Kevin House beginning to slow, the competition to start in one of the wide receiver positions is between Cox, Anderson and Michael Young. The senior player is Henry Ellard, a beautiful, rangy runner, who led the wide receivers in all three categories of receptions, yardage and touchdowns in 1987. For once, the Rams have no big-name tight end on their books, but any one of former Chargers player Pete Holohan, Damone Johnson and Greg Baty could make some headlines. The offensive line does not look as powerful as usual, but it still needs to be treated with respect. The starting lineup will have Irv Pankey and Jackie Slater at tackles, Tom Newberry at left guard, with Doug Smith at center. If Mike Schad does not develop, Duval Love would be the obvious choice to move in at right guard.

Defense

On defense, the Rams ranked 21st in the NFL, but there is no real weakness which can be identified. Perhaps the secondary did look a little lifeless on occasion, and that would have to go down as a major observation, for the secondary is not an area where the Rams might expect to be weak. As a general philosophy, the Rams have two distinct formations, one an orthodox 3-4 formation and the other a complex 'Nickel Defense' which, belying its name, has six defensive backs including a 'dime'. Also, there is much substituting of personnel. Nonetheless, it still is possible to identify LeRoy Irvin, Jerry Gray, Nolan Cromwell, Johnnie Johnson and Vince Newsome as first-rate players who could find their way onto any pro roster. Irvin, Gray and Cromwell are either current or former AFC-NFC Pro Bowlers, and Johnson, who is an outstanding run forcer, ought to have been. 1987 saw the introduction of three young players, rookies Clifford Hicks and Michael Stewart, and second-year cornerback Mickey Sutton. There's a settled look about the group at linebacker, which is respectable against the run. The nominal starters in the orthodox system are Mel Owens, Carl Ekern, Jim Collins and Mike Wilcher. Ekern and Collins, the latter who led the team in tackles, are former AFC-NFC Pro Bowlers. Kevin Greene is a backup but he comes into his own in the 'Nickel' as a pass rusher, a role in which he registered 6.5 quarterback sacks to rank second on the team behind defensive end Gary Jeter's seven. Fred Strickland, who played at inside linebacker in college, was drafted in the second round. Lining up on first down, the Rams will have Doug Reed and Shawn Miller at defensive end, with Greg Meisner at nose tackle. Only Reed remains in the 'Nickel', shifting to defensive tackle, where he is paired with Jeter. Greene and Fred Stokes take over at defensive end.

1988 SCHEDULE OF GAMES	September	
	4 at Green Bay	12:00
	11 DETROIT	1:00
	18 at Los Angeles Raiders	1:00
	25 at New York Giants	4:00
	October	
	2 PHOENIX	1:00
	9 at Atlanta	1:00
	16 SAN FRANCISCO	1:00
	23 SEATTLE	1:00
	30 at New Orleans	12:00
	November	
	6 at Philadelphia	1:00
	13 NEW ORLEANS	1:00
	20 SAN DIEGO	1:00
	27 at Denver	2:00
	December	
	5 CHICAGO (Mon.)	6:00
	11 ATLANTA	1:00
	18 at San Francisco	5:00

Special Teams

Mike Lansford and Dale Hatcher take care of the kicking game, whilst Ellard and Hicks handle the punt returns. The Rams will miss Brown's kickoff returns, not so much for his consistency, but more for the panic he used to induce every time he circled underneath the falling ball. He was always likely to run it back all the way.

1988 DRAFT

Round	Name	Pos.	Ht.	Wt.	College
1.	Green, Gaston	RB	5-10	192	UCLA
1.	Cox, Aaron	WR	5-9	178	Arizona State
2.	Newman, Anthony	DB	6-0	198	Oregon
2.	Anderson, Willie	WR	5-11	170	UCLA
2.	Strickland, Fred	LB	6-2	240	Purdue
3.	Piel, Mike	DT	6-3	260	Illinois
5.	Delpino, Robert	RB	5-11	198	Missouri
5.	Washington, James	DB	6-1	192	UCLA
6.	Jones, Keith	RB	5-9	187	Nebraska
6.	Knapton, Jeff	DT	6-4	242	Wyoming
8.	Franklin, Darryl	WR	5-10	186	Washington
9.	Foster, Pat	DT	6-3	240	Montana
10.	Mullin, R.C.	T	6-5	310	Southwestern Louisiana
12.	Beathard, Jeff	WR	5-9	190	Southern Oregon

VETERAN ROSTER

No.	Name	Pos.	Ht.	Wt.	NFL Year	College
57	Bartlett, Doug	LB	6-2	257	1	Northern Illinois
84	Baty, Greg	TE	6-5	241	3	Stanford
42	Bell, Greg	RB	5-10	210	5	Notre Dame
92	Brown, Richard	LB	6-3	240	2	San Diego State
95	Byrne, James	NT	6-3	280	1	Wisconsin-LaCrosse
50	Collins, Jim	LB	6-2	230	7	Syracuse
72	Cox, Robert	T	6-5	258	2	UCLA
21	Cromwell, Nolan	S	6-1	200	12	Kansas
8	Dils, Steve	QB	6-1	191	9	Stanford
55	Ekern, Carl	LB	6-3	222	12	San Jose State
80	Ellard, Henry	WR-PR	5-11	175	6	Fresno State
87	Embree, Jon	TE	6-2	230	2	Colorado
34	Evans, Donald	RB	6-2	256	2	Winston-Salem State
11	Everett, Jim	QB	6-5	212	3	Purdue
35	Francis, Jon	RB	5-11	207	2	Boise State
25	Gray, Jerry	CB	6-0	185	4	Texas
91	Greene, Kevin	LB	6-3	238	4	Auburn
44	Guman, Mike	RB	6-2	218	9	Penn State
5	Hatcher, Dale	P	6-2	200	4	Clemson
38	Heimuli, Lakei	RB	5-11	192	2	Brigham Young
28	Hicks, Clifford	CB	5-10	188	2	Oregon
	Holohan, Pete	TE	6-4	235	8	Notre Dame
83	House, Kevin	WR	6-1	185	9	Southern Illinois
47	Irvin, LeRoy	CB	5-11	184	9	Kansas
59	Jerue, Mark	LB	6-3	229	6	Washington
77	Jeter, Gary	DE	6-4	260	12	Southern California
86	Johnson, Damone	TE	6-4	230	3	Cal Poly-SLO
20	Johnson, Johnnie	S	6-1	186	9	Texas
52	Kelm, Larry	LB	6-4	226	2	Texas A&M
1	Lansford, Mike	K	6-0	190	7	Washington
67	Love, Duval	T-G	6-3	280	4	UCLA
90	McDonald, Mike	LB	6-1	235	4	Southern California
24	McGee, Buford	RB	6-0	206	5	Mississippi
69	Meisner, Greg	NT	6-3	265	8	Pittsburgh
12	Millen, Hugh	QB	6-5	216	2	Washington
98	Miller, Shawn	DE	6-4	255	5	Utah State
66	Newberry, Tom	G	6-2	279	3	Wisconsin-LaCrosse
22	Newsome, Vince	S	6-1	179	6	Washington
58	Owens, Mel	LB	6-2	224	8	Michigan
75	Pankey, Irv	T	6-5	280	8	Penn State
93	Reed, Doug	DE	6-3	250	5	San Diego State
82	Richardson, Craig	WR	5-11	189	1	Eastern Washington
26	Riley, Eric	CB	6-0	177	1	Florida State
76	Schad, Mike	G	6-5	290	2	Queen's, Canada
78	Slater, Jackie	T	6-4	275	13	Jackson State
61	Slaton, Tony	C	6-3	265	5	Southern California
56	Smith, Doug	C	6-3	260	11	Bowling Green
96	Smith, David	LB	6-6	235	1	Northern Arizona
23	Stewart, Michael	S	5-11	195	2	Fresno State
65	Stokes, Fred	DE	6-3	262	2	Georgia Southern
49	Sutton, Mickey	CB	5-8	165	3	Montana
32	Tyrrell, Tim	RB	6-1	201	5	Northern Illinois
51	Vann, Norwood	LB	6-1	237	5	East Carolina
73	Walker, Jeff	T	6-4	295	3	Memphis State
41	Wattelet, Frank	S	6-0	190	8	Kansas
33	White, Charles	RB	5-10	190	8	Southern California
54	Wilcher, Mike	LB	6-3	235	6	North Carolina
99	Wright, Alvin	NT	6-2	265	3	Jacksonville State
88	Young, Michael	WR	6-1	185	4	UCLA

Jerry Gray underlined his class in 1987.

NEW ORLEANS SAINTS

Address 1500 Poydras Street, New Orleans, Louisiana 70112.

Stadium Louisiana Superdome, New Orleans.
Capacity 69,723 *Playing Surface* AstroTurf.

Team Colours Old Gold, Black, and White.

Head Coach Jim Mora – third year.

Championships None.

History NFL 1967-69, NFC 1970-

Offense

Following the Saints' Week Seven loss to the 49ers, head coach Jim Mora was not pleased. Looking at everyone in the Saints' organisation but at no one in particular, he said, 'I've had enough of listening to how we woulda, coulda, shoulda . . . ' The Saints won their next nine games and, in that short period, confirmed that after 21 years of trying, they'd arrived in this league. With the defense able to take care of itself – they ranked fourth in the league – Mora used four of his top five draft options to select players for the offense. They were hardly in need at running back, but it may be that Rueben Mayes takes time to regain his former powers following knee surgery, and anyway, the opportunity to pick Craig (Ironhead) Heyward was just too good to miss. Heyward is one of only eight players in college football history to rush for 100-or-more yards in all eleven regular-season games. A healthy Mayes, Dalton Hilliard and Heyward should give the club outstanding productivity, with Barry Word and Buford Jordan sharing the blocking at fullback. As expected, Bobby Hebert established a seniority over Dave Wilson and he shows every prospect of improving as the rest of the offense gains in stature. Wilson is a perfectly adequate backup. At wide receiver, Eric Martin emerged as the most productive receiver, leading the team both in receptions and yards. Also, he has the speed to go deep. Former Vikings player Mike Jones, a steady player, is the other starter. Last year's second-round draftee, Lonzell Hill, did not make an immediate impact. This year, the Saints went looking again and came up with Brett Perriman, whose blazing speed was not put to full use at the University of Miami, where Michael Irvin was the preferred target. The offensive line confirmed its position as a team strength and even left guard Brad Edelman, who went to the AFC-NFC Pro Bowl, can not be certain of holding on to his starting spot. It may go to Steve Korte, the former center who is returning from injury but might not be able to displace Joel Hilgenberg. Rookie Steve Trapilo moved up to start at right guard whilst Stan Brock underlined his class at right tackle. Former first-rounder Jim Dombrowski should be better for having been roasted a few times at left tackle. At tight end, both Hoby Brenner and John Tice are solid blockers, and Tice showed an unexpected flair for finding the end zone – six of his 16 receptions were for touchdowns!

Defense

Even without defensive end James Geathers, who missed most of the year through injury, the line was particularly ungenerous. Bruce Clark, Tony Elliott and Jim Wilks brunted the run to good effect. Frank Warren, who logged six sacks, is a fine situation pass rusher. The return of Geathers and the continued development of last year's first-round pick, Shawn Knight, would present Mora with an embarrassment of riches. That's already true at linebacker, which grades out to be the strongest area of the defense ahead of the defensive line. A cocktail of two former USFL players, Sam Mills and Vaughan Johnson, 1986 third-round draftee Pat Swilling, and the great Rickey Jackson, can have heady results. Swilling came through to lead the club with 10.5 quarterback sacks, one more than Jackson. Jackson missed out on AFC-NFC Pro Bowl selection for the first time since the 1983 season whilst Mills, an undersized run-stuffer, earned his first trip. Reassuringly, in the likes of former first-round pick Alvin Toles, Joe Kohlbrand and James Haynes, there is excellent reserve strength. It is the quality of the front seven which helps to carry a relative weakness at defensive back. Of the competitors for starting spots, ninth-year cornerback Dave Waymer, who shared the team lead with five pass interceptions, has the best credentials. Reggie Sutton has some weaknesses but when opposing quarterbacks went after him they were punished as he, too, picked off five passes. He has great potential but has yet to establish himself and will compete with Van Jakes to start at right cornerback. Antonio Gibson, a former starter at strong safety, should be back from injury and will battle with Gene Atkins for his old position. At the end of last season, Brett Maxie was the starter at free safety, but he faces increasing pressure from Toi Cook, who, as a 1987 rookie, had some good moments.

1988 SCHEDULE OF GAMES	September	
	4 SAN FRANCISCO	12:00
	11 at Atlanta	1:00
	18 at Detroit	1:00
	25 TAMPA BAY	12:00
	October	
	3 DALLAS (Mon.)	8:00
	9 at San Diego	1:00
	16 at Seattle	1:00
	23 LOS ANGELES RAIDERS	12:00
	30 LOS ANGELES RAMS	12:00
	November	
	6 at Washington	4:00
	13 at Los Angeles Rams	1:00
	20 DENVER	12:00
	27 NEW YORK GIANTS	7:00
	December	
	4 at Minnesota	12:00
	11 at San Francisco	1:00
	18 ATLANTA	12:00

Special Teams

It would be a major shock were placekicker Morten Andersen, the NFL all-time field goal efficiency leader, to be anything less than excellent, and dual-purpose kick returner Mel Gray, who was the NFL leading punt returner with an average of 14.7 yards, must be on the verge of AFC-NFC Pro Bowl selection. Punter Brian Hansen slipped a little but he is hardly under threat.

1988 DRAFT

Round	Name	Pos.	Ht.	Wt.	College
1.	Heyward, Craig	RB	6-0	265	Pittsburgh
2.	Perriman, Brett	WR	5-9	182	Miami
3.	Stephens, Tony	NT	6-2	298	Clemson
4.	Carr, Lydell	RB	6-0	224	Oklahoma
5.	Scales, Greg	TE	6-3	250	Wake Forest
5.	Taylor, Keith	DB	5-11	192	Illinois
6.	Sims, Bob	G	6-3	270	Florida
7.	Forde, Brian	LB	6-2	235	Washington State
8.	Derby, Glenn	T	6-6	290	Wisconsin
9.	Nunn, Clarence	DB	5-9	177	San Diego State
10.	Santos, Todd	QB	6-1	206	San Diego State
10.	Fizer, Vincent	LB	6-4	220	Southern
11.	Couch, Gary	WR	5-9	170	Minnesota
12.	Jurgensen, Paul	DE	6-5	240	Georgia Tech

VETERAN ROSTER

No.	Name	Pos.	Ht.	Wt.	NFL Year	College
40	Adams, Michael	CB	5-10	195	2	Arkansas State
7	Andersen, Morten	K	6-2	221	7	Michigan State
28	Atkins, Gene	S	6-1	200	2	Florida A&M
83	Benson, Cliff	TE	6-4	240	4	Purdue
85	Brenner, Hoby	TE	6-4	240	8	Southern California
67	Brock, Stan	T	6-6	292	9	Colorado
59	Campen, James	C	6-3	260	2	Tulane
75	Clark, Bruce	DE	6-3	275	7	Penn State
89	Clark, Robert	WR	5-11	175	2	North Carolina Central
	Coffman, Paul	TE	6-3	225	11	Kansas State
66	Commiskey, Chuck	G-C	6-4	290	3	Mississippi
70	Contz, Bill	T	6-5	270	6	Penn State
41	Cook, Toi	S	5-11	188	2	Stanford
26	Dawsey, Stacey	WR	5-9	154	2	Indiana
72	Dombrowski, Jim	T	6-5	298	3	Virginia
63	Edelman, Brad	G	6-6	270	7	Missouri
99	Elliott, Tony	NT	6-2	295	7	North Texas State
38	Evans, Vince	RB	5-10	216	1	North Carolina State
11	Fourcade, John	QB	6-1	208	2	Mississippi
46	Gajan, Hokie	RB	5-11	230	5	Louisiana State
97	Geathers, James	DE	6-7	290	4	Wichita State
27	Gibson, Antonio	S	6-3	204	3	Cincinnati
77	Gilbert, Daren	T	6-6	295	4	Cal State-Fullerton
37	Gray, Mel	RB-KR	5-9	166	3	Purdue
10	Hansen, Brian	P	6-3	209	5	Sioux Falls, S.D.
80	Harris, Herbert	WR	6-2	192	3	Lamar
92	Haynes, James	LB	6-2	233	5	Mississippi Valley St.
3	Hebert, Bobby	QB	6-4	215	4	Northwestern St., La.
61	Hilgenberg, Joel	C	6-2	252	5	Iowa
87	Hill, Lonzell	WR	5-11	189	2	Washington
21	Hilliard, Dalton	RB	5-8	204	3	Louisiana State
57	Jackson, Rickey	LB	6-2	243	8	Pittsburgh
22	Jakes, Van	CB	6-0	190	5	Kent State
53	Johnson, Vaughan	LB	6-3	235	3	North Carolina State
86	Jones, Mike	WR	5-11	183	6	Tennessee State
23	Jordan, Buford	RB	6-0	223	3	McNeese State
71	Kaplan, Ken	T	6-5	270	4	New Hampshire
78	Knight, Shawn	DE	6-6	288	2	Brigham Young
55	Kohlbrand, Joe	LB	6-4	242	4	Miami
60	Korte, Steve	C-G	6-2	269	6	Arkansas
24	Mack, Milton	CB	5-11	182	4	Alcorn State
84	Martin, Eric	WR	6-1	207	4	Louisiana State
39	Maxie, Brett	S	6-2	194	4	Texas Southern
36	Mayes, Rueben	RB	5-11	200	3	Washington State
51	Mills, Sam	LB	5-9	225	3	Montclair State
88	Pattison, Mark	WR	6-2	190	2	Washington
29	Sutton, Reggie	CB	5-10	180	2	Miami
56	Swilling, Pat	LB	6-3	242	3	Georgia Tech
69	Swoopes, Patrick	NT	6-4	280	2	Mississippi State
82	Tice, John	TE	6-5	249	6	Maryland
54	Toles, Alvin	LB	6-1	227	4	Tennessee
65	Trapilo, Steve	G	6-5	281	2	Boston College
73	Warren, Frank	DE	6-4	290	8	Auburn
83	Waters, Mike	TE	6-2	230	3	San Diego State
44	Waymer, Dave	CB	6-1	188	9	Notre Dame
94	Wilks, Jim	DE	6-5	266	8	San Diego State
18	Wilson, Dave	QB	6-3	206	7	Illinois
34	Word, Barry	RB	6-2	220	2	Virginia

Dalton Hilliard rushed at an average of 4.1 yards in 1987.

SAN FRANCISCO 49ers

Address 711 Nevada Street, Redwood City, California 94061.
Stadium Candlestick Park, San Francisco.
  Capacity 61,891 *Playing Surface* Grass.
Team Colours Forty Niners Gold and Scarlet.
Head Coach Bill Walsh – tenth year.
Championships Division 1970,'71,'72,'81,'83,'84,'86,'87;
  Conference 1981,'84; Super Bowl 1981,'84.
History AAFC 1946-49, NFL 1950-69, NFC 1970-

Offense

The 49ers now hold the longest current sequence of playoff appearances, five, but their exit at the hands of Minnesota in the divisional playoffs means that there may be changes to the starting lineup, even one which ravaged more than a few of its opponents last year. It seems more and more likely that Steve Young will make a serious bid to oust Joe Montana, even though the winner of two Super Bowl MVP awards has just secured the first NFL passing title of his career. Certainly, it would be wrong to suggest that Montana could not do the same effective job, but he will be given a serious challenge by Steve Young, a brilliant, spontaneous athlete, whose different style may expose new and unexpected skills in the rest of the offensive strike players. Protecting him will be an offensive line with plenty of talent available, but whose exact form will not become clear until late in the preseason. The 49ers ended the regular season with Bubba Paris and Harris Barton at tackle, Jesse Sapolu and Bruce Collie at guard and Randy Cross at center. It meant that Fred Quillan and Guy McIntyre were relegated to reserve status, but, together with Jeff Bregel, they do make a fine set of back-ups. Another change saw the replacement of former Pro Bowl tight end Russ Francis by John Frank, who holds a slight edge over Ron Heller. There are no questions to be asked at wide receiver, where Jerry Rice has just enjoyed a campaign unparalleled in league history. The marvel is that in catching 22 touchdown passes, he hardly seemed to be under any kind of pressure, and it seems well within his capabilities to raise the record by another half-dozen or so. He demands double-teaming, and that must help Dokie Williams, who came in a trade with the Raiders and will probably be the other starter. Mike Wilson, a player not blessed with great speed, has disciplined moves and great concentration. Behind these three is John Taylor, a good athlete with terrific speed, who is being groomed as a future starter. As usual, the offensive backfield would be expected to make a significant contribution to the passing game. It was another of the changes which saw Roger Craig move to halfback, ahead of Joe Cribbs, whilst Tom Rathman took over at fullback, where he is supported by Harry Sydney. Terrence Flagler and Doug DuBose will be expected to be more prominent after going through learning seasons.

Defense

The 49ers may just have the best defensive secondary in pro football, but the club is in the process of revamping the front seven. Last year it was the offense which was helped by the top four picks, and this year, excluding draftee punter Barry Helton, they went to the defense. Top pick Danny Stubbs is listed as a defensive end, but it is most likely that he will play the role of specialist pass rusher, which forms such an important part of the 49ers' system. Second pick Pierce Holt was selected for his toughness against the run. It is not likely that Holt could displace current starting nose tackle Michael Carter, but Stubbs might share significant time with Charles Haley. They may even be used in tandem. The starting line probably will see Jeff Stover and Dwaine Board either side of Carter. At linebacker, the 49ers are solid without being dramatically spectacular. Todd Shell, one of their better blitzers, was restricted to just two starts because of injury. He is projected to share time with Keena Turner, probably on passing downs, at right outside linebacker. On the other side, Milt McColl has great poise and is considered by the club to be one of their most consistent performers. There will be a competition for the inside spots with Michael Walter, Jim Fahnhorst and Riki Ellison as the principal contenders. Head coach Bill Walsh feels that Walter has all-star potential, an observation which suggests that he will start. Ellison, who started all sixteen games in 1986 but who did not regain his full powers after suffering a broken arm in the 1987 season opener, would appear to have an edge over Fahnhorst. Turning to the secondary, we see Ronnie Lott, who is regarded as the NFL's premier free safety, the reliable Jeff Fuller at strong safety, and the NFC's best cornerback pairing of Tim McKyer and Don Griffin. Former Pro Bowlers Carlton Williamson and Eric Wright should be back to full fitness after their injuries, completing a formidable array of talent.

1988 SCHEDULE OF GAMES		
September		
4	at New Orleans	12:00
11	at New York Giants	1:00
18	ATLANTA	1:00
25	at Seattle	1:00
October		
2	DETROIT	1:00
9	DENVER	1:00
16	at Los Angeles Rams	1:00
24	at Chicago (Mon.)	8:00
30	MINNESOTA	1:00
November		
6	at Phoenix	2:00
13	LOS ANGELES RAIDERS	1:00
21	WASHINGTON (Mon.)	6:00
27	at San Diego	1:00
December		
4	at Atlanta	1:00
11	NEW ORLEANS	1:00
18	LOS ANGELES RAMS	5:00

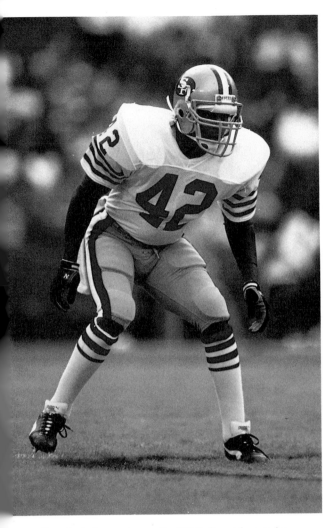

Ronnie Lott remains as the NFL's finest free safety.

Special Teams

Punter Max Runager has the kind of precise placement for which the 49ers ask, and there's nothing wrong with kicker Ray Wersching that isn't counterbalanced by his composure. Joe Cribbs doubles as a fine kickoff returner, but, despite ranking second in the NFL, punt returner Dana McLemore has been released.

1988 DRAFT

Round	Name	Pos.	Ht.	Wt.	College
2.	Stubbs, Danny	DE	6-3	252	Miami
2.	Holt, Pierce	DT	6-4	276	Angelo State
3.	Romanowski, Bill	LB	6-3	228	Boston College
4.	Helton, Barry	P	6-2	195	Colorado
7.	Bryant, Kevin	LB	6-4	210	Delaware State
8.	Clarkson, Larry	T	6-7	298	Montana
9.	Bonner, Brian	LB	6-1	227	Minnesota
10.	Foley, Tim	K	5-9	228	Georgia Southern
11.	Brooks, Chet	DB	5-11	192	Texas A&M
12.	Mira, George	LB	6-0	230	Miami

VETERAN ROSTER

No.	Name	Pos.	Ht.	Wt.	NFL Year	College
79	Barton, Harris	T	6-4	280	2	North Carolina
23	Berry, Ed	CB	5-10	183	2	Utah State
76	Board, Dwaine	DE	6-5	248	9	North Carolina A&T
65	Bregel, Jeff	G	6-4	280	2	Southern California
95	Carter, Michael	NT	6-2	285	5	Southern Methodist
69	Collie, Bruce	G-T	6-6	275	4	Texas-Arlington
59	Comeaux, Darren	LB	6-1	227	7	Arizona State
52	Cooper, George	LB	6-2	225	2	Michigan State
33	Craig, Roger	RB	6-0	224	6	Nebraska
83	Crawford, Derrick	WR-KR	5-10	185	2	Memphis State
28	Cribbs, Joe	RB-KR	5-11	193	8	Auburn
51	Cross, Randy	C	6-3	265	13	UCLA
57	Dean, Kevin	LB	6-1	235	2	Texas Christian
25	DuBose, Doug	RB	5-11	190	2	Nebraska
50	Ellison, Riki	LB	6-2	225	6	Southern California
75	Fagan, Kevin	DE	6-3	260	2	Miami
55	Fahnhorst, Jim	LB	6-4	230	5	Minnesota
32	Flagler, Terrence	RB	6-0	200	2	Clemson
86	Frank, John	TE	6-3	225	5	Ohio State
49	Fuller, Jeff	S	6-2	216	5	Texas A&M
11	Gagliano, Bob	QB	6-3	195	5	Utah State
2	Gamache, Vince	P	5-11	176	3	Cal State-Fullerton
93	Glover, Clyde	DE	6-6	280	2	Fresno State
29	Griffin, Don	CB	6-0	176	3	Middle Tennessee St.
54	Hadley, Ron	LB	6-2	240	2	Washington
94	Haley, Charles	LB-DE	6-5	230	3	James Madison
89	Heller, Ron	TE	6-3	235	2	Oregon State
46	Holmoe, Tom	S	6-2	195	6	Brigham Young
	Jones, Brent	TE	6-4	230	2	Santa Clara
67	Kugler, Pete	DE	6-4	255	6	Penn State
48	Lewis, David	TE	6-3	235	5	California
92	Lilly, Kevin	DE	6-5	265	1	Tulsa
42	Lott, Ronnie	S	6-0	200	8	Southern California
84	Margerum, Ken	WR	6-0	180	7	Stanford
53	McColl, Milt	LB	6-6	230	8	Stanford
62	McIntyre, Guy	G	6-3	265	5	Georgia
22	McKyer, Tim	CB	6-0	174	3	Texas-Arlington
97	Mikolas, Doug	NT	6-1	270	2	Portland State
16	Montana, Joe	QB	6-2	195	10	Notre Dame
88	Nicholas, Calvin	WR	6-4	208	1	Grambling State
20	Nixon, Tory	CB	5-11	186	4	San Diego State
77	Paris, Bubba	T	6-6	306	6	Michigan
15	Paye, John	QB	6-3	205	1	Stanford
56	Quillan, Fred	C	6-5	266	11	Oregon
44	Rathman, Tom	RB	6-1	232	3	Nebraska
80	Rice, Jerry	WR	6-2	200	4	Mississippi Valley St.
91	Roberts, Larry	DE	6-3	264	3	Alabama
4	Runager, Max	P	6-1	189	10	South Carolina
61	Sapolu, Jesse	G	6-4	260	3	Hawaii
90	Shell, Todd	LB	6-4	225	4	Brigham Young
72	Stover, Jeff	DE	6-5	275	7	Oregon
24	Sydney, Harry	RB	6-1	217	2	Kansas
82	Taylor, John	WR	6-1	185	2	Delaware State
60	Thomas, Chuck	C	6-3	280	3	Oklahoma
41	Thomas, Sean	DB	5-11	192	2	Texas Christian
58	Turner, Keena	LB	6-2	222	9	Purdue
74	Wallace, Steve	T	6-5	276	3	Auburn
99	Walter, Michael	LB	6-3	238	6	Oregon
14	Wersching, Ray	K	5-11	215	16	California
	Williams, Dokie	WR	5-11	185	6	UCLA
27	Williamson, Carlton	S	6-0	204	8	Pittsburgh
85	Wilson, Mike	WR	6-3	215	8	Washington State
21	Wright, Eric	CB	6-1	185	7	Missouri
8	Young, Steve	QB	6-2	200	4	Brigham Young

✩✩✩✩✩✩✩✩✩ **CHAPTER EIGHT** ✩✩✩✩✩✩✩✩✩

1988 NATIONAL FOOTBALL LEAGUE SCHEDULE

(All times local)

FIRST WEEK
Sunday, September 4 — Kickoff

Atlanta at Detroit	1:00
Cleveland at Kansas City	3:00
Dallas at Pittsburgh	1:00
Houston at Indianapolis	3:00
Los Angeles Rams at Green Bay	12:00
Miami at Chicago	12:00
Minnesota at Buffalo	1:00
New York Jets at New England	4:00
Philadelphia at Tampa Bay	1:00
Phoenix at Cincinnati	1:00
San Diego at Los Angeles Raiders	1:00
San Francisco at New Orleans	12:00
Seattle at Denver	2:00

Monday, September 5

Washington at New York Giants	9:00

SECOND WEEK
Sunday, September 11

Chicago at Indianapolis	12:00
Cincinnati at Philadelphia	4:00
Detroit at Los Angeles Rams	1:00
Kansas City at Seattle	1:00
Los Angeles Raiders at Houston	3:00
Miami at Buffalo	1:00
New England at Minnesota	3:00
New Orleans at Atlanta	1:00
New York Jets at Cleveland	4:00
Pittsburgh at Washington	1:00
San Diego at Denver	2:00
San Francisco at New York Giants	1:00
Tampa Bay at Green Bay	12:00

Monday, September 12

Dallas at Phoenix	6:00

THIRD WEEK
Sunday, September 18

Atlanta at San Francisco	1:00
Buffalo at New England	1:00
Cincinnati at Pittsburgh	1:00
Denver at Kansas City	12:00
Green Bay at Miami	1:00
Houston at New York Jets	1:00
Los Angeles Rams at Los Angeles Raiders	1:00
Minnesota at Chicago	12:00
New Orleans at Detroit	1:00
New York Giants at Dallas	3:00
Philadelphia at Washington	1:00
Phoenix at Tampa Bay	1:00
Seattle at San Diego	1:00

Monday, September 19

Indianapolis at Cleveland	8:00

FOURTH WEEK
Sunday, September 25

Atlanta at Dallas	12:00
Chicago at Green Bay	12:00
Cleveland at Cincinnati	1:00
Los Angeles Rams at New York Giants	4:00
Miami at Indianapolis	12:00
New England at Houston	12:00
New York Jets at Detroit	1:00
Philadelphia at Minnesota	12:00
Pittsburgh at Buffalo	1:00
San Diego at Kansas City	3:00
San Francisco at Seattle	1:00
Tampa Bay at New Orleans	12:00
Washington at Phoenix	1:00

Monday, September 26

Los Angeles Raiders at Denver	6:00

FIFTH WEEK
Sunday, October 2

Buffalo at Chicago	12:00
Cincinnati at Los Angeles Raiders	1:00

Cleveland at Pittsburgh	1:00
Denver at San Diego	1:00
Detroit at San Francisco	1:00
Green Bay at Tampa Bay	1:00
Houston at Philadelphia	1:00
Indianapolis at New England	1:00
Kansas City at New York Jets	4:00
Minnesota at Miami	4:00
New York Giants at Washington	1:00
Phoenix at Los Angeles Rams	1:00
Seattle at Atlanta	1:00

Monday, October 3

Dallas at New Orleans	8:00

SIXTH WEEK
Sunday, October 9

Chicago at Detroit	1:00
Denver at San Francisco	1:00
Indianapolis at Buffalo	1:00
Kansas City at Houston	12:00
Los Angeles Rams at Atlanta	1:00
Miami at Los Angeles Raiders	1:00
New England vs. Green Bay at Milwaukee	12:00
New Orleans at San Diego	1:00
New York Jets at Cincinnati	1:00
Pittsburgh at Phoenix	1:00
Seattle at Cleveland	1:00
Tampa Bay at Minnesota	12:00
Washington at Dallas	12:00

Monday, October 10

New York Giants at Philadelphia	9:00

SEVENTH WEEK
Sunday, October 16

Atlanta at Denver	2:00
Cincinnati at New England	1:00
Dallas at Chicago	12:00
Detroit at New York Giants	1:00
Green Bay at Minnesota	12:00
Houston at Pittsburgh	1:00
Los Angeles Raiders at Kansas City	12:00
New Orleans at Seattle	1:00
Philadelphia at Cleveland	1:00
Phoenix at Washington	1:00
San Diego at Miami	1:00
San Francisco at Los Angeles Rams	1:00
Tampa Bay at Indianapolis	12:00

Monday, October 17

Buffalo at New York Jets	9:00

EIGHTH WEEK
Sunday, October 23

Cleveland at Phoenix	1:00
Dallas at Philadelphia	1:00
Denver at Pittsburgh	1:00
Detroit at Kansas City	12:00
Houston at Cincinnati	1:00
Indianapolis at San Diego	1:00

Los Angeles Raiders at New Orleans	12:00
Minnesota at Tampa Bay	1:00
New England at Buffalo	1:00
New York Giants at Atlanta	1:00
New York Jets at Miami	4:00
Seattle at Los Angeles Rams	1:00
Washington vs. Green Bay at Milwaukee	12:00

Monday, October 24

San Francisco at Chicago	8:00

NINTH WEEK
Sunday, October 30

Atlanta at Philadelphia	1:00
Chicago at New England	1:00
Cincinnati at Cleveland	1:00
Green Bay at Buffalo	1:00
Kansas City at Los Angeles Raiders	1:00
Los Angeles Rams at New Orleans	12:00
Miami at Tampa Bay	1:00
Minnesota at San Francisco	1:00
New York Giants at Detroit	1:00
Phoenix at Dallas	12:00
Pittsburgh at New York Jets	1:00
San Diego at Seattle	1:00
Washington at Houston	7:00

Monday, October 31

Denver at Indianapolis	9:00

TENTH WEEK
Sunday, November 6

Buffalo at Seattle	1:00
Dallas at New York Giants	1:00
Detroit at Minnesota	12:00
Green Bay at Atlanta	1:00
Kansas City at Denver	2:00
Los Angeles Raiders at San Diego	5:00
Los Angeles Rams at Philadelphia	1:00
Miami at New England	1:00
New Orleans at Washington	4:00
New York Jets at Indianapolis	4:00
Pittsburgh at Cincinnati	1:00
San Francisco at Phoenix	2:00
Tampa Bay at Chicago	12:00

Monday, November 7

Cleveland at Houston	8:00

ELEVENTH WEEK
Sunday, November 13

Chicago at Washington	1:00
Cincinnati at Kansas City	12:00
Cleveland at Denver	2:00
Houston at Seattle	1:00
Indianapolis at Green Bay	12:00
Los Angeles Raiders at San Francisco	1:00
Minnesota at Dallas	7:00
New England at New York Jets	1:00
New Orleans at Los Angeles Rams	1:00
New York Giants at Phoenix	2:00

Philadelphia at Pittsburgh	1:00
San Diego at Atlanta	1:00
Tampa Bay at Detroit	1:00

Monday, November 14

Buffalo at Miami	9:00

TWELFTH WEEK
Sunday, November 20

Atlanta at Los Angeles Raiders	1:00
Chicago at Tampa Bay	1:00
Cincinnati at Dallas	12:00
Denver at New Orleans	12:00
Detroit vs. Green Bay at Milwaukee	12:00
Indianapolis at Minnesota	12:00
New England at Miami	8:00
New York Jets at Buffalo	1:00
Philadelphia at New York Giants	4:00
Phoenix at Houston	12:00
Pittsburgh at Cleveland	1:00
San Diego at Los Angeles Rams	1:00
Seattle at Kansas City	12:00

Monday, November 21

Washington at San Francisco	6:00

THIRTEENTH WEEK
Thursday, November 24 (Thanksgiving Day)

Houston at Dallas	3:00
Minnesota at Detroit	12:30

Sunday, November 27

Buffalo at Cincinnati	1:00
Cleveland at Washington	1:00
Green Bay at Chicago	12:00
Kansas City at Pittsburgh	1:00
Los Angeles Rams at Denver	2:00
Miami at New York Jets	1:00
New England at Indianapolis	4:00
New York Giants at New Orleans	7:00
Phoenix at Philadelphia	1:00
San Francisco at San Diego	1:00
Tampa Bay at Atlanta	1:00

Monday, November 28

Los Angeles Raiders at Seattle	6:00

FOURTEENTH WEEK
Sunday, December 4

Buffalo at Tampa Bay	1:00
Dallas at Cleveland	1:00
Denver at Los Angeles Raiders	1:00
Green Bay at Detroit	1:00
Indianapolis at Miami	1:00
New Orleans at Minnesota	12:00
New York Jets at Kansas City	3:00
Phoenix at New York Giants	1:00
Pittsburgh at Houston	7:00
San Diego at Cincinnati	1:00
San Francisco at Atlanta	1:00
Seattle at New England	1:00

Washington at Philadelphia	1:00

Monday, December 5

Chicago at Los Angeles Rams	6:00

FIFTEENTH WEEK
Saturday, December 10

Indianapolis at New York Jets	12:30
Philadelphia at Phoenix	2:00

Sunday, December 11

Atlanta at Los Angeles Rams	1:00
Cincinnati at Houston	12:00
Dallas at Washington	1:00
Denver at Seattle	5:00
Detroit at Chicago	12:00
Kansas City at New York Giants	1:00
Los Angeles Raiders at Buffalo	1:00
Minnesota at Green Bay	12:00
New Orleans at San Francisco	1:00
Pittsburgh at San Diego	1:00
Tampa Bay at New England	1:00

Monday, December 12

Cleveland at Miami	9:00

SIXTEENTH WEEK
Saturday, December 17

New England at Denver	2:00
Washington at Cincinnati	12:30

Sunday, December 18

Atlanta at New Orleans	12:00
Buffalo at Indianapolis	1:00
Detroit at Tampa Bay	1:00
Green Bay at Phoenix	2:00
Houston at Cleveland	1:00
Kansas City at San Diego	1:00
Los Angeles Rams at San Francisco	5:00
Miami at Pittsburgh	1:00
New York Giants at New York Jets	1:00
Philadelphia at Dallas	12:00
Seattle at Los Angeles Raiders	1:00

Monday, December 19

Chicago at Minnesota	8:00

Postseason

Saturday, Dec. 24	AFC First Round Playoff
Monday, Dec. 26	NFC First Round Playoff
Saturday, Dec. 31	AFC and NFC Divisional Playoffs
Sunday, Jan. 1	AFC and NFC Divisional Playoffs
Sunday, Jan. 8	AFC and NFC Championship Games
Sunday, Jan. 22	Super Bowl XXIII at Joe Robbie Stadium, Miami, Florida
Sunday, Jan. 29	AFC-NFC Pro Bowl at Honolulu, Hawaii

STOP PRESS

Below are listed several player movements which we were unable to include in the team scouting reports.

Just when it seemed certain that the Raiders would go with veteran quarterback Marc Wilson, he was abruptly released. However, such are the subtleties of contractual arrangements that it would be no surprise to see Wilson back in harness with the 'Silver and Black', though at a much lower salary than his reported $1,000,000 of the 1987 season. At the time of writing, there are rumours that he is having discussions with the Green Bay Packers. In the continuing search for depth at cornerback, the Raiders acquired Russell Carter from the Jets in the exchange for a 1989 sixth-round draft option. Carter may even win a starting spot. It was not widely known that Houston running back Alonzo Highsmith had undergone major surgery on his left knee in January, and for a time it was felt that his career may be in jeopardy. Currently, early July, he is undergoing daily exercise and, thankfully, there is every prospect that he will be back to full strength by the middle of August.

One factor in the Oilers' emergence has been the development of the pairing of Jeff Donaldson and Keith Bostic in the safety positions. Free safety Bo Eason, whose injury gave Donaldson his chance, could not regain his former starting spot and asked to be traded. Shortly afterwards he was signed by the 49ers in exchange for a conditional 1989 fifth-round draft option. With Jerry Rice, Dokie Williams and Mike Wilson, the 49ers hardly needed any more wide receivers, but they jumped at the chance to trade for the Chargers' former AFC-NFC Pro Bowler, Wes Chandler, in a straight player swap for center Fred Quilland.

As expected, former Dallas all-pro running back Tony Dorsett obtained his release and has joined Denver in exchange for a 1989 conditional fifth-round draft option. Dorsett, who will be reunited with Dan Reaves, a former Cowboys assistant coach, could have a major role in the Broncos' backfield. Somewhat surprisingly, Tampa Bay has released three former starters, guard George Yarno, inside linebacker Scot Brantley and strong safety Bobby Kemp. Subsequently, Brantly was signed up by Cincinnati, almost concurrently with the release of their backup inside linebacker, Kiki DeAyala.

In the cycle of things, Buffalo's Eugene Marve, a former starting inside linebacker, was traded to Tampa Bay for an undisclosed 1989 draft option. Kansas City defensive end Art Still has been traded to Buffalo for an undisclosed draft option, thus rejoining head coach Marv Levy, who, in his first year as the Chief's head coach (1978), drafted Still in the first round (he was the second player selected behind the great Earl Campbell). Strong safety Todd Bell is another who has rejoined his former mentor. Bell, who went to the 1985 AFC-NFC Pro Bowl, was released by Chicago and has signed for Philadelphia, whose head coach, Buddy Ryan, installed the Bears' '46 Defense'.

Placekicker Mick Luckhurst has announced his retirement in order to take up the post of presenter for Channel Four's coverage of the NFL in the 1988 season. His departure will be a major blow to the Falcons, who had come to rely on his trusty boot.

ALL-TIME HEAD-TO-HEAD RESULTS

	Buffalo	Indianapolis	Miami	New England	N.Y. Jets	Cincinnati	Cleveland	Houston	Pittsburgh	Denver	Kansas City	L.A. Raiders	San Diego	Seattle
Buffalo		17-17-1	9-34-1	23-32-1	27-28-0	5-9-0	2-7-0	10-18-0	4-6-0	14-9-1	15-12-1	11-13-0	9-17-2	0-2-0
Indianapolis	17-17-1		10-27-0	16-19-0	18-18-0	5-5-0	6-12-0	6-4-0	4-10-0	1-6-0	3-6-0	3-4-0	3-6-0	2-0-0
Miami	34-9-1	27-10-0		25-19-0	24-20-1	8-3-0	3-4-0	10-10-0	8-3-0	5-2-1	7-7-0	3-15-1	5-9-0	3-2-0
New England	32-23-1	19-16-0	19-25-0		24-31-1	6-4-0	2-7-0	15-13-1	3-5-0	12-14-0	7-11-3	13-12-1	13-12-2	5-2-0
N.Y. Jets	28-27-0	18-18-0	20-24-1	31-24-1		8-4-0	3-8-0	10-15-1	0-9-0	11-10-1	13-13-0	11-12-2	7-14-1	3-7-0
Cincinnati	9-5-0	5-5-0	3-8-0	4-6-0	4-8-0		17-18-0	21-16-1	15-20-0	6-9-0	8-9-0	4-12-0	7-11-0	5-2-0
Cleveland	7-2-0	12-6-0	4-3-0	7-2-0	8-3-0	18-17-0		23-12-0	45-31-0	3-10-0	5-5-1	2-10-0	5-6-1	2-7-0
Houston	18-10-0	4-6-0	10-10-0	13-15-1	15-10-1	16-21-1	12-23-0		11-26-0	19-11-1	12-21-0	10-22-0	13-17-1	4-2-0
Pittsburgh	6-4-0	10-4-0	3-8-0	5-3-0	9-0-0	20-15-0	31-45-0	26-11-0		5-8-1	10-5-0	6-9-0	9-4-0	4-3-0
Denver	9-14-1	6-1-0	2-5-1	14-12-0	10-11-1	9-6-0	10-3-0	11-19-1	8-5-1		21-34-0	18-36-2	27-28-1	13-9-0
Kansas City	12-15-1	6-3-0	7-7-0	11-7-3	13-13-0	9-8-0	5-5-1	21-12-0	5-10-0	34-21-0		23-32-2	27-27-1	10-9-0
L.A. Raiders	13-11-0	4-3-0	15-3-1	12-13-1	12-11-2	12-4-0	10-2-0	22-10-0	9-6-0	36-18-2	32-23-2		35-20-2	11-11-0
San Diego	17-9-2	6-3-0	9-5-0	12-13-2	14-7-1	11-7-0	6-5-1	17-13-1	4-9-0	28-27-1	27-27-1	20-35-2		9-9-0
Seattle	2-0-0	0-2-0	2-3-0	2-5-0	7-3-0	2-5-0	7-2-0	2-4-0	3-4-0	9-13-0	9-10-0	11-11-0	9-9-0	
Dallas	3-1-0	6-3-0	2-4-0	6-0-0	4-0-0	2-1-0	9-15-0	4-1-0	11-12-0	3-2-0	2-1-0	1-3-0	3-1-0	3-1-0
N.Y. Giants	2-2-0	3-7-0	0-1-0	2-1-0	3-2-0	0-3-0	16-26-2	3-0-0	41-26-3	3-2-0	4-1-0	1-3-0	3-2-0	3-2-0
Philadelphia	4-1-0	5-5-0	2-4-0	4-2-0	4-0-0	0-4-0	11-29-1	3-0-0	42-25-3	3-2-0	1-0-0	2-3-0	2-2-0	2-1-0
St. Louis	3-2-0	5-4-0	0-5-0	4-1-0	2-1-0	1-2-0	10-30-3	3-1-0	20-29-3	0-1-1	1-3-1	1-1-0	1-3-0	2-0-0
Washington	3-2-0	6-15-0	2-5-0	3-1-0	4-0-0	3-1-0	8-31-1	2-2-0	40-27-3	3-2-0	1-2-0	2-4-0	4-0-0	3-1-0
Chicago	2-1-0	14-21-0	0-4-0	3-2-0	2-1-0	1-2-0	3-6-0	2-2-0	14-4-1	4-4-0	3-1-0	3-3-0	1-4-0	1-4-0
Detroit	1-1-1	16-17-2	1-2-0	2-2-0	2-2-0	2-2-0	12-4-0	2-2-0	13-9-1	2-4-0	2-3-0	2-4-0	3-2-0	1-3-0
Green Bay	1-2-0	18-17-1	0-4-0	1-2-0	1-4-0	2-4-0	8-5-0	2-3-0	16-11-0	1-3-1	2-1-1	1-5-0	3-1-0	3-2-0
Minnesota	4-1-0	5-12-1	1-4-0	1-2-0	1-3-0	2-3-0	7-2-0	2-2-0	6-4-0	3-2-0	2-2-0	2-5-0	3-3-0	1-3-0
Tampa Bay	3-1-0	1-3-0	1-2-0	0-2-0	1-3-0	1-2-0	0-3-0	1-2-0	0-3-0	0-2-0	2-4-0	0-2-0	0-3-0	0-2-0
Atlanta	2-2-0	0-9-0	1-4-0	2-3-0	2-2-0	1-5-0	1-7-0	4-2-0	1-7-0	3-3-0	0-2-0	1-4-0	2-0-0	0-3-0
L.A. Rams	3-1-0	15-20-2	1-4-0	1-3-0	3-2-0	2-3-0	7-9-0	3-2-0	13-4-2	3-2-0	3-0-0	1-4-0	2-1-0	3-0-0
New Orleans	1-2-0	1-3-0	1-4-0	0-5-0	1-4-0	3-3-0	2-8-0	3-2-1	5-4-0	0-4-0	2-2-0	0-3-1	0-3-0	1-2-0
San Francisco	1-2-0	15-21-0	2-4-0	4-1-0	4-1-0	5-1-0	5-8-0	4-2-0	6-7-0	2-3-0	3-1-0	2-3-0	1-3-0	2-1-0